**Psychology
and the
Teacher**

D0294009

Psychology
and the
Teacher

Dennis Child

Senior Lecturer in the Psychology of Education
University of Bradford

Holt, Rinehart and Winston
London · New York · Sydney · Toronto

Copyright © 1973 Holt–Blond Ltd
all rights reserved
ISBN 0 03 910138 X

Printed in Great Britain
Photo-litho reprint by
W & J Mackay Ltd, Chatham
from earlier impression

It is illegal to reproduce, except
by special permission of the
copyright owners, any part of
this publication. Reproduction
of this material by any duplication process whatsoever,
without authorization, is
a violation of copyright.
Reprinted July 1973
Reprinted December 1973
Reprinted July 1974
Reprinted January 1975

Preface

This book was written as an introductory text for students in colleges and departments of education. It should also serve those who are embarking on advanced courses in education and who wish to renew their acquaintance with basic concepts in the psychology of education.

The central aim of the book is to introduce teachers to elementary ideas in psychology which have some relevance for their work with young people. In addition to drawing on my own experience in teaching and teacher-training, I have benefited greatly from the publisher's findings in making contact with education lecturers in a number of colleges and departments of education and sounding out their opinions about the most important elements in a course involving educational psychology. From their comments, it has been possible to build up a picture of current curriculum content and aspirations. The text aims to include those topics which are representative of this picture.

Growth in the application of psychological principles to educational problems has become rapid and diverse in recent years. New and illuminating lines of approach are born out of, or become grafted on to, old ones. Occupational development and choice, creativity and curriculum development and design are but a few which have established such a firm place in educational psychology that they merit inclusion in a basic text.

The book has several special features which I hope will appeal to lecturers and students. I have deliberately started with a chapter introducing the meaning of psychology in educational settings in order to put the book in context. The choice of further topics has been governed by my conception of the role of the teacher. The better-established work of biologists on the biological bases of behaviour forms the foundation for a study of the less certain factors in educational practice. Chapters on motivation, perception and attention then lead into the core of the text which examines theories of learning and concept formation and shows how the effects of individual differences in intelligence and personality can be assessed and taken into account. With this knowledge the teacher should be in the position to create a stimulating learning environment in the classroom. He will then be called upon to evaluate the results of his efforts using standardized tests and examinations, and to give guidance in occupational and curriculum choice. The last chapter on psychological research in education is intended to act as a bridge between this introductory text and the more advanced and more recent approaches which the reader will meet during his studies.

By using the traditional topic approach of child psychology I have made it possible for students to dip in at a particular point to supplement lecture material or to find guidance for further study and reading. But the reader will soon become aware, from the extensive notes and cross-references, that the topics are interdependent. It could not be otherwise because human attributes are also interdependent.

A textbook is not the last word, but the beginning of several additional activities. With this in mind I have concluded each chapter with references and notes, further reading and points for enquiry and discussion. Experience with college and postgraduate students convinces me that they are not in possession of the statistical and methodological sophistication which would enable them to read, evaluate and use the information contained in research papers at the time when they need a basic text in educational psychology. I have therefore tried to select the less onerous examples which will aid students who wish to study a topic in greater detail.

The enquiry and discussion sections are intended to stimulate the investigation of important questions such as reward and punishment, incentives, self-fulfilling prophesies and streaming. These can be pursued in seminars and tutorial groups and particularly during teaching practice or on school observation. Several questions relate to the work of students in colleges in the belief that it is important to examine our own assumptions and arrangements with the same fervour as we would examine any other sector of education.

I also hope that the student will get personal satisfaction from a knowledge of psychology both as a discipline and as a means of exploring his own qualities as a person as well as a potential teacher.

No book of this kind could possibly be written without the help and encouragement of others. Amongst these I particularly want to thank Mick Adams of Endsleigh College of Education for reading the first draft and making many significant suggestions. To students and colleagues past and present I owe a debt of gratitude for their participation in sharpening my thinking in psychology. Michele Benjamin deserves a special word of thanks for her part in collecting opinions and information about curriculum content in a sample of colleges of education and in making smooth the tricky operation of compiling the finished article. Being a two-fingered and sluggish typist, I simply could not have coped without the help of Joyce McGregor who typed the whole manuscript. I am greatly indebted to her.

Acknowledgements relating to references, quotations and examinations material will be found at the appropriate point in the text.

University of Bradford
January 1972

Dennis Child

Contents

1   Psychology and education

THE STUDY OF PSYCHOLOGY

Understanding ourselves and others has probably always been a human preoccupation. Certainly from the time when man produced his first written record, he has shown a deep interest in human and animal behaviour. Yet his ideas were almost entirely unsystematic and unrepresentative. Even now we casually watch others or listen with prejudiced ears to conversation and from this evidence build up distorted rules of thumb about human nature. In this way, the earliest explorers of man's nature (1) produced a number of 'armchair' theories which became established as a branch of philosophy. Although this kind of theory is still in evidence and still finds a place in contemporary theorizing, it has gradually been replaced from the last century onwards by a serious attempt to adopt the methods of the natural sciences in order to make the study of behaviour more systematic. Outstanding examples of founder members of this movement are Wundt (2) in experimental psychology, Galton in devising and applying statistical procedures to the study of genius, and Freud, who in his own way tried to build a model of the causes and cures of mental illness from careful observations of his patients. But it is to the present century that we must turn to see a marked and rapid growth in the application of scientific methods to behavioural problems.

Psychology is concerned with a wide area of interest. It has been defined as the scientific study of animal and human behaviour and covers all kinds of pursuits from making dogs salivate at the sound of a bell to a study of the growth of intelligent behaviour in humans. The term 'behaviour' on the one hand includes all those aspects of human activity which we can observe. In effect it represents the outward life of individuals which is public knowledge and which can be noted dispassionately. Behaviour also involves personal experience which can only be studied by asking individuals to express their feelings and thoughts. This method of *introspection*, attempting to expose the private knowledge of persons by asking them to recount their attitudes, opinions or values, is regarded with suspicion by some (the *behaviourists* for example), but it does constitute a widely used technique in some fields of psychology.

BRANCHES OF PSYCHOLOGY

The study of animal or human behaviour can take many forms. Some psychologists are concerned with general principles about *normal* or *animal* psychology without particular regard for the application of these principles. As the physicist attempts to discover the laws which govern planetary motion, so the psychologist might try to discover the laws which govern learning in organisms. At this broad level, the psychologist concentrates on *animal* behaviour either for its own sake or in the belief that if man has emerged from the animal kingdom as part of the evolutionary process, he will bring with him some of the characteristics of animals. Therefore a study of animals might give a clue, at a rudimentary level, to man's nature.

Some psychologists prefer to look at the *physiological psychology* of animals and man, to study body structures and their bearing on behaviour. In our study of the brain and central nervous system, we shall find many examples of physiology being used to discern body–behaviour connections. *Social psychology*, the study of social institutions and their impact on the behaviour of individuals, concentrates on the external agencies which influence man, whilst physiological psychologists are more interested in the internal agencies. Social psychologists would be interested in, for example, the psychological characteristics of people in particular social settings such as the family or a village, the role of the headteacher in a school or the effect of family background on achievement at school. *Child psychology* is yet another example of a broad field of interest in which the physical, emotional and intellectual characteristics and development of youngsters from the prenatal stage onwards are studied. Clearly, educational specialists draw extensively on this knowledge for its possible relevance to teaching. All these branches have their interconnections and it would be futile to attempt to devise a classification without recognizing this.

A number of applied fields have developed which draw on the findings of general, physiological, social and child psychology. Thus, *clinical psychology* is the study of abnormal mental life and is of interest to psychiatrists and clinical psychologists. It has not only used the findings of other branches of psychology but has offered useful criteria for defining the attributes of normal mental life (3). *Occupational psychology*, the study of such problems as vocational development and job satisfaction, has rapidly grown into a prominent applied field and a chapter of this book has been devoted to the problem of vocational development and guidance in schools. Other examples of applied branches are *industrial psychology* and *cybernetics* which is the study of machine simulation of human functions such as appear in the automaton or 'George' the automatic pilot in aircraft. For the purposes of student teachers, the most significant applied field is *educational psychology*.

EDUCATIONAL PSYCHOLOGY

Traditionally, educational psychology has endeavoured to apply the findings of general, social and child psychology to assist in a better understanding of learning processes. (The term 'learning processes' includes social and moral as well as factual learning.) It seeks to discover, by studying the mental, physical, social and emotional behaviour of children and adults, the factors which influence the quality and quantity of learning; it offers to replace 'common sense' or trial and error notions about learning and teaching with a variety of hypotheses regarding learning environments derived from systematic studies of individuals in those environments. The application of psychology in education, therefore, gives us a means of appraising individual children's similarities and differences when attempting to create more efficient learning environments for them. It provides us with a means of making evaluations of our own strengths and weaknesses as learners and teachers. Other benefits also accrue which might help us as parents or in the context of our daily lives and dealing with others.

In this book an attempt is made to define and elaborate those aspects of psychology which would seem to illuminate the work of teachers. Psychology teaches us about people—how they think, respond and feel, why they behave as they do and what initiates and sustains their actions. Such fundamental processes are so central to our understanding of children's learning that they cannot help but form a substantial part of a course in teacher-training. We cannot rely on our independent observations alone. When we observe children in class or at play, it is deceptively easy to draw conclusions based on isolated incidents and to make generalizations about all children from these incidents. This is called *anecdotal evidence*. It is sometimes helpful as a starting point for more systematic observations or as confirmation of a general principle, but anecdotes cannot serve as the sole criteria for making decisions about the education of children. Psychologists, on the other hand, try to formulate generalizations based on representative groups of people, or animals where they think the findings can be validly transferred to human situations. There are, nevertheless, shortcomings even in these tightly controlled experiments and we shall return to a discussion of these in chapter 17.

There are so many questions of common concern to psychologists and teachers that a single book cannot possibly touch on them all. Value judgements have to be made as to the most significant contributions. The first chapters deal with physical, emotional and cognitive growth in children and adults in which there is an extensive literature. By starting with a consideration of the brain and central nervous system, we are recognizing that the physical and mental life of children take their origin from biological mechanisms. The fascinating story of brain function and its possible connection with the day-to-day learning skills and problems in the classroom has only just begun to unfold. We know in a general way that the nervous system is closely related to mental functioning, memory, emotional development and behaviour and this has been a source of feverish research activity. Whilst the findings at present offer no direct help to a teacher in dealing with children, knowledge of the biological mechanisms provides a background context in which he can consider the behaviour processes of his charges.

It is a platitude to say that the child (or man) must be motivated before he will learn, and psychologists have progressed beyond this point. We are, for example, beginning to specify some of the conditions which give variations in levels of motivation both in terms of individual differences and in the environmental settings of the child. Other important questions connected with this relate to the effects of attention and perception in the classroom. There are also chapters in this book which look at the development of thinking skills in children and the influence of home and school on language acquisition—important in an essentially verbal world.

What have theorists to say about the processes of learning? So far, they have not been too revealing. The basic data they are working on are the same, but the theoretical explanations are confusingly disparate. But the student teacher who understands the origins of the present position concerning learning theories is in a stronger position when it comes to making decisions in class and to evaluating the innovations he reads in contemporary research than a student who is ignorant of them. Innovation and speculation in learning, as in any other field, are more likely to succeed when they are informed by sound theoretical frameworks.

Exciting new developments in the study of individual differences of intelligence and personality continue to shed light on the teacher's work. Part of the time, the teacher is dealing with a group. More frequently he deals with individuals each possessing a unique blend of mental, emotional, physical and social attributes. An awareness of the possible differences, even in cases where no precise measure is available, is an important asset when it comes to determining the motives and achievement of children and in making decisions about how to handle learning and behaviour problems. Intellectual, behavioural and emotional variability is the order of the day for all teachers, especially in these days of unstreamed classes. The teacher must know what to look for and what action to take.

There comes a time when the teacher has to take stock, when he has to determine whether his ambition to encourage and develop children's learning has been realized. For this, he needs to be knowledgeable in the art and science of evaluation. Examining the work of children is a skilled task if it is to be reliable and valid.

Of recent vintage as experimental areas in psychology with obvious application in schools are vocational development and guidance, and curriculum planning. The former is, perhaps, of more concern to those in secondary and higher education, but the latter is of crucial concern to everyone in education. In one sense, it might have figured at the beginning rather than the end of the book, but the technicalities of the subject are better considered after a grounding in other more fundamental topics in the psychology of education.

READING THE RESEARCH LITERATURE

Keeping up to date in a rapidly expanding market of research literature associated with the psychology of education is difficult for professional researchers let alone teachers in training. Libraries are splitting at the seams with the onslaught of new periodicals and books reporting research—which, if nothing else, is a testimony to the increasing vitality and enthusiasm for pursuing answers to our many questions. Therefore, it might be of help to the student to say a few words about reading research papers.

Much of what follows in the book is based on research findings which are reported either in learned journals or books. Several references to these sources appear at the end of each chapter. The student will, quite understandably, find a lot of the technical papers almost unreadable. Children become 'subjects'; classes of children become 'biased samples' of size 'N'; 'variables' are manipulated using 't-tests', 'chi-square' or 'correlation coefficients', and so on. Fortunately, most journals use a similar format for the presentation of research, of which the summary, consisting of a few hundred words at the beginning or the end of an article and intended to give a brief impression of the major findings, should prove to be the most readable part. Also towards the end of a paper will be found a discussion section which endeavours to summarize the findings and make suggestions about their implications. Summary and discussion sections do not normally contain too much statistical terminology, and provided the student can pick his way through the technical jargon of the subject matter of the paper, he should gain something from his reading.

The list of educational research journals is very long indeed. To get some idea of the British journals, the student should look at the *British Education Index* (4) where a list of periodicals appears on the first page. This Index is also a most useful starting point for a project which requires recent research references. The Index and most of the major journals it refers to are usually available in college and university libraries. To mention just a few of the most significant ones: *Educational Research* (and the leaflet *Educational Research News*) is produced by the National Foundation for Educational Research as a review of research for the benefit of teachers. This organization also publishes research reports in book form [see note (5) for two illustrations]. *The British Journal of Educational Psychology* published for the British Psychological Society contains many useful papers, although the statistical sophistication will probably limit the student to summaries and discussion sections in the absence of a college or university course on research methods and statistics.

Other journals of psychological interest are *Educational Review* (University of Birmingham), *Durham Research Review* (University of Durham) and *Research in Education* (University of Manchester). At a more popular level, *Forum* and *Trends in Education* sometimes contain useful papers of psychological significance. In any case, these latter contain many relevant articles on the contemporary educational scene. The American research literature is vast and no attempt will be made here to select journals. Students are advised to browse in the library to discover for themselves the range and scope of this literature.

SUMMARY

Psychology is the study of behaviour in man and animals and therefore has an obvious contribution to make in our understanding of education problems relating to the learner, the processes of learning and the conditions of learning. Much of the information has been applied from specialist branches such as child, social, physiological and clinical psychology. As a scientific enterprise, the psychology of educational matters has still a long way to go (see Further Reading and chapter 17), and the message of this chapter has consequently been one of cautious optimism for the application of psychology to the daily routines of the teacher. Whilst it cannot provide unequivocal or black and white answers to the teacher's problem, it nevertheless provides an essential ingredient in the diagnoses and decisions of classroom practice.

ENQUIRY AND DISCUSSION

1. First impressions often become a means of deciding on the nature of others. Consider the dangers of this approach, particularly when faced with a group of children having differing intellectual skills, personalities and social experiences.

2. What do you think will be the difficulties in building up a profile of individual pupils?

3. How do teachers keep up to date in the psychology of education?

4. Next time you visit the library, look out for the research journals in education. Select one or two psychological journals to get some idea of the format. At this stage you may find only the summaries are readable.

5. As a group discussion with a tutor, examine some of the most influential educational experiences which you had as pupils. As the course unfolds, it is hoped that many of these experiences will be explored for their psychological significance.

NOTES AND REFERENCES

1. Educational theory prior to the nineteenth century was largely conducted from the comfort of the theorist's armchair. Jean-Jacques Rousseau, in his *Emile*, theorizes on the subject of child development, and Hippocrates (and Galen) speculates about personality typologies (chapter 11) without the advantages of experimental evidence. Ancient Greece is regarded as the source of these methods of deductive reasoning. Aristotle's name, for instance, is usually associated with the technique of using syllogisms as a means of arguing a case. For a definition of these earlier methods, read K. Lovell and K. S. Lawson, *Understanding Research in Education*, University of London Press, London, 1970.

2. Sir Francis Galton is recognized as the founder of psychological studies of individual differences. His book, *Hereditary Genius*, in 1869 marked the beginning of a movement applying scientific and mathematical methods to the study of human capacity. Wilhelm Wundt, a German physiologist, turned his scientific training to a study of psychology and established the first experimental laboratory in 1879. At the turn of the century, Sigmund Freud founded the school of psychoanalysis. As a qualified doctor and neurologist interested in the mentally ill, Freud was prompted to direct his energies to curing the mentally disordered.

3. We shall see in the chapter on personality that Eysenck used the symptoms of the mentally ill, particularly neurotics and psychotics, for defining the dimensions of personality believed to be common to us all. His claim is that the mentally ill are simply extreme examples in a continuum of personality qualities which are approximately normally distributed in the population.

4. The *British Education Index* is published three times a year by the British National Bibliography. It contains a catalogue of references to research in Great Britain which might be of interest to educationists.

5. Two recent examples of books produced by the NFER are: J. C. Barker Lunn, *Streaming in the Primary School*, 1970, and R. Sumner and F. W. Warburton, *Achievement in Secondary School*, 1972.

FURTHER READING

S. W. Bijou, 'What psychology has to offer education—now', *J. appl. behav. Anal.*, **3**,

65–71 (1970). This paper gives a summary of the main ways of applying psychology to education and goes on to discuss a behaviourist approach. Chapter 17 also contains further reading on the question of new approaches.

H. J. Butcher and H. B. Pont (Eds), *Educational Research in Britain*, vol. 1 (1968) and vol. 2 (1970), University of London Press, London. These volumes, and there are more to come, will give the student an idea of the scope and scale of research at present of interest to psychologists. A glance at the contents page and a dip into one or two of the articles will suffice at this stage.

E. G. S. Evans. *Modern Educational Psychology: An Historical Introduction*, Routledge and Kegan Paul, London, 1969. The writer gives an historical perspective to our present educational psychology scene. This is the kind of book the student can return to as the course proceeds.

2 The nervous system and the brain

The most important scientific enterprise of all time is now well under way: the search for human nature within the living tissues of the brain. The machinery inside our heads does not yield its intricate secrets easily but new discoveries and ideas about how it works are already displacing the simple-minded psychological theories of past decades.

Nigel Calder in *The Mind of Man* (1)

Human nature is an extremely complex affair. The variety of possible human experiences and their impact on our development is in itself a vastly intricate subject of which we are only just beginning to scratch the surface. At the core of the problem is an organism whose biological equipment sets the scene for the immense potentialities of each person's life style. The statement by Calder with which the chapter began is, however, an over-statement. It is important to reflect on the possible dilemma (Joynson, 1) that if human behaviour is ultimately capable of being explained in terms of the physiology of the brain and nervous system, then there will no longer be an independent science we can call psychology! With this teasing philosophical problem, let us take a cautious look at some of the biological equipment of man.

It is now firmly established that certain body structures are closely linked to the behaviour we can observe in animals and man. The brain and central nervous system are undoubtedly most important structures in this respect. Injuries to specific parts of the brain, as we shall see presently, cause specific behaviour changes and disorders; severing nerve fibres in the front part of the brain can bring about obvious and some-times radical changes in the personality of individuals; abnormalities in brain or nerve structures at birth bring with them a corresponding variation in, or absence of, behaviour consistent with normal brains. But our knowledge of the precise causal connections between behaviour and body mechanisms is far from complete. We have, for instance, only a gross and sketchy notion of the part played by the brain in emotional activity, perceiving or memory. What little we do know is important for any student of human behaviour.

THE NERVOUS SYSTEM

Two systems of particular interest to us are the nervous and endocrine systems. The latter will be dealt with later in the chapter. At present we will look at the reception, transmission and control mechanisms of the nervous system. For a detailed but straightforward description of the structure and functioning of these systems the student is recommended to read a basic text in biology or psychology (2).

There are several ways in which the nervous system has been classified. These depend on the location or function of the various portions of the system. Common to all these classifications is the *central nervous system* (often abbreviated to CNS) comprising the brain, brain stem and spinal cord. The CNS is sometimes considered along with the nerve fibres (*receptor fibres*) leading to it from the sense organs and the fibres (*effector fibres*) from it to the muscles. This combination of CNS plus the receptor and effector fibres is called the *somatic nervous system*. It is responsible for (i) transmitting impulses set up in the sense organs by external or internal stimuli (sights, sounds, pain, and so forth) to the brain; (ii) interpreting and responding to these receptor impulses within the brain; and (iii) transmitting the effector impulses from the brain through the spinal cord to muscles which then contract if required. The final phase represents a response to the stimulus.

The somatic nervous system can be brought under the direct control of an individual. A hungry child when he sees an inviting apple might reach out, pick it up and eat it. The stimulus through the sense of sight has set up impulses transmitted through the optic nerve fibres to the brain from which effector impulses are transmitted to bring about an appropriate response pattern of muscular movements necessary for grasping and lifting the apple. Conduction paths from sense organs in other parts of the body, as in the case of pain, temperature and kinaesthetic sensory regions (the *periphery*), pass through the spinal cord to the brain and back to the musculature by the same route.

This, of course, is an over-simplified version of what goes on inside our bodies. The effects of socialization, to mention just one complication, may prevent the child from taking the apple if it belongs to someone else. Something intervenes between the stimulus and the response to inhibit the child from taking the apple. What precisely goes on in the brain in this case is still a complete mystery. In our discussion on motives we shall raise this matter again.

There is a way in which the receptor and effector organs are connected directly without necessarily involving interpretive functioning of the brain. This is called the *reflex arc*. Man and animals are born with certain reflexes such as swallowing, eye blinking and knee jerking in response to the presence of threatening stimuli. A puff of wind directed at the eye will cause the lids to close automatically to protect the delicate surface of the eye. Swallowing prevents unwanted particles from passing into the air passages leading to the lungs.

Another important system, the *autonomic nervous system* (ANS), supplies the glands and various organs of the body. As the term implies, the autonomic, or self-controlling, system operates without a deliberate effort on the part of an individual. Organs such as the heart, lungs, stomach, intestines, bladder and glands (tear and salivary) continue to throb, expand, contract, open and close quite independently of our conscious control. Routine operations are managed by the system, having their origins in the hypothalamus (see later) and passing from there to the organs via the spinal cord. Two divisions known as the *sympathetic* and *parasympathetic* have been identified. The sympathetic portion innervates and stimulates organs which enable the organism to respond rapidly, especially in circumstances which spell danger or create fear. A frightening experience, as readers well know, causes increased and irregular breathing and heartbeat, sweating, pallor and the hair to stand on end. The extra supply of oxygen and release of energy-giving chemicals (glycogen from the liver for instance) provide the excess energy enabling the organism to escape or fight. The parasympathetic section also innervates the same organs, but has the opposite effect on them by acting as a braking system to the sympathetic nerves and slowing down the body mechanisms.

Implicit in all we said in the previous paragraph is the assumption that the organs regulated by the autonomic nervous system may not be brought under the control of the will. This, however, is not the case. At a simple level, it is possible to arrest lung action and bring about a change in heartbeat. More sophisticated control is achieved by those on the stage who can think themselves into emotive states (weeping, anger) without really 'feeling like it'. Devotees of yoga are able to control their metabolic rates so as to reduce the amount of oxygen needed for body functioning. Several yogis (3) have been known to survive in confined spaces for much longer than would be possible in normal circumstances. Controlled experiments in the United States by Miller (4) support the view that autonomic functions are susceptible to conscious control. By a system of rewards in the form of a pleasant buzzer sound, he encouraged high blood pressure patients to think about reducing their heart rate. When the heart rate had reached a predetermined lower level, the buzzer sounded. In this way, the patients were able to lower the rate to quite a marked extent.

RECEPTORS

Our lives are filled with testing the environment with our senses. In fact, our continued existence depends on our sensitivity to the environment and the appropriateness of our responses. To receive this information from the surroundings, there are groups of cells which are receptive to light, sound, touch, taste, smell, movement, heat and the like. The cells are known as *receptors* and some groups of cells form the sense organs such as the eyes, ears, taste buds on the tongue and areas in the nose; less obvious receptors of pain, temperature change and movement (kinaesthetic sense), are widely distributed both outside and inside the body. The complex structure of these organs is a subject which need not detain us here (5).

In general terms, a receptor cell will operate when there is a change or difference in the environment. The change is known as a *stimulus*. The difference in light intensity between the dark letters and the white background of this page you are reading enables you to observe the stimulus of the letters. When an object vibrates sufficiently it sets up a disturbance in the surrounding air. The disturbance spreads out in all directions from the source and on striking the ear-drum sets it in sympathetic motion. In turn this is transmitted to the sound-sensitive points in the inner ear. A change in pressure or temperature on the body surface is soon detected. Where a change does not reach a perceivable *threshold*, obviously it will not be detected. By threshold we mean a level of stimulation below or above which we are not aware of the stimulus. Dogs respond to high sound pitches whilst man is insensitive to them. Regular background stimulation often goes unnoticed—as the ticking of a clock or the pressure of clothes on the body. This provides a sound reason why teachers should vary their voices and take note of the colours used on blackboards or visual aids. There are also variations in the threshold levels from one person to the next. It is thought that some people have low pain thresholds and soon succumb by showing marked anxiety symptoms. Some children are more upset by pain than others, although the differences arise probably from experiential as much as constitutional sources.

Vision   It has been shown that vision in the new born is very rudimentary. Its eyes are sensitive to light and they can adapt to darkness. Colour discrimination may also develop very quickly in the first few months. But the eye lenses cannot alter (accommodate) readily to focus on objects at different distances. The eye movements are not coordinated. In fact, each eye can move independently at first in a fashion disturbing to unsuspecting mothers and fathers. They need not worry because it is not an abnormality and eye movements ultimately become coordinated.

Colour blindness is the inability of some people to distinguish particular colours— chiefly red and green which look greyish. Four in every hundred people are colour blind so that on average there will be one pupil in every class you might take who is unable to distinguish some portions of those colourful visual aids, colour reading or colour factor so lovingly prepared.

There are several ways in which the eyes move according to their usage. *Pursuit movements* occur when we watch a moving object such as a car; *compensatory movements* happen when we fix our attention on an object and move our heads from side to side. A third kind of movement is *convergence* or *divergence* when an object travels towards or away from an observer. Finally, and most significant for the teacher of reading, is *saccadic movement* which occurs when the eye moves along a line of print. The present sentence might require on average eight to ten eye movements, one every two words. But length and difficulty of the words, coupled with the reading speed of a person, will govern the number of eye movements required by each person (6). The following sentences demonstrate the possible positions at which the eyes fixate as they jump along the line of words. The fixation points are shown as black dots.

A slow reader's movements with a small 'visual' span, that is the number of words he takes in at each fixation point, would look something like this:

The eye only sees when it is stationary.

For a fast reader, the following might apply:

Therefore the more you take in at each jump the bigger can be the jumps.

Reading efficiency is directly related to saccadic movement because the distance between each fixation of the eye will govern the pace of reading—but *not* necessarily the understanding of the reading material. Pace is also affected by other mechanical aspects such as fixing for long periods at each point, using too many jerky forward and backward movements over the words already viewed or by the arrangement of the print. Courses for improving reading speed concentrate some of their time on these factors.

Hearing   Research with babies as the subjects is plainly a precarious business. Because they cannot communicate or since their motor skills are still rudimentary it is not always possible to plot the progress in some aspects of their development. Response to sounds seems to be fairly general in that babies do not appear to discriminate readily between types of sound. Of course they react to sounds of varying intensity. Loud sounds may well produce a startle reaction. There could be dissimilar reactions to the same loud sound. But we have to wait until the baby is several months old before he begins to respond to his mother's voice in a different way to other similar sounds.

Hearing, along with sight, are the two important communication senses for the teacher. Faulty hearing or eyesight in children can, and often does, go unnoticed by parents and teachers. The effect of these deficiencies on learning is obvious. The teacher can do much to improve the situation by judiciously placing children who have partial hearing or seeing defects in suitable positions in the classroom.

Touch   The sense of touch in infancy is our first hard evidence of reality. We probably underrate the importance of tactile experience for our children. Our human preoccupation with the written and spoken word has led to our neglecting the sense of touch which includes the detection of pressure, pain and temperature. Many primary school teachers now give their children opportunities to manipulate various materials or identify objects hidden from view using only the sense of touch—as in the 'feeling' boxes or bags used in primary schools. Some regions of the body are devoid of the sense of pain; some areas are more sensitive to pressure than others. The finger-tips are particularly sensitive ,whilst the sole of the foot is comparatively less discriminating (7).

TRANSMISSION

Reception of stimuli from outside or inside the body is only the beginning. Impulses set up by the receptors need to be conveyed to the brain for interpretation and possible response.

The impulses are the result of electrical and chemical changes passing along the length of the nerve fibres with great rapidity. The slowest is around three feet per second and the fastest approaches 300 feet per second. Witness the speed with which a pin prick which excites the pain receptors on the body will give rise to withdrawal of that area from the painful stimulus.

The tissues making up the nervous system are living cells of various shapes and sizes, depending on the work they do. Our bodies contain roughly 30 000 000 000 of these cells. Scientists are now able to study their structure using the powerful magnifying properties of the electron microscope.

The figure 2.1 gives an indication of a nerve fibre magnified many times. The whole nerve cell, or *neuron*, consists of the *cell body* with fine hair-like processes called *dendrites* and a drawn out portion which is the nerve fibre or *axon* ending in similar processes to the dendrites. The tips of the processes end in knobs referred to as *synaptic knobs*. They form connections with the next neuron or with muscle fibres (end plates). The dendrites from one cell interlace with the synaptic knobs from an adjacent cell. Note from the diagram that they do not actually touch the dendrites. The minute gap (roughly a millionth of an inch) is known as the *synaptic gap* or *cleft* and the surrounding area as the *synapse*. Electrical impulses are conveyed along the neurons by means of electrical potential differences between the inside and outside of the neuron membrane.

On reaching the synaptic gap the signal does not pass across in electrical form but by chemical means. On arriving at the gap (see figure 2.1) the electrical impulse encourages the release of a chemical from the end feet into the synaptic material which either excites or inhibits the dendrite processes of the next neuron. The sum total of those excitatory or inhibitory impulses governs whether the impulse will or will not pass along the next neuron and this is known as *facilitation* or *inhibition*. There appear to be no half measures. The neuron either fires or it does not fire, a phenomenon known as the 'all or nothing' principle. The chances of an impulse reaching the brain depend on the strength of the incoming signals such that the stronger the signal the more rapid is the impulse rate. The presence of inhibitory processes enable many possible courses

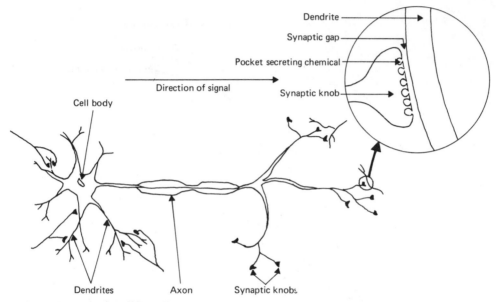

Figure 2.1   A simplified diagram of a neuron or nerve cell

of action (or simple inaction). It also helps to deal with all the extraneous perceptions in the field of view or hearing by eliminating them and preventing the brain from having to cope with an excess of information from the senses (8).

THE STRUCTURE OF THE BRAIN

The brain is a massive concentration of nerve cells representing about a third of all the nerve cells in the body. The outer layer, or *cortex*, consists of many folds (*convolutions*) so as to confine a large surface area into a small volume. The finished article looks like a walnut. Brain tissue has one of two shades depending on its composition. Where there is an abundance of nerve cells the resulting tissue is called *grey matter*. The outer cortex consists of grey matter. Where there are many nerve fibres, which are normally surrounded by a white sheath, the tissue is called *white matter*. The cells require a constant and rich supply of oxygen otherwise they die within one or two minutes. In instances where oxygen supply is limited, as when the windpipe is blocked or more directly in stroke conditions, serious and permanent mental impairment can result. Well-ventilated classroom conditions are an obvious necessity to enable normal oxygen supply and brain activity.

Viewed from the side, as shown in figure 2.2, there are two conspicuous folds which act as convenient boundary lines for the division of the brain. Bear in mind that we are looking only at one side. The other side, because of the approximate bilateral symmetry of the body, looks very much the same. The fold running across the top and a little way down the sides is the *central fissure*. The second at the sides is the *lateral fissure* (or fissure of Sylvius). Figure 2.2 also gives an idea of the positions of these

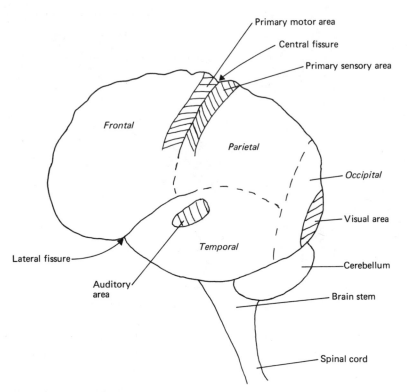

Figure 2.2 A side view of the brain

fissures. Viewed from above, the brain appears to be divided into two equal parts by a deep groove, the *median fissure*, running the length of the brain. Using these fissures as boundary lines, the figure 2.2 shows how the surface cortex has been divided into *frontal*, *parietal*, *temporal* and *occipital* regions or lobes. These lobes have corresponding partners on the other side of the brain. It is worth noting that these are only broad divisions partly reminiscent of the functional aspects of the brain.

If the brain is divided down the median fissure to expose the central organs, we find the termination of the spinal cord forming the *brain stem* and at the rear we find the *cerebellum*. The cortical region normally enveloping the brain stem (sometimes referred to as the *cerebrum*) can be seen as a thick and extensive covering of nerve cells. A curious crossover of nerve fibres occurs between each side of the brain so that the left-hand side supplies the right-hand side of the body and vice versa for the other side. Consequently, damage to the motor region on one side of the brain will bring about a corresponding malfunctioning of the motor activity on the opposite side of the body.

BEHAVIOUR AND THE BRAIN

Our chief concern in the next few sections will be a consideration of parts of the brain mentioned above and their bearing on behaviour as revealed by recent research. Although the picture is at present blurred, it does constitute an important and exciting area of study for the student of human behaviour. But first let us see what methods researchers have been able to apply in their explorations of brain–behaviour connections using both man and animal as subjects.

With animals, and in certain kinds of human brain surgery, portions of brain tissue have been removed. This technique is called *extirpation* or *ablation*. Observations could then be made to note the changes in behaviour accompanying extirpation. Severing nerve tracts can also give rise to observable differences in behaviour. Later we shall look at the effects of cutting these connections between the frontal lobes (leucotomy).

Electrical activity of the brain is also used. As we saw above, the impulses in the nervous system are the outcome of electrical and chemical changes and the surface of the brain exhibits voltage changes which can be picked up using small plate-like electrodes placed against the scalp. These voltage changes are translated and recorded as a wavy ink line drawn by a pen moving along a rotating drum. The instrument (9) is known as the *electroencephalogram* (EEG) and erroneously regarded as a lie-detector recording 'brain-waves'. The size of the waves and the number per unit of time are employed to estimate the level of arousal of the brain. *Electrical stimulation of the brain* (ESB), when an external electrical impulse can be passed through electrodes which have been implanted in specific regions of the brain, has been most successful in identifying functions of deep regions of the brain as well as in studying emotion in animals. Brindley in this country (10) has been studying the effect of ESB in the vision region at the rear of the brain on blind patients. He has managed to get blind patients to report having 'seen' spots before their eyes and is hopeful that sight may be restored sufficiently for reading purposes. Probes can be used, whilst an animal is conscious and without pain, to detect the activity of individual cells. This has been accomplished using micro-electrode control (11) where movements of a few thousandths of a millimetre are possible.

Post mortem operations following the death of a brain-injured or -diseased patient can often reveal a tie up between behavioural patterns prior to death and the damaged portion of the brain. With conspicuous nerve tracts it is possible to trace the paths using careful dissection techniques. Hebb's work, to be mentioned in the section on intelligence (12), showed that fairly substantial proportions of the frontal regions of the brain in adults could be removed without seriously diminishing the intellectual performance, although the same is *not* true of children.

A relatively new line of attack has been the study of *brain chemicals* and we shall say more of this in the discussion of memory and the brain at the end of this chapter.

The brain stem

In figure 2.2 the brain stem is shown as a deep-seated portion of the brain and in an evolutionary sense it is the oldest part of the brain. Crudely it is a hollow tube of nerve tissue at the top of the spinal cord through which all impulses from the cord must pass en route to the brain. It consists of two areas, the *medulla* on the outside surrounding the inner core or *reticular formation* which lines the hollow tube and runs through to connect with the hypothalamus and thalamus. The reticular formation has two systems— the *descending reticular system* for motor functions and the *ascending reticular activating system* (ARAS) for sensory functions. This latter system is of particular importance. In broad terms its function is to monitor the impulses coming from the senses. Stimuli are selected or ignored so as to prevent overloading the brain with too much incoming information. Selective attention, therefore, is accomplished by the ARAS. Interestingly, the receipt of sensory information is very necessary for normal functioning of the brain. If sensory cues are eliminated, as in many experiments where the subject's arms are encased in tubes and his eyes and ears are shut off from the surrounding stimuli, the subject becomes disoriented and distressed. University students (13) have been bribed with money to undergo this kind of experiment only to abandon it after a day because of the intense frustration. It seems, then, that we must have sensory stimulation or spontaneous body activity. Man and animals must satisfy what appears to be their basic need to explore, driven by curiosity. This fact has obvious implications for the teacher who must take advantage of the ready-made inquisitive nature of children.

The brain stem is also related to the cycle of sleep and wakefulness. Different areas of the stem appear to be responsible for the states of waking, sleeping and dreaming. Operations on the brains of rats (14) have enabled the identification of specific regions relating to alertness (reticular formation), sleeping (raphe nuclei) and dreaming (locus coeruleus). If it so happens that the raphe nuclei are destroyed by operation or accidental brain damage in animals or man, the victims are unable ever to sleep as we know it. However, in the normal mechanism of sleep and waking there appears to be a built-in *biological clock* which has its first settings laid down by the control of the individual and partly from habits formed in childhood. Babies spend a fair proportion of their lives snoozing or sleeping in the day, and the habit carries over to reception classes where teachers are well acquainted with their children dropping off during the afternoon.

Hypothalamus

Near the top of the brain stem and close to the pituitary gland we find the hypothalamus. The organ contributes to starting, maintaining and stopping behaviour associated with satisfying the basic body needs such as food, water intake, temperature control. The balance between need and satisfaction is called *homeostasis*. When 'fuel' is running low in our bodies, the homeostatic balance is said to be disturbed. Sensations of hunger leading to food-seeking activity will occur until the balance is restored by eating. The hypothalamus also exerts some control over the activities of the pituitary gland which is an endocrine gland controlling the hormone-producing glands of the body.

Much research using electrode stimulation of the brain (ESB) has enabled us to pinpoint sites in the hypothalamus responsible for excitation accompanying hunger, thirst, temperature variation, sex, pleasure and aggression. There are sites which act as counterparts to excitation once the organism is satisfied. Anand and Brobeck (15) are largely responsible for this research and the theory of centres in the hypothalamus. With a hungry animal the 'eating' site brings about excitation which initiates eating. A corresponding satiation site begins to inhibit eating as the animal becomes satisfied. ESB of the hunger excitation site will, in fact, elicit eating long after the animal would normally be satisfied. Delgado (16) also uses ESB techniques to control the aggressive behaviour and movement of animals—including bulls!

One alarming point about ESB is its immediate effect on specific behaviour patterns to which the recipient has little resistance. Movements and feelings can be affected and consequently a detailed study of emotions and abnormal mental life have been studied. Already epileptics and those suffering from narcolepsy (irresistible feelings of drowsiness) have been helped.

Thalamus

The thalamus surrounds the top of the brain stem and has nerve connections from its position deep in the brain to the cortex in the roof of the brain. Fibres from all sense organs except the olfactory organs (sensitive to odours) pass through this region. It provides a centre for sorting and directing information from sensory organs to specific sensory and motor regions in the roof of the brain.

The limbic system

The limbic system appears as a lining to the roof of the brain and surrounds the top of the brain stem. The important functional units are the hippocampus, amygdala, the septal area and cingulate gyrus. Damage or stimulation to these units gives rise to perceptual changes and disorders such as an inability to distinguish visual cues (caused when the cortex in contact with these units is removed), impairment of recent memory (hippocampus) and the disappearance of avoidance behaviour—as when a person no longer appears to be afraid of painful stimuli (amygdala). Broadly speaking, the limbic system exercises some control over motivational and emotional behaviour.

Cerebral hemispheres

In this brief, whistle-stop, tour of the brain we have now reached the extensive outer cover described above as a highly convoluted grey mass of nerve cells. The outer layer is called the *cerebral cortex* with a conspicuous median fold appearing to divide the brain into two *cerebral hemispheres*. We also noted four regions which will help us in defining some of the functions associated with the cortex (see figure 2.2).

First notice the *primary motor* and *sensory* areas bordering the central fissure. The motor strip, of all brain regions, has been explored in great detail by such men as Wilder Penfield (17). Motor control of the left toe can be located at the top of the strip in the median fissure in the *right* hemisphere and as we work down the strip, motor control regions progress from the lower to the upper parts on the left-hand side of the body. The sensory strip on the other side of the central fissure is responsible for the senses of touch, pain and kinaesthesia. Note the separate regions for sight and hearing. A knock on the back of the head will make one 'see stars'. This is caused when the visual area impinges on the rear of the skull.

Regions outside these areas are known as the association areas. They are divided into the *frontal association area* sited in the frontal lobes and the *PTO association area* made up from portions of the parietal, temporal and occipital lobes.

The frontal association area has eluded the efforts of scientists to determine, with some precision, the purposes of the tissues. In man, extensive damage to frontal tissue seems in most cases to have had little effect on performance in conventional intelligence tests. Hebb (13), on the other hand, has noted that similar kinds of damage in children appear to have a lasting effect. It may be that frontal tissue is particularly relevant in establishing, in a diffuse manner, intellectual schemas in children. Damage at this stage will have a more potent, lasting effect on intelligent behaviour than when the schemas are well established and dependent on a wide distribution in the brain tissues. Some have claimed the frontal association areas to be the seat of man's highest intellectual powers (18); others (13) are more cautious, as we have seen. Certainly the size of the frontal lobes seems to be proportional to the intellectual complexity of animals. But this by itself does not tell us much about the workings of the lobes.

Teuber (19) supposes that frontal lobes have something to do with willed or purposeful aspects of activity. If the side of the frontal lobe is stimulated the head moves sideways leaving the eyes looking in the same direction. The conclusion from the experiment is that the eyes must have compensated, that is, they have rotated in their sockets in order to maintain their original position. Luria (20) has supported this point of view in his work on brain-damaged patients. Damage to certain areas of the frontal association region gives rise to incongruous behaviour and loss of power to control behaviour in some circumstances. These symptoms are known as the 'silliness syndrome'.

Deep in the frontal region we find areas which have a direct bearing on personality. *Frontal leucotomy*, or severing certain connections between the frontal lobes, has been used in the past to alleviate patients suffering from morbid conditions such as acute depressive states. The method is rarely used now because the damage to other surrounding tissues which accompanied the operation gave rise to complications which became manifest in such behaviour as carefreeness to the point of inconsequentiality. Several patients were not cured at all and some suffered post-operational epileptic fits. Recently, Knight (21) has replaced the surgeon's knife with radioactive 'seeds' planted in specific locations in the brain and the radiation from these seeds is just sufficient to destroy surrounding tissue in minute quantities which would be impossible to deal with using surgery. Clearly, this reduces damage to surrounding tissue and has proved extremely effective in curing suicidal and psychoneurotic conditions.

The PTO association area governed by the thalamus has been described as the *sensory* or *cognitive* association cortex. It covers those remaining portions of the brain chiefly the parietal, temporal and occipital lobes not already mentioned, but with the exception of a region in the temporal lobe known as the *interpretive association cortex*.

Damage to the cognitive association cortex results in speech and language deficiencies collectively known as *aphasia*. Sensory and motor aphasias are possible. On the sensory side we find *auditory aphasia*, an inability to understand speech, and *visual aphasia* (alexia), an inability to read or understand the written language. This does *not* mean that all children who cannot read suffer from brain damage in this region. Far from it, for there may be many other causes. Motor aphasia appears in three forms: *verbal* (cannot pronounce words), *manual* (cannot write) and *nominal* (cannot name objects).

Curiously, there is a dominant side to everyone's brain, usually the left side in right-handed people. Not only is it dominant in controlling speech, but there is a 'language lump' making the temporal lobe on that side a little larger. This has been found from brain-damaged patients and by injecting into the left or right side of the brain some sodium amytal which discloses the dominant side by disrupting speech. Bogen (22), from a series of studies using brain-damaged people, maintains a laterality of the brain in which the left hemisphere is related to verbal skills and the right hemisphere to spatial skills. After brain damage, a person's right hand was able to write but unable to copy a geometric figure. The left hand could cope with the figure but could not write at all.

Penfield has used ESB methods to tap the temporal lobes. From his work patients have claimed to experience vivid 'flashbacks' to their past. He supposes this to be evidence that the brain retains in the interpretive cortex a record of conscious experience which can be revived, randomly, with electrical stimulation. Removal of the temporal cortex impairs visual learning where discrimination is required, as happens for instance where coloured or shaped objects have become linked with food rewards in animal experiments. Symptoms similar to those described for a malfunctioning limbic system are also in evidence.

Cerebellum (or little brain)

The conspicuous lump of tissue at the rear of the brain and under the occipital lobes (see figure 2.2) is known as the *cerebellum*. ESB studies of Sir John Eccles (23) using micro-electrodes have attempted a minute exploration of this part of the cat brain. His conclusion is that it is responsible for the control of movement in routine activities such as walking and balancing. Damage to this region leads to coarse, clumsy and inaccurate movements. Eccles has refined his method to such a point that he can now detect information from a particular part of the body through the nerves to a specific cell in the cerebellum.

MEMORY AND THE BRAIN

Memory is one of those eye-catching subjects of interest to most of us and its study has been the centre of considerable research effort over the years. At a simple, but inaccurate level, the workings of the brain in the recall of information have been likened to a computer's storage banks. The analogy breaks down when we realize that information stored in a computer has a precise location and is retrieved in exactly the same form each time. 'Information' storage in the brain seems to be much more diffuse and can be of different natures as in short- or long-term memory.

Answers to questions such as how and where are memories stored, or what part does the brain play in thinking and reasoning remain unanswered, although several intriguing leads have come to light in recent years. Earlier experiments by Lashley (24) were unsuccessful in finding locations for these activities. However, we now know that if the hippocampus (part of the limbic system) is destroyed, individuals can no longer lay down long-term memories. Memories previous to damage are preserved and short-term memories are still possible, such as recalling a telephone number for a few minutes, but no lasting learning is possible without the agency of the hippocampus. We have also seen various aphasic conditions when the PTO association area is damaged and the impairment of visual learning when the temporal cortex is removed.

Perhaps the most exciting advance in the last few years is the prospect of a chemical explanation of learning and memory. The electrical activity in the brain can be detected using the EEG and there is no doubt about chemical processes occurring in the synaptic clefts. Further, when animals are taught to run a maze and the animals' temperatures lowered to halt the electrical activity, the animals can still remember how to complete the maze task. This has forced scientists to conclude that memory storage is more likely to depend on chemical than on electrical factors. Baldwin at Cambridge has injected into the brains of goats drugs contrived to have a disruptive effect on electrical activity; yet this has no effect on short-term memory and strengthens the case for a chemical theory of learning.

But the evidence which has caused most concern amongst brain scientists emerges from the work of McConnell (25). In 1966 he reported that if flatworms (not related to ordinary worms and much simpler in body design) were taught to turn in a given direction, killed and their tissues injected into another untutored flatworm, the latter was able to learn the task much quicker than could non-injected animals. The theory behind this extraordinary result is that learning has been accompanied by a chemical change which has been transmitted with the cells into the host flatworm. More recently, hampsters have been taught to enter a feeding box at the sight of a flashing light. RNA (short for a chemical found in all cells and known as ribonucleic acid) was extracted from the brain tissue and injected into rats. The rats apparently turned toward the boxes when the light was flashed. Many explanations are possible and the conclusion that there has been some chemical transfer of the stored information which, by injection, has found its way into the brain of the host is only one. Replications of this research afford little support for the original findings (26).

The most recent and stimulating report of possible chemical–memory connections comes from Hydén and Lange (27) in Sweden who were able to show differences in the RNA content of cells before and after a learning task. An ingenious method was devised to contrast the left and right sides of the hippocampus part of brain. By teaching normally 'right-handed' rats to carry out tasks with their left paws and comparing the chemical nature of the RNA content of the cells on the left and right side of the brains of control and experimental groups, they were able to show that RNA was being manufactured more profusely on the relevant side for the paw in use. This research has been extended to demonstrate that a special protein molecule (S100) suddenly appears in the cells extracted from the 'active' side of the brain. Many scientists are sceptical of these conclusions, particularly the connection between the specific chemical and learning. These researches, if nothing else, indicate how important chemical activity and protein manufacture are to the normal functioning of the brain tissue. But we have a long way to go before the problem is resolved.

EMOTION AND THE BRAIN

You have just settled down in the carriage of a train. The train begins to move off and suddenly you notice your suitcase standing on the platform. Intense feelings quickly take over along with a sudden burst of action or frozen dread. Our language is rich with expressions one might use to describe your state of mind and body—astonishment, alarm, panic, despair and many others. In cases of this kind we are said to be experiencing emotions. Disgust, joy, hopefulness, pity and a whole range of experiences from highly pleasant to deeply unpleasant sensations are described, although the hard evidence from physiology or psychology for the separate existence of these supposed emotional states is not yet available. One simple classification by Watson embraced fear, rage (anger) and love. More recently some have postulated (28) that as neonates we experience only excitement which becomes differentiated as we grow older, first as distress (further divided into anger, disgust and fear) and then as delight (elation and affection).

All these reactions, whether we attempt to distinguish different patterns of response for dissimilar circumstances or not, have their beginnings in internal physiological changes assisted by the sympathetic nervous system and the endocrine secretions (29). A general definition of emotion would be 'physiological and psychological responses that influence perception, learning and performance' (30).

The classical interpretation of emotive activity and responses was that after a stimulus has been received which is interpreted as threatening or pleasing, the body reacts via the nervous and endocrine systems and these give rise to feelings of emotion. Fear, anger, joy, tenderness were said to be the outcome of body secretions and nerve action. Fear was then made manifest by increased breathing and heartbeat, drying of the mouth, hair on end, and so forth. James and Lange (31) independently contested this hypothesis and suggested quite the reverse. They maintained that the outward reaction of the body to an emotive stimulus—running, crying, fighting—gave rise to sensations of fear, anger, etc., expressed in the well-known James–Lange theory of emotion. James, summarizing his views, says 'we are afraid because we run, we do not run because we are afraid'.

Cannon (31) provided evidence to confound the James–Lange Theory. When the nerve connections between the organs influenced by the autonomic system and brain are severed, organisms still show fear, rage, affection and other emotional states. The Cannon–Bard theory (again independent investigators coming to much the same conclusions from their researches) was proposed. According to this the impulses from incoming stimuli pass through the thalamus, sensitizing it, passing the impulses to the cortex, organs and muscles. The cortex input represents conscious knowledge of an emotive state and the feelings which accompany emotions. The organs and muscles would be responding at the same time.

From our viewpoint, it is probably more helpful to think of emotional behaviour in terms of three dimensions in preference to numerous specific states which are loosely tied in our minds to ill-defined terms which exist in our language to describe our feelings. The three dimensions proposed by Murray (30) are intensity, pleasantness–unpleasantness and approach–avoidance. Intensity is related to the level of arousal and is widely recognized by psychologists (see the section on drive and performance in chapter 3). The second dimension helps to remind us of the infinite variety of experiences from complete ecstasy to utter terror (whilst being vaguely reminiscent of the hedonistic theory of man as a pleasure-seeking–pain-avoiding animal). The third dimension concerns the feeling of attraction towards, or repulsion from, emotively charged objects or

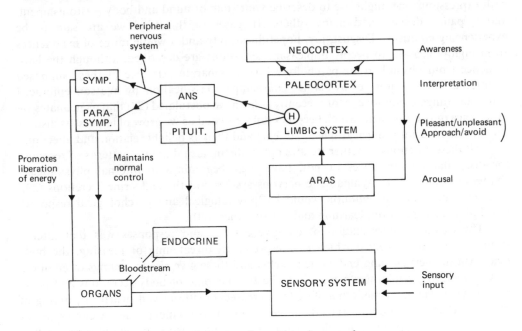

Figure 2.3 Representational diagram of emotional arousal sequence
(H = Hypothalamus)

situations. Fear arising from unpleasant experience may give rise to either fight or flight.

Returning to the place of the brain in emotional response, we know that two systems are involved. One is the limbic system, including parts of the thalamus and hypothalamus, ar 1 the inner portion of the cortex (old cortex or paleocortex). Stimulation of this system, as we have observed, is associated with fear, anger, aggression and many other reactions. The second is the ascending reticular activating system (ARAS) in the brain stem already identified earlier in the chapter as responsible for arousing the cortex and moderating messages from the sensory systems. Its function is not directive but energizing.

The sequence of events might be easier to follow from diagram 2.3. A sensory stimulus is received by receptor organs and transmitted to the brain via the ARAS. Arousal of the latter is noted by the cortex and also by the hypothalamus in the limbic system. As the hypothalamus transmits to the ANS and pituitary gland, the sympathetic and endocrine systems are alerted. Organs which might aid in escape by the provision of additional sources of energy are activated, and this is recorded by internal sensory systems. Thus we are made aware not only of the external stimulus, but also of our internal body reactions. The exact point at which the body as a whole responds by approaching or avoiding the stimulus is not fully understood, but it may take place when the ARAS is arousing the cortex along with internal emotional reactions subsequent to ANS and pituitary stimulation.

The utility of emotional states is obvious. Increased supplies of sugar for the body metabolism with more oxygen and increased rate of blood circulation from lung and heart action are all essential for improved performance. Cannon has claimed that emotional activity has survival value by aiding 'emergency reaction'. Duffy (32) goes further in seeing emotional arousal as *the* source of energy for body mobilization for normal, as well as emergency, activities. However, the view is not supported by evidence and we shall discuss some implications of anxiety states and their beneficial or disruptive effects on learning and performance in the next chapter.

HEREDITY (33)

An important biological fact is that the human race has a vast pool of characteristics which can be transmitted from generation to generation during the process of reproducing its kind. In our discussions of such complex human qualities as intelligence and personality, we will frequently have cause to wonder to what extent the potential for individual characteristics is inherited and to what extent the life experiences of individuals shape the outcome of these inherited properties. At this stage, it is necessary to give readers a brief idea of the biological mechanisms of inheritance.

It is common knowledge that the basic structures for reproducing human characteristics are the germ cells (female ovum, or egg, and male sperm). Within each is found a nucleus which contains the *chromosome* material—long thread-like structures now known to be made up of complex chains of chemicals. The basic unit for the transmission of characteristics from parent to offspring is the *gene*. Using powerful chemical and electron-microscopic techniques, biologists have found that each gene is a specific area along the chromosome with a unique chemical composition. The mechanism of gene reproduction and interaction is a rather detailed biological phenomenon which need not concern us here. But we do need to discuss the broad ideas underlying the transmission of physical and mental qualities.

One way of regarding the process of evolution and inheritance is to think of the genes, with their enormous potential for variety, as a *population*. Within this population, we would find a pool of characteristics for a given trait ranging from one extreme, let us say intense blue eyes, to the other, deep brown eyes, and in the middle of the range would be found hazel eyes. Each new generation brings with it a selection from this pool which depends on the particular genes carried by the parents. Strains which are beneficial to survival will continue, other strains which are maladaptive will die out. This is, crudely, the Darwinian theory of the survival of the fittest by which the natural environment will only support those who are best suited to that environment. This reshuffling of gene content is one way of producing variety in a species. There is a second method called *mutation* which arises from sudden, often accidental, alterations in the gene structure and gives rise to unique characteristics. Mutations are known to be caused by exposure to radioactive fall-out and many examples have been reported from the A-bomb aftermath in Japan. Fortunately, in well-established species, many mutations do not survive.

An intriguing example of positive adaptation by a mutant is provided by the resistance of certain strains of bacteria to streptomycin. Normally, a population of a bacterium called *E. colli* can be destroyed when exposed to streptomycin. However, very occasionally a mutant appears which is quite resistant. The fact that it is a mutant strain and not a question of the bacteria becoming resistant has been shown quite conclusively.

Note that the offspring do not inherit a mixture of the parents' gene contributions. In other words, if dad has brown eyes and mum has blue eyes, the sons and daughters will *not* inherit hazel eyes. Each parent carries in the germ cells certain possibilities for a given characteristic which he or she, in turn, has inherited from parents. So there is some element of luck attached to the specific characteristic which has been 'drawn' from the parents' pool. Should the contributions from the parents be in conflict (father-brown, mother-blue), then one gene will be dominant in its influence. At the same time, the child now possesses the dominant gene from father's side *and* the *recessive* gene from mother. When the child is about to pass on the characteristics, once more there will be two possibilities.

Later in the book we shall refer to heredity and intelligence. Here we are dealing with a very complex genetic make-up; in fact, intelligence is probably partly dependent on several interrelated genes (*polygenic* condition) and not just one gene. Therefore, the inheritance of intelligence is far more subtle than that of physical characteristics. The environment also plays a significant part in permitting intellectual potential to be realized and this point will be taken up in chapter 9.

MATURATION

Behaviour changes in man are brought about by the interaction of both external and internal agencies which he brings to each situation. For convenience, the origins of these changes are separated into *learning* and *maturation* (2). Learning is due to environmental influences, that is influences external to us which can affect development. The teacher's job is plainly an instance of environmental influence intended to bring about learning. Maturation, on the other hand, is a built-in tendency in all members of a species to grow and age in an ordered sequence of events. The changes should occur in the absence of experience. As Wright (2) declares, the central function of maturation 'is to refer to genetic control of the patterning and sequential ordering of development'.

The physical growth pattern of children is a clear example of maturation. However, there are other kinds of development said to be maturational. Skill in locomotion which starts with crawling and ends in walking is one. Gesell (34) studied the motor development of children and postulated several landmarks of motor competence in normal development. More recently, norms of physical development have been published (34, Davie *et al.*) along with information about differences occurring between children from dissimilar socio-economic backgrounds. As we shall see in the course of this book, there are several maturational theories relating to speech development, cognitive development, vocational development, and so on. We will notice that in all cases there is said to be a systematic unfolding of competence which follows a predictable path, which varies from one individual to another in quality and quantity but is, nevertheless, present in some degree.

SUMMARY

The mind of man has puzzled the philosophers and psychologists for many years. In studying the functioning of the brain and central nervous system, there is an assumption that we may discover some biological explanations for man's behaviour, although this idea should be tempered with the possibility that man's behaviour is more than the sum of the actions of his physiological parts and that conscious life is more than an epiphenomenon arising from body functioning.

Certainly the important body mechanisms which bring us into sensory contact with, and help us to respond to, our surroundings are located in the central nervous and brain systems. A brief description of the structure of the CNS and brain was given to illustrate the nature of the systems. In this description, we looked at the receptor, transmission and brain processes, relating them to activities of general interest to teachers.

Several sections were concerned with behaviour and the most significant parts of the brain. Whilst this has no direct bearing on the day-to-day workings of an educational system, nevertheless, it provides a background of factual information which fits the physical body into a behavioural context. Some may be quite difficult for the non-biologist, though he should at least attempt to understand the functioning of the brain stem, homeostasis and the hypothalamus, the higher regions of the brain including aphasic conditions and the lack of bilaterality in the cerebral hemispheres.

Memory and brain action involved a somewhat speculative look at current theories intended to give the reader a glimpse into the research of the near future. The subject of memory comes up again in chapter 4. Emotion and the brain was dealt with from the point of view of the arousal sequence involving hypothalamus action and the organization of the sympathetic and parasympathetic nervous systems.

The final two sections on heredity and maturation were included in this 'biological' chapter as a basis for later elaboration of such important considerations as intelligence, personality, cognitive and language development and the earlier theories of vocational development.

ENQUIRY AND DISCUSSION

1. Read the relevant parts of R. Davie, N. Butler and H. Goldstein, *From Birth to*

Seven, Longmans, London, 1972, and use this as a starting point to consider the physical growth, sensory development and the use made of medical services in relation to socio-economic background.

2. Discuss in seminar the distinction between maturation and learning. Of what significance is this distinction to the teacher?

3. Review the literature and draw up a list of the major sensory defects which are likely to affect the work of schoolchildren. How might the teacher discover these abnormalities? Discuss with tutors the action which must be taken when a teacher finds children in his classroom who suffer from sensory defects.

NOTES AND REFERENCES

1. This BBC publication, the outcome of a programme on the mind of man, was compiled by Nigel Calder. For beginners it should prove to be a most stimulating and readable book which attempts to introduce the layman to some of the numerous and intricate researches relating to the workings of man's mind. N. Calder, *The Mind of Man*, BBC Publications, London, 1970. But also see R. B. Joynson, 'The return of mind', *Bull. Br. psychol. Soc.*, **25**, 1–10 (1972).

2. A particularly helpful and thorough text for the beginnner has been written by D. S. Wright, A. Taylor, D. R. Davis, W. Sluckin, S. G. M. Lee and J. T. Reason, *Introducing Psychology: An Experimental Approach*, Penguin, London, 1970. Several other specific and technical books are given in the Further Reading list.

3. Mentioned in the reference of note (1).

4. N. E. Miller, 'Learning of visceral and glandular responses', *Science*, 434–445 (1969). See also the Report of the 17th International Congress of Psychology in London, 1969.

5. Any basic biology text will contain details of the structure of sense organs. Have a look at C. G. Mueller, *Sensory Psychology*, Prentice-Hall, New Jersey, 1965.

6. Several books have been written on the subject of improving reading efficiency. For those interested, have a look at C. Mares, *Teach Yourself Efficient Reading*, English Universities Press, London, 1964 or M. and E. De Leeuw, *Read Better, Read Faster*, Pelican, London, 1965.

7. A measure of contact sensory discrimination is accomplished by touching various places on the body with a pair of dividers and measuring the distance between the points at which the subject can identify the separate points of contact without seeing the dividers. For example, compare the finger-tip with the sole of the foot.

8. For an excellent, simplified version of neuronal action, see reference given in note (1) above.

9. D. Hill and G. Parr (Eds), *Electroencephalography*, Macdonald, London, revised 1963.

10. G. S. Brindley and W. S. Lewin, 'The sensations produced by electrical stimulation of the visual cortex', *J. Physiol.*, 479–493 (1968).

11. Sir John Eccles, probably the world's most renowned neurophysiologist, has established a large research team in Canada. His book, *The Neurophysiological Basis of Mind*, Oxford University Press, London, 1953, is a standard work in this field. See also J. C. Eccles, M. Ito and J. Szentagothai, *The Cerebellum as a Neuronal Machine*, Springer, New York, 1967.

12. D. O. Hebb, 'The effect of early and later brain injury upon test scores, and the nature of normal adult intelligence', *Proc. Am. Philos. Soc.*, **85**, 275–292 (1942).

13. D. O. Hebb, *The Organization of Behavior*, Wiley, New York, 1966 (8th Impression).

14. M. Jouvet, 'The states of sleep', *Scientific American*, **216**, 2, 62–72 (1967).

15. B. D. Anand and J. R. Brobeck, 'Hypothalamic control of food intake', *Yale J. biol. Med.*, **24**, 123–140 (1951).

16. Some ESB research is quite spectacular and is a common topic for popularization. The work of José Delgado is particularly remarkable. His book *Physical Control of the Mind*, Harper and Row, New York, 1970, contains a summary of his findings.

17. W. Penfield and T. Rasmussen, *The Cerebral Cortex of Man*, Macmillan, New York, 1950.

18. W. C. Halstead, *Brain and Intelligence*, University of Chicago Press, Chicago, 1947.

19. H.-L. Teuber, 'The riddle of frontal lobe function in man', in J. M. Warren and K. Akert (Eds), *The Frontal Granular Cortex and Behavior*, McGraw-Hill, New York, 1964.

20. A. Luria, *Higher Cortical Functions in Man* (translated by Haigh), Tavistock, London, 1966. *Traumatic Aphasia* (translated by Critchley), Macdonald, London, 1970.

21. G. Knight, 'Stereotactic surgery for the relief of suicidal and severe depression and intractable psychoneurosis', *Postgraduate Med. J.*, **44**, 1–13 (1969). The operation using radioactive seeds goes by the unrepeatable title of 'bi-frontal stereotactic tractotomy'.

22. See 'Factors of the brain', by J. McFie, pp. 11–14, and 'The educational significance of recent research on brain bisection', by I. Macfarlane-Smith, p. 60, in *Bull. Br. psychol. Soc.*, **25**, January (1972).

23. See note (11) and *The Physiology of Nerve Cells*, Johns Hopkins Press, Baltimore, 1957.

24. K. Lashley, one of the first in this field of brain surgery and memory, carried out numerous extirpations to discover the precise location in the brain for memory storage. He was entirely unsuccessful in this venture and concluded that learning

ought to be impossible! A summary of his work appears in *Brain Mechanisms and Intelligence*, University of Chicago Press, Chicago, 1929.

25. J. V. McConnell, *New Evidence for the Transfer of Training Effect on Planarians*, 18th International Congress of Psychology, Moscow, 1966, Symposium on Biological Basis of Memory Traces.

26. See p. 118–126 of the reference in note (1).

27. H. Hydén and D. W. Lange, 'A differentiation in RNA response in neurons early and late during learning', *Proc. Nat. Acad. Sci.*, **53**, 946–952 (1965). Also H. Hydén and E. Egyhazi, 'Nuclear RNA changes in nerve cells during a learning experiment in rats', *Proc. Nat. Acad. Sci.*, **48**, 1366–1372 (1962).

28. K. Bridges, 'Emotional development in early infancy', *Child Dev.*, **3**, 324–341 (1932).

29. The endocrine glands secrete special chemicals called *hormones* into the bloodstream. The glands are ductless, in other words, they pass their secretions directly into the bloodstream without the aid of tubular ducts (in contrast to the salivary glands). The important glands, their position and the function of their hormones are:

    pituitary—suspended beneath the hypothalamus—controls the action of the endocrine system.

    thyroid—in the front of the neck—secretes thyroxin which aids in growth and metabolic control.

    adrenals—near each kidney—continuously secrete adrenalin and noradrenalin to mobilize various organs already mentioned in connection with the ANS; also exudes excessive quantities of the hormones in emergency and emotive states.

    pancreas—level with kidneys—secretes insulin which is responsible for sugar control in the body; the well-known disease of diabetes occurs when insufficient insulin is secreted, therefore, the body must be supplied artificially by injecting insulin into the bloodstream.

    gonads—testes or ovaries—the sex glands which control the appearance and maintenance of secondary sexual characteristics such as face, chest and pubic hair, voice breaking and body stature in men and the menstrual cycle and breast formation in women.

    Deficiencies or excesses of the hormonal secretions give rise to various diseases, the nature of which can be read about in any standard biology textbook containing human physiology.

30. E. J. Murray, *Motivation and Emotion*, Prentice-Hall, New Jersey, 1964.

31. C. Lange and W. James, *The Emotions*, Williams and Wilkins, Baltimore, 1922; W. B. Cannon, *Bodily Changes in Pain, Hunger, Fear and Rage*, Appleton-Century-Crofts, New York, 1929.

32. E. Duffy, *Activation and Behavior*, Wiley, New York, 1962.

33. C. D. Carter, *Human Heredity*, Penguin, London, 1962.

34. A. Gesell and F. L. Ilg, *Child Development*, Harper, New York, 1949. See also

J. M. Tanner, *Growth to Adolescence*, Blackwell, Oxford, 1962, and a most important recent report of development in early childhood by R. Davie, N. Butler and H. Goldstein, *From Birth to Seven*, Longman, London, 1972. One important conclusion reached by this report is that 'equality of educational opportunity cannot be achieved solely by improving our educational institutions. The child is often handicapped both physically and mentally before he reaches school as a result of deficits in opportunities at home'.

FURTHER READING

C. V. Brewer, *The Organization of the Central Nervous System*, Heinemann, London, 1965 (reprint).
J. H. Burn, *The Autonomic Nervous System*, 4th ed., Blackwell, Oxford, 1971.
N. Calder, *The Mind of Man*, BBC Publications, London, 1970.
A. N. Davison and J. Dobbing (Eds), *Applied Neurochemistry*, Blackwell, Oxford, 1968.
C. G. Mueller, *Sensory Psychology*, Prentice-Hall, New Jersey, 1965.
D. E. Wooldridge, *The Machinery of the Brain*, McGraw-Hill, New York, 1963.
D. S. Wright *et al.*, *Introducing Psychology: An Experimental Approach*, Penguin, London, 1970.

3　Human motivation

INTRODUCTION

The increased complexity of living in our society has made it necessary to cultivate in the young the will to acquire many varied cognitive as well as physical skills. In fact, schools are created as artificial arrangements whereby we require our children to carry out all kinds of activities which, for many of them, would not have been a significant part of their young lives and which would certainly not have occurred to them spontaneously. Left to themselves, the majority of children would not learn to read or pore over arithmetic problems without prompting from adults. Those teachers who have taken a bewildered group of little ones in reception class fresh from the security of home to the uncertainty and properness of the school setting, or taught a class of school-leavers with their minds on worldly things, will know all about the problems of prompting the young.

A study of motivation is, therefore, crucial for a teacher. Without a knowledge of the ways and means of encouraging children's learning, of knowing about their 'appetites' in the widest sense of the word, of being sensitive to their interests, the teacher's task would be impossible. For this purpose, most teachers would place an understanding of motivation very high on their list of priorities.

A working definition of motivation would be that it consists of internal processes which spur us on to satisfy some need. We shall return to examine some of these 'processes' and 'needs' shortly, but first it is necessary to look at some of the broader issues. In some cases we may be fully aware of a particular need and our actions will be quite deliberate in attempting to satisfy it. Hunger has fairly obvious symptoms and well-tried cures. A hungry child eats food in the full knowledge that this will relieve his feeling of hunger. On the other hand, we may be quite oblivious of the underlying causes when we, say, undertake a course of training to enter the teaching profession. The analysis of those causes which drive us to engage in such complicated activities embodied in a course of training is very difficult. Simpler creatures with a limited span of behaviour for detecting and imbibing food or reproducing their own kind have fairly inflexible and obviously essential mechanisms for their survival. As we pass through the animal kingdom to man we find that the origins of motivation become obscured by complicated patterns of behaviour. Satisfaction of basic body requirements such as food, air and water is still essential, but it gives way to, or is possibly built into, an intricate network of other activities designed to satisfy acquired needs.

In all the instances we have cited here, the source of activities is not fully understood primarily because the internal process cannot be observed directly. We have to guess or infer that certain internal processes must exist from the behaviour we observe or experience. What people do can be observed; why they do it is still a matter for speculation.

MOTIVATION THEORIES

In the study of motivation we can identify at least three important questions:
(a) what spurs us to be active?
(b) why, when we are active, do we behave in one way rather than another?
(c) how does one bring about a change in the direction of any activity?
Let us look at these in more detail.

(a) Because we have to speculate about the internal springs of action, several explanations in the form of theories of motivation have arisen. No one theory has been found which is entirely satisfactory, and the main value of these theories to the teacher is in providing a background against which he can tentatively evaluate his experiences of motivational problems in the classroom. One way of looking at these theories is to view them as a continuum from *biogenic* (having origins in biological processes) to *sociogenic* (having origins in social processes). Biogenic theories, favoured by physiologists (1), emphasize innate biological mechanisms such as instincts or biological needs as being the templates which define our actions. Sociogenic theories lay stress on the moulding influence of cultural determinants. Between these extremes we find moderate views which find a place for both biological and social influences. We shall look at four of these theories spread along the continuum of instinct, physiological, psychoanalytical, field and culture-pattern theories. There are, of course, those like Skinner (2) who find no place in their theories for speculations about what might be going on inside our bodies. They are more impressed by stimulus and response mechanisms which can be observed and manipulated in the study of such problems as habit formation or the effects of punishment, reward and deprivation.

(b) The short answer to the second question relates to *habit*. We behave, by and large, in characteristic ways because we have discovered through experience that some responses are (in the short or long term) more effective than others. Where a desire has been fortified in the past by adopting certain behaviours, it seems reasonable to suppose that the same pattern is likely to be repeated in similar circumstances.

(c) The third question is of the utmost importance to a teacher. By the process of extrinsic manipulation it is possible to alter patterns of behaviour. Habits can be 'broken' and alternatives substituted in their place. New patterns take the place of old ones by rewarding (or *reinforcing*) the former and not rewarding or punishing the latter. The questions posed in (b) and (c) above are the subject of the latter part of this chapter and the section on learning. But let us first look briefly at some theories which attempt to answer the question regarding the source of motivated behaviour.

Prior to the eighteenth century it was generally held that man was able to exercise complete control over his actions. As a rational creature he had the power to direct, redirect or inhibit his passions at will. These ideas were bound up with the early philosophies relating to religion and morals. Man was seen as a pleasure-seeking, pain-avoiding creature (*hedonistic* outlook). Animals, on the contrary, were activated by instincts—inborn mechanisms which gave rise to fixed ways of satisfying animal needs. Darwin's *Origin of Species* (1853) then came as a nasty shock to those who thought than man and animals were completely unalike in their motives.

McDougall (3) in 1908 saw the arguments of Darwin as confirmation of his 'hormic' or *Instinct Theory* which postulated that man's actions, as well as those of the animals to whom he was related, were the outcome of instincts—innate, unlearned tendencies to behave in specific ways in response to various biological and social needs (4). The idea that man was tied down to fixed patterns of behaviour was heavily criticized and he modified his view by suggesting that man was endowed with 'pro-pensities' rather than animal instincts. Burt (5) defines a propensity as a 'complex inherited tendency, common to all members of a species, impelling each individual (a) to perceive and pay attention to certain objects and situations; (b) to become pleasurably or unpleasurably excited about those objects whenever they are perceived; (c) thereupon to act in a way likely in the long run to preserve the individual by so acting'.

The theory in its original form has very little support nowadays. Vernon (6) was amongst many who had harsh things to say about man's behaviour having its beginnings in inborn rituals of survival value. The main argument against the instinct theory was that human beings do not display stereotyped patterns of unlearned behaviour. One need only contrast the rigid antics apparent when a baby bird is being fed by a mother, or the courtship rites of many species of birds and animals, with similar events in man to realize how unlike an instinctual drive our behaviour is. Only the simplest reflexes of man are invariable in nature. Support for this stems from the work of social anthro-pologists (7) who claim that the dominant instincts of aggression, acquisition and sex vary considerably from tribe to tribe. Again, our motives become so overlaid with secondary and acquired desires that it makes the theory of inherited tendencies impossible to validate. Allport (8) recognized this and coined the phrase 'functional autonomy' to describe the acquisition of new motives derived from more fundamental motives which ultimately become independent of the latter. Drug-taking, smoking or developing professional attitudes (high standards of craftsmanship) are examples of activities which continue to give satisfaction long after they have become divorced from the initial starting motive.

A revival of the concept of instinct as applied to man has been brought about by the work of Lorenz and Tinbergen (9), two famous ethologists (students of character formation in animals), but their findings [some details are discussed in note (9) and chapter 6] remain of theoretical interest at present. Their main contention is that man, being a biological organism and subject to evolutionary development as in the remainder of the animal kingdom, is possessed of instinctive urges which if studied would give a sound scientific basis to human behaviour.

A second approach, variously referred to as *Physiological* or *Behaviour Theories*, has the central tenet that all our actions have their roots in our efforts to satisfy organic *needs* such as food, water, air, pain avoidance and body temperature maintenance for personal survival, and courtship, mating and parenthood for species survival. More complex behaviours at first sight seem far removed from the simple gratification of body needs; however, many followers of these theories believe that they also arise from the struggle for survival. Satisfaction of the basic or *primary needs* is brought about by *primary drives* [Hull (12)]. *Acquired* or *secondary reinforcers* appear as by-products of the satisfaction of basic needs. Money is a secondary reinforcer because it can provide the means of satisfying a number of primary needs (13).

Mention has been made of physiological states of disequilibrium when the body is deficient of basic needs. When deficiencies occur, the body registers the imbalance through the agencies of the blood and arousal systems in the brain (hypothalamus). Thus Hull equates psychological drive with physiological need by the process of *homeostasis*—a term we have already met. This mechanistic view of behaviour has met with strong opposition from psychologists and we shall return to this in the section on learning.

Historically and developmentally the theory expounded by Freud (10), referred to as *Psychoanalytical* (*Depth psychology* or *Psychodynamic*) theory goes some way to bridging the instinctual views of McDougall and the physiological theories. The framework set up by Freud will be given in chapter 11, but for the present we shall look very briefly at his hypothesis that there are two basic instincts (more accurately 'moving forces') of *life* and *death*. These originate from bodily needs. The life instincts include (a) sexual instincts (*libido* instincts) required for reproducing the species and (b) instincts relating to hunger and thirst which are required for life preservation and maintenance (*ego* instincts). The death instincts are never properly defined but are loosely incorporated as inner processes. The only one specifically defined by Freud was the aggressive instinct. He believed these instincts to be there at birth—a 'cauldron' of instinctual energy referred to as the *Id*. The constraints placed on the expression of these basic desires by conscious effort on the part of individuals or as a result of social pressures, chiefly parental influences, lead to repression of the desires. The 'taming of the passions' of the Id is made possible by the *Ego*, such that many *defence mechanisms* replace the immediate gratification of basic desires so that the motive energy is used in more socially acceptable ways. Exclusion from the conscious mind of less desirable solutions to instinctive cravings does not mean that they have disappeared altogether. Freud creates the *unconscious* mind which contains the traces of unpleasant and repressed memories. Behaviour is hereafter influenced whenever similar circumstances to the original experiences occur, but the individual is not aware of the source of his behaviour. The root cause of motives will only break through in special circumstances such as hypnosis, dreams, drugs or in a psychotherapeutic session when the defences are down. For a fuller discussion of Freudian and similar views, the student should read the relevant part of chapter 11 where a number of criticisms are also considered. For the moment, it is sufficient to note how Freud accounts for the source and direction of our motivation.

The instinct, physiological and the earlier psychodynamic approaches to motivation undervalue the influences of social pressures and patterns of culture into which a child is born and reared. *Culture-pattern* and *Field* theories have sprung into being over the past forty or so years in response to this omission. Social anthropologists have already been mentioned in the notes (7) at the end of the chapter. Their concern is the effect which culture patterns might have on the rearing of children and the subsequent behaviour patterns which arise from these motivational precursors.

The research of Harlow and Zimmerman (11) is important in this context, as well as illustrating the social development of young monkeys and the theory of *critical periods*, that is the period during which particular aspects of growth to maturation are most effectively developed [see note (9)]. These investigators placed newly born monkeys with two substitute (or 'surrogate') mothers. They were not live mothers but made of wire and cloth. One was kept as a plain wire shape with a feeding bottle protruding at the front, whilst the other was surrounded by a soft material though without a feeder. The young ones always preferred cloth surrogate mothers and would even cling to the cloth whilst reaching across to the wire model for milk. When frightened, the babies would leap onto the cloth rather than the wire surrogate. This response is said to give 'contact comfort' which Harlow and his co-workers believe to be an essential basic need of young animals including human babies. There was some evidence of a *critical period* [see note (9)] between roughly the 30th and 90th days after birth when attachment became strong and security firm. Another important observation was the distorted emotional development of monkeys raised in wire cages or with wire mothers. The monkeys tended to be (a) lacking in affection; (b) lacking a will to cooperate; (c) aggressive; and (d) deficient in sexual responses to other monkeys.

Allied to the culture patternists are the more inclusive field theories, particularly those of Lewin (11). Interaction of all the factors of the present environment, including personality characteristics, is stressed as the dominant criterion governing behaviour. Lewin (11) thinks that 'the behaviour of a person or group is due to the distribution of forces in the social situation as a whole, rather than to intrinsic properties of the individual'. Thus the dynamic aspects of our present experience are the all-important things. However, this leaves a teacher somewhat empty-handed when he wants to use his knowledge of social and individual differences in order to determine the factors which may assist him in motivating his children.

COMMON GROUND BETWEEN THEORIES

To help us in our understanding of the sequence of events which might occur when a person is motivated to action, let us use a simple model and extract from it some relevant ideas. In a straightforward diagrammatic form it might look like this:

need → drive → activity → satisfaction → drive reduction

←————— learning occurs —————→

To illustrate a successful sequence, take an example of modelling in the classroom. We all *need* to explore and manipulate our environments. Few but the senile and ill can sit motionless and uninterested for long. If you distribute modelling clay to a class of seven year olds there will be few who do not take up the challenge to shape the clay. Most children enjoy this kind of manipulation (for many reasons) and feel a *drive* to constructive (or sometimes destructive) *activity* with the material. *Satisfactions* appear when a recognizable shape emerges, when the teacher shows approval or just from the feel of the material. The challenge does not last indefinitely. The initial desire to model wanes (again for many reasons) and we might conclude that the *drive* has been *reduced*.

The likelihood of the cycle of events being repeated is high when there is success. Where a child has produced a useful, attractive or personally satisfying object, *reinforcement* of the sequence is possible. The child's need for social approval may also be fulfilled where the teacher or other children praise the finished article.

Successful sequences lead to learning. Manipulative and perceptual skills in this case are encouraged. But learning also occurs from unsuccessful sequences even if one learns not to repeat the task because it gives little satisfaction. Children soon learn that some kinds of activity also lead directly to disapproval. In this event, the sequence will be inhibited—a process known as *extinction*. The teacher's task is to find alternative sequences to arrive at satisfying and educative ends. Whatever the teacher's objective might be, whether it is the improvement of manipulative, perceptual or learning skills, routes must be found which offer the chance of satisfaction and need reduction in order to facilitate positive learning. Punishment, whilst necessary in certain circumstances, often has the effect of cutting short a sequence without replacing it with an alternative, acceptable sequence.

Let us now look in more detail at the various stages of the sequence of motivation suggested above.

Needs

Much has been written about human needs (14). We have already briefly encountered primary, secondary, biogenic and social needs earlier in the chapter. A most useful model has been expounded by Maslow (15). He sees a hierarchy of needs shown here in figure 3.1 as a pyramid. He distinguishes the needs in order of their importance and therefore prepotence, so that physiological deficiences must be satisfied before we fully attend to safety needs. The significance of the pyramid shape is not only to demonstrate the hierarchical arrangement, but to show the broad base of physiological and safety factors necessary before other possible needs are likely to be considered. Note also the broad categories of, first of all, personal, then social, and finally at the highest level, intellectual needs. Progress through the hierarchy only occurs as more important needs are satisfied. Obviously, these levels are not exclusive. Food-seeking in primitive tribes when food is scarce would be accompanied by some regard for body safety, although greater risks would probably be taken where physiological drives are strong.

Sexual behaviour—courtship, mating, parenthood—is not classified in the physiological needs because the urges do not arise from homeostatic imbalance in the same way as do food or oxygen deficiency. The behaviour has more to do with social and species survival than with personal survival. A corollary of this possibility is that humans in extreme hardship as in prisoner of war camps during the Second World War experienced atrophy of the sex organs and consequently no desire for sexual or social behaviour (16). Hungry humans think of little else but food—all the human capacities, such as intelligence, memory, dreams, are put to work in trying to seek satisfaction relating to hunger (17).

Once the organic needs are satisfied, 'higher' needs emerge to be satisfied. The safety needs, that is protection from potentially threatening objects, situations or illness come to the fore. Children are especially susceptible to unfamiliar surroundings. They seek refuge in routines because too much open-ended and ambiguous experience may constitute a threat to their safety. Tolerance to ambiguity may well be an acquired characteristic depending for its quality and extent on child-rearing and childhood encounters. Inconsistency in the expectations and demands of parents and teachers can give rise to disturbing and insecure feelings amongst children.

The 'love needs' assert themselves when physiological and safety needs are reasonably well gratified. Most humans appear to need to give and receive affection. They need the feeling of belonging which has nothing to do with sexual desire. To some extent the feeling of belonging adds to our safety needs. Parents and teachers, inadvertently, can bring powerful pressure to bear on children who feel insecure from lack

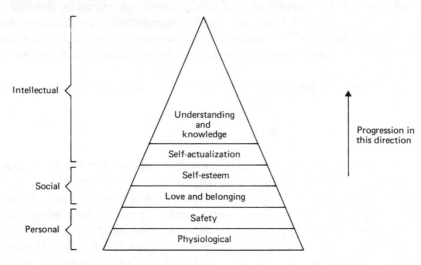

Figure 3.1 A hierarchy of needs
Based on A. H. Maslow, 'A theory of human motivation', *Psychol. Rev.*, **50**, 370–396 (1943)

of affection. On a wider front, 'society' can exact high levels of social control and conformity by the implicit threat of social isolation (prison, borstal, secret societies, religious sects—where it is possible to purchase a good conduct ticket in this world for a place on the next). Psychotherapy places great faith in the influence of thwarted love needs on the conscious life.

Maslow sees two sets of 'esteem' needs. First there is the desire for strength, achievement, adequacy, confidence in front of one's fellows, independence and freedom. Secondly, he posits the desire for reputation and prestige, recognition, attention, importance and appreciation by others. The first is the desire for confidence in onself; the other is a wish for prestige and respect from others. Thwarting of opportunities for these desires to be realized is said to produce feelings of inferiority, weakness or helplessness.

The next step in the pyramid, self-actualization, refers to the desire to fulfil one's potentiality. Maslow declares 'What a man *can* be, he *must* be'. Self-actualization is also dependent on self-realization. We have to know what we can do before we know we are doing it efficiently. The role of the teacher in providing for this is clear. The school has a major part to play in discovering, encouraging and advertising each child's capabilities. At the peak of the hierarchy comes the acquisition of knowledge and understanding. The role of curiosity, exploration, and our search for meaning in a muddled world are well known. Note also that in Maslow's view knowledge and the assimilation of information precedes understanding.

Plainly, there are implications for the teacher. If the model has any validity, it has abundant applications for the major preoccupation of the teacher, that is, the transmission and understanding of knowledge which comes at the very end of a long list of human needs. Hungry or frightened children are less likely to aspire to the requirements of school than well-fed and secure children. Children starved of affection at home are less likely to cope than those from emotionally well-balanced home backgrounds. This list of applications is extensive and students might sit back and work out some of these applications for themselves.

Drives

Drive can be defined as an aroused state which leads to action. This topic need not detain us for long. Our knowledge of the source of motive power is scant and there is certainly little information on which the teacher can capitalize. We are aware of internal stimuli—the organs, the brain—and external stimuli—the sight of food or general arousal caused by a frightening condition which is related to emotional states (see chapter 2). Beyond this, we have no clear picture of internal and external drive states.

Activity, satisfaction, drive reduction

These stages are treated together because they are important to learning. When a sufficient level of arousal is reached, mobilization of the body or mind takes place. The resulting activity is referred to by some as *goal-seeking behaviour*. Thus the internal demands of drive states are such as to impel the individual to seek for a means of gratification. The body need not necessarily move, since the arousal might be connected with the solution of a mathematical problem requiring no more than an alert mind. Reading a book to acquire knowledge is another case of covert activity. 'Goal-seeking' assumes that a direction has been taken. The teacher's function is to provide the direction, and much of his scheming in lesson preparation hinges on devising ways in which children will fruitfully acquire knowledge. Badly organized goal-seeking and goal-planning might have disastrous effects on children's morale. 'Discovery' techniques, if poorly devised, can produce frustrated children with no idea of what they are intended to discover, busy pooling their combined ignorance (class participation in which the teacher plays no part) and often feeling needlessly insecure on such open-ended paths to the acquisition of knowledge. Drive reduction may unfortunately be attained by alternative and less acceptable forms of activity where children become desperate.

MOTIVATION IN EDUCATION

Sufficient has been said about theories and models of motivation to convince the reader that many assumptions have to be made in attempting to give meaning to our observations in both the description and explanation. Peters (18), a philosopher, has little to say in favour of all-inclusive theories. Along with many teachers, he feels that we should classify the *goals* of man if we want to make man's actions intelligible. For the teacher, the external, situational and manipulable factors of human motivation are the primary concern. In the following pages we will explore some of the topics found to be of significance in classroom practice from the point of view of their *outcomes* rather than their *origins*.

Curiosity, exploration and manipulation

We started the chapter by suggesting that the classroom was far from a natural setting. Teachers have to sell their wares. In Maslow's terms, we are at the highest point of the hierarchy and have to depend upon *cognitive drive* [to coin a term from Ausubel and Robinson (19)]. We are very much dependent on the child's will to know and understand and his manipulative and physical awareness (modelling, craft, physical exercise, games). Often the teacher will appeal to needs lower in Maslow's scheme. Illustrations are the child's desire for self-esteem, confidence in the presence of others or in himself, the need for approval and his social needs.

Collectively the activities of exploration, manipulation and curiosity are known as *attention needs*. They depend for detection or satisfaction on the senses and the extent to which we pay attention to our surroundings. You will recall from Hebb's experiment in chapter 2 [note (13)] that almost total inaction has serious disorientating effects on the mind. Even before this stage is reached, people subjected to prolonged inaction become extremely frustrated. Belief in these as components of human behaviour reflects an active rather than a passive view of life with man as a goal-oriented animal actively engaged in exploring his environment. Children, once they can move, do not lie or sit around waiting for information to wash over them; they actively seek out and manipulate. Mothers and teachers in primary schools are fully alive to this. The idea of an active, experience-seeking child is prominent in Piaget's theory of cognitive growth (see later).

Play is regarded by some psychologists as a manifestation of the attention needs. It is a universally spontaneous activity especially amongst the young of most higher animals. Many theories have arisen to explain the purposes it serves (20), but we are still not really certain. Regardless of theory, it is plain that play can be of significance in the physical, social and moral development of children and can be converted to therapeutic and educational ends. Body tone (muscles, organs, circulation) is kept in trim by the exercise afforded in play. Cooperation and competition provide an opportunity for social development. Initially, children appear to prefer solitary play or, at the most, playing side by side without mixing (parallel play). Later, they engage in associative and cooperative play in which the rules of procedure and coexistence with others are gradually observed or taken into account. Thus play also gives children the chance to develop moral judgements, as Piaget has shown (see chapter 5). Play also opens up the opportunity for children to manipulate the materials of their environment. to discern shape, texture, size, weight and the like and to assist them in differentiating the real from the imaginary.

Amongst the theories, we find the 'surplus energy' theory which regards play as the inevitable outlet for the abundant energy of youth made available for the survival of the species. Once the business of survival has been catered for, the surplus is used in exploratory activities. 'Recreative' theories emphasize the therapeutic, hedonistic aspects of play. We play for pure joy, pleasure and relaxation. Play has also been thought of as a rehearsal for adult roles (girl with doll = mother with baby) in which life is played out in miniature. These views are sometimes referred to as 'instinct' or 'preparatory' theories. 'Achievement-mastery' and a desire to have physical mastery over the environment has also been seen as having some bearing on the motivation to play. Finally, a view which now has few supporters is the 'recapitulation' theory and this supposes that play follows a series of stages similar to the evolution of the species; thus the behaviour of young children is reminiscent of the early stages in man's development.

The use of play in education, the *playway* as it is sometimes called, has its origins in the belief that all children want to play and that learning will occur at the same time— as a bonus, in a sense. By suitably shaping the order and nature of the materials, devising situations in which children can play and learn as well and having a keen sense of the things which children enjoy doing, play can be pressed into productive service in the process of learning. However, long periods of unstructured, unguided, 'accidental' practice are wasteful, frustrating and unnecessary. The gravest disservice to our young would be to transmit, by default, the idea that learning does not require personal effort and sacrifice. As students well know, learning has its enjoyment, but it also involves hard work.

Need to achieve

The motive to achieve, whilst having no well-established origins in primary needs, is, nevertheless, a useful concept which has some face validity in the classroom. Ausubel (19) perceives at least three components in achievement motivation. They are (1) *cognitive drive* which is *task-oriented* in the sense that the enquirer is attempting to satisfy his need to know and understand (see Maslow), and the reward of discovering new knowledge resides in the carrying out of the task; (2) *self-enhancement* which is *ego-* or *self-oriented* and represents a desire for increased prestige and status gained by doing well scholastically and which leads to feelings of adequacy and self-esteem; and (3) a broader motive of *affiliation* which is a dependence on others for approval. Satisfaction comes from such approval irrespective of the cause, so that the individual uses academic success simply as a means of recognition by those on whom he depends for assurances. Parents play an active part in the young child's affiliation needs. Later the teacher often becomes another source of affiliation satisfaction.

Another direction of exploration arises from the work of McClelland (21). He introduced the term 'need for achievement' or 'nAch' for short. The persistence of both children and adults to master objects and ideas would suggest that they have a strong desire to achieve. Whatever the cause, its presence is a constant source of hope and encouragement to teachers. McClelland adopted 'projection' techniques (see chapter 11) to differentiate the levels of need to achieve following from a variety of experimental conditions. In one research there were two stages to the experiment; the first stage consisted of seven pencil-and-paper verbal and motor tests; the second stage followed with a test of 'creative imagination' where the subjects had to write stories about several pictures (projecting their achievement motive) from which a measure of achievement motivation was taken. Six experimental conditions were chosen.

1. relaxed: The students were told that the research had been devised to improve the quality of the tests. In other words, the tests and not the students were being tested;
2. neutral: Again, the tasks were oriented towards the tests rather than the students, but in this instance they were asked to take the tests seriously and to do their best;
3. success: The first of the seven tests was first completed and scored as a carefully timed exercise. Students were then asked about their individual class marks and positions, IQ and a personal estimate of their ability. They were also told that the present series of tests were measures of intelligence in which students at a rival institution had excelled. After these false statements the students were given some invented 'norms' for the first test making it look as though most had done well. Similarly, results of the next six tests were announced to maintain the impression that the group had been successful;
4. achievement oriented: Instructions were the same for this group as for the 'success' group except that no norms were given;
5. failure: Similar instructions to the 'success' group were used except that the invented norms after the first and the next six tests were so high as to make it appear as though most of the group had failed;
6. success–failure: The norms announced after the first test were low so that almost everyone was successful, whilst very high norms followed the six tests.

The results are expressed diagrammatically in figure 3.2. The order in which the conditions appear bears some profitable information for the teacher. Note the relative position of 'relaxed' and the other forms of motivation. The results seem to show that the difference between the 'success' and the 'success–failure' groups is statistically significant.

This brings us to a discussion of a complementary concept to nAch, that is the *fear of failure*. Much important recent research by Birney (22) points to the paradox in our society, with its overriding respect for those who strive and succeed, that an advance towards achievement is also a retreat from the fear of failure. Notice in McClelland's work the highest levels of nAch are obtained by those who think they have failed, especially those who have tasted success. As Birney observes, 'success and failure can best be understood *only in an interpersonal context*. . . . In an achieving society, success is highly instrumental in gathering esteem and respect, while failure is a standard way of losing esteem.' Fear of failure may have many causes, but three important ones are lessening of self-esteem, lowering of public image and the loss of rewards accompanying poor attainment. Where self-ratings on a questionnaire are used (23) to show differences in expressed attitudes towards achievement motivation and actual performance, those with high achievement professed to being self-confident, diligent, serious, singleminded and conformist.

Children need to succeed. In catering for this we have to keep a close watch on their abilities and potential when devising their classroom work. Herein lies one of the important reasons for individual attention of children: that we can set goals for each child in accordance with what the teacher sees as within the capabilities of that child, thus ensuring that the child tastes success as well as failure.

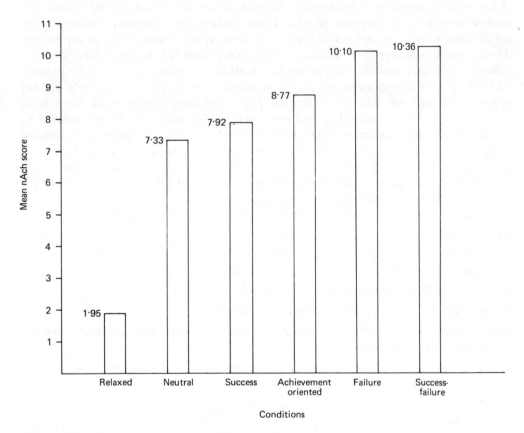

Figure 3.2 Need-achievement in different circumstances
From the work of D. C. McClelland *et al.*, *The Achievement Motive*, Appleton-Century-Crofts, New York, 1953

Level of aspiration

In the light of experience and advice, we all set ourselves standards of achievement. These can be referrred to as *levels of aspiration*. Plainly the level at which we set our sights has an important bearing on our levels of performance. Children without a challenge are less likely to improve their skills than those who are encouraged to strive for better performance.

In a well-known study by Sears (24), fourth, fifth and sixth grade children (ten to twelve year olds) were divided into three groups of those who had been successful, unsuccessful and 'differentially' successful in school subjects including arithmetic and reading. The differential group had succeeded in reading, but had done badly in arithmetic. Under familiar, normal classroom conditions the children were given several tasks in arithmetic and reading. After a task each child was asked to give an estimate of how long it would take for him to carry out the next task; this was taken as a measure of his level of aspiration. Discrepancies between actual time taken and estimated time needed were used to compare groups. Three particularly interesting findings were: (a) children with a background of success set themselves realistic levels of aspiration; (b) those with a background of failure tended to set unrealistic levels of either over- or underestimates; (c) the differential group were realistic in reading, their normally successful subject. In a continuation experiment in which each group was randomly divided into two, one half was falsely told they had performed badly in their most recent tasks and the other half was told they had done well. Self-estimates of the time needed to complete the tasks were again requested of the pupils. In this case, Sears was interested in the short-term effects of success and failure for those who usually experience long-term effects. The results showed that (a) the short-term success group tended to set realistic levels of aspiration; and (b) short-term failure had little effect particularly for those in the group normally experiencing long-term success.

Several helpful pointers can be gleaned from this and other evidence.

(a) repeated failure does not enable children to make a reasonable estimate of their capabilities. Naturally, if a child has no idea what he can do successfully, he cannot possibly be in a position to set himself realistic goals;

(b) the effects of intermittent failure are more varied than those of success;

(c) unexpected failure gives lowered levels of aspiration;

(d) continued failure produces a decline in levels of aspiration—nothing enhances failure better than failure;

(e) a combination of failure and success (see McClelland's work earlier in the chapter) raises levels of aspiration and need to achieve;

(f) where there is knowledge that a goal has been achieved, a child will often be inspired to set his sights higher on the next occasion—his levels of aspiration are raised;

(g) the greater the success of a child, the stronger is the tendency to raise levels of aspiration;

(h) however, where success comes too easily, levels are frequently lowered;

(i) highly cherished goals may be reflected in lowered levels of aspiration so as to ensure some success;

(j) unexpected success often leads to raised levels of aspiration.

In conclusion, the judicious use of success and, to a limited extent, failure must form an important element in classroom practice. Children need help in discovering their capacities and setting realistic goals for themselves.

The self-fulfilling prophecy

Once we have made up our minds about the capabilities of each child, to what extent does this decision adversely influence our treatment of the child? Do children perform in the way we expect them to perform? In a recent survey of the literature and research by Rosenthal and Jacobson (25), it appears that performance and attainment in school subjects was significantly improved where improvement was anticipated. They go on to speculate that

> by what she said, by how and when she said it, by her facial expressions, postures, and perhaps by her touch, the teacher may have communicated to the children of the experimental group that she expected improved intellectual performance. Such communications together with possible changes in teaching techniques may have helped the child learn by changing his self-concept, his expectations of his own behaviour, and his motivation, as well as his cognitive style and skills.

The opportunities for these unintentional influences abound in every classroom. Presumably the reverse effect of inadvertently depressing a child's performance by setting goals which are too low is yet another possibility. In many ways, the self-fulfilling prophecy can be used to advantage by adopting an optimistic attitude toward the performance of children in the hope that they will learn more than was deemed possible at first sight.

INCENTIVES

To this point, no clear distinction has been made between internal drive states, the 'push' from within which is supposed to have energizing properties, and incentives, that is objects external to us which act as a 'pull' from without. Desire for organic satisfaction (food, air, water), security, approval, attention, companionship or achievements are assumed to have some intrinsic motivational origins. Nevertheless, there are many extrinsic factors such as teacher personality, work conditions, teaching techniques, rewards and punishments which determine the course of events in the classroom.

Whilst accepting the value of intrinsic motivation for long-term rewards, all teachers are obliged to press into service extrinsic motivating systems of immediate rewards or incentives. The knowledge that children delight in exploratory or manipulative activities and that they have a need to achieve and set themselves goals, must act as a potent starting point for a teacher. Sometimes the inherent interest in school work is sufficient to arouse the children to cognitive activity. But often it will be necessary to apply external stimuli.

Knowledge of results

Obtaining information about how successfully one is performing ('feedback'), as we have seen, has high motivational value, especially when the news is good. Skinner (26), as we shall see in the section on learning, makes much of the idea that pupils should have *immediate* knowledge of their performance for the knowledge to have any value. The longer the time between completing work and getting to know the verdict, particularly if it is favourable, the less chance there is of the results having a motivational impact on the pupil. This applies equally well to essays at any level of education. Skinner applied the idea in constructing the linear teaching programme (see chapter 6) where the response given by a pupil is evaluated immediately. As we have seen, knowledge of failure can be equally devastating, hence Skinner suggests that the steps taken in the programme should be short and give a slow build up in level of difficulty so as to ensure a high level of success.

Reward and punishment

In a classic experiment by Hurlock (27) in 1925, ten year olds were given practice in a series of addition tests all of equal difficulty. Four groups were formed: (1) a *control*

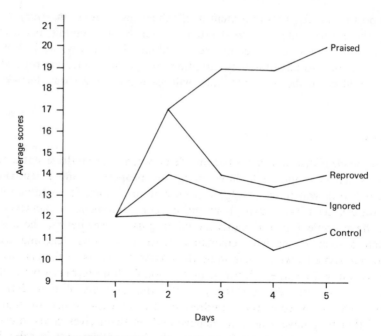

Figure 3.3 Effects of praise and reproof as incentives
Adapted from E. B. Hurlock, 'An evaluation of certain incentives
used in school work', *J. educ. Psychol.*, **16**, 145–159 (1925)

group given no special motivation and kept separate from the other groups; (2) a *praised* group who were complimented on the preceding day's work irrespective of the level of performance; (3) a *reproved* group who were chided for poor work, careless mistakes or lack of improvement—in fact, any pretext by which to chastise individuals; and (4) an *ignored* group who were neither praised nor reproved but were present in the same room with the praised and reproved groups so that they could hear comments made to other children. The diagram in figure 3.3 displays some clear differences between the performance of the groups over the five days of the research.

The conclusion is that whilst the performance of the pupils on the first day was the same, the praised group outstripped all others in subsequent performance. The reproved group do improve in the short term, but continued harassing tends to have a deleterious influence. It may be that where standards are too exacting, where teachers are perfectionists, study and performance suffers because the pupils, unable to live up to the impossibly high standards, just capitulate. The complacency of the ignored and control groups is worth noting. This research was repeated by Schmidt (28) with rather less success because the variations in settings in which praise or reproof can occur also have a marked effect on the extent to which they influence performance as well as the level of anxiety experienced by the pupil (see later section on drive and performance).

The misfortune is that we tend to dichotomize reward/punishment. There is doubtless a continuum of feedback mechanisms employed between teacher and taught (from high praise through mild words of caution to much more serious rebuking on the punishment side) which induces a whole spectrum of pupil reaction (29). Given the limitation to Hurlock's work, it does support the contention that both praise *and* reproof are more effective in their different ways in a classroom than a neutral discourse. Operational conclusions also arising from this work are that the balance along the continuum of reward and punishment should be tipped in favour of reward. The problem with punishment is in its effects. They tend to be less predictable than for rewards and to indicate to the pupil what *not* to do. It is important to provide at the same time as the punishment a clear indication of what should have been done.

Errors need to be pointed out; misbehaviour which is antisocial should be corrected; but the teacher should always attempt to ascertain the reasons for failure or blatant misconduct before applying punitive methods. Personal problems, home circumstances, misjudgements in the standard of work being given to a child (either too hard or too easy) and many other causes may be at the roots of underachievement (performance below that expected from previous performance or standardized tests). Therefore, one should not be too hasty in applying pressure until valid and reasonable causes have been eliminated.

Cooperation and competition

Research into the relative merits of cooperative and competitive methods in class has not been particularly illuminating. To begin with, we have the dilemma of encouraging both cooperation and competition within the same teaching systems. The only generalization which emerges from a mass of research is that in none of the studies does competition yield more effective learning than cooperation (30). Nevertheless, the one thing that seems certain is that both devices are valid motivators (31). Provided the level of competitive antagonism is not too high performance appears to be improved (30). Where the stakes are very high, children opt out or resort to cheating. Self-competition has already been alluded to as an effective means in our discussion of nAch and levels of aspiration. The matter of social motives (32) such as dependence, affiliation and desire for approval have likewise a great deal to do with encouraging children to participate in cooperative ventures.

DRIVE AND PERFORMANCE

Throughout the present chapter several terms have been used which suggest that motivation involves some kind of tension state. We talk of 'fear of failure', anxiety and drive states, conflict, frustration or emotional tension all implying some kind of disturbance or dissonance. What we have not discussed is the connection between the 'amount' of drive present and the nature and extent of the activity ensuing. Is there a straightforward link between drive and performance such that an increase in one gives rise to a

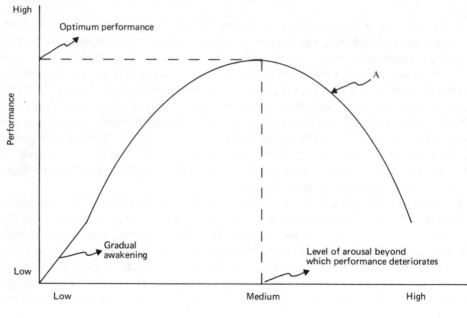

Figure 3.4   Idealized representation of the Yerkes–Dodson Law

corresponding increase in the other? Or are there times when a maximum level of performance is reached beyond which no amount of drive will increase output? Will highly motivated (or highly anxious) performers invariably do better than moderately motivated ones? The answers to these questions are not simple. The factors involved are many and of devious influence. But two factors of primary importance which have been examined are the *level of motivation* or *arousal* and the *difficulty* of the task. As long ago as 1908, Yerkes and Dodson (33) found from their work with rats that as the level of motivation is increased for a given task an optimum is reached beyond which performance increasingly deteriorates. Figure 3.4 is a theoretical graph of this statement. As we pass from one kind of task to another, the difficulty of each task also affects the optimum level of arousal at which learning and performance are adversely influenced. A general statement of this finding is that as the difficulty of tasks increases, the optimum motivation for learning or performance decreases. This became known as the Yerkes–Dodson Law. The law is beautifully demonstrated by Broadhurst (34) using three levels of difficulty for tasks performed by rats as shown in figure 3.5.

Everyday examples of achievement being influenced by the level of difficulty are not hard to find. Very simple tasks (shelling peas) are not likely to cause us concern under normal circumstances, whereas highly provoking tasks where emotional arousal is in evidence do not need to become too complex before we begin to make silly mistakes (as when sitting examinations or taking a driving test). However, there are dangers in

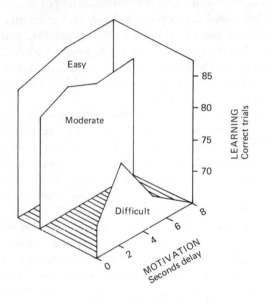

Figure 3.5   The Yerkes–Dodson Law
Reprinted from P. L. Broadhurst, 'Emotionality and the Yerkes–Dodson Law', *J. exp. Psychol.*, **54**, 348 (1957) with the permission of the American Psychological Association

drawing direct analogies between the moderately simple activities required of rats in maze-running or food-seeking problems and the highly intricate tasks required of children or students. The relationship could not be as clean-cut as the Yerkes–Dodson effect. The curvilinearity (the inverted U-shape of figure 3.4) applies to rat performance. What little evidence we have for complicated tasks will be considered in more detail in chapter 11, but we have cause to believe that those in highly provoking situations, or high anxiety-prone people as measured in tests of neuroticism, may experience disruptive influences from the very outset of task performance. In other words, as the stress in a situation mounts, our performance deteriorates immediately. Representing this graphically, the starting point of our graph in figure 3.4 would be at point A which is beyond the peak of performance.

It would be premature to draw generalizations about class practices from the evidence presented above. A little tension or 'dissonance' might well be essential for arousal and learning. What we do not know is the limit of the tension which can be tolerated by individuals in given circumstances. The main point is to be wary of creating a classroom atmosphere which is too stressful (35).

SUMMARY

Children abound with vitality and an urge to satisfy many kinds of human need. It is armed with this knowledge that teachers are able to make the formal setting of school into an environment where children can learn and develop conducively and efficiently. The process of motivation sees the release of energy which can be utilized for, and directed towards, educational objectives. Where a child is physiologically satisfied, where he feels secure and wanted and where he has the opportunity to grow in confidence, independence and self-esteem through achievement, there is every likelihood that he will go on to seek the intellectual satisfactions provided at school.

For our purposes, the important emphasis is in the testable outcomes of our methods in the classroom, rather than in seeking the elusive origins of human needs. For example, we know that young children become puzzled by their surrounds; they poke around, question, and show inquisitiveness; they manipulate and inspect most things that come within reach. The classroom should, therefore, be designed to take advantage of these ready-made characteristics. Children also strive to succeed or achieve in their attempt to master environmental obstacles (material, social or intellectual). Man would not have survived if this had not been so. Of course, the conditions for achievement are varied and research shows that a skilful combination of success and failure is more favourable for stimulating positive achievement than a distant or 'neutral' atmosphere. Children tasting success and failure—in that order—are most likely to continue the struggle to achieve. They also set themselves goals; teachers must ensure that these goals are adequate and realistic for each child. The teacher must beware, however, of prejudging the capabilities of a child to the point where the teacher consistently under- or overestimates them. It is so easy to 'give a dog a bad name'.

Extrinsic motivators in the form of incentives are a very necessary part of a teacher's life. Children, as with adults, like to know how they are faring in relation to their own previous performance and to the performance of others. Research tells us that the sooner a person knows the outcome of his work, the more likely it is that he will be reinforced to continue learning—always provided he meets with sufficient success, because knowledge of repeated failure is not likely to stimulate further activity. As we observed above, positive achievement must be part of the teacher's design. Praise and reproof from a respected teacher are powerful incentives. Children delight in approval in the presence of their peers.

A knowledge of childhood motives is one of the essentials of teaching skill. When children are pursuing purposeful activities in class because they feel the need and want to learn, their teacher is clearly well on the way to an understanding of these motives.

ENQUIRY AND DISCUSSION

1. Using Maslow's theory as a possible framework, consider the varied conditions of home and school likely to affect the highest desire of man to satisfy his need for knowledge and understanding.

2. On school observation, carefully note those activities which children in particular age groups most enjoy. Can these be turned to good effect in class? What criteria have you used for detecting interest and enthusiasm amongst children? Discuss with your tutors whether these are valid criteria.

3. Observe children at play and note the differences according to age. Is play a 'natural' educator? How can it be canalized to good effect in school work? Where should teachers draw the line between 'play' and 'work'?

4. In the text we talked about 'a continuum of feedback mechanisms' running from high praise to severe punishment. Explore this continuum of possible 'rewards' and 'punishments' using your knowledge of schooldays, school observation and parental control. Which do you think are effective at particular ages and why? Discuss this matter with children.

5. Read *Pygmalion in the Classroom* [note (25)]. What can a teacher do to avoid the self-fulfilment of adverse prophecies?

6. Note the use made by teachers of incentives. Compare the relative merits of incentives in particular age groups and, where possible, with different ability ranges.

7. The previous suggestions for enquiries could be pooled for group discussions with your tutor. At the same time, discuss the extent to which your findings fit in with previous work.

NOTES AND REFERENCES

1. D. O. Hebb, 'The role of neurological ideas in psychology', *J. Personality*, **20**, 29–55 (1951).

2. B. F. Skinner, *Science and Human Behaviour*, Macmillan, New York, 1953.

3. W. McDougall, *An Introduction to Social Psychology*, Methuen, London, 1908.

4. McDougall claimed that the 'human mind has certain innate or inherited tendencies which are the essential springs or motive powers of all thought and action'. He posited fourteen such human instincts, some with a corresponding 'sentiment' which was the emotional disposition characteristic of individuals and arising from their particular experience and training in coping with each instinct. Those such as food-seeking and gregariousness have no obvious corresponding sentiments. Here are some:

instinct	sentiment
food ⎱ -seeking water ⎰	?
gregariousness	?
acquisitiveness	?
constructive	?
aggression	anger
mating	sexual desire
curiosity	wonder
self-assertion	elation
maternal	tenderness
repulsion	disgust
escape	fear
self-abasement	submission

5. C. Burt, 'Is the doctrine of instincts dead?' A Symposium. I—The case for human instincts. *Br. J. educ. Psychol.*, **11**, 155–172 (1941).

6. P. E. Vernon, 'Is the doctrine of instincts dead?' A Symposium. II. *Br. J. educ. Psychol.*, **12**, 1–10 (1942).

7. The much quoted work of M. Mead, *Sex and Temperament*, Routledge, London, 1935, showed major differences in child-rearing practices which lead to obvious differences in the characteristics of the tribes. The Arapesh of New Guinea, we are told, were peace-loving and not particularly concerned about taking on the roles of leadership. Children were reared with great tenderness, given every attention and suckled at the breast for as long as mother could hold out. The Mundugumour were aggressive, warlike, ruthless and their babyhood was likewise made into a struggle between parent and child. Babies had to fight for the breasts for the short time they were available, were starved of affection and handled roughly if rarely. One is left wondering how much of the adult characteristics are the outcome of direct teaching from the parents, not so much as a baby, but later when the child could begin to understand the language and learn the tribal mores. Again, the fertility or hostility of the environment, which was easy for the Arapesh and harsh for the Mundugumour, may have determined the particular traits which would assist the tribes to survive. Thus, the question of whether we are dealing here with inherited or acquired characteristics is wide open. See also R. Benedict, *Patterns of Culture*, Routledge, London, 1935.

8. G. W. Allport, *Personality*, Holt, New York, 1937.

9. The most recent elaboration of the ethologists' work can be found in N. Tinbergen, *A Study of Instinct*, Oxford University Press, Oxford, 1951. W. H. Thorpe also has a readable summary in *Learning and Instinct in Animals*, Methuen, London, 1956.

Two concepts central to their work are the *sign* or *environment stimulus* and the *innate releasing mechanism* (IRM). Largely by analogy from animal studies, Lorenz considers that humans have a parental instinct which can be released by various cues. The sight of a doll (environmental sign stimulus) elicits parental behaviour in female children (innate releasing mechanism). The pattern of stimulation which brings about the release of instinctive parental responses are thought by Lorenz to consist of the dolls' short face, large forehead, chubby cheeks and disjunctive limb movements. This is reminiscent of Burt's definition of innate propensities mentioned earlier in the chapter. Tinbergen thinks that, at the very least, patterns of locomotion, sexual behaviour, sleep, food-seeking, care of the body surface and parenthood are instinctive in man. Lorenz would add social and aggressive drives to this list. One further idea which may have some application in human learning is animal *imprinting* and *critical periods*. It would seem that many animals become attached to objects other than parents soon after birth if those objects are seen first. Birds have become attached to humans who were the only living things present at hatching. This special social attachment is termed imprinting and the time over which imprinting is keenest is known as the critical period. Imprinting occurs in many species of bird and animal including monkeys. Some have suggested that it may also appear in a rudimentary form in human infants. E. H. Hess in a chapter in *New Directions in Psychology*, Holt, Rinehart and Winston, New York, 1962, suggests that orphans who grow to be incurably unsocialized do so because they have missed out on social contact during an early critical period. See W. Sluckin, *Imprinting and Early Learning*, Methuen, London, 1964.

For a recent statement showing Lorenz's adaptation of animal instincts to human behaviour see K. Lorenz, *On Aggression*, Methuen, London, 1967.

Xenophobia, or the hatred existing between human races, has been described by Robert Ardrey, in *The Territorial Imperative*, Collins, London, 1967, as an example of an inborn biological tendency, akin to the animal's desire to protect its territory against predators. We are said to dislike foreigners because they constitute a threat to survival or to our way of life.

10. Sigmund Freud (1856–1939) was a prolific writer and thinker. His gift to psychology and in turn to education is not so much a theory of motivation or personality, but a way of thinking about the mental life of man. His postulates, in the main, do not lend themselves to verification; his theory is an act of faith. For his views on instincts see 'Instincts and their vicissitudes' (1915) in *A Collection of Papers of Sigmund Freud*, vol. I (translated by Riviere), Hogarth, London, 1949.

11. H. F. Harlow and R. R. Zimmerman, 'Affectional responses in the infant monkey', *Science*, **130**, 421 (1959). Also see the work of the field-theorist K. Lewin, *Principles of Topological Psychology*, McGraw-Hill, New York, 1936.

12. C. L. Hull, *Principles of Behavior*, Appleton-Century-Crofts, New York, 1943. For a clear summary see W. F. Hill, *Learning: A Survey of Psychological Interpretations*, Methuen, London, 1963.

13. In a series of experiments with chimpanzees, J. B. Wolfe, managed to teach the animals to 'work' for counters which could be used to withdraw raisins from a slot machine. The counters became valued objects as long as the chimps were hungry. The animals had learnt that the counters were an *incentive* to work. When we work, hunger is not necessarily present. Thus, for us, money can also be a *secondary reinforcer*. For the chimp experiments see J. B. Wolfe, 'Effectiveness of token rewards for chimpanzees', *Comp. Psychol. Monogr.*, **12**, 5, Whole No. 60 (1936), and J. T. Cowles, 'Food tokens as incentives for learning by chimpanzees', *Comp. Psychol. Mongr.*, **14**, 5, Whole No. 71 (1937).

14. C. N. Cofer and M. H. Appley, *Motivation: Theory and Research*, Wiley, New York, 1964. See also the Further Reading, particularly M. D. Vernon's book.

15. A. H. Maslow, 'A theory of human motivation', *Psychol. Rev.*, **50**, 370–396 (1943).

16. Planarians, small, simple creatures very low in the animal kingdom, absorb their reproductive organs back into the body tissue when there is no food. It almost seems as though reproduction is taken as pointless when basic body needs cannot be satisfied. There is no purpose in bringing young into the world if they cannot be fed. But, this would endow the planarian with the ability for conscious control, whereas the absorption of the reproductive organs is entirely physiological.

17. Usually known as the Minnesota Starvation Studies, 26 normal men were put on a six month semi-starvation diet. In all other respects, such as living quarters, social life and exercise, their provisions were normal. All were soon preoccupied with food. A few extreme cases displayed serious mental disorders. A. Keys, 'Experimental induction of psychoneuroses by starvation', *The Biology of Mental Health and Disease*, 27th Animal Conference: Milbank Memorial Fund, Harper and Row, New York, 1952.

18. R. S. Peters, *The Concept of Motivation*, Routledge and Kegan Paul, London, 1958. Although he lays emphasis on providing for an examination of human motivation by starting with the classification of man's observable goals and, as it were, working back, Peters does see a place for causal theories particularly in looking at devious cases.

19. D. P. Ausubel and F. G. Robinson, *School Learning*, Holt, Rinehart and Winston, New York, 1969.

20. For background reading on theories of play have a look at M. Lowenfeld, *Play in Childhood*, Gollancz, London, 1935, or more recently C. Hart, 'Exploration and play in children', in P. A. Jewel and C. Loizes (Eds), *Play Exploration and Territory in Mammals*, Academic Press, London, 1966.

21. An enormous volume of research has sprung from D. C. McClelland's concept of nAch. Some of this is summarized in his book *Studies in Motivation*, Appleton-Century-Crofts, New York, 1955, but the most detailed statement of his view is to be found in D. C. McClelland, J. W. Atkinson, R. A. Clark and E. L. Lowell, *The Achievement Motive*, Appleton-Century-Crofts, New York, 1953. For a recent

report see R. C. Birney, 'Research on the achievement motive', in E. F. Borgatta and W. F. Lambert (Eds), *Handbook of Personality Theory and Research*, Rand McNally, Chicago, 1968.

22. R. C. Birney, H. Burdick and R. C. Teevan, *Fear of Failure*, Van Nostrand Reinhold, New York, 1969.

23. H. G. Gough, 'What determines academic achievement of high school students?', *J. educ. Res.*, **46**, 321–331 (1953).

24. P. S. Sears, 'Levels of aspiration in academically successful and unsuccessful children', *J. abnorm. soc. Psychol.*, **35**, 498–536 (1940).

25. R. Rosenthal and L. Jacobson, *Pygmalion in the Classroom*, Holt, Rinehart and Winston, New York, 1968. See also D. A. Pigeon, *Expectation and Pupil Performance*, NFER, Slough, 1970.

26. B. F. Skinner, *The Science of Human Behaviour*, Macmillan, New York, 1953.

27. E. B. Hurlock, 'An evaluation of certain incentives used in school work', *J. educ. Psychol.*, **16**, 145–159 (1925).

28. H. O. Schmidt, 'The effect of praise and blame on incentives to learning', *Psychol. Monogr.*, **53**, No. 240 (1941).

29. I. Johannesson, 'Effects of praise and blame upon achievement and attitudes in schoolchildren', *Child and Education*, Munksgaard, Copenhagen, 1962.

30. C. B. Stendler, D. Damrin and A. C. Haines, 'Studies in cooperation and competition: I: the effects of working for group and individual rewards on the social climate of children's groups', *J. genet. Psychol.*, **79**, 173–197 (1951).

31. There is a long literature on this subject stretching back to J. C. Chapman and R. B. Feder, 'The effect of external incentives on improvement', *J. educ. Psychol.*, **8**, 469–474 (1917). See also J. Vaughn and C. M. Diserens, 'The experimental psychology of competition', *J. exp. Educ.*, **7**, 76–97 (1938).

32. Imbalance and its remedy is a widely used concept in psychology and sociology. We have already met homeostatic imbalance. Piaget used the term *equilibration;* Bruner spoke of *mismatch*; L. Festinger has developed a seminal idea with his *cognitive dissonance* in a text entitled *A Theory of Cognitive Dissonance*, Row Peterson, Evanston, Illinois, 1957. His basic theme is concerned with the motivational value of tension which accompanies 'dissonance'. Dissonance, according to Festinger, occurs when we are aware of differences between the related 'elements' in a situation. If a child who regularly does well in the school football team has a bad day, dissonance arises because of the incongruity between previous experience and present performance. The tension arising from this dissonance may be dissipated in a number of ways. If the footballer has an injury, is feeling ill or has another problem on his mind, these may be used to disperse the tension. His central hypotheses are that dissonance is psychologically uncomfortable and will therefore

motivate individuals to reduce the dissonance. Secondly, when dissonance is in evidence, individuals will do all they can to avoid meeting with information which is likely to increase the dissonance.

33. R. M. Yerkes and J. D. Dodson, 'The relation of strength of stimulus to rapidity of habit-formation', *J. comp. neurol. Psychol.*, **18**, 459–482 (1908).

34. P. L. Broadhurst, 'Emotionality and the Yerkes–Dodson Law', *J. exp. Psychol.*, **54**, 345–352 (1957).

35. It has been claimed by Biggs in research on the teaching of mathematics in primary schools that very high levels of anxiety are regularly created by inadequate teaching of the subject (partly because the teachers are not themselves numerate). The outcome is a widespread dislike of the subject because pupils associate high tension with it. See J. B. Biggs, The Psychological Relationships Between Cognitive and Affective Factors in Arithmetic Performance. *Ph.D. Thesis*, London University.

FURTHER READING

C. N. Cofer and M. H. Appley, *Motivation: Theory and Research*, Wiley, New York, 1964. A technical book, but very thorough.

A. H. Maslow, 'A theory of human motivation', *Psychol. Rev.*, **50**, 370–396 (1943).

E. J. Murray, *Motivation and Emotion*, Prentice-Hall, New Jersey, 1964. Concise and well written.

M. D. Vernon, *Human Motivation*, Cambridge University Press, London, 1969. A detailed, well-balanced book with plenty of value for a teacher.

4   Attention and perception

The ceaseless, simultaneous bombardment of stimuli on the sense organs and their subsequent treatment in the nervous system and brain was discussed in a previous chapter without considering the prevention of overloading (see, for example, the section on the brain stem in chapter 2). Clearly we could not possibly cope with every stimulus that falls on the eyes in a given instant, let alone those falling on all the other senses at the same time. Just consider for a moment all that is happening around you at this very instant. Your eyes are taking in the print impressions (and I hope the brain is translating them into a meaningful pattern!), as well as the peripheral images of other nearby objects on the table or of your hand gripping the book. You may be the victim of audible noises from other students, vehicles, building in progress, and so on. There may be perfume or other chemicals in the air. Your body is experiencing pressure from contact with clothes, and objects such as this book, the chair and table. Along with many other sensory possibilities, the brain would have to deal with a phenomenal number of sensations. The study of attention is concerned with finding an answer to the question of how the body manages so many signals and why an individual selects certain stimuli for attention and ignores others.

Again, having selected stimuli for attention what do we make of them? If, for example, we looked at the same object or listened to the same piece of music would we interpret the sensory stimuli in precisely the same way? It is more than likely we would not. There may be cultural differences in the way we perceive objects because of differences in our sensory experience (see the section on illusions later in the chapter), or the combination of notes in the music may be recognized as a tune by some and an indescribable, formless noise by others. Most important is the fact that the interpretation of present sensory information is dependent on our past experiences. As Kant once said, 'we see things not as they are but as we are'. A consideration of sensory interpretation, or perception, will be the second major concern in this chapter.

THE MEANING OF SENSATION, ATTENTION AND PERCEPTION

First let us distinguish between three terms, sometimes confused, which frequently recur in this chapter. They are sensation, attention and perception. *Sensation* is said to occur when any sense organ (eye, ear, nose) receives a stimulus from the external or internal environment. This can, and frequently does, occur without our knowledge. Sound waves for instance are impinging on the ear-drum and causing disturbances which we do not register. If you listen attentively for a moment you will soon discover many sounds which would have passed you by had you not made a search for them.

With so many senses being activated at the same time, how is it that we are only aware of one stimulus at a time? One possible explanation is that a selection mechanism operates which is either voluntary—where we make a deliberate effort and search for a particular kind of stimulus—or involuntary—where some peculiar quality of the stimulus arrests our attention. The ability of human beings to process some part of the incoming sensations to the sense organs and to ignore everything else is referred to as *attention* [Russian Pavlovian psychologists use the term *orientation reaction* (1)].

Receiving and attending to a noise or the touch of a material is only part of the story because we need to interpret the selected sensations in the light of our past experience. This internal analysis of sensations by the brain is termed perception. Although these three terms are defined separately it is clear from the definitions that they are closely connected and constitute an integral part of human information processing.

A common and inaccurate belief is that the sensations picked up from our surroundings are selected, received, interpreted and reproduced by the brain like a photograph or gramophone record of sights and sounds—as if there was a little man sitting in the recesses of the brain taking in exact reproductions of incoming signals. This is not the case. The physical images received by the sense organs must first be translated (encoded) into a form compatible with nerve impulses previously received and stored so that the incoming impulses can be matched with past experience. Consider how many ways you have experienced the concept 'rose'—spoken word, written word, touch, smell, sight, etc. In the spoken word alone you will have heard many accents, voice pitches and intensities, but all have been transformed to a common code. So there is a wide latitude within which sensory experience is given a common meaning (perceptual constancy). Therefore, the nervous system must carry out appreciable transformations of the input of physical images in order for perception to take place.

ATTENTION

At the beginning of the present century, James (2) generated considerable interest in attention amongst psychologists. Experimentation was not his strong point, but his insights into the processes of attention and perception served until the early 1950s when Broadbent (3) revitalized interest with his seminal researches and speculations. Much of what is to follow in this section is based directly or indirectly on the ideas of Broadbent.

Above we defined attention in a rather specific fashion. It refers chiefly to *selective* or *voluntary* attention when the individual is actively seeking for some signals and ignoring others. Sometimes the term is used to describe search behaviour as in vigilance tasks where the individual is required to identify specified signals on a screen or clock. 'Set' is also used to describe a predisposition to perceive certain signals and ignore all others. Sometimes our attention is demanded rather than controlled, as when we hear an unusual sound, see contrasting colours on a blackboard or sense a harsh smell. But the work we shall describe deals with purposeful attention.

Broadbent's filter theory

Broadbent's work on selective attention forms a productive model from which we can derive some profitable applications for the teacher (4). Basically, the filter model (see figure 4.1 p. 58) is taken from communications theory, including much of the jargon, and provides an explanation of how selective attention is managed. The sense organs and nervous system receiving and transmitting impulses are referred to as the *input channels*. Several input channels are operating simultaneously in parallel. However, the amount of information passing along the channels is far too much for the brain to cope with at any one time because overloading would occur if all the information was assimilated. Thus, to regulate the intake Broadbent supposes that there is a filter followed by a bottleneck (*limited capacity channel*) which selects some of the incoming impulses for processing in the brain. The input not selected may be held in a *short-term storage* system and can be taken out of store provided this is done within a very short time (a few seconds at the most). However, the stored input signals grow weaker with time and when 'a line becomes available' for one impulse through the limited capacity channel, the remaining stored impulses suffer a further weakening effect. The phenomenon of short-term memory accounts both for our ability to recall a very recent incident and the deficit in information when it has been stored for a short time compared with the moment of reception. In other words, we have a temporary and limited capacity for remembering events which the sense organs have received but to which we have not given our immediate attention.

Transmissions through the limited capacity channel are processed by a perceptual system possessing at least the *long-term memory* store and a *decision-making system*. The latter is subsequently responsible for *effector* activity and *output*.

Several modifications have been recommended to accommodate subsequent research findings. For example, the model assumes that selection of input takes place *before* the interpretation of its meaning which confines the selection to the physical sensory characteristics of the input. Treisman (5) questions this stage at which Broadbent places selection and argues from her researches that a more complex analytical mechanism operates to filter out levels of increasing complexity. Thus, starting with physical characteristics, let us say of spoken sentences, one voice sound is chosen from all others. Then comes a test of that sound for syllables, words, grammatical structure and finally meaning. Therefore, the sentence input is progressively attended to and defined. Peripheral input is stored temporarily in the short-term memory and *attenuated* ('subdued' or 'reduced' in value). Nevertheless, most psychologists are agreed about the inevitability of a filter at some stage to regulate input.

The factors which influence attention

Workers in this field are agreed that both the observer and the stimulus possess characteristics which are likely to influence attention. The following are of particular relevance for the teacher. For convenience let us divide them into external and internal factors.

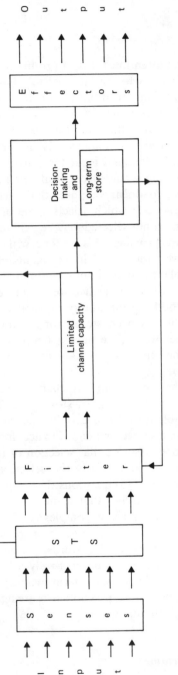

Figure 4.1 Adapted from D. E. Broadbent, *Perception and Communication*,
Pergamon, London, 1958
STS = Short-term store

External factors

1. Selection of information does not occur in a random fashion. The *intensity* of a stimulus for instance can attract attention. Loud noises, bright colours, strong odours, high pressure on the skin are compelling stimuli.

2. *Novel* stimuli attract attention. Any unusual or irregular event is liable to distract us. The reason for using italics in a textbook or colour on a blackboard is to draw your eye to key concepts by printing the words in an irregular form. Ringing the changes of methods of presenting subject matter in school has obvious possibilities of catching children's attention.

3. A *variable* or *changing stimulus* demands our attention. Animals stalking their prey (cats for instance) move as little as possible so as not to attract attention. Teachers quickly discover how to use their voices by frequently changing the intonation. Wall charts and aids should be changed regularly, otherwise they no longer attract the children's interest—the children become *adapted* to the aids in the same way as happens with the ticking of a clock to which one becomes accustomed and takes for granted.

4. *Regularity* of stimuli presented in space (spatial) or time (temporal) has an effect on attention. Distributed presentations, again to avoid becoming adapted, have a better chance of becoming noticed than rapid, regular presentations.

5. Certain *colours* are more attractive than others. Infants are much more interested in coloured than in grey backgrounds, and both children and adults pay more attention to red and white designs in preference to black and white.

6. *High sounds* are more likely to be regarded than low sounds when the two are presented simultaneously.

7. *Conditioned* and habitual stimuli are likely to be picked out from other stimuli. When your name is announced in the midst of other names or conversation, you will pick it out. This is called the 'cocktail party' effect because it is often possible to hear a familiar phrase or name over and above the chatter of conversation at a party.

Internal factors

Physical and mental dispositions are necessarily important influences of attentiveness. The fact that people in identical or very similar physical circumstances display striking differences in the degree to which they attend to stimuli is partly a matter of internal dispositions. The following are amongst the most important.

1. *Interest* is clearly a factor likely to cause differential attention. Events in which a child has already gained an interest are more likely to attract attention than events which have not previously been of interest. Attitudes and prejudices also affect the extent to which we are drawn to pay heed to events or ideas.

2. Physical or social *deprivations* pertaining to basic human needs (see chapter 3) have a marked effect on the direction and intensity of attention. Extreme deprivation frequently leads to excessive orientation of all the senses toward the satisfaction of the deprived need. Excessive starvation ultimately gives rise to all manner of unusual manifestations where the individual dreams of, fights for, has hallucinations about, and directs all his physical and mental energies towards food [see the Minnesota Starvation Studies, chapter 3, note (17)].

3. *Fatigue* has a detrimental effect on attentiveness. It stands to reason that as our

physical reserves become depleted, our vigilance in any sense modality will be correspondingly reduced. Fatigue can occur in a general way where the whole body is affected, or it can occur in one or some of the senses which have been over-used. A child short of sleep or exhausted from strenuous physical or mental activity is less likely to attend in class.

4. In the chapter on motivation (and subsequently in our discussions of personality) we met with a theory of drive which states that performance improves with increased *arousal* up to a point. Beyond this point, performance begins to deteriorate until at high levels of arousal the quality of performance is extremely poor. A graph of this relationship (figure 3.4) approximates to an inverted U-shape. Attention is also thought to be affected in a similar way as the arousal level increases. A basic level is needed in the first place for attention to be attracted (a threshold of arousal), and once this level has been surpassed, the individual's attention increases usefully. Beyond an optimum level, which varies with the sense in use and the intensity of the external and internal factors mentioned above, attention becomes adversely affected.

5. *Personality characteristics* have a differential influence. Students will be introduced later to a theory of personality structure involving several personality types. One type defined by the dimension of extraversion and introversion will be considered in more detail then. For the present, suffice it to point out that many behavioural distinctions exist between extraverts and introverts. Extraverts need more *involuntary rest pauses* whilst performing tasks requiring concentration. Consequently, their vigilance suffers in comparison with introverts who do not require so many pauses. Extraverts also accumulate inhibition to the continuation of a repetitive task and therefore cannot attend as consistently as introverts (6). The sensory thresholds (levels of stimulation required for us to be aware of the stimulus, mentioned in chapter 2) tend to be lower for introverts than extraverts. The implications for the class teacher are that children with extravert qualities are more likely to wilt and become distracted during long periods of attentive activity and to work at a lower level of sensory susceptibility than introverts.

ATTENTION AND MEMORY

Sperling (7) argues that there are at least three stages of memory. These are (a) *sensory images* of immediate events; (b) *short-term (or primary) memory* (STM) with a limited capacity for information from the immediate sensory images; and (c) a more *permanent long-term (or secondary) memory* (LTM) system with a vast capacity.

(a) Short-term memory of sensory images has been explored in studies of 'span of attention' or 'apprehension' where a person is required to recall a stimulus (objects on a table, dots on a sheet of paper) exposed for a brief interval (8). On average, people can recall between 6 and 10 objects, numbers or letters arranged at random. So a telephone number heard or seen for a short time would be within the competence of most people. Where learning is required, teachers are well advised to note the limitations of immediate memory span.

In an amusing discussion by Miller (9) it is suggested that our *span of absolute judgement*, which is somewhere about 7 objects at once, can be radically improved by a process known as 'chunking'. This consists of grouping items into chunks numbering no more than seven. The technique is widely used in learning subjects like morse, typing and chemistry where items (dots and dashes, letters or chemical symbols) are brought together and learnt as groups.

(b) We have already met the concept of short-term memory, in Broadbent's model, enabling individuals to recall recent sensory events. Fading of these events occurs rapidly and, as we noted above, the act of recalling one aspect of an event in STM interferes with the recall of remaining events. Briefly then, the STM store is seen as a temporary storage of a limited amount of information. Unattended information occurring simultaneously with that to which we are attending can be retrieved with diminishing accuracy as time goes by. Close your eyes and try to recall the objects on the desk. You should have some success in recalling peripheral images of surrounding objects which have impinged on the senses without your having consciously recorded them.

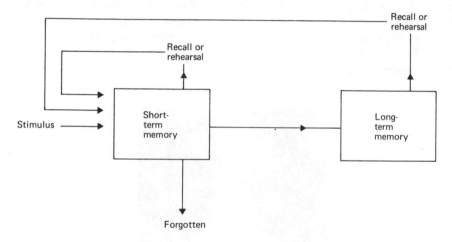

Figure 4.2 Adapted from N. C. Waugh and D. A. Norman, 'Primary memory', *Psychol. Rev.*, **72**, 92–93 (1965)

A current popular view of the relationship between short-term and long-term memory (10) is summarized in figure 4.2.

Recall or rehearsal of information in the short-term store is thought to occur by passing the information through the limited capacity channel and re-entering it to the short-term store. In other words, rehearsal is closely related to rote learning as when we repeat a telephone number, a shopping list or historical details. The more this cycle is repeated, the more likely it is that information will pass into the long-term store (10). There are probably telephone numbers or car registrations lurking in our long-term memory from years ago arising from repeated recall.

(c) A more detailed discussion of LTM appears in chapter 7. There are several characteristics of information received by our sensory system which have a decisive effect on the prospects of survival in the LTM (10). These have been alluded to in various ways above, but we shall summarize them here. They amount to (a) the length of the message; (b) the content of the message; (c) the opportunity and extent of initial learning; and (d) the interaction between successive messages. A concise summary of the relevance of these four characteristics to the problem of effective instruction can be found in an article by Dale, 'Memory and effective instruction', *Aspects of Education* [See note (10) for details of reference]. He concludes that

> for material to enter long-term storage it has to survive an initial period during which retention loss can be extremely rapid. In order to survive, the amount of material should be small; it should be as free as possible from inter-item accoustic confusions; it should be varied so that interference between successive messages is minimised; also an opportunity for a brief period of silent rehearsal should be provided after each component message is presented.

PERCEPTION

We cannot help making sense of our world. How this might be done varies from one to another. The basic sensory signals from objects are the same, but the way we apprehend them differs because of the circumstances in which similar sensory experiences have occurred. The newborn child with crude sensory equipment and next to no backlog of experience against which to evaluate incoming signals builds up, from recurring stimulus

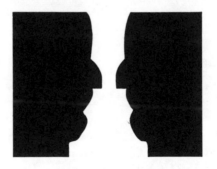

(a)

Figure 4.3 (a)   Figure–ground reversal

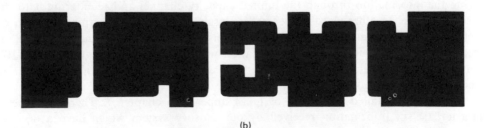

(b)

Figure 4.3 (b)   Figure–ground reversal

patterns presented in a multitude of sizes, shapes, colours, distance from the eye, etc., a perception of his surroundings.

In effect we impose structure on our environment by building models from our sensory experience. In doing this we scan a scene or listen to sounds and pick out particular features which become *the figure*. The background against which the figure is observed is known as *the ground*. Thus, in identifying a shape, the contour outline is most important. It is probably aspects of the figure which pass through the filter to the brain and the immediate ground which is stored temporarily in the short-term memory. Figure–ground discrimination applies in all the sense modalities. For example, music can be picked out and understood against a background of other moderate sounds. Tomato sauce is identified against a background of other foods in one's mouth. When one tries to discriminate one taste from another, they successively take on figure and ground by conscious selection.

Attempts to find a figure against a background are usually not difficult, but occasionally we can be deceived. Figure 4.3(a) in one instant is seen as a candlestick, in the next as the side view of two faces looking at each other. Note the decisiveness with which the figure is *either* a candlestick *or* faces and not a mixture of both. We automatically select a figure. Moreover, when it is a candlestick the brain fills in the lines at the top and bottom. You may even get the impression that the candlestick is of a brighter nature than the surrounding white page, so strong is the tendency to distinguish figure from ground in terms of previous models (a candlestick in this case). Figure 4.3(b) has a similar effect. You may at first only notice meaningless shapes like a plan of a housing estate. It should transpose into a word which will suddenly leap out of the page when you realize what it is.

The nature of perception

Theories of how we establish perceptions and how things appear to us are basically of two kinds. At one extreme it is commonly believed that apart from in-built tendencies to distinguish figure and ground, we gradually learn to identify and interpret objects or arrangements of objects. Hebb (11) proposes that sensory experience is registered in the brain cortex in the form of 'cell assemblies'—groups of neurons which become associated with particular sensory events and which change structurally as a result. As sensory patterns become more complex and stable, whole sequences of cells 'fire' in conjunction in response to stimulation. These larger sequences are known as 'phase sequences'. Thus, Hebb sees perception as an acquired characteristic.

A second and more widely used view was founded in Germany earlier this century and held that perceptual organization is inborn. Psychologists such as Wertheimer, Koffka and Köhler created a school of thinking known as the *Gestalt School* of psychology. The word 'gestalt' is German for 'pattern' or 'form' and the theory emphasizes our ability to perceive patterns as *wholes*. The motto for this movement could well be that 'the whole is more than the sum of the parts'. In other words, we perceive and give meaning to objects by their characteristics *in toto* and not by considering a jumble of the parts which go to make up the total figure.

Several criteria affect the meaning we ascribe to objects. Four arrangements seem to be of primary assistance in recognizing and determining the dominant pattern of the figure in order to form a 'good' pattern or gestalt. The formation of 'good' perceptual patterns is referred to as the *Law of Prägnanz*. They are (a) similarity, (b) proximity, (c) continuity, (d) closure.

(a) *Similarity*.   Where a figure consists of similar elements we tend to group them to form a pattern. Details such as similar shape, size and colour tend to be grouped. In figure 4.4(a) we are more likely to see four columns of Xs or Os than rows of XOXO even though we normally read horizontally. We prefer to order and arrange similar objects in rows rather than at random to avoid the uncomfortable sensation which randomness creates. Instruments, violins in an orchestra for instance, are heard as an entity and not as separate instruments.

(b) *Proximity* applies where similar objects appear close together. In figure 4.4(b) the pattern would most probably be described as three groups containing 3, 2 and 1 Xs respectively and not as six crosses. The morse code relies on the close proximity of dots and dashes.

(c) *Continuity and symmetry*.   Similar parts of a figure which appear in lines (straight or curved) tend to stand out. When they make recognizable shapes such as circles or squares they become conspicuous. The illustration given in figure 4.4(c) will be seen as a square, not as twelve Xs. We spontaneously join up the Xs to make lines. Music is perceived as a continuous rather than a separate system of sounds.

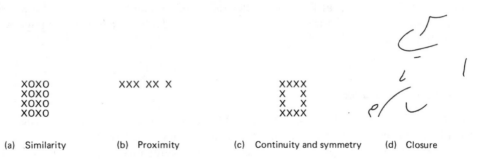

| (a) Similarity | (b) Proximity | (c) Continuity and symmetry | (d) Closure |

Figure 4.4   Patterns which assist in forming *gestalten*

(d) *Closure*.   Closed or partially closed figures are more readily perceived than open figures, except when the open figure has an acquired meaning such as the letters of the alphabet (letter C for example is open but recognized as a letter). Figure 4.4(d) is incomplete, but it will doubtless be recognized from previous models as a man's face. In this recognizable instance we have closed the figure in order to give it a familiar meaning.

Visual illusions and perceptual constancy

Evidence that we tend to perceive in 'gestalten' rather than building up the separate elements of an object is provided from the study of *visual illusions*. They are false perceptions of reality. The three illusions of figure 4.5 are well known. If the book is held so that you are looking along the vertical lines of (A) they will be seen to be straight and parallel. (B) is the Müller–Lyer illusion with (a) and (b) exactly the same length. The third illustration (C) looks as though the lines are curved. But if you look along them from the direction of the arrow they will be seen to be parallel and straight. Even when we know the details it will still be impossible to compensate. One explanation for the illusion (12) is that we are compensating for perspective. Take the Müller–Lyer illusion (B). The outward-pointing arrow (a) could be taken as a near corner jutting out and (b) as a far corner. Consequently we compensate for this possible perspective by perceiving the drawing (b) as larger than it is. *Perceptual constancy* is another case of compensation where we allow for the distance of an object from our senses when judging its magnitude. A man seen at a distance may look as if he is three inches high, but we allow for the distance.

Actually, the more experience we have of perspective in our daily routines, the more we are taken in by illusions. African tribesmen who live in round huts are less prone to the Müller–Lyer effect. The essential point about illusions is that, no matter how hard we try, it is impossible to separate out the parts of the figures. We invariably perceive the figure as a whole.

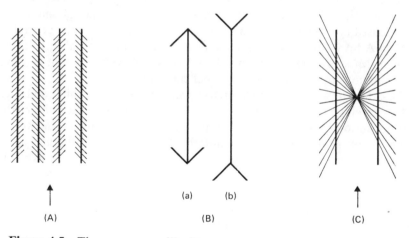

Figure 4.5 Three common illusions
(A) Zölner illusion; (B) Müller–Lyer illusion; (C) Hering illusion

Bruner and Goodman (13) found that young children from poor socio-economic conditions tended to underestimate the size of coins whilst children from favourable conditions were accurate in their judgements. This was regarded by Bruner and Goodman as evidence for cultural experience being a significant influence in perception. Selective attention as an outcome of a particular upbringing (parents who encourage their children to observe the behaviour of animals) is similarly thought to be a factor in perceptual development.

Perception and the teacher

We have still much to learn about perception in human beings. What we do know of value to a teacher will now be summarized.

1. The idea of the Law of Prägnanz in perceptual matters is thought to apply equally well to mental activity. Having clear organization and classification of intellectual experience would therefore obey the same rules as perceptual phenomena; therefore, the field of learning should be structured.

2. Pupils should be given opportunities to use closure. This amounts to leaving something for pupils actively to complete for themselves. Attempting to give meaningful structure to concepts helps to implant them in long-term memory (see the work of Piaget later).

3. Perception is always carried out in the light of previous experience. Therefore, it is essential to start from a point in the presentation of material which enables the pupil to call on previous experience. Understanding rather than rote learning is important in the formation of clear perceptions and is more likely to assist in long-term memory. The teacher should emphasize that the learning process consists of discovering meanings, building up patterns of knowledge and meaningful relations.

4. Some have argued that learning by getting the total picture rather than learning material piecemeal is more efficient. Methods of learning a poem by re-reading it throughout until it is learnt, or the 'look and say' (and not the 'phonic') method of reading are based on 'whole' rather than 'part' learning. However, the generalization is questionable. A lot would depend on the type and extent of material to be assimilated. As we saw in Miller's work, 'chunking' does have its place in learning and even then there are limitations to the amount of channel capacity.

5. The extent to which young children perceive their surroundings and themselves is subject to developmental limitations. Piaget has proposed that the child *centres* on a particular dimension of his sensory field to the exclusion of all others. In two- or three-dimensional problems the young child is not able to free himself from the single dimension to make judgements about changes or constancies in such matters as volume and area (see chapter 5).

6. False perceptions can arise because:
 (i) sensory information is inadequate or inaccurate. Auditory, visual or tactile materials should be plentiful, appropriate and unambiguous;
 (ii) attention is not full or the direction is misguided—we have already given several reasons why attention might stray. Another cause may be that too much latitude is provided in the perceptual field so that models cannot begin to be formulated;
 (iii) the existing percepts are inadequate for incoming sensory experience—this should soon be evident to the teacher who is evaluating his or her work as an on-going process;
 (iv) the wrong 'set' is present, that is, the pupil is looking out for the wrong sensory cues.

SUMMARY

Sensory reception, attention and analysis have an important place in the work of teachers. Needless to say, without the pupils' attention the teacher might as well retire. But gaining their attention is not just a question of insisting on their looking and listening to what is going on. There are many factors conspiring to distract or fatigue the child at a subtler level than this. We have noted that external factors such as intense, novel, changeable, colourful, high-pitched and conditioned stimuli can operate to assist or defeat the teacher's intentions. Internal variables of interest, fatigue, need deprivation, arousal state and personality qualities are likewise of relevance.

Memory was considered in chapter 2 from the point of view of physiological functioning. In this chapter, we explored the subject using a speculative model derived from Broadbent's filter theory of attention. Short- and long-term memory storage was discussed in relation to the nature of the input information. The prospect of this information 'reaching' the long-term memory store was seen to depend on at least four aspects of the information. These were (a) its length; (b) its content; (c) the opportunity for initial learning; and (d) the activity taking place between successive units of information.

As every student knows, long messages are less likely to be remembered than short ones. Technical messages, the level of familiarity, the particular sense or language of a message are all significant for long-term storage. Revision is clearly going to assist pupils in transferring information from the STM to the LTM. Multiple ways of presenting the same material, permitting active recall between each unit of information and reducing the speed of presentation will help in this respect. The effect of introducing a distraction at the outset of a revision session, or producing interference (pro- and retro-active—see chapter 7) before, during or after a learning session can have a devastating effect on the amount recalled. Vocalization as a means of revision helps in the short term.

Of the theories of perception, the most influential to date has been that proposed by the Gestalt School. Perceptual discrimination is seen to be more than just the sum of sensory experiences. Questions of interpretation are often distorted by the acquired perceptual characteristics of one's culture or sub-culture (i.e. we learn *how* to look at things and *what* to look at as an outcome of cultural inheritance). The deceptions of illusions are partly a question of cultural experience. It is also believed that social class background can affect the perceptions of children [Bruner and Goodman note (13)].

Finally, we gave several suggestions from research on perception which should be of assistance to the teacher. These included (1) the importance of structure in the presentation of material; (2) the need to leave children to complete some part of their learning, provided they are in possession of sufficient knowledge to do this (closure); (3) the importance of starting with familiar perceptual experience from which to derive the unfamiliar; (4) 'whole' learning, in some cases, as more valuable than learning 'in bits'; (5) a consideration of the developmental level of the child; and (6) some common sources of false perceptions.

ENQUIRY AND DISCUSSION

1. Read through the suggestions given under the heading of 'Perception and the teacher' and use these in your observations at school. Analyse the content and presentation of lessons or class activities with these in mind. Try to seek out examples for each suggestion.

2. With the help of your tutor, see if you can devise a series of experiments to show that

the intensity, novelty, variability, distributed regularity, colour and conditioned stimuli are variables in arresting our attention. In what ways can this information be used in the classroom?

3. Read 'Memory and effective instruction' by H. C. A. Dale in *Aspects of Education*, No. 7 (1968), follow up the important references he gives and draw up some conclusions which you as a teacher might find useful.

4. Examine the literature to discover if there are any important differences in the extent to which we use our senses (e.g. do we tend to use our eyes more than our ears?). Do we tend to learn through one sense more than another? How do your findings help in deciding on the arrangement and emphases of lesson presentation? Are there differences according to the age of pupils?

NOTES AND REFERENCES

1. R. Lynn, *Attention, Arousal and the Orientation Reaction*, International Series of Monographs in Experimental Psychology, Pergamon, Oxford, 1966.

2. W. James, *The Principles of Psychology*, vol. I, Holt, New York, 1890. The reference is given for those interested in early ideas in modern experimental psychology. This man made some remarkable introspections, some of which have only recently been put to the test.

3. D. E. Broadbent, *Perception and Communication*, Pergamon, London, 1958. The book gives a detailed review of research prior to the 1950s and evidence from his own researches which has provided innumerable lines of exploration in attention and perception.

4. Most recent experimentation in perception has involved the technique of *shadowing*. This means presenting, usually aurally, a message through head-phones which the listener has to repeat whilst some other distraction (often another message) is given either in the same ear, in both ears, or in the opposite ear to the shadowed message. N. Moray, *Listening and Attention*, Penguin, London, 1969, describes several shadowing experiments.

5. A. M. Treisman, 'Verbal cues, language and meaning in selective attention', *Am. J. Psychol.*, **77**, 215–216 (1964).

6. H. J. Eysenck, *The Biological Basis of Personality*, Thomas, Illinois, 1967.

7. G. Sperling, 'The information available in brief visual presentations', *Psychol. Monogr.*, No. 498 (1960).

8. You may frequently see the term *tachistoscope* whilst reading about visual perception. This is the instrument which has a controlled exposure time and operates like the shutter of a camera.

9. G. A. Miller, 'The magical number seven, plus or minus two: some limits in our

capacity for processing information', *Psychol. Rev.*, **63**, 81–97 (1956)—or 'the 7 $\pm$ 2 paper'.

10. N. C. Waugh and D. A. Norman, 'Primary memory', *Psychol. Rev.*, **72**, 92–93 (1965). It is assumed in this model that short- and long-term memory are capable of being treated as separate entities. Some psychologists would argue against this fragmentation of the processes of memory. H. C. A. Dale, 'Memory and effective instruction', *Aspects of Education*, **7**, 8–21 (1968).

11. D. O. Hebb, *The Organization of Behaviour*, Wiley, New York, 1966, 8th Impression.

12. R. Gregory, *Eye and Brain: the Psychology of Seeing*. Weidenfeld and Nicholson, London, 1966.

13. J. S. Bruner and C. C. Goodman, 'Value and need as organizing factors in perception', *J. abnorm. soc. Psychol.*, **42**, 33–44 (1947).

FURTHER READING

D. E. Broadbent, *Perception and Communication*, Pergamon, London, 1958. A technical book, but well worth attempting as it gives a thorough review of research to its date of publication.

N. Calder, *The Mind of Man*, BBC Publications, London, 1970. Gives several of the more spectacular findings in perception.

R. H. Day, *Human Perception*, Wiley, New York, 1968.

R. Lynn, *Attention, Arousal and the Orientation Reaction*, International Series of Monographs in Experimental Psychology, Pergamon, Oxford, 1966. Very technical and only for those who need depth in this field.

N. Moray, *Listening and Attention*, Penguin, London, 1969.

D. A. Norman, *Memory and Attention*, Wiley, New York, 1966. A very clearly written book combining previous research with present speculations.

M. D. Vernon, *The Psychology of Perception*, Penguin, London, 1962. Introduces developmental approach to perception as well as experimental work.

5 Concept formation and attainment

In the chapter on perception, we assumed the existence of internal mental processes as a necessary step in the analysis of sensory experiences. One simplified interpretation suggested was a long-term store of past experiences which are made available when we need to appraise incoming signals, the outcome of which is to regulate our behaviour. The mental activity which we assume is taking place is defined by the familiar term *thinking*. Vinacke (1) suggests that thinking involves 'internal processes which bring the organization laid down in past learning to bear upon responses to current situations, and which shape these responses in keeping with inner needs'. The existence of these inner processes is supported from observations we make of our own thought processes (introspection) and from the simple fact that our responses to problem situations have much more in them than the original information with which we are provided. In this chapter we shall concentrate on the building-blocks of thought, the 'organization laid down in past learning' to use Vinacke's phrase.

Unfortunately, 'thinking' has become a confused and multipurpose term; it has even come to mean different things to different psychologists. However, one broad distinction which we can draw is between *perceptual* and *ideational* thinking. Perceptual thinking is the term we apply to the mental activity occurring during problem-solving which relies on the presence of the object or objects involved in the problem. Much of Piaget's work with very young children calls for an understanding of perceptual thinking (see later in the chapter). Ideational thinking, on the other hand, is much more complex and relies on the existence of a symbolic form such as a language or number system, and does not necessarily rely on the presence of cues from the environment. We shall meet with both these types of thinking in our discussion of concept formation later in the chapter. Other uses of the term are mentioned in note (2) at the end of the chapter. But first we must turn to a consideration of the means whereby thinking is made possible.

CONCEPTS

If man were not able to classify the things and events around him he would find it impossible to carry out the highly complicated mental operations of which he is capable. By classifying and discriminating what he perceives, man is able to represent the world to himself by the formation of *class* (or *category*) *concepts*. But two essential conditions are needed for concept formation. Firstly, he must perceive and abstract the common elements of objects or events to construct generalizations; secondly, he must at the same time be capable of discriminating between elements which are relevant and those which are irrelevant to the accurate formation of his concepts. Hence, we talk of classification *and* discrimination when forming concepts. Flowers, for example, have certain things in common; they all serve the same purpose in providing for the production of seeds; they have, by and large, similar structures such as petals, stamen and pollen grains. These *critical attributes* which connect one flower with the next enable a classification to take place. But classification is not enough. We must also be in a position to specify the limits of our classification. Young children, for instance, are particularly prone to over-generalization because they have not yet learnt the limits of classification. Any part of a plant, be it a leaf, root, stem or whatever, is likely to be labelled as a flower. By the same token, all men may be 'daddies' to a young child because the critical attributes of father-hood have not yet been established in his mind. At a more advanced level, refined distinctions will be necessary before a child can discriminate between different kinds of flowers and daddies.

The speed and inevitability of concept attainment in the young, despite varied child-rearing practices and in some cases alarming cultural disadvantages, has led many to believe that we are born with a predisposition to order our perceptions into concepts. However, though the *act* of concept formation might be inborn, the substance of the concepts is acquired from experience and it is this vital point which is of concern to teachers. Both parents and teachers constitute reference groups for assisting children in abstracting and classifying concept attributes.

In the early stages, concepts become established as images. *Imagery* is the term we use to describe calling up a mental replica (using any sense modality) of an object or event which we have previously experienced. If I said 'call up the image of a bell ringing', you would imagine the sound of an actual bell which you have heard sometime in the past. Bruner (see next chapter) supposes that we actually recall a composite sound by combin-ing previous similar experiences. He calls this *iconic* representation. Piaget (later in this chapter) refers to imagery as *internalized imitation;* in other words, we take in the actual sensory events and reproduce some aspects of them on request. *Eidetic imagery* is an extreme case of the ability to recall a sensory event in great detail. This is done by casting an actual image of what is seen onto a surface and using it to identify parts of the total scene. Children are especially prone (about 6 per cent) to exhibit the skill. Probably the talent becomes redundant because it is not put to use. The phenomenon is sometimes known as 'photographic memory', although the images are rarely as perfect as a photograph.

Images can be used as the basis for simple reasoning. For example, the simpler scientific and geometrical concepts involving apparatus and figural arrangements can occasionally be manipulated as an image in our minds. It is also possible that animals use imagery as an aid in their responses. They also try out their reactions to the environ-ment physically rather than by manipulating mental concepts because, it is believed, animals have more highly developed and organized sensory organs than man.

But many concepts cannot even be imagined because they are far too complex or abstract. We cannot imagine 'energy' or 'honesty'. We might be able to conjure up an image of a body moving and therefore possessing energy, or perhaps the picture of someone stealing (and by implication what an honest person should not do), but these are only instances (*exemplars*) of some aspect of the concepts. Man's ability to deal with problems in the absence of material evidence or mental images, and to reach higher levels of complexity in his appreciation and response to the environment (in contrast to animals), is entirely due to the use of *symbolic languages*. These include number systems as well as the spoken and written word. By classifying and labelling with words and phrases, man can represent the world economically whilst at the same time freeing himself from the need for material evidence in his reasoning. Through the acquisition of concepts, from the simplest discrimination and classification of objects to the complex moral, mathematical or scientific concepts, we order our experiences. In the process, language plays a vital role and we shall devote the next chapter to a consideration of this aspect. For the time being, it is important to remember that words are not concepts; they only stand for concepts. In the case of class concepts a word is a label which represents, symbolically, a class of objects.

Some characteristics of concepts (3)

To help us in our understanding of the development of thinking in children, let us first take a closer look at some of the more important characteristics of concepts.

1. As we have seen above, concepts are generalizations (4) built up by abstracting particular sensory events, the critical attributes, and classifying them. They are not the actual sensory events, but representations of some aspects of these events. With most concepts there are wide margins of attribute acceptability, that is a leaf is a leaf whether it is small, glossy, dark green and prickly like a holly leaf or large, dull, light green and harmless like a chestnut leaf. In some cases, the boundaries which distinguish concepts are hazy and ill defined (some of the abstract concepts we have to deal with in the study of human behaviour are of this nature). But generally speaking there is a large measure of agreement in the definition of most class concepts within a given culture.

2. Concepts are dependent upon previous experience. We have noted that home background and educational opportunity are possible variables in the formation of concepts. There are likewise emotional as well as perceptual connections associated with concept formation [see paragraph 5(b) on the intentional use of concepts].

3. Concepts are symbolic in human beings. The concept 'bee' can be called to mind from numerous stimulus sources. The sight of the insect or the word 'bee', a relentless droning sound, honey, a piece of music ('The Flight of the Bumble Bee') can all trigger off the concept 'bee'. Words, numbers, chemical symbols or physical formulae have symbolic significance beyond the simple meaning normally associated with the actual symbol. For the chemist, the symbol 'O' is not just a circle; it represents the element oxygen. Sometimes objects have complex symbolic meaning such as the crucifix, a V sign, or road signs.

4. Concepts can form 'horizontal' or 'vertical' organizations. An example of a horizontal classification would be if we gave children some examples of reptiles—snakes, lizards, crocodiles and prehistoric reptiles. They all belong to the same major group of animals because they possess certain attributes in common. However, they also differ in some other minor respects thus permitting us to classify them into separate groups *within* the same level in the animal kingdom.

Vertical classification results from the presence of hierarchies, that is categories which increase in complexity as we proceed through the classification. A dog belongs to the family of animals called *canis*, which is subordinate to the order of animals called *carnivora* (along with cats, bears, otters and seals), which is subordinate to the class of animals called *mammals*, which in turn are *vertebrates* (with backbones), which are *animals*. You will notice the increasing inclusiveness of the groups as we pass up the hierarchy of the animal kingdom.

Some higher-order concepts are very complicated. Try working out the number of subordinate concepts required to understand the concept of 'force', the theorem of Pythagoras, the ten commandments or the causes which led to the fall of the Roman Empire.

5. Concepts function in at least two ways—extentionally and intentionally.

(a) The *extentional* use of concepts applies where the meaning given is the widely acknowledged one defined in terms which are patently clear to anyone observing the object or event. Concept usage arises from common agreement and acceptance of the objective attributes of the object. A particular variety of plant or animal, let us say a lupin or a giraffe, has a 'public' meaning which we all accept.

(b) The *intentional* use of concepts can vary considerably from one person to another. In this case, the concept is defined as a result of personal, subjective experiences accompanying the formation of the concept. A rose might arouse pleasant associations or unpleasant ones if one has suffered the thorns during pruning. A botanist might view the plant from a technical standpoint, an artist from a creative, aesthetic angle or a cricket fan in Yorkshire as an emblem of his county in the 'roses match'. In all these cases, special significance has become attached to the object which has no universal acceptance.

6. Some concepts can be irrational. Superstitions (black cats, ladders, opening an umbrella indoors, lucky numbers and colours) provide many illustrations of irrational concepts. Their origins are obscure, but they are certainly not based upon the usual methods of concept formation from raw reality.

7. Many concepts are formed without our conscious awareness. Values established by our culture and which regulate our daily conduct have often been formed as habits in our childhood without us realizing it. Aversions and prejudices are frequently stamped into our repertoire of responses in this way. Dislike of animals, racial prejudice, attitudes towards religion or politics are imperceptibly planted during a lifetime.

In our discussion of concepts it has been argued that concept formation is dependent upon several psychological processes. Firstly, a young child has to be able to *differentiate* the attributes of his environment. By this we mean that he must have sufficient perceptual skills to distinguish the characteristics he observes in order even to begin the process of classification. As we observed before there will be a time when a child may refer to all men as 'daddy' or all four-legged creatures as 'doggy' because of the child's inability to limit the scope of his generalizations.

Secondly, having consolidated his ability to differentiate features, a child has to perceive *groupings*, that is, he needs to recognize structural or functional similarities.

Finally, he has to *classify* the groupings into hierarchies thus devising classes of experience with increasing levels of complexity and abstractness.

PIAGET'S THEORY OF CONCEPT FORMATION

Contemporary views on the nature of concept formation have been vastly influenced by the work of one man. He is Jean Piaget (born 1896), a one-time biologist, who turned his energies to a study of the evolution of children's thinking. His impetus from the Universities of Paris and Geneva has led to a worldwide search for important factors in concept development. His particular line of thinking and the abundant research it has generated is sometimes known as the *Geneva School* of thought to distinguish it from the *Harvard School* in the United States typified by the work of Bruner who we will mention shortly, and the *Russian School* founded by Vygotsky and Luria. He has never claimed in any of his numerous books (5) that his work would be of direct application to learning or teaching. Nevertheless, his findings have probably done more to influence educational practices in this country than most theories. He would claim that *epistemology* has been his primary interest, that is, the study of how we know what we know and the extent of this knowledge.

His method of investigation has been the clinical approach—detailed face-to-face discussion and questioning of individual children in many problem situations (he used his own children in the first experiments in the 1920s). The method aims to discover, by analysing the verbal introspections of the children, the quality and nature of concept attainment at a particular time in their lives. The work has led to a descriptive analysis of development of basic physical, logical, mathematical and moral concepts from birth to adolescence (concept growth in such things as number, time, space, velocity, geometry, chance and morality).

At heart, his theory is:

(a) a genetic one in that higher processes are seen to evolve from biological mechanisms which are rooted in the development of an individual's nervous system [compare this view with Hebb (6)];

(b) a maturational one because he believes that the processes of concept formation follow an invariant pattern through several clearly definable stages which emerge during specific age ranges;

(c) a hierarchical one in that the stages he proposes *must* be experienced and passed through in a given order before any subsequent stages of development are possible.

Piaget also maintains that three factors are of special importance in ensuring the appearance of the stages of cognitive development. These are (i) biological factors which account for the regularity and inevitability of the stages he postulates much in the same way as we see the appearance of sexual characteristics during a given period in the development of boys and girls before we are justified in saying they are mature adults; (ii) educational and cultural transmission which, according to Piaget, account for the discrepancies in the chronological ages at which his stages appear as we pass from one individual to another; and (iii) the activities in which children engage. Piaget takes an 'active' rather than a 'passive' view of the part played by children in their own development. The child's self-directed motor activity is seen as a necessity in cognitive development.

His earlier preoccupation with biology and logic is reflected in the widespread use he makes of the technical language used in these subjects. It will be necessary, therefore, to sort out some of these terms first before we describe his developmental theory.

In the first days of life, a baby responds to his surroundings by reflex activity which, as we know, is *not* acquired. Very soon, the baby develops beyond reflex action and begins to react to his surroundings in a way which leads us to suspect purposeful behaviour. He seeks his mother's nipple, he grasps objects in contact with the palm of his hands, his general body movement begins to show signs of coordination. These actions, which become organized into distinct patterns of behaviour, Piaget refers to as *schemata* (schema is the singular, schemata or schemas the plural). Note the key to the formation of schemata is *action* on the part of the baby in attempting to *adapt* himself to the demands of his environment. Once a schema has appeared, it becomes directed to similar, parallel situations—somewhat like transfer of training (see chapter 6). For example, arm movement, grasping, then lifting toward the mouth is a cycle of activity which is likely to happen to any object which comes within range of the child.

The process, described in the last paragraph, of incorporating new perceptions to form either new schemata or integrating them into existing schemata is termed *assimilation* by Piaget (analogous to humans taking in a variety of foods which the body uses to build into existing tissue). When the child is capable of modifying existing schemata to meet new environmental demands, he is said to experience *accommodation*. (Using the biological analogy again, the infant being weaned from milk to solids will have to accommodate to the change in the nature of the food in order to assimilate the food for use by the body.)

In summary, Piaget considers that conceptual growth occurs because the child, whilst actively attempting to adapt to his environment, organizes his actions into schemata through the processes of assimilation and accommodation.

The schema is an important element in Piaget's theory. Bartlett (7) coined the expression to describe 'an active organization of past actions'. Hebb (6) uses 'cell assemblies' as the counterpart of Piaget's schemata. In effect, the mental framework of past experiences is the substance of Broadbent's long-term memory store (see chapter 4). When the actions become replaced by symbols (words, numbers, etc.) they become known as *representational schemata*. When a child is able to represent his world mentally, by means of memory, imagery or symbolic language, he is said to have *internalized* these experiences.

Thought or thinking, according to Piaget, has its origins in actions physically performed and then internalized. Bluntly then, thought is internalized actions. The starting point of cognitive development must therefore be activity on the part of the neonate, not passive reception of sensory data. The child's striving to adapt and structure his experience enables patterns of actions to be formed. At a primitive level, the patterns may be simple perceptual patterns which become internalized. When these are recalled, they reappear as images of the origin experience. We have already mentioned this phenomenon as imagery (internalized imitation).

Once symbolic language frees the child from the need to manipulate raw reality in order to form schemata, he can begin to develop logical thinking. He is able to reason using representations of the facts. The ability to carry out activities in one's imagination is known as an *operation* and, as we shall see presently, the child's growth to intellectual maturity depends on his capacity to carry out these mental operations.

In the developmental description which follows, we shall see how Piaget accounts for the gradual unfolding of thinking skills starting with simple sensory and motor activities in babyhood and gradually being superceded by internal representation of actions carried out by the child; then, through the agency of language, reaching the highest form of logical thinking, at first in the presence of objective evidence and finally by mental reasoning.

Piaget's stages of development

We argued above that Piaget's theory was genetic, maturational and hierarchical. Adaptation takes place in a set sequence of stages associated with successive mental (not chronological) ages. Several schemes representing the stages exist. The outlines in table 5.1 are the two most popular.

Table 5.1   Outline of Piaget's stages of development

Period		Stage	Mental age range in years
Sensori-motor	I	Sensori-motor	0–2
Preparation for, and use of, concrete operations	II	Pre-operational (A) Pre-conceptual (B) Intuitive	2–4 4–7
	III	Concrete operations	7–11$\frac{1}{2}$
Formal operations	IV	Formal operations	11$\frac{1}{2}$–

I: The sensori-motor stage (mental age approximately 0–2 years).   Developmentally, the first two years of life are very important and full. So much is achieved in motor and mental skills by way of walking, talking, playing and establishing a self-identity. Yet, at birth, actions are severely limited to reflex grasping, sucking and general body movement. Within the first months, the reflexes become adapted to very simple tasks. The first schemata involve grasping or sucking anything which comes in contact with hand or mouth.

As the senses and limb movements rapidly improve and coordinate, cycles of activity are discovered and repeated by the infant. He may, for example, combine an arm movement with placing his thumb in his mouth and sucking it. These cycles of action Piaget calls *primary circular reactions*. They are significant because their appearance gives the first clues to the existence of a primitive memory. Note, however, that the voluntary motions of the infant are extensions of reflex action and not purposive movements. Equally, the movements are directed towards his own body rather than objects outside his body. These rudimentary habitual schemata are called 'primary' because they are at first built into the baby's inherent reflex systems.

Soon, new activities appear with less and less apparent connection with reflexes. Around four to eight months the baby begins to direct his activities towards objects outside his body and this enlarges his range of actions. Increasing visual–motor coordination enables him to carry out these tasks. With each new object, the baby carries out his party pieces with schemata already assimilated. These are called *secondary circular reactions* where patterns of action become generalized to any object within reach. Up to one year of age the secondary circular reactions are coordinated and applied to new situations. There is every sign of purposeful behaviour as sequences of movements seem to be directed toward the attainment of goals. He will, for example, move objects out of the way to obtain a desired toy, which implies that schemata are being assimilated and coordinated by combining secondary circular reactions.

Accommodation has played a minor role up to this point in his life. The child has been preoccupied with the assimilation of schemata. Initially, when an object is hidden, even in the presence of the child, he will not pursue it—out of sight, out of mind! There is no suggestion of reasoning as we know it. Life is all go!

From twelve to eighteen months, however, the child becomes capable of inventing new ways of attaining ends. Circular reactions may be repeated with several variations. In other words he is beginning to accommodate to new situations by modifying and experimenting with existing schemata. These are called *tertiary circular reactions*.

Towards the end of the sensori-motor stage, the youngster is beginning to represent his world in mental images and symbols. The onset of language enables the child to represent objects in their absence. Playing bricks become cars or real building bricks in the child's imagination. Play becomes very important. For Piaget, play enables the child to assimilate. Imitation, on the other hand, is an example of accommodation because the child is attempting to modify his behaviour to become someone or something else. *Deferred imitation* is the ability to copy someone else in their absence and represents a great advance because it shows that the child is now able to form images of events which can be recalled for future reference.

II A: Pre-conceptual stage (mental age approximately 2–4 years). The direct link between sensory experiences and motor activity, so apparent in the first of Piaget's stages, gradually becomes obscured by the intermediate process of mental activity. This occurs largely because the child is internalizing imitations and actions.

As the term 'pre-conceptual' implies, children are not yet able to formulate concepts in the same way as older children and adults. Concept formation which relies on abstracting and discriminating the characteristics of objects or situations in order to form generalizations is known as *inductive* reasoning. Where generalizations are used to describe particular instances, we call the process *deductive* reasoning. Children at this stage tend neither to induction nor deduction. Instead, they use *transductive* reasoning. By this Piaget means that children reason by going from one particular instance to another particular instance in order to form *pre-concepts*.

One or two illustrations of transductive reasoning should help to show how pre-concepts are formed.

My daughter, Louise, at 3 years 6 months saw her mother combing her hair. She said, 'Mummy is combing her hair. She is going shopping'. I asked her why mummy was going shopping and apparently she had noticed that on the previous day the two events had been linked. Louise had reasoned transductively by going from the particular to the particular. Mummy combs her hair on many occasions for many reasons—similarly she goes out on many occasions for many reasons—but the coincidence of these two events had created a pre-concept. In summary, A occurs with B once, therefore A occurs with B always. The pre-concept 'all men are daddies' has been formed by the child who has only used one characteristic (voice or clothing or features) which all men have in common. We tend to play on this fact in the Father Christmas confidence trick. Young children are not sophisticated enough to distinguish between the men dressed up and appearing in different places. For children, they are all one man. In short, the child cannot successfully form classes of objects.

The period is also progressively dominated by symbolic play; dolls become babies, flowers become rows of children. Similarly imitation of what other people are doing is in evidence. *Egocentricism* predominates because the child is unable to view things from another person's point of view. He does not appreciate that if he and another person were looking at an object from different angles, the two views would be different. We shall see the importance of egocentric speech (rehearsing with oneself) in the next chapter.

II B: Intuitive stage (mental age approximately 4–7 years).   The child begins this period of his intellectual development very much dependent upon superficial perceptions of his environment. He forms ideas impressionistically—hence the name of the 'intuitive' stage. This arises because he appears to be unable to account for all aspects of a situation simultaneously. Also his outlook is dominated by the perceptual field in that he fixates on one dimension of an object or event to the exclusion of all others. Piaget calls this phenomenon *centering*. The child grasps only one relationship at a time.

A simple experiment described by Piaget will demonstrate the notion of centering. Two plasticine balls are rolled until the child agrees that they are the same size. One ball is then chosen and rolled into a sausage-shape as in figure 5.1 and put alongside the other ball. If a five year old is asked if they are the same size (or does one ball have more plasticine in it than the other) the child will most frequently say that the sausage is bigger. If asked why, he usually says, 'because it is longer'. Occasionally, a long narrow shape is taken as being smaller because it is narrower. In the first case, the child has 'centered' on the length dimension of the sausage shape and compared it with the width of the other ball to arrive at the conclusion that the former is more. In the second case, where the child claims that the sausage is smaller, he has centered on the width.

To explain this, Piaget says that children, by centering on a single aspect of a problem and ignoring all others, lack the ability for *conservation of quantity* (plasticine or water would be described as a 'continuous' quantity, beads as a 'discontinuous' quantity). An inability to conserve arises because children at this stage of their development seem unable to reverse the situations they are observing. Whilst watching a ball being rolled into a sausage-shape, they 'center' on one dimension changing in length without being capable of reversing the process back to the point of origin and realizing that the actual quantity of material is unchanged.

Another example of irreversibility in a conservation experiment is afforded by filling two identical vessels with water to the same level. They must be accepted as similar in level by the child. One vessel is taken and the contents poured into a vessel of a different shape—tall and thin or small and squat as in figure 5.2(a). Children who cannot reverse and therefore conserve would claim that there was more liquid in vessel C than in A (or less in D than in A). When asked why, the children soon display that they have

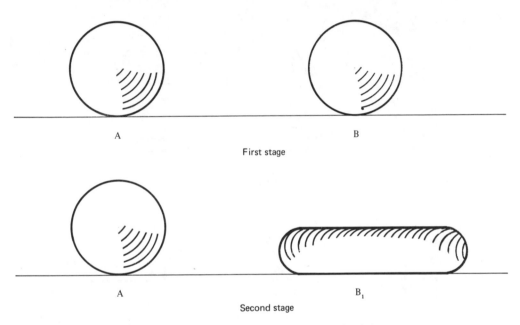

Figure 5.1 To demonstrate conservation using balls of plasticine
First stage: balls appear equal in quantity
Second stage: to conservers, balls still accepted as equal in quantity; to non-conservers, B₁ is more than A

centered on length or width without compensating for changes in the other dimensions.

An interesting modification reported by Bruner (8) is shown in figure 5.2(b). The third vessel C was chosen to be the same height as the other two and all but the tops of the vessels hidden from view using a screen. When asked which vessel, A or C, had the most drink in, younger children (four to five year olds) did no better than chance (half were correct), 90 per cent of the five to six year olds got the correct answer, whilst 100 per cent of six to seven year olds came up with the answer. It would seem that the younger children who can see what is going on are overwhelmingly influenced by the perceptual field and when this is partly removed, they resort to intuitive guesswork.

According to Piaget the act of repeating the sequence of activities performed in these experiments in one direction, makes it very difficult for the child to reverse the process. Therefore, reversibility is a central skill which frees the child from intuitive impressions, enabling him to appreciate the *invariance* of materials undergoing a change in physical dimensions without changes in total quantity.

Another interpretation of Piaget's findings has recently been made by Bryant (9) in this country. He has questioned the basic assumptions of conservation and has

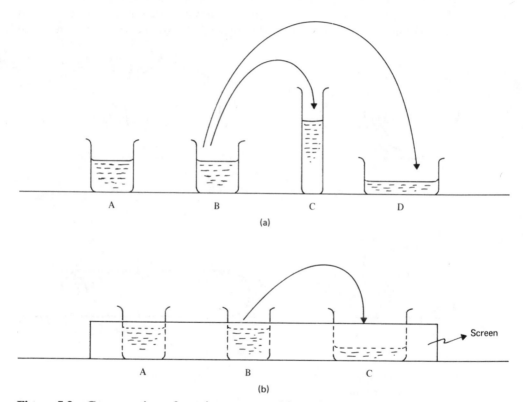

(a)

(b)

Figure 5.2 Conservation of continuous quantities using vessels of water

(a) the conserver appreciates that the quantities in C and D are the same as in A. The non-conserver says there is more in C and less in D when compared with A;

(b) Bruner's experiment

offered alternative explanations which have far-reaching implications for education, if they are correct. The central issue is the question of invariance. Piaget, as we have seen, claims that children who cannot conserve have not yet learnt the invariance principle. Bryant challenges this position in the following way. In all the conservation experiments there are usually three steps. First, the child establishes a hypothesis about the equality of the plasticine balls or amounts of liquid in our particular examples. In other words, the child appreciates that A = B [for plasticine in figure 5.1 and for the vessel of water in figure 5.2(a)]. Furthermore, he is consistent in his appraisal of equality which shows that he has made a definite hypothesis. At the next step, he applies the invariance principle such that he sees $B = B_1$ (plasticine) or $B = C$ or D (water). Finally, to solve the problem correctly, he coordinates these first two stages to establish a final hypothesis that $A = B_1$ (plasticine) or $A = C$ or D (water). Unfortunately young children without knowledge of counting, weighing or measuring must rely on some other criterion, possibly estimates of length or width in the case of the experiments above. Therefore, there is a conflict of hypotheses between the first ($A = B$ using length) and the last (A is not equal to B, C or D again using length). Faced with this conflict, the child chooses his most recent deduction and says that A is not equal to B, C or D. Bryant goes on to substantiate his conflict-hypothesis theory by experiment (9). His major conclusion is an optimistic one for education because, unlike Piaget, he believes that teaching hypothesis-testing and memory-training would serve a useful purpose. 'Piaget's experiments effectively demonstrate that young children find transitivity problems difficult, but these difficulties are simply the result of *inadequate strategies of recall*' (the author's italics). In effect, we must teach children how 'to distinguish correct hypotheses about quantities and numbers from incorrect ones' and thus avoid failures of memory (not to be confused with failures in logical thinking).

III: Concrete operations (mental age approximately 7–11 years).   As we have seen, an operation for Piaget is internalized action. At first the child's reasoning is almost exclusively tied to concrete experience. He may be able to formulate in his mind a hypothesis which takes him one step beyond the concrete evidence available to him, but he is in large measure dependent on the perceptual facts before him. The child at this stage *describes* his environment; at the highest levels of abstract reasoning he tries to *explain* it. This distinction will be clarified later in the section describing the pendulum experiment.

Conservation, irrespective of number, shape or quantity transformations, is crucial for reasoning at the concrete stage of operations. For example, a child would have to be aware that no matter how one presented the problem $2 + 4 + 3$ ($4 + 2 + 3$, etc.), it would still add up to the same quantity. Similarly, he would need to achieve reversal of number such that he could solve any combination of the problem $2 \times 6 = 12$ or $\frac{12}{6} = 2$ or $\frac{12}{2} = 6$, all of which requires a knowledge of reversal. There are numerous properties capable of being conserved and these, according to Piaget, appear in a particular sequence. Conservation of substance, for instance, occurs around the age of seven to eight years and precedes the conservation of weight (around nine to eleven years) which in turn precedes the conservation of volume at about twelve years of age. Number conservation appears before area. Another essential process mentioned previously is that of *decentering*. This involves the realization that the same fundamental quantity, be it number, volume, area, weight or whatever, exists no matter how the dimensions might be altered—the child's attention is no longer fixed on one dimension.

A second important operation in the development of concepts is the formation of consistent *classifications*. Previously, we saw how the child tended to form pre-concepts by passing from the particular to the particular (transductive reasoning). Now, the formation of valid concepts depends on accurate sorting out of similar and irrelevant properties.

Allied to classification is another process known as *seriation*, that is the ability to cope with the ordering of similar objects according to, say, size or position. A child who can count (cardination) may not necessarily be capable of appreciating the ordering of objects (ordination). Given six sweets arranged in a row, the pre-conceptual mind may not be able to select the '4th' from a specified end. Classification and ordination are plainly interdependent, so much so that a child is not able to operate at the concrete level until he can cope with both these processes. Seeing relationships between groups and understanding similarity and subordination of classes are essential skills (10) in concrete operational thinking.

IV: Formal operations (mental age approximately 11 to adolescence). Nine and ten year olds are quite capable of dealing with concepts involving such things as weight, number, area, distance or temperature provided they can operate in the presence of first-hand reality. Concepts involving an understanding of, for instance, volume, density, justice or cruelty are not well formed. These require more subtle levels of reasoning which we call *formal operations*. These highest levels of thinking of which man is capable develop once he can follow the *form* of an argument without needing the concrete materials making up the substance of the argument.

At the formal level of operations, the individual can reason hypothetically and in the absence of material evidence. He sets up hypotheses and tests these to determine real solutions to problems amongst a number of possible solutions. This is known as *hypo-thetico-deductive reasoning*.

To illustrate the difficulties in hypothesis-testing experienced by children at the concrete stage as contrasted with those at the formal level, let us take an actual illustration. My eldest son, Paul, at 9 years 6 months was given the pendulum problem originally used by Inhelder and Piaget (11). With one or two minor modifications this consisted of a length of string with a lump of plasticine on the end. The string could be changed in length and more plasticine made available for adding to, or removal from, the existing lump. Paul was required to discover the factor or factors which governed the time of swing of the pendulum we had made.

His first reaction was to say that the higher one raises the lump before release the longer it takes to slow down because gravity (a concept vaguely mentioned at home and school) gradually pulls it 'slower and slower towards the middle' (of the swing). After a good deal of somewhat random exploration with the length, amount of plasticine and method of release (either pushing with different forces or releasing freely) and with little regard for accurate measurement, he concluded that altering the length, weight on the end, force of release and 'gravity' would change the time of swing. I then put it to him that of the possible variables he had suggested, only one made much difference to the time of swing; how, then, would he set about discovering which of the four variables he had suggested was the important one?

His first proposition was to alter the length whilst varying the 'push'. What happens about the other variables? He would include those as well. After some trials and tribulations trying to arrange an experiment involving all the variables at once, he concluded 'I'm completely lost. There are too many, what do you call them—variables'.

Paul's responses were typical of concrete operational thinking. He was capable of sorting out the factors which might vary by making direct observations of the apparatus. He pinpointed length, weight, gravity and method of release. He could also carry out seriation—as the string gets longer and longer, the pendulum swings slower and slower. But he could not at this stage manage to *test hypotheses* which were unambiguous by considering only one variable whilst holding the others constant. In fact, his mind boggled at the prospect of having to change the variables simultaneously. For formal operations he would need not only to theorize about the *possible* influences of all factors, but then to design an experiment to test the influence of each one in a systematic way whilst keeping the others invariant.

There is a second characteristic of formal reasoning, not too well illustrated by the pendulum experiment, that is the *setting up of hypotheses* (12). We saw how hypotheses were tested in the experiment, but the relevant variables were fairly obvious and the child had no need to go much beyond the raw materials in front of him to discover the attributes necessary for hypothesis-testing. Length, weight or 'push' are self-evident. Frequently, formal reasoning requires more subtle processes of abstracting the important criteria from the objective evidence. Moreover, the reasoning must go beyond the tangible and perceivable to the construction of propositions about objects and events from the attributes extracted. Piaget calls these 'second-order operations' to distinguish them from the 'first-order operations' of the concrete stage. Second-order operations, then, are operations on first-order operations. Problems involving proportion require second-order operations because we must first establish the relationship from the information given (first-order), and use this to discover a second relationship.

Some criticisms of Piaget's theory

Like so many theories in psychology, Piaget's has not been without its critics. Before pointing to the implications of his work, we must first consider the commonest objections raised by psychologists (13). American psychologists have been very sceptical of the clinical methods he adopts. They are said to depend too much on the verbal introspections of immature minds. Behaviourists much prefer evidence to be independent of attitudes and self-reports. Nevertheless, replications using all kinds of adaptions to overcome the shortcomings of introspection have yielded results which are very similar and coherent. Children from very different social and ethnic backgrounds with varying degrees of verbal talent still appear to give the developmental pattern described by Piaget.

The stages propounded are not so rigidly coupled with age according to recent work (14). The conservation of substance, for instance, appears at different ages in children. Moreover, appearance of the ability to conserve in a child is not sudden or all-embracing. There is a gradual emergence of the ability to conserve which varies from one property to the next. This point has considerable value for teachers. Individual differences in children's conceptual development will greatly influence the design of the curriculum by the teacher who is aware of the criteria for determining when certain conceptual possibilities can be entertained.

The bulk of Piaget's theorizing has been applied to mathematics and science with much less regard for other school subjects. Naturally, concept formation extends far beyond the bounds of maths and science and this has to some extent been rectified over the past few years by an increase in research and curriculum development in other areas of interest to schools (15).

Some [Bruner (16) and Bryant (9)] place greater emphasis on the part played by experience than Piaget. It is argued that the consistency of the stages is a function of the regularity of a culture's child-rearing patterns rather than of some in-built and inevitable sequence of development. However, 'training programmes' designed to ring the changes of these patterns and accelerate development have not, as yet, produced more than minor deviations in Piaget's developmental sequence. His earliest sample sizes were also criticized, although this has since been rectified.

IMPLICATIONS OF PIAGET'S WORK FOR THE TEACHER

Whilst admitting that there are limitations to the work of Piaget, there is still much we can learn which is of service in teaching. Some of the more relevant aspects are discussed below.

1. The existence of a maturational unfolding of conceptual skills being linked with certain periods in the lives of children has an obvious bearing on curriculum planning. Piaget is quite clear in his belief that neurological development and a progression of concept-forming skills must appear before full intellectual maturation is possible. The theory implies that certain periods are critical in mental growth. Teachers should, therefore, be aware of what is possible and what is not possible in the concept formation of their children. This does not mean that we must stick rigidly to a programme of teaching based exclusively on Piaget's sequence of concept development. Such a philo-sophy is too pessimistic if it leads us to sit back and wait for the next stage to appear. We should continue to explore teaching environments crucial to concept formation and hypothesis testing (9, 16). In this respect, mental age is a more valid concept than chronological age because we are concerned here with intellectual and not physical development.

2. Teaching at Middle and Upper School level should begin from concrete con-siderations, building up, where applicable, to more abstract reasoning. This is reflected in many teaching programmes in mathematics and science which begin with experi-mental, practical aspects before attempting deductive work (recommendations of the Mathematical Association and Nuffield Science are very much concerned with this approach).

The idea of active participation is in keeping with Piaget's view that concept forma-tion arises from the internalization of actions. Building up schemata requires practical experience of concrete situations, as far as possible, so as to encourage active assimilation and accommodation.

It is probably true to say that most of us most of the time are operating at the concrete level. Less able secondary school children may rarely, if ever, reach the heights of abstract thinking (17). Even university students have their problems (18). Discretion must be exercised in the presentation of abstract concepts particularly where they are of such an order of abstraction as to require an understanding of several subordinate concepts.

3. With primary school children and less able secondary children, be on the look out for intuitive, pre-operational thinking. Again, practical as well as verbal experience must assist the formation of concepts. Note also that operational thinking in some aspects of school work is by no means an indication of similar competence in other related aspects. Remember that research has shown marked irregularities for individuals in both the character and level of concept attainment.

4. Cognitive development is a cumulative process. The hierarchical nature requires the formation of lower-order schemata on which more advanced work can be built. If, therefore, cognitive frameworks depend on what has preceded, it is important to regulate the difficulty level and order of presentation of material. To apply an ordered sequence of work is to admit that we can monitor children's progress. Therefore we can use the pattern of development in each child as a means of assessing attainment both in respect of the child's own progress and in relation to the expectations of his mental age group.

5. Verbalization is very important. Language aids internalization and consequently the formation of concepts. Verbal interchange between teacher and child or parent and child constitutes an important communication channel by which the world is defined. More will be said about its role in the next chapter.

CONCEPT ATTAINMENT

Piaget is by no means the only person to attempt an analysis of concept formation. But there are differences in emphasis which distinguish the researchers in this field. Piaget is interested in the structural side of concept growth. But other psychologists, notably Vygotsky and Bruner, have concentrated more on function than structure. Vygotsky (19) carried out several ingenious investigations into concept formation using a method which did not depend on the language skills already acquired by the child. His main purpose was to examine the relationship between language and thought.

Briefly, his materials consisted of 22 wooden blocks varying in colour, shape, height and size. These *attributes*, as they are called, occurred in a variety of combinations derived from five colours, six shapes (square, triangle, circle, semi-circle, six-sided figure and trapezium), two heights (tall or flat) and two sizes of horizontal surface (large or small). Each block had a nonsense syllable written on the underside so that the subject could not see it. Only four syllables were used, LAG, BIK, MUR, CEV representing specific combinations of attributes (e.g. LAG is written on all tall, large blocks). Colour is not used as an attribute but is included as a distraction. The experimenter thinks of a concept and exposes a syllable on the underside of one block (called the *sample*) and asks the subject to pick out all the other blocks having the same syllable on them, that is the subject must deduce the critical attributes of the block which make up the concept (in this case tallness and largeness). When a wrong choice is made, the experimenter shows the subject an inaccurate block and the game proceeds until the subject tracks down the concept.

In the course of this research, Vygotsky and his co-workers arrived at conclusions about concept formation in close agreement with Piaget. Three stages were isolated; first, there is the *vague syncretic* (syncretic in this context means random rather than reasoned groupings of blocks) in which the child at an early stage of development piles the blocks into heaps without any recognizable order. The groupings result from trial and error, random arrangement or from the nearness of the blocks.

The second stage is called thinking in *complexes*. These are a kind of primitive concept in which the child groups attributes by criteria which are not the recognized properties which could be used for the classification of the concepts. Five sub-stages were identified. Classification of the blocks was drawn up (a) according to one common characteristic—*associative complexes;* (b) in collections like a square, a circle and a semi-circle (similar to the idea of having a knife, fork and spoon); (c) as *chain complexes* where the child first picks out some triangles and notices that the last one chosen was, say, green and this in turn makes his next series of selections green, etc.; (d) *diffuse complexes* consisting of chains which are unrelated such as green–blue–black, and so forth; and (e) *pseudo-concepts*. These latter arise when the child perceives superficial similarities based on the physical properties of objects without having grasped the full significance of a concept. The formation of pseudo-concepts is not spontaneous, but determined by the meaning given to a word by adults. In effect, the pseudo-concept is the product of mechanical and rote learning without an understanding of the underlying attributes and led Vygotsky to place more weight on the role of experience in concept formation than Piaget.

The third stage identified by Vygotsky is called the *potential concept stage* in which the child can cope with one attribute at a time, but is not yet able to manipulate all the attributes at once. When he can, he has reached maturity in concept attainment.

The description of how children progressed from haphazard grouping through pseudo-concept to full concept formation is illuminating. One can spot the grave difficulties presented to the infant and primary school child when faced with classification problems. We must be wary of creating too many pseudo-concepts using drill methods without first providing a rationale. Verbal labels are too readily acquired from adults with insufficient exemplars to aid in the construction of class concepts. Children often use terms which give the appearance of understanding, yet on closer inspection it becomes obvious that they do not really know the concepts involved. The shift in emphasis from traditional to modern mathematics and the use of structured apparatus (Cuisenaire rods, Dienes apparatus, colour factor) is a recognition of the need to establish an understanding of number operations as well as manipulative skills with numbers.

Bruner's strategies

We have dealt in some detail with concept development from birth to mid-adolescence. We shall now look briefly at some work which attempts to answer the question as to how adolescents and adults, who already have well-formed concepts, expand on these in order to acquire more elaborate concepts. Bruner and his colleagues (20) devised a method seeking to discover the routes used by people who are attempting to expand, modify and adapt existing concepts to meet new demands.

To do this, Bruner, like Vygotsky, used objects having several attributes; using well-defined attributes such as colour, shape, size or number which can have different *values* and combining these to create concepts which were drawn on cards, Bruner asked subjects to deduce the concept which he had chosen. Peel (2) provides a reduced version of the task in his book *The Pupil's Thinking*. Using verbal reports from subjects and by watching the direction taken by them in trying to arrive at a solution, Bruner distinguished two broad strategies or plans of action. These are *scanning* and *focusing* strategies.

To elucidate their meaning, let us take a simple illustration. We shall use three attributes of human beings, each with two values. These are sex [boy (B) and girl (G)], size [tall (T) and short (S)] and hair colour [fair (F) and dark (D)]. To simplify the presentation, each attribute value will be given a letter of the alphabet—these are shown after each value. Cards containing these attributes are then presented to someone as displayed in figure 5.3. We have used words instead of a card carrying a picture of the attributes. The cards contain all the possible combinations of the three attributes. Given the values, we can arrange them to form concepts containing three, two or one attribute values. Thus with the values:

B	oy	G	irl
T	all	S	hort
F	air	D	ark

we can get the following combinations:
8 three-attribute concepts by combining (see figure 5.3)

BTF, BTD, BSD, BSF
GTF, GTD, GSD, GSF

12 two-attribute concepts by combining

BT, BF, BS, BD, GT, GF, GS, GD, TF, TD, SF, SD

6 one-attribute concepts from

B, G, T, S, F, D

making 26 concepts in all.

The tester now thinks of one of the concepts (let us say the two-attribute concept of *fair girl* GF) without telling his subject. The former then selects one of the eight cards (the sample card) which includes the concept (let us say card GSF). The subject tries to deduce the concept by pointing to another card which he thinks is another instance of the concept. The tester answers 'yes' or 'no' to the selections until the subject is able to specify the precise combination of attributes making up the concept.

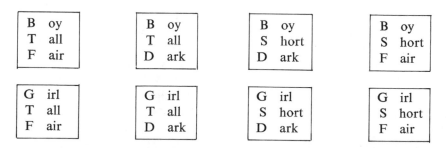

Figure 5.3 Sample cards containing the attributes of sex, size and hair shade

Returning now to the strategies observed by Bruner, in the scanning strategies a person works out hypotheses from the information given. In the case above, he has been shown GSF and he can now assess the combinations of attributes still open to him. Of the concepts, there are seven remaining possibilities: GSF, GS, GF, SF, G, S, F. With these in mind, he can adopt a completely logical approach known as *simultaneous scanning* by holding in mind all the combinations whilst setting up further hypotheses. To cut down the range of options still further, let us say the subject now chooses GTF, to which the experimenter says 'yes' because it contains GF. The number of alternatives is now reduced since the only common values in the two selections GSF and GTF are G and F. This, therefore, leaves three concepts, namely girls (G), fair girls (GF) and fairness (F). By a process of elimination, it would not take long to track down the correct concept. However, simultaneous scanning can be a tedious and uneconomic procedure putting a premium on having a good memory especially when there are a lot of attributes. A less exacting variation is *successive scanning* by which a person takes one step at a time. In our example at the stage where GTF is picked, the subject would then go on to look at each attribute in turn noting the positive instances only (in simultaneous scanning, negative instances are also taken into account). Guesswork and anticipation (two popular ploys with us all) are used in the early stages of this method.

Focusing does not involve hypothesis-testing. The individual proceeds by altering one attribute value at a time (*conservative focusing* which can be a long-winded affair) or more than one attribute at a time (*focus gambling*). The safest, or most conservative, method is to change and test the attribute values one at a time. In our example using GSF as the sample card, if a person wishes to test the presence of *girl* in a concept he might point to the card containing BSF. By this means he is holding SF constant. Building up to two and three values, if necessary, will finally enable the concept to be specified. The focus gambler, as the term implies, chances his arm by varying two attributes at each choice to test, in the first place, for single attribute concepts. He might, in our example, offer BSD as his first choice to test the significance of the size attribute. Lack of success would lead him to test double and ultimately treble attribute concepts.

Teachers will soon recognize the tactics employed by pupils (and themselves) in trying to solve problems involving attribute discrimination. The more concrete methods of successive scanning and particularly the focusing methods are the commonest. Note the rapid increase in task difficulty as one increases the number of attributes. At any level of mental operations it is important to avoid unduly overloading the problems with variables where simultaneous scanning is important (many physics problems, for example, can be approached in this way, as in the pendulum experiment mentioned earlier). There is also a suggestion (21) that strategies adopted by individuals are a function of the conditions in which they work. As a laboratory exercise, the games mentioned above are more likely to induce focusing techniques, whilst every day problems appear to encourage scanning. As yet, research has not been able to provide any precise information about the appropriateness of strategies for particular kinds of problem.

SUMMARY

Much of man's experience is assimilated in the form of concepts and expressed in a symbolic form as in verbal and mathematical modes. Thus, by the processes of classification and discrimination of the critical attributes of objects and events, man can organize his percepts and employ symbol forms to represent these experiences. Concepts have several distinctive characteristics of which the following are amongst the most important. Concepts are (1) generalizations arrived at by abstracting and distinguishing the critical attributes of objects and events; (2) they are subject to experiential influences; (3) they are symbolic; (4) they can be used either in a way which is widely accepted by everyone (extentionally), or in a highly personal way (intentionally); (5) they form hierarchies of increasing complexity (think of the classification of animals as an illustration of hierarchical structure); (6) they can be irrational as in superstitions and phobias; (7) they may be formed without the conscious knowledge of an individual.

Concept formation has been one of the special provinces of the French psychologist, Jean Piaget. His researches have led him to postulate a theory of qualitative changes during cognitive development from birth to adolescence which take place in a definite, inevitable sequence of maturational steps starting with biological mechanisms and culminating in a highly developed system of abstract operations. The child, whilst he strives to come to terms with his surroundings, organizes his activities into schemata by the processes of assimilation and accommodation. Piaget suggests four stages from birth to adolescence consisting of the sensori-motor, pre-operational (composed of pre-conceptual and intuitive sub-stages), concrete operations and formal operations.

A particular contribution of Piaget's theory to the educational scene is in drawing attention to the child as an active participant in his own concept-learning processes. Moreover, curriculum planning needs to be informed by the stages he postulates, but without being too rigid and ignoring the variations in individual concept growth. With new topics at any stage, one should proceed from the concrete and practical to the more difficult abstract. With younger children, there may be little success in going beyond the concrete aspects of a topic. Where concepts are cumulative, the order of presentation must be carefully worked out so as to build up schemata in a logical and orderly sequence.

Language is most important for the internalization of concepts. The work of Vygotsky pays attention to the build up of concepts alongside the acquisition of verbal symbols representing the concepts. His developmental theory was similar in many respects to that of Piaget, but see chapter 8 for a discussion of the function of language in concept growth. Bruner's main interest was to elucidate the thinking strategies of adults who already had a grasp of concepts. He concluded that there are four basic ways of attaining concepts in the form of simultaneous scanning, successive scanning, conservative focusing and focus gambling.

ENQUIRY AND DISCUSSION

1. It is very important for student teachers to meet children from all ages. With care, several of Piaget's original experiments can be repeated with the children (not particularly at school, but whenever or wherever the occasion presents itself). The materials are usually inexpensive and readily available. Try to choose a range of ages likely to include youngsters from each stage of cognitive development. As a guide to materials, procedures and characteristic findings see K. R. Fogelman's book *Piagetian Tests for the Primary School*, NFER, Slough, 1970.

Do not forget to let the children know where they have gone wrong once the experimentation has been completed. You will find this a particularly exacting task, especially where the developmental stage of the child clearly falls short of that required for an understanding of the problem.

2. Explore Bruner's strategies using materials indicated in *The Pupil's Thinking* [note (20)].

3. Using as a starting point the references in note (15), read up and examine in terms of learning and teaching techniques the theories of concept growth associated with those of the following which are of particular interest to you: science; mathematics; history; geography; moral judgement; religion.

NOTES AND REFERENCES

1. W. E. Vinacke, *The Psychology of Thinking*, McGraw-Hill, New York, 1952.

2. E. A. Peel, in *The Pupil's Thinking*, Oldbourne, London, 1960, presents a number of different ways in which the term 'thinking' has been used. He classifies them under four headings of *thematic* (imaginative thinking in creative writing, painting or music where one is not bound by a given problem), *explanatory* (describing and explaining events and things), *productive* (applying knowledge in new situations giving rise to new inventions or products) and *coordinating* or *integrative* thinking (seen in the discovery of new theories and systems of thought). The work of Bogen mentioned in chapter 2 also points to a distinction between *spatial* and *verbal* thinking which may even be specific to a certain hemisphere of the brain.

3. Vinacke's book in note (1) gives a thorough discussion of concept characteristics. R. Thomson, *The Psychology of Thinking*, Penguin, London, 1959 also provides a summary.

4. R. H. Forgus, *Perception: The Basic Process of Cognitive Development*, McGraw-Hill, New York, 1966. He classifies four schools of thinking as to how these generalizations might arise. There are those psychologists who believe that concepts are formed by choosing *identical* elements. Others believe that *common relationships* define a concept. For example, apple, pear, banana, orange and plum all share the relationship of 'fruitiness'. A third basis for concept formation is *similarity of function*. The example listing fruits also serves to illustrate a functional concept. Finally, we have what Osgood refers to as the *common mediation process* which we shall deal with in chapter 8.

5. J. Piaget's books are generally very difficult to understand. One of his most recent and relevant books entitled *Science of Education and the Psychology of the Child*, Longman, 1970 is amongst the easiest to understand. Readers who would like to sample his earlier writing should consult *The Child's Conception of Number*, Routledge, London, 1952 or B. Inhelder and J. Piaget, *The Growth of Logical Thinking from Childhood to Adolescence*, Routledge, London, 1958. There are now

many introductory texts interpreting Piaget for the benefit of students and some of these are given in the Further Reading list.

6. D. O. Hebb, *The Organization of Behaviour*, Wiley, New York, 1949.

7. F. C. Bartlett, *Remembering*, Cambridge University Press, London, 1932.

8. J. S. Bruner, 'The course of cognitive growth', *Am. Psychol.*, **19**, 1–15 (1964).

9. Some of these experiments look so simple to the adult, and the child's errors so incredibly naïve. In an experiment of Piaget's, several sweets or counters are arranged in equal rows, some for the child, and an opposite row for another person.

child

· · · · ·

· · · · ·

other person

When the child's row is spread out,

· · · · ·

· · · · ·

he will say, if he is at the intuitive level of development, that he has more than the other person. A contracted row is said to be smaller and contain less. We again meet up with a transitivity problem involving invariance similar to those described in the body of the textbook. The child uses length as his criterion of quantity and is immediately faced with a conflict of hypotheses.

Bryant attempted to remove the conflict in a research reported in the following: P. E. Bryant, 'Cognitive development', *Br. Med. Bull.*, **27**, 200–205 (1971), and P. E. Bryant and T. Trabasso, 'Transitive inferences and memory in young children', *Nature*, **232**, 456–458 (1971). If the arrangement of counters is such that the child has more as indicated in the illustration beneath:

· · · · · ·

· · · · ·

he will, even at the intuitive level, set up the correct hypothesis by saying he has more than the other person (by, as yet, some unsubstantiated method). If the second stage is now made indeterminate by placing the counters into two identical glass containers such that they appear the same height (in other words two counters have not made an appreciable difference to the height), the child, according to Bryant, still says that he has more than the other person regardless of the fact that he can see the heights are equal. Why? Because, says Bryant, the child has been able to establish a 'definite hypothesis' at the first stage, can appreciate the invariance principle in the transformation to the second stage and is not so perceptually dominated at this second stage as to say that the quantities are equal when the heights are equal. When equal numbers of counters are used in the same experiment but arranged to give unequal lengths in the rows, as in the second part of the illustration at the beginning of this note, the child sets up the incorrect, but definite, hypothesis of a difference in the quantities and maintains it throughout even though, as in the first case, the heights in the glass vessels look equal. Bryant's conclusion is that we ought to concentrate on how children arrive at definite hypotheses rather than debate the invariance issue.

10. The grouping of operations is carefully defined by Piaget. For a summary, the reader might like to refer to R. M. Beard, *An Outline of Piaget's Developmental Psychology*, Routledge and Kegan Paul, London, 1969, pp. 81–83 or J. L. Phillips, Jr., *The Origins of Intellect: Piaget's Theory*, Freeman, San Francisco, 1969, pp. 69–75. These groupings are seen by Piaget as an essential prerequisite to concrete operations.

11. B. Inhelder and J. Piaget, *The Growth of Logical Thinking from Childhood to Adolescence*, Routledge and Kegan Paul, London, 1958.

12. A chapter on 'Formal reasoning' by E. A. Lunzer, in E. A. Lunzer and J. F. Morris (Eds), *Development in Human Learning*, vol. 2, Staples, London, 1968 gives a clear analysis of hypothesis-construction and -testing by children at the concrete and formal stages of development.

13. A useful summary of objections to the Piagetian position is given in D. G. Boyle, *A Student's Guide to Piaget*, Pergamon, London, 1969, chapter 10.

14. For example, see the work of K. Lovell and E. Ogilvie, 'A study of the conservation of substance in the junior school child', *Br. J. educ. Psychol.*, **30**, 109–118 (1960), and 'A study of the conservation of weight in the junior school child', *Br. J. educ. Psychol.*, **31**, 138–144 (1961).

15. Over the last twenty years, several workers have looked at concept growth in particular subject areas. For a summary up to the mid-60s have a look at J. G. Wallace, *Concept Growth and the Education of the Child*, NFER, Slough, 1965. The growth of religious concepts has been examined by R. Goldman, *Religious Thinking from Childhood to Adolescence*, Routledge and Kegan Paul, London, 1964. Also look at G. Jahoda, 'Children's concepts of time and history', *Educ. Res.*, **15**, 87–104 (1963); K. Lovell, *The Growth of Basic Mathematical and Scientific Concepts in Children*, University of London Press, London, 1968; W. B. Sloan, The Child's Conception of Musical Scales: a Study Based on the Developmental Theory of Piaget, *M.Sc. Dissertation* (Unpublished), University of Bradford, 1969; G. Jahoda, 'The development of children's ideas about country and nationality', *Brit. J. educ. Psychol.*, **33**, 47–60, 143–153; R. Hallam, 'Piaget and the teaching of history', *Educ. Res.*, **12**, 3–12 (1969); W. Kay, *Moral Development: A Psychological Study of Moral Growth from Childhood to Adolescence*, Allen and Unwin, London, 1968.

16. J. S. Bruner believes that children are remarkably flexible in their ability to acquire concepts. He places instruction and experience at a higher level of priority as potent influences in concept development than would Piaget. See his book, *Toward A Theory of Instruction*, Norton, New York, 1966.

17. K. Lovell, 'A follow-up study of Inhelder and Piaget's *The Growth of Logical Thinking*', *Br. J. Psychol.*, **52**, 143–154 (1961).

18. M. L. J. Abercrombie, *The Anatomy of Judgment*, Hutchinson, London, 1960.

19. L. S. Vygotsky, *Thought and Language*, M.I.T. Press, Cambridge, Mass., 1962 gives a detailed examination of the impact of language and concept formation.

20. J. S. Bruner, J. J. Goodnow and G. A. Austin, *A Study of Thinking*, Wiley, New York, 1965. For a simplified version of the research see E. A. Peel, *The Pupil's Thinking*, Oldbourne, London, 1960 or R. Thomson, *The Psychology of Thinking*, Penguin, London, 1959.

21. N. E. Wetherick, 'Bruner's concept of strategy: an experiment and a critique', *J. gen. Psychol.*, **81**, 53–58 (1969).

FURTHER READING

R. M. Beard, *An Outline of Piaget's Developmental Psychology*, Routledge and Kegan Paul, London, 1969. A detailed commentary on Piaget's work.

D. G. Boyle, *A Student's Guide to Piaget*, Pergamon London, 1969. An introductory text.

B. Inhelder and J. Piaget, *The Growth of Logical Thinking from Childhood to Adolescence*, Routledge and Kegan Paul, London, 1958. An historical work, but hard going for those interested in introductory books.

N. Isaacs, *New Light on Children's Ideas of Number: The Work of Professor Piaget*, Ward Lock, London, 1960, and *The Growth of Understanding in the Young Child*, Ward Lock, London, 1961. These two books are brief and to the point.

K. Lovell, *The Growth of Basic Mathematical and Scientific Concepts in Children*, University of London Press, London, 1968.

E. A. Peel, *The Pupil's Thinking*, Oldbourne, London, 1960. A thorough and technical text with several detailed descriptions of experimental work.

J. L. Phillips, Jr., *The Origins of Intellect: Piaget's Theory*, Freeman, San Francisco, 1969. One of the best introductory texts available.

R. Thomson, *The Psychology of Thinking*, Penguin London, 1959.

J. G. Wallace, *Concept Growth and the Education of the Child*, NFER, Slough, 1965. A detailed survey of researches on concept formation.

6 Learning theory and practice

Previous chapters have made it abundantly clear that learning is a very necessary activity for living things. Their survival depends on it. For man, the versatility of his adaptation to diverse environments and the joys of abstraction in art and science are founded on his phenomenal learning capacity. Whilst there is no complete agreement amongst psychologists about the details of learning processes, they do accept the basic premise that learning occurs whenever one adopts new, or modifies existing, behaviour patterns in a way which has some influence on future performance or attitudes. Unless there were in fact some influence, we would not be able to detect that learning had taken place. This view of learning excludes certain kinds of reaction which are thought to be inborn such as, for example, reflex action or innate release mechanisms (IRM mentioned in chapter 3) where these have not undergone modification in the course of growth. But the definition includes learning which occurs without deliberate or conscious awareness, bad as well as good behaviour and covert attitudes as well as overt performance. The importance of studying learning processes is self-evident since one of the central purposes of the teacher's task in formal educational settings is to provide well-organized experiences so as to speed up the process of learning, thus enabling pupils to make reasoned choices in solving life's problems.

Whether we recognize it or not, every parent and teacher has a personal theory or theories about how learning best takes place. In the home, the nature and severity of punishments or rewards tell us something about parental theories of learning. In the use of corporal punishment, some believe that actions almost invariably speak louder than words; others never beat their children because to apply corporal punishment to children would be to show them that violence is one acceptable way of solving problems; most people manage to strike a balance between these extreme views of the place of physical punishment in teaching children to behave, although even here the particular occasions chosen on which to apply punishment reveal something of a parent's philosophy of learning.

In the classroom we constantly observe methods which depend on assumptions about the process of learning. What assumptions are teachers making who use question and answer techniques, rewards (sweets, marks, class positions, etc.), i.t.a. or traditional orthography, 'look and say', 'phonic' or 'alphabetic' methods of teaching reading, 'Nuffield' or traditional methods of science teaching, learning tables or the alphabet to *exercise* the memory, deductive or inductive methods of teaching, the direct method of teaching modern languages, and teaching social sciences to increase social awareness (transfer of training)?

As with so many complex issues in psychology, no one theory has provided all the answers to the kinds of questions of concern to teachers. Some theorists, as we shall see, have cornered the market in particular aspects of learning (Skinner and programmed learning for example), but no single theory has yet been formulated which satisfactorily accounts for all the facts. Nevertheless, it is worthwhile looking at the main tenets of some theories because we must have a background against which to examine our own suppositions about learning in the light of existing experimental evidence, and to illuminate the origins and development of commonly held views about learning amongst professionals. For an excellent summary of the major theories, readers should look at W. Hill's book entitled *Learning* (1).

THE TASK OF LEARNING THEORISTS

Let us attempt to summarize the major problems of importance to teachers which any comprehensive theory of learning should be capable of answering (2).

(a) How can we determine the limits and influence the capacity of learning in the individual? In this respect, what is the influence of inheritance, age, intelligence, maturational level, environmental opportunities, aptitudes, personality, motivation or practice (see the relevant chapters)?

(b) What is the influence of experience, that is the effect of early learning or later learning? How are cognitive strategies and habits assimilated and how are they affected by future experience?

(c) There should be a place for an explanation of the complexities of symbolic learning in man (see chapter 8).

(d) What is the connection between animal and human learning and is a compromise between them possible without investing animals with human qualities, or vice versa (*anthropomorphism*)? As we shall see, Skinner has managed to build a most elaborate theory of human learning using animals such as rats and pigeons.

(e) Because learning takes place as part and parcel of body mechanisms, any theory should be capable of incorporating physiological and ethological findings (see chapter 2).

(f) Practice has a central function in learning, but we still need to know far more about the conditions which favour or adversely affect achievements after practice. Is there a threshold of practice beyond which one cannot improve? Under what circumstances are massed or distributed practice most effective?

(g) What is the place of drives, incentives, rewards and punishments in learning programmes (see chapter 3)?

(h) Is it possible to transfer learned skills from one activity to another (transfer of training)? In other words, to what extent can our learning in specific situations be generalized to other similar, but non-identical, situations?

(i) What happens when we retain or forget information (see chapter 7)? What part do attention or perception play in the processes of remembering and forgetting (see chapter 4)?

(j)   What is the importance of 'understanding' in attempting to learn? Some things we seem able to do without any apparent 'understanding', such as physical movements of muscles (in writing, and eye movements in reading), whilst to understand the beatitudes or differential calculus requires a long, arduous mental effort involving the accumulation of simpler concepts.

Most of the salient questions posed in the above list are elaborated in other chapters. In this chapter we shall deal with the rudimentary propositions of the major theories of learning. The behavioural phenomena are there for all to see; the divergence between the theories occurs in the interpretation of the causal processes which give rise to that behaviour. Of the many theories of learning extant, we have chosen the following because between them they form the foundation stones on which several views of teaching and learning in schools have been built. But we must hasten to add that the contribution of learning theories *per se* has, up to now, been only marginal to the successful formulation of educational programmes.

SOME IMPORTANT THEORIES

Lunzer (3) has suggested a fruitful two-way classification of approaches to the study of learning (table 6.1). In the first place we have the widely accepted classification which runs from *connectionist* (or *behaviourist*) to *cognitive* (or *field-cognition*) theorists. The basic differences are that on the one hand the connectionists treat learning as a matter of links between stimulus and response (S–R for short). The individual develops certain responses to given stimuli and the connectionist is interested in observing those S–R bonds and the ways in which experience with other stimuli can change them. Inferences are made by direct observation of the effects of 'input' and 'output' variables applied to animal and human situations. On the other side, the cognitive psychologists place greater store by the functioning of the brain (internal processes including perception and attitudes) and the cognitive structures which man might acquire from experience and which modify his present behaviour. Much greater stress is placed on man being aware of the surroundings and being flexible in the solutions he adopts.

The second classification involves the place of the stimulus as an explanatory concept of physical or mental activity. Some regard the stimulus (any source of disturbance which might affect any sense organ) as the initiator of behaviour—without stimulation, they say, there would be no response. Lunzer refers to this view as *reactive* because responses are held to occur only when an organism needs to 'react' to a stimulus. Another approach, the *structural*, sees the organism as spontaneously activated. 'Behaviour is responsive to stimuli, but it is not made up of responses to stimuli. If there were no stimuli (in the environment), the organism would seek stimuli. There is no end-state for behaviour in general, for the organism is constantly active'. The difference, then, between a reactive and a structural point of view is the difference between a passive and an active philosophy of the role of organisms in their environments.

In both these classifications we find those who take up an intermediate position. Thus we can generate a table, as shown here, which contains nine points of view.

Table 6.1 Modified from E. A. Lunzer, *The Regulation of Behaviour*, vol. I, Staples, London, 1968, p. 120

		connectionist	intermediate	cognitive
	reactive	Watson Thorndike Hull		(Locke)
Role of the stimulus	intermediate	Pavlov	Tolman	Gestalt psychologists
	structural	Skinner	Lorenz (and ethologists) Broadbent Lunzer	Piaget (Lewin)

As Lunzer is careful to indicate, precise classification into a ninefold table obscures the fact that there is a considerable overlap in the points of view expressed by those mentioned in the table. So we must expect to find shades of opinion within the classification. Let us look in more detail at the theories expounded by those mentioned in the table.

THE CONNECTIONISTS

(a) J. B. Watson

Before the last century, man had never really been the subject of honest scientific experiment. The establishment of a psychological laboratory by Wundt in Germany in 1879 saw the beginning of a more objective attack on the study of animal and human behaviour and the impetus thus given soon created a firmer foundation for psychology. At the turn of the century, Pavlov in Russia, and Watson and Thorndike in America directed their attention to a detailed study of *what* and *how* animals and man behaved in given laboratory circumstances rather than relying on introspective beliefs or feelings. The earliest and most extreme 'behaviourist', as the connectionists are sometimes called, was Watson (1878–1958). His fundamental conclusion from many experimental observations of animal and childhood learning was that stimulus–response (S–R) connections are more likely to be established the more *frequently* or *recently* an S–R bond occurs. A child solving a number problem might have to make many unsuccessful trials before arriving at a correct solution. Of the many responses he can possibly make in his efforts to solve the problem, the unsuccessful ones will tend not to be repeated, thus there will be an increase in both the frequency and recency of successful responses until a correct S–R pattern appears immediately the same or similar problem reappears. The process of trying alternative paths in the solution of problems of any kind is known as *trial and error* learning.

(b) E. L. Thorndike

Thorndike, working about the same time (1874–1949), similarly held that we *stamp in* effective S–R connections and *stamp out* those responses which are useless. Using cats, dogs and chickens, he devised experiments in which an animal was placed in a cage from which it could escape to reach food. The food was visible but not accessible from the cage and the hungry animals soon began to seek after the lure. The door of the cage could only be opened by pulling a cord hanging within reach outside the cage. In an endeavour to reach the food the animal clawed, banged and prowled around the cage, occasionally touching the release cord. In this 'trial and error' fashion some animals hit on the solution to their problem. Successive attempts by the same successful animals took shorter periods of time by cutting out the useless activities. From this work Thorndike derived several 'laws' of learning which he believed applied equally well to man as to animals.

Whereas for Watson the important thing was the simultaneous presence of stimulus and response (*contiguity* theorist), Thorndike gave more weight to the end effects of the response. Satisfying and gratifying outcomes from a response are more likely to lead to that response reappearing, in other words, the S–R connection is *reinforced* whenever satisfying results are apparent. The statement that satisfaction serves to strengthen or reinforce S–R bonds is known as Thorndike's *Law of Effect*. Note also in this connection that dissatisfaction does not necessarily extinguish responses; rather, it causes the respondent to look for alternatives and seek out satisfactory solutions by trial and error. Of course, Thorndike accepted Watson's position and it appears in the *Law of Exercise* which states that bonds are strengthened simply by the same stimulus and response repeatedly occurring together, whilst a reduction in a response weakens the S–R bond to the point where it finally becomes redundant. The relevant point here is that exercise or practice alone is not enough. Knowledge of results must follow for reinforcement to take place, so the Law of Exercise is a corollary or consequence of the Law of Effect.

The particular contribution of Thorndike to learning theory and to teaching is his insistence on the use of scientific measurement as a means of examining learning skills amongst children and his belief in motivation through the agency of rewards rather than punishment as an efficient means of establishing good learning habits. Punishment may, however, have an indirect influence for the better by redirecting the attention of pupils from their existing ineffective S–R bonds to more suitable ones, and this is where the teacher can assist by providing appropriate alternative S–R routes. Whilst the laws are somewhat rudimentary and limited in their usefulness to teachers, nevertheless they contain the germs of reinforcement theory prevalent in the work of later connectionists such as Skinner and Hull.

(c) I. P. Pavlov (4)

Though his major findings are of limited pragmatic value in the classroom, it would be difficult to put the present behaviourist position into perspective without reference to the physiological work of Ivan Pavlov. Like Thorndike and Watson, he viewed behaviour as responses initiated by stimuli—a reactivist, but unlike them his interests were strictly to do with physiological reflex actions, in particular the salivation reflex in dogs. Quite by accident he discovered (*circa* 1880) that dogs would salivate when some other pre-viously neutral stimulus besides food was present, provided that on some previous occasions the stimulus had appeared at or just before the presentation of food. From this finding he set about intentionally teaching dogs to associate salivation with neutral stimuli—a process known as *classical conditioning*. In one such experiment, a hungry dog was placed in a harness in a sound-proof room and a tuning fork sounded. Very soon after, meat powder was presented causing the dog to salivate. Observe that learning has already taken place because the reflex action of salivation normally occurs initially in response to food in the mouth and not from the sight of food. However, the dog soon learns to anticipate food in its mouth and experiences anticipatory salivation from the signs (sight, smell) of the food. Pairings of the tuning fork followed by the presentation of meat powder ultimately lead to the dog salivating at the sound of the tuning fork in the absence of the meat powder. The time lapse between the tuning fork and meat powder stimuli is critical because the greater the time gap between the stimuli the less likely it is that the dog will connect the two events. The salivation is an *unconditional response* (UR) innately governed and available when food, in this case meat powder, is presented as an *unconditional stimulus* (US). The tuning fork acts as a *conditional stimulus* (CS) giving rise to salivation as a *conditional response* (CR)—'conditional' because the salivation is conditional on the continued presentation of food from time to time. The relationship is sometimes shown diagrammatically as:

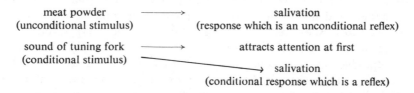

meat powder ⟶ salivation
(unconditional stimulus) (response which is an unconditional reflex)

sound of tuning fork ⟶ attracts attention at first
(conditional stimulus) ⟶ salivation
(conditional response which is a reflex)

Whenever the tuning fork is sounded along with food, *reinforcement* takes place. But several abortive soundings of the tuning fork will lead to a lessening of the quantity of saliva and ultimately *extinction* of the conditional S–R link.

A human condition which displays classical conditioning is a child's visit to the doctor for an injection (or the dentist). The unconditional situation is:

pain ⟶ 'activation syndrome' (heart increases in beat along with other
(US) autonomic reactions, UR)

If the child experiences pain when he is injected by doctors, the waiting room may act as a conditional stimulus for the activation of autonomic reactions. Where the child continues to experience pain on each visit, the conditioning is reinforced, otherwise the absence of pain will bring extinction of the fear.

doctor's surgery ⟶ general interest
(CS) ⟶ activation syndrome

Classical conditioning is rooted in the reactions of involuntary systems in the body such as the organs and emotional reactions controlled by the autonomic nervous system (see chapter 2), and reflex actions such as salivation, eye blinking, knee-jerks and pupillary constriction in response to light intensity changes. Learning takes place by acquiring responses through conditional ties to these reflexes. Fear has been a popular experimental condition. Watson in the 1920s made successful attempts to condition or extinguish children's responses to fear-provoking events. By pairing pleasant and feared objects with each other or with a neutral stimulus, Watson was able to condition children. 'Little Albert' (5) was conditioned to fear a white rat. Whenever the eleven month old Albert reached out to touch the rat a loud bang was created behind the child. In time, Albert was petrified by the sight of the white rat.

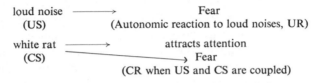

Extinction of a fear or phobia can sometimes be accomplished by pairing the conditional stimulus with a pleasurable stimulus. Albert's white rat might have been gradually introduced and brought progressively nearer at meal times. Bribes to persuade children who have built up a conditional fear of school to go to school can be of a similar nature. This special variety of extinction is called *reciprocal inhibition*. In chapter 2 we discussed the relationship between the sympathetic and parasympathetic parts of the autonomic system and it is believed that reciprocal inhibition results from the para-sympathetic system (responsible for putting a brake on the energy-producing mecha-nisms of the body) overriding the sympathetic system (activates and excites body mecha-nisms which produce the symptoms of fear) and encouraging de-conditioning. Some-times a supposed extinguished conditional response suddenly reappears after a lapse of time in which the US has not been in evidence. This is called *spontaneous recovery*.

How exact must the conditioning stimulus be each time it is presented? In fact some stimuli can have pretty wide limits within which a response is instigated and we call this *stimulus generalization*. The frequency of the tuning fork in the experiment described above does not have to be exactly the same each time; there is usually a range of effective frequencies. The animals used in the reciprocal inhibition experiments with children can vary in size and shape and still produce the desired effect. Children who fear starting school are not particular which school. In chapter 5 we noted that the definition of a particular concept is not easy because our generalizations require a knowledge of the limits within which a classification is possible. Poodles and Irish wolf hounds can elicit the same response 'dog' even though there are staggering differences in size, shape, colour and habits. We also met with generalization at the beginning of chapter 4 in the discussion of encoding. In some way our reception system seems to have a built-in tolerance to divergence in percepts either presented through the various sense modalities or, as mentioned above, in the written and spoken word. There are, of course, limits to stimulus generalization and it becomes necessary to draw distinctions between similar, but non-identical, stimuli especially when the discrimination of response is a matter of adaptive survival. This is known as *stimulus discrimination*. For a rat running a maze in order to obtain food or a child classifying the attributes of the concept of colour (see chapter 5), there has to be differentiation of superficially similar stimuli before satis-factory responses materialize.

Extinction, spontaneous recovery, stimulus discrimination and generalization emphasize the complexity of S–R connections. However, classical conditioning is limited to reflex mechanisms and in turn to emotional reactions. Unfortunately the effect of, say, reward and punishment is complicated by learning processes of a higher order than a reflex. Fear of failure and pleasure from praise, whilst they might be regarded as potent unconditional responses, are probably the result of much more complex acquired reactions than can be explained from Pavlovian conditioning.

(d) B. F. Skinner

Amongst contemporary behaviourists, the American psychologist B. F. Skinner is undoubtedly the best known. His contributions to programmed learning and behaviour therapy are widely publicized. His main interest, like Pavlov, has been conditioning, but his special brand is termed *operant conditioning*. Initial laboratory experiments involved hungry rats placed in 'Skinner boxes' and these consisted of levers which when pressed would cause the release of food pellets. Exploratory activity of the rat in confined space would usually end up in a chance contact with a lever. After two or three accidental lever contacts the rat would display a dramatic change in behaviour by intentionally pressing the lever, often very quickly, to obtain food. We have here another example of trial and error learning. More important is the rat's instrumental or 'operant' behaviour whereby he produces his own reward or *reinforcement* by converting a productive accident into an intentional behaviour pattern. When the rat obtains a pellet of food every time it presses the bar Skinner refers to it as *continuous reinforcement*. When the rat is sometimes rewarded and sometimes not it is known as *intermittent reinforcement*. In the early stages of conditioning continuous reinforcement is needed to establish the S–R link. However, perseverance wanes when hunger is satisfied and intermittent reinforcement can then be introduced with gradually increasing intervals between each reward. In TV advertising of popular goods (soap powders, etc.), gambling where the winnings are intermittent or the judicious use of praise in the classroom we have examples of the powerful effects of intermittent reinforcement.

A second important series of experiments using pigeons will help to elucidate some of the basic principles of learning derived by Skinner. A hungry pigeon was to be taught to walk in a figure of eight. At first sight this is a difficult task because the bird must walk first in one direction then the opposite direction in order to complete the figure. A pellet of food was given immediately the bird began to move in a clockwise direction. Once the movement was initiated, intermittent reinforcement was used to reward extensive clockwise movements until the bird walked or ran in a clockwise circle. By carefully planning the reinforcement it was found possible to introduce rewards for anticlockwise movements because the pigeon on those occasions when it was not given a food pellet for a clockwise motion would tend to explore other kinds of movement including anti-clockwise motion. Apparently, it takes a surprisingly short period of time to encourage the pigeon to walk in a figure of eight provided the pellet rewards are carefully planned; this planning of rewards by the experimenter is known as a *schedule of reinforcement*.

From many similar animal and human experiments, Skinner drew several valuable conclusions about learning:

(i) each step in the learning process should be short and should grow out of previously learned behaviour;

(ii) in the early stages, learning should be regularly rewarded and at all stages should be carefully controlled by a schedule of continuous and intermittent reinforcement;

(iii) reward should follow quickly when the correct response appears. This is referred to as *feedback* and is based on the principle that motivation is enhanced when we are informed of our progress. This is allied to (i) since to ensure a high success rate the steps in the learning process must be sufficiently small and within the capacities of the learner;

(iv) the learner should be given an opportunity to discover stimulus discriminations for the most likely path to success. In the pigeon experiment the bird has to perceive the difference between clockwise and anticlockwise motion.

Two distinctions exist between classical and operant conditioning hinging upon the nature of the response and the source of reinforcement. In Pavlovian conditioning the response is controlled by the experimenter because he determines when and what to present as the stimulus. Thus, the response is *elicited* using existing reflex action either inborn or acquired. In a sense the individual's role is passive since the response must await a particular stimulus to appear—*respondent behaviour*. On the other hand, in Skinnerian conditioning, we must wait for the desired response to appear before learning can proceed. Only when this response is *emitted* can reinforcement occur. Therefore the individual must act or operate on his environment in order to be rewarded—*operant behaviour*. The second difference is in the action of the reinforcement. In classical conditioning the unconditional stimulus is correlated with reinforcement, so that the meat powder in Pavlov's work acts as an encourager for the repetition of behaviour. In operant conditioning, the response acts as the source of reinforcement; when a reward follows a response (lever pressing in rats, or pigeon movements), the response is more likely to be repeated.

With regard to reinforcement there are at least two kinds we can identify. *Differential reinforcement* occurs when only responses surpassing some specific criterion are recognized for reward. A certain pressure might have to be applied to a bar lever in the Skinner box before a food pellet is expelled. Children might have to reach a given mark in school subjects before a teacher gives praise. Alternatively, we can condition by reinforcing each bit of behaviour which approximates to that required, a technique known as learning by *successive approximation*. The method used for teaching the pigeon to walk in a figure of eight demonstrates this technique.

Operant conditioning is far more prevalent in both animal and human learning than Pavlovian conditioning, and examples applicable in education will be discussed later in the chapter. One commonplace example is animal training in circuses. Note that Skinner is not unduly concerned to know what happens 'inside' an organism when learning proceeds. Such intermediate or intervening variables involved in physiological or cognitive processes which might affect the nature and direction of learning are not subject to direct observation and do not figure in Skinner's psychology. Observable and modifiable stimuli and responses for the control and delineation of behaviour are the key variables for him. The stimulus may be an accident, but the overt response constitutes the means whereby the organism *operates on its environment*. We see now the reason for regarding Skinner as a 'structural' rather than a 'reactive' psychologist in table 6.1 at the start of the chapter.

(e) C. L. Hull

Clark Hull was another influential American theorist who created a complex hypothetical model of learning which, as yet, has found little or no outlet in the day-to-day work of the teacher. Like other behaviourists we have encountered, except Skinner, Hull believes that S–R bonds depend on elicited responses and not emitted responses to stimuli. But his major theme involves the inner states in man for he sets great store by the *intervening variables* (6) occurring in the formation of S–R bonds in an effort to predict responses from given stimuli. Symbolically, his view is expressed as S–O–R to signify the importance of the intervening happenings in the organism O. Like Freud, he has provided a theoretical conceptual framework the terms of which, for want of better, have become an inescapable part of psychology. We have already met his theory of primary and secondary drives in chapter 3 and we shall refer to the intervening variables of *excitatory potential* (the tendency to make a response to a stimulus) and *reactive inhibition* (the tendency not to repeat a response which has just been made) in chapter 11 on Personality. The only other term we need to mention is his theory of *need reduction*. When a deprivation exists such as food or water, or a secondary need derived from primary needs as indicated in chapter 3, responses which lead to a reduction of the need are likely to produce an S–O–R connection. The need reduction provides the reinforcement for the connection. Learning, then, takes place as part and parcel of the process during which animal or human needs are being satisfied—which, even if we argue with the details, is not an unreasonable generalization.

COGNITION THEORIES

One of the cardinal problems raised by the behaviourist approach is whether it is possible to evaluate total human or animal response by teasing out, observing and analysing bits and pieces of the behaviour. To what extent is it necessary to account for an organism's perception of a situation as a basis for responding to stimulation? Wertheimer, the earliest worker to attempt a cognitive interpretation, thought that breaking down behaviour into constituent parts obscured or possibly obliterated the full meaning of that behaviour. Along with Köhler and Koffka he founded the school known as *Gestalt psychology* which concentrates on a study of perception for a better understanding of learning. Some of the basic principles of this school have already been dealt with in the section on perception in chapter 4.

 The greatest single contribution of Gestalt psychologists to learning is their study of *insight*, a term now popularly used to mean 'intuitive'. But to Gestalt psychologists insightful learning is more than this. It occurs as a sudden solution to a problem in a way which can readily be repeated during a similar event in the future and which has some transfer to new situations. Köhler's first demonstrations of insightful learning took place when he was a World War I internee on the Canary Islands. Using chimpanzees as subjects he arranged a number of problems where bananas were placed out of arm's reach outside their cages. The chimpanzees were provided with short sticks which, whilst not long enough to reach the bananas singly, could be made to do so when slotted together. Sometimes bananas were hung from the roof of the cage and obtainable by piling up boxes strewn about the cage. In both instances *some* animals, after unproductive exploratory activity, suddenly got the 'idea' of how to solve the problem. This sudden, immediate, repeatable and transposable behaviour he called *insight*. Trial and error might be evident in the early stages of animal exploration, but once the animal had seen the task as a whole he could restructure or reorganize the perceptual field in ways which afforded solutions to his problem.

Apart from the differences in interpretation of learning which exist between connectionist and cognitive theorists referred to above, there is a very fundamental distinction in the experimental organization. As Köhler points out, if you cage a starved rat in a puzzle box with levers or press buttons about which it has no conceivable knowledge whatever, it is clear you will evoke trial and error learning. In other words, the structuring of the problem situation dictates the nature of the problem-solving. The puzzle box is so difficult for a rat that it can do little else but learn by trial and error.

On several occasions in the book we refer to the work of Piaget, in particular his theories of cognitive development (chapter 5) and the place of language in the intellectual growth of children (chapter 8). Whilst his observations may not be recognized as a theory of learning, he nevertheless has quite a lot to say about the steps which lead to the acquisition of knowledge. The primary, secondary and tertiary circular reactions build on to reflex activity of babies, the role of imitation, the internalization of actions to become thought and the place of language as a mediator in intellectual growth and learning skills are but a few of his most important suggestions which are pointers to learning processes.

One further name of note is Tolman. His major work (7) attempts to marry the objectivity of behaviourism to a cognition theory. For him, behaviour is purposive, that is to say most of our behaviour is a striving toward a particular goal. Organisms learn to recognize *cues* or *signs* and the relationship of these cues to the satisfaction of specific goals. Rats solving a maze to reach food or Köhler's chimpanzees are not just connecting or associating particular responses with particular stimuli, they are assimilating signs which will most effectively lead to solving a problem (reaching a goal in Tolman's words). These assimilated signs are known as *cognitive maps* of meanings (not movements) by which we acquire whole patterns of behaviour (*sign-gestalts*). In simple language, organisms learn from experience that purposeful behaviour based on cues and previously learnt plans of action will lead to the attainment of goals. The creature acquires expectations of his environment (intervening variables again as in Hull's case) from present and previous perceptions and learning consists essentially in modifying these expectations in the light of new experience.

A STRUCTURAL INTERPRETATION OF LEARNING

Tolman's theory provides an uneasy compromise between the behaviourist and cognitive views outlined above. His theory, along with most others, especially those incorporating an explanation using intervening variables, seems singularly oblivious to the findings of neurophysiology. There is just no connection at all between the neurological findings outlined in chapter 2 and the hypothetical internal behaviour used by Hull or Tolman to account for the links between stimulus and response. A recent attempt to provide a model which finds a place amongst the structural theories whilst taking up an intermediate position between the behaviourist and cognitive approaches has been made by Lunzer (8). Though it is still only of academic interest at present, it has special significance in drawing together a number of contemporary strands in psychological thinking and research especially the work of the ethologists (Lorenz, Tinbergen, Deutsch), those interested in perception and attention (Broadbent) and the cognitive theories of Piaget. The model is much too elaborate for a basic textbook and only the main tenets will be mentioned here. Further details can be found in note (8).

Two kinds of intervening mechanism between stimulus and response are postulated. Lunzer compares these to the well-known mechanical devices of the teleprinter and computer. In one we may find the teleprinting system which faithfully interprets all the information fed in (stimulation) as print-out (response). The same input gives identical output. In the second type we find a computer which already possesses a programme of instruction before the input (data) is supplied to the computer. Even then, the data are not fed directly to the computer as input, but must be 'read' first. Whether data are operated on or not depends on the adequacy of the programme. Hence the data are not automatically treated as in the teleprinter. The operation of the teleprinter is crudely analogous to the stimulus–response theories, whilst the computer is analogous to structural theories. In the first case the stimulus is said to trigger off the response (S–R theory of Thorndike for example) or to trigger off reactions in the organism which determine the response (Hull and Tolman's S–O–R theories). The second analogy assumes from the outset that the organism is an active initiator of behaviour sequences which are programmed from birth (nervous and endocrine systems) to channel reactions to stimuli and to modify the programme in the light of experience (learning). No two programmes are identical (natural variation of inherited characteristics) and they are vital for perceptual categorization, or *what is perceived*. For Lunzer the most conspicuous 'characteristic of perception is the decision-making to which it gives rise' growing out of previous perceptual experience. Reinforcement comes from the decision itself [or, as other psychologists call this decision, the 'strategy' (Bruner), 'learning set' (Harlow), 'plan' (Miller, Galanter, Pribram) or 'schema' (Piaget)] and not from the stimulus or the response as proposed by other behaviourists.

The key to a creature's springs of action comes from ethological work and relates to the *innate release mechanism* (IRM). This we defined in chapter 3 as an inborn tendency to carry through a sequence of actions triggered off by some external or internal stimulus. The mating habits of animals have frequently been studied as illustrating IRM. Male sticklebacks have a regular cycle of behaviour consisting of territory isolation, building a nest, seeking out a mate by courting rituals, mating, fanning fresh water over the fertilized eggs in the nest and keeping watch over the territory. The satisfactory completion of one stage in the cycle seems to herald the start of the next stage and we have a hierarchy of behaviour organization in which progress through the sequence depends on ordered emergence and completion of each stage. Sticklebacks and gulls seem a far cry from human learning, but Lunzer suggests that we too have IRMs from birth. However, they differ in 'their greater susceptibility to modification'. We now see the tie up between the computer programme to which we can apply modifications and corrections as experience teaches us more effective ways of using the programme and Lunzer's modifiable IRM model of human learning.

There is much more to the theory than has been outlined here, but further theoretical discussion will not serve our present purposes. Before leaving the topic it should be reiterated that Lunzer believes there to be brain structures which are 'differentially sensitive to cues', whilst at the same time the organism actively filters (see Broadbent's work in chapter 4) established and recognizable perceptions in accordance with the 'programme' settings. These latter are in turn alterable in the light of further experience.

SOCIAL LEARNING

The study of learning as a consequence of social interaction and imitation has become a primary contribution of Bandura and his co-workers (9) who have postulated that we all, especially children, acquire large units of behaviour through watching and imitating others. There are, according to Bandura, at least three effects of exposure to *models* (parents, teachers, friends, famous people) which give rise to behavioural change. Firstly, children may copy an entirely new response pattern not in their behaviour repertoire. This is called the 'modelling effect'. The unit of behaviour is frequently complete at an early stage of imitation and seems to bear little resemblance to the trial and error or successive approximations of stimulus–response theory. A now famous research by Bandura, Ross and Ross (9) presented several children with a film showing aggressive adults. Without prompting or reinforcement of any kind, the children quickly began to display similar aggressive behaviour. Secondly, observation of behaviour of a model may lead children to alter their own established responses by strengthening or inhibiting the responses. In this way, children adjust the 'limits' of their behaviour as they discover, through watching others, the tolerance levels in particular situations. For example, if children see a certain kind of behaviour going unpunished which they previously regarded as punishable, they are less likely to inhibit their behaviour on subsequent similar occasions. These effects are called 'inhibitory' or 'disinhibitory effects'.

The third behavioural change arises from what Bandura calls the 'response facilitation effect' (sometimes known as 'eliciting effect'). Behaviour is sometimes initiated in an observer by the cues given to him from a model. The process has much in common with the ethologists' explanation of innate release mechanisms (see chapter 3) except that the patterns of social behaviour are not regarded by Bandura as inborn. The child matches the behaviour he observes in others with behaviour already in his repertoire. It appears as if the behaviour of the model acts as a releaser for parallel behaviour in the observer.

The distinctive styles of the teacher as a model of social behaviour, that is his aggressiveness, friendliness, aloofness, cooperativeness, calmness, and so forth, will act as the initiators of novel behaviour changes in the child or will modify or trigger off existing patterns. The teacher is clearly a potent figure in the social behaviour modifications of children. Once language has been acquired, the models need not necessarily be actual but pictorial or verbal. The acquisition of certain kinds of language usage and meaning are thought by Bandura to be partly the result of modelling from adult conversation (see the work of Bernstein in chapter 8). Some children from working-class backgrounds have difficulty in compromising between their home models and those of their middle-class teachers.

The holistic rather than the 'bit-by-bit' approach to social learning is emphasized by Bandura who concludes:

> It is evident from informal observation that vicarious learning experience and response guidance procedures involving both symbolic and live models are utilized extensively in social learning to short-circuit the acquisition process. Indeed, it would be difficult to imagine a culture in which the language, mores, vocational and avocational patterns, familial customs, and educational, social, and political practices were shaped in each new member through the gradual process of differential reinforcement without the response guidance of models who exemplify the accumulated cultural repertoires in their own behaviour. In social learning under naturalistic conditions responses are typically acquired through modelling in large segments or *in toto* rather than in a piecemeal, trial-and-error fashion. [Note (9), Bandura, 1970]

LEARNING THEORIES AND TEACHING CHILDREN

We have made the point that no one learning theory provides us with all the answers. Furthermore, all the theories put together do not provide us with all the answers. The only course we can justifiably take is a pragmatic one—choosing amongst the experimental findings the points of clear relevance to our task. In most cases, psychologists are not really arguing about the findings so much as the interpretations of those findings.

Motivation   It would be safe to say that all theorists in the field of learning either explicitly or by implication argue that a motivated creature is more likely to learn than one which is not. The matter is so important that we have already devoted a whole chapter to it. Pavlov had to starve his dogs and Skinner his rats and pigeons to ensure they would learn. Children need to satisfy their desire to explore and manipulate their surroundings; they need the approval of others (affiliation) and to achieve; they pursue success and eschew failure. Incentives in the form of rewards (words of praise, encouragement, recognition), immediate knowledge of satisfying results (not always possible of course), cooperation and self-competition or competition with others are potent sources of motivation for learning. As we have seen elsewhere (chapter 3) motivation must not be too intense otherwise performance suffers as a result of distracting emotional conditions such as pain, fear or anxiety. Controlled reward also appears to be a more profitable motivator than failure or punishment. Hilgard concludes from his analysis of learning theories that tolerance of failure is best realized after a history of success because it helps to compensate for the failure.

Optimum interest can be gained where information is unambiguous and the curriculum designed to engage children in pursuits having everyday relevance. Current misgivings about the raising of the school-leaving age are caused by our inability to motivate young people who would sooner be earning a living. 'Everyday relevance' for them is highly instrumental in terms of work when they leave school, preparation for adulthood and leisure. Whatever designs we might have about higher-order educational objectives— enhancing intellectual skills, encouraging social awareness, preserving our habitat, using leisure time, and so forth—they must be superimposed on the down to earth, 'bread and butter', outlook of our young adults.

Habits and learning sets (10)   A term in common usage is *habit*. We talk about forming bad or good habits in many everyday activities in both social and educational contexts. Habits are automatic response patterns elicited by particular stimulus situations and are generally acquired by repeating a sequence of activities (the Law of Exercise) until the sequence is spontaneous. Many of our daily practical routines such as dressing, and eating are carried out in a regular pattern of events without any apparent conscious effort. Parents and teachers are inevitably concerned with encouraging children in the formation of habits—habits relating to common courtesies, habits of cleanliness and survival, habits of number and letter recognition, and so on. As Thorndike has shown, the more frequently a pattern of activity is successfully completed, the more likely it is to be repeated. Repetition to the point of overlearning, that is rehearsing a task beyond the point of successful accomplishment, as in the case of concert pianists who continue to practise familiar pieces, or actors who continue to recall their lines long after they know them, helps not only to substantiate the material, but enables the performer to concentrate on the refinements of presentation.

Apart from habits of doing things, we also develop habits of thinking—characteristic ways of tackling problems (see chapter 10). Studies with human and animal subjects have revealed that an ability to learn *how* to solve problems of a given kind can be developed with sufficient practice on tasks of a similar nature. This ability is known as *learning set* or *learning to learn*. There is another, more limited, sense in which we use the concept of transfer known as 'transfer of training' which we shall deal with in chapter 7. But this wider, more general, application in the formation of learning sets is the outcome of Harlow's work (10) with monkeys and young children. He found that routines formed in the solution of certain tasks were readily adapted for use in the solution of other similar tasks. Teaching children sets and matrices in modern mathematics syllabuses is rooted in the notion that by establishing routines about the fundamental understanding of the nature of number, children will have a better chance of coping with more complex mathematics. Learning how to learn a subject, as well as acquiring the rules to be applied to the subject matter, is a crucial classroom activity. The child's whole approach to problem-solving depends on the learning sets he brings to the solution. His experience at home and at school, his attitudes and values all predetermine how he will characteristically organize his responses.

Knowledge of results   Most theorists and practitioners are agreed that favourable feedback about performance has a positive effect on subsequent performance. Skinner calls it reinforcement, Thorndike calls it the Law of Effect. In human terms, there must be some reassurances about levels of success and, to be a really effective reinforcer in educational achievement, knowledge of results must follow quickly upon completion of a task for it to have maximum influence on future performance. School work should be dealt with and commented on as soon as possible after children have completed work; children's progress should be up to date and fed back to them whilst it is still fresh in their minds and still likely to have a reinforcing effect. Skinner claims that the steps taken in a learning programme should be sufficiently small to ensure high success rates amongst children (nothing succeeds like success). Knowledge of poor results for some children could be devastating, and this is why Skinner suggests that we should try to strike the right level with each child to ensure high success rates. Nevertheless, we should avoid the fallacy of trying to make out that a child's performance is good when it is not. This only leads to low personal standards being set and maintained. By insisting on realistic goals and thus ensuring some measure of success for each child, we are increasing the likelihood of reinforcement.

Whole or part learning   A theoretical debate surrounds the subject of whether it is better to learn by small steps (Skinner) or large chunks (Gestalt psychologists). For the teacher, there is clearly a time and a place for both approaches. Later we shall see that programmes of learning can be constructed using either technique. With some children, especially the mentally dull, small steps are useful because with a limited 'channel capacity' there is more chance that the information will be held in mind. Part learning by small steps, however, might be a disadvantage where the material is connected in some way. Poetry, theories or laws of science, for example, really need to be presented in their entirety, otherwise the relationship between the parts is lost. Learning a poem line by line was a popular compulsory pastime for schoolchildren not so long ago, and it is surprising how difficult it was to put the whole poem together without a conscious effort to establish connections between the end of one line and the beginning of the next in order to preserve the continuity. Where total context is important, 'whole' learning is an advantage because taking parts of the content out of context may lead to the material being meaningless. When to use whole or part learning is a matter which the teacher must judge from his or her experience of the content.

Schematic vs. rote learning   Schematic learning (this means using organizations of past actions which become the seed bed for interpretation and development in future learning) is thought by Skemp (11) to be underrated in importance. In an intriguing experiment, using a set of symbols he had invented to represent attributes capable of being combined to give more complex forms (for example, O = container, $\rightarrow$ = moves, therefore $\frac{O}{\rightarrow}$ = vehicle), he showed that schemata were absolutely essential even in relatively straightforward learning tasks because of the meaning they gave to the learning in hand. In any new field, the initial schemata first formulated have a lasting consequence on future learning in that field (see learning sets). Therefore, the first and most important task for any teacher is to discover and carefully define the elementary schemata required to enable the most productive assimilation. He should proceed from a familiar framework to unfamiliar knowledge. Overlapping lesson content and teaching by analogy, that is using familiar instances to exemplify unfamiliar ones, have much to commend them. A second conclusion of Skemp's was that schematic learning can be more efficient than rote learning where one builds systematically on previously acquired knowledge. Rote learning in the absence of understanding precludes the logical acquisition of further meaningful knowledge.

Active vs. passive learning and learning by discovery   The role of pupil participation in the learning process and the place of the teacher in this process has been a recurring issue in this book. There are times when children want and need to sit back and listen; there are times when they need actively to be engaged in work. Piaget has suggested that schemata are laid down in the course of active involvement and not by the passive absorption of sensory data. Model making, visits and well-organized project work plainly encourage the child to active participation in learning.

The place of learning by discovery, either in a 'pure' form where children are left to find out things entirely for themselves (a very rare method one would imagine) or in a partially structured and guided setting, has been a hot-potato in educational psychology particularly since the Second World War. These methods, or their variants, have been adopted by some teachers as an alternative to verbal reception of ready-made learning schemes (learning-by-rote approaches). The processes of learning by discovery have been interpreted and applied in many ways. For an excellent discussion of the dilemmas thrown up by this subject, students should read *Learning by Discovery: A Critical Appraisal* edited by Shulman and Keislar (12) in which several famous American psychologists conferred and debated the numerous issues involved. The process of learning by discovery involves (a) *induction* (taking particular instances and using them to devise a general case) with the minimum of instruction; and (b) *'errorful'* learning employing trial and error strategies in which there is a high probability of errors and mistakes before an acceptable generalization is possible.

Bruner cites some useful illustrations (12) which demonstrate both these activities. One describes a class of fifth graders (ten to twelve years of age) who were handed charts of North Central America containing nothing but the major rivers, lakes and natural resources. The pupils were asked to indicate where they thought we might find the principal cities, the railways and the major roads. The children were not allowed to use other maps or source books. Naturally, the children were not starting from scratch because they would have some prior knowledge of geography, but this knowledge was now required to be pooled in an effort to find the answers to the question. In the discussion which followed, the children had to justify their choices. By piecing together the particulars they had accumulated from previous geography lessons, the children formed for themselves generalizations from which to locate the positions (both induction and deduction). When the actual chart was exposed at the end of the exercise, the children discovered their mistakes, and in so doing they had learnt, by induction, that cities arise where there is water and other natural resources, where materials can be shipped, where climatic conditions and land shape are congenial.

One of the confusions presented by the term 'learning by discovery' is whether it is intended to imply the means—to give practice at discovering in order to acquire knowledge—or to imply the end product—to develop the ability to discover. In fact, will the programmes of 'free' or 'guided' discovery embarked on in schools produce an *ability to learn in particular ways* as well as enabling an accumulation of knowledge (quality of learning as well as quantity of learning)? One needs, therefore, to discern what a teacher can do to encourage the process, what the pupil must do in discovery learning and what is achieved by the procedures encouraged and adopted. These variables are still the focus of research work. In one research by Rowell *et al.* (12), the relative effectiveness of discovery and verbal reception programmes using the kind of material adopted by Skemp and mentioned in the previous section was tested. In common with several other researches, Rowell and his associates found that verbal instruction techniques had significant merit, more so than is often given credit for by those who take up an extreme 'discovery method' position. Further, the verbal reception technique produced relatively superior results, both in the short and the long term, to the discovery approach when used with students who had reached the formal operational stage of Piaget's theory of mental growth. One possible explanation offered was that 'discovery learning, even guided discovery, requires that the student first discover and organize any new subject matter before internalization in schematic form is possible. For verbal reception learning, however, the student has only a minimum of reorganization of the material before he can internalize the schema, provided that the material has been carefully structured to meet his requirements.' The findings are, of course, limited to particular forms of schemata with students who have reached mental maturity in an educational system which is essentially oriented to verbal reception techniques. The students, in effect, are more familiar with, and probably better at, verbal reception than any other strategy of learning.

Ideally, the teacher who favours learning by discovery hopes to produce problem-solving skills, especially those involving inductive reasoning; he assumes that discovery learning is intrinsically more satisfying and therefore of greater motivational value than rote learning; he hopes that pupils will learn the art of modifying generalizations in the light of new evidence, i.e. pupils will not accept propositions without examining them; he expects that his pupils will become more self-sufficient and resourceful and will not have to rely too much on the transfer of ready-made solutions from others; he anticipates that discovery learning helps in rule-finding at a time when knowledge is expanding at a phenomenal rate, and thus by learning the rationale of a subject, knowledge acquisition is made easier. But these aspirations remain as intuitions and speculations in need of investigation using meaningful material from current curricula.

'Insightful' learning   The special contribution of Gestalt psychology to education is in emphasizing that we should structure our learning. Learning must involve organization of the material. The Law of Prägnanz (chapter 4), which states that we try to impose the best possible pattern on a new perceptual experience, should be a constant source of consolation to teachers. The insightful 'penny dropping' experience is quite common in perceptual events and has a remarkable effect in discovering meaning. An experience common to the author illustrating the sudden appearance of a solution to a perceptual problem may be familiar to other readers. The 'instant artist' in programmes such as 'Vision On' (BBC TV) has this uncanny knack of being able to reach an advanced stage in a painting before it suddenly dawns on the viewer what the painting is about. When

this happens, the lines, blotches and smudges miraculously become railway lines, signal boxes, signals, trains, platforms, and so forth. The transformation from confusion to almost complete recognition is quite startling. Structure has given meaning to parts previously incomprehensible. Those interested in the experimental work surrounding insightful learning in children should read Wertheimer's book *Productive Thinking* (13).

PROGRAMMED LEARNING

One of the first direct applications of laboratory psychology has come largely from the work of Skinner (14) using his techniques of operant conditioning schedules of reinforcement for controlling and shaping human behaviour. The system has been used to reshape the behaviour of autistic children and delinquents as well as to form a basis for teaching machines and programmed instruction.

The main symptom of autism is an apparent inability on the part of the child to communicate with others. He even finds looking at another person very difficult. To improve this condition, Skinner advised the use of a schedule involving food and drink as a reward. A therapist is seated opposite the autistic child who is rewarded with a spoonful of food or a drink each time he attempts to look in the direction of the therapist. Next, the therapist concentrates on rewarding sounds or lip movements, then words and finally sentences. The technique has much in common with the experiment described earlier where a pigeon was taught to walk in a figure of eight. Note the need in both schedules to use a step-wise reward system until the total behaviour required has been pieced together. The method works, although it has its critics who feel it to be an inhuman way of dealing with children, particularly when the long-term effects are not completely known, even if it does work better in many cases than other methods.

Work with a group of delinquents in a Washington reform school provides another application of operant conditioning. Forty young criminals, including murderers, rapists and other serious offenders, were submitted to a schedule involving their living conditions. Leisure activities, food and living quarters were used as incentives for improving their behaviour and learning a trade. At worst, the offender could sit around doing little of interest, live on a boring frugal diet and sleep in a dormitory. Good behaviour and learning using teaching machines, however, were rewarded by better food, private quarters, colour TV and a free day out. By the time they were due out, many had learnt useful skills from the programmed learning texts—a feat they had abandoned at school. Normally, most delinquents are in trouble within three years of leaving a reform school in America. In Skinner's sample only 45 per cent were in trouble within three years.

Programmed instruction using teaching machines (15)

Skinner's greatest single contribution is in the realm of teaching machines and programmed learning, although he is not the only contributor. In 1926, Pressey produced the first recognizable teaching machine involving multiple choice answers to each item of information. It was not until 1954 that Skinner applied his findings from animal conditioning to the production of the first *linear* teaching programme. However, before we discuss the kinds of programmes available let us define some important concepts.

Where a machine is used there are two main constituents, namely the *hardware* and the *software*. Hardware is the mechanical device designed to provide a means of controlling the presentation of information and checking the responses of the pupil. These now appear in various shapes and sizes from small cardboard or wooden boxes to TV-type machines.

The really important part in the whole process is the software, which is the programme containing the subject matter organized in a carefully arranged progression of information, questions and answers. Each unit of information appearing before the pupil is called a *frame*. Machines are not the only presentation device. It is becoming popular nowadays to use *scrambled textbooks*, each page being a frame of information or an answer, and these are scattered throughout the book rather than in page order to discourage cheating.

At least six components are needed for an efficient mechanical teaching device. These are (i) a subject matter store; (ii) a display system; (iii) a response system for the pupil; (iv) a marking or evaluation system; (v) a response store; and (vi) a control for the presentation of information which governs the rate of progress of the pupil.

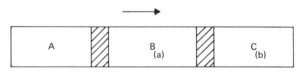

Figure 6.1

If we add to the above components the essential requirements of an operant conditioning schedule we have the makings of a *linear programming* system. The requirements are:

(i) small pieces of subject matter presented in a logical sequence at such a pace as to pretty well guarantee success on the part of the pupil;

(ii) active responses on the part of the learner. This, called 'constructed response', usually entails writing a word or phrase in answer to a question;

(iii) immediate knowledge of the accuracy of the response, which is usually correct if (i) is followed;

(iv) the pupil can work at his own pace. Often bright children can be bored and dull children left behind where formal settings prevail.

The linear programme, therefore, consists of a series of frames each containing a small item of information to which the pupil must respond. Frames also contain the answer to the problem set on the preceding frame. There will be overlap of information from one frame to the next and revision from time to time. Diagrammatically the system can be represented as in figure 6.1, where capital letters represent information frames and small letters the answers. An extract from a linear programme is given on p. 114.

1. If learning is defined as a change in behaviour, teaching is an *interaction*   (Frame)
   with the student that effects this _____ .   (response)

   _____ (end of frame)

   change in behaviour   (answer)

2. Teaching generally entails an _____
   with the student.

   _____

   interaction

3. In order for a program to teach effectively, it must _____with the student.

   _____

   interact

4. The basic unit of a program is a frame. The f_____teaches by interacting
   with the student.

   _____

   frame

5. A program is composed of chapters which are composed of sets which are composed of
   frames. The basic unit of a program is the _____ .

   _____

   frame

6. Interaction in a frame means that activity is required of the _____as well
   as from the program.

   _____

   student

7. A frame consists of a stimulus, a response and feedback. A frame is the _____
   of the program.

   _____

   basic unit

8. The frame acts by providing a stimulus and feedback. The student acts by r_____
   to the stimulus.

   _____

   responding

9. The three principal parts of a frame are s_____ , r_____
   and f_____ .

   _____

   stimulus, response, feedback

(From J. L. Becker, A Programed Guide to Writing Auto-Instructional Programs, RCA
Service Co., N.J., 1963, pp. 49–51).

Branching programmes are an alternative to the linear type and differ in several
important respects. Crowder's name is linked with this kind of programming because
he developed the first *branching* (or *intrinsic*) system for use in the United States Air
Force in 1955. In these programmes the frames of information are larger and are
followed by questions offering several answers of which only one is correct, that is
multiple choice responses (see chapter 13). The alternative answers are chosen either
because they are plausible (though inaccurate) or they represent common errors. A
student choosing the right answer will be passed on to the next frame of information.
Inaccurate answers lead to a detour, a remedial loop, intended to show the pupil the
source of his error. He is then returned to the original frame so as to give him another

opportunity to respond. This use of remedial loops is called *wash back*. A diagram of the system might be as shown in figure 6.2.

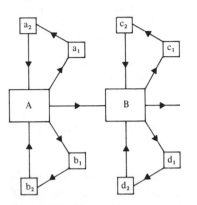

Figure 6.2   Branching programme with three alternative answers, two leading to remedial loops, the third to the next frame

There are, however, many ways in which branching can take place involving the remedial sub-sequences of differing length and difficulty. The following is an example of a branching system.

1. Branching can be considered a separate idiom of programing or merely a technique. This branching idiom, called intrinsic programing by Dr Norman Crowder, differs radically from linear programing. It is based on the belief that a person can learn effectively even from his mistakes provided they are quickly followed up by proper guidance. A high error rate is unhealthy in a linear program but not necessarily unhealthy in an intrinsic program.
    In intrinsic programing much emphasis is placed on the student's covert reorganization of material. Thus, it is important to point out why the student is right and why he is wrong. To a linear programer, however, branching is not so much a way of teaching as it is a means of providing for individual differences.
    The linear idiom considers branching as:
    (a) an opportunity for guidance (see frame 7);
    (b) a method of teaching (see frame 3);
    (c) a means of providing for individual differences (see frame 5).

7. Your answer to frame 1 was (a): an opportunity for guidance. You are probably answering from what you think should be the case but notice that we asked 'what the linear idiom considers to be the purpose of branching' and we have already told you that.
    Reread page 1 carefully and select another response.

3. Your answer to frame 1 was (b): the linear idiom considers branching as a method of teaching.
    You are not correct.
    Perhaps you are confusing the linear with the branching idiom. The linear idiom is based on the belief that the student learns best when he is making correct responses that are reinforced. With the branching (intrinsic) idiom it is believed that the student will learn regardless of the valence of his response, provided that the reason for his response is properly explained.
    Do you see now that intrinsic programs use branching as a means of teaching? But branching is only incidental to the method of teaching in an intrinsic program.
    Go back to frame 1.

5. Your answer to frame 1 was (c): the linear idiom considers branching as a means of providing for individual differences.

You are correct.

Teaching is accomplished in a linear program chiefly by reinforcing correct responses;
branching then is employed only for the important job of providing for individual differences, differences in intelligence, in interests, level of accomplishment or previous achievement.

The intrinsic idiom also uses branching to provide for individual differences but
branching is used chiefly to point out the reason for errors and to guide the student in
organizing the material for himself.

Go to frame 4.

(From J. L. Becker, A Programed Guide to Writing Auto-Instructional Programs, RCA
Service Co., N.J., 1963, pp. 149–151).

Apart from the obvious differences in the arrangement of frames between linear
and branching techniques and the point made in the programme above, there are three
other distinctive features which rest on different psychological beliefs. Skinner believes
that knowledge of results is central, whilst Crowder gives students knowledge of results
incidentally. The important part for Crowder is information—information about
incorrect responses as well as new matter. So there is regard for the reinforcement except
that it includes information about errors as well as successes. Secondly, Skinner avoids
error as much as possible. He makes the steps small, with a gradual increase in difficulty
to minimize errors. Crowder uses errors as the starting point of information to the
student and as an opportunity to revise the subject matter of the frame. The third
distinction is the size of the information given. Skinner uses small amounts of information, whilst Crowder programmes appear to favour the gestalt view that one must see
the whole context to make the parts more meaningful; therefore, the frames contain
much more information.

The multiple choice branching method has probably been the most popular. It has
the advantage of enabling the student to adapt his knowledge because there are several
alternative routes each attempting to account for different levels of understanding.
Nevertheless, constructing programmes, especially those containing plausible alternatives, is an extremely arduous task. One has to specify characteristics of the *target
population* (the pupils who are going to use the programme) with some precision in
terms of age, ability, previous experience, so as to design the subject matter around this
information. As we shall see in chapter 13, finding alternative solutions to a multiple
choice question which are not distractors is not easy. Detailed breakdown of the syllabus
is required and this constitutes a very salutary exercise for anyone who has not tried it.
Certainly a good programme requires a very sound knowledge not only of subject
matter but of the difficulties encountered by pupils and the many pitfalls to which they
are prone. It is always wise to try out the programme on a *pilot sample* which is representative of the target population.

The place of programmed instruction in schools

In a comparatively short period of time, programmed learning techniques and teaching machinery have spread from the psychologists' laboratory through the business world into education. Circulars and periodicals now abound with information relating to soft- and hardware. In all, a formidable campaign has been launched to convince teachers that programmed teaching aids can play a major part in improving our standards of education and serve as a remedial device, whilst also providing the teacher with a bonus of free time for more creative activity.

But there lurks in the minds of some teachers the feeling that a price (literally and metaphorically) may have to be paid for introducing too much inanimate machinery into the classroom. They have asked whether programmed learning is the antipathy of creative thinking in not allowing the pupil sufficient opportunity for self-expression. In turn, does this mean that programming is more appropriate for some subjects which are more factual in content (science, mathematics) than for other subjects which are more evaluative (English literature)? The less practical minds amongst teachers may boggle at the thought of having to maintain the machinery. Again, is the time made available for 'creative activity' going to be spent in proliferating time-consuming programmes? Motivation of pupils is another source of concern for it would seem that once the novelty of the method has worn off, some pupils do express a feeling of boredom and monotony, especially those using linear programmes. Again, when pupils can work at their own pace, there is no guarantee that they are working to the best of their ability. It might be seen as an opportunity for slacking.

We have already pointed out some good features such as immediate knowledge of results, pupils working at their own pace and by themselves thus avoiding the embarrassment and humiliation of displaying ignorance in front of the class. A good programme becomes widely available for all to use (but, equally, so does a bad one!). In addition, the protagonists of programmed instruction have marshalled a convincing array of research in support of their case. It is claimed from the research by one company (16) that programmed learning 'is as effective as teaching by conventional methods, is usually faster, and usually achieves better results'. In a system which espouses discovery methods and encourages strategies which must meet the needs of individual children, one requires an army of teachers far in excess of the number likely to be appointed. We must, therefore, find and exploit additional modes of communication with the children. This is particularly clear with bright pupils who outstrip their classmates and need to be given a chance of progressing faster than the rest, as well as with children in need of remedial help where a programme (provided they can read) would serve to reduce the repetitive work of the teacher. Wisely used, programmed instruction should make a valuable contribution in our schools.

SUMMARY

In this chapter we have looked briefly at some of the major theories of learning and tried to extract from them some common ground and guidelines which might be of service to teachers. The next chapter on learning, retention and recall also continues the discussion. When we face a classroom full of children, what important matters do we need to consider in order to effect behavioural changes in directions which we might prescribe? In other words, how do we encourage children to learn? In other chapters throughout the text, we have considered the influence of body mechanisms such as the brain and central nervous system, motivation, language, cognitive development, intelligence and personality on the learning process. Here we have tried to provide a framework of theory as a background to these other influences.

The connectionists, or behaviourists, led by Watson and Thorndike are predominantly concerned with the relationship between stimulus and response. Behaviour, according to them, is acquired or changed when the organism, be it a hungry rat or a child in school, builds up connections between S and R. The connections may arise because of the closeness of S and R (contiguity theory favoured by Watson), or by satisfaction which comes from giving a correct R to a given S (reinforcement theory favoured by Thorndike). Of the other behaviourists, the work of Pavlov and Skinner is outstanding. Pavlov's contribution was to show that animals and men can be taught to respond to a stimulus, chosen by the experimenter, which may not have any apparent resemblance to the response. The well known salivation response of dogs to the sound of a bell or tuning fork is an illustration. This is known as classical conditioning. In operant conditioning, enunciated by Skinner, a response sometimes arises spontaneously and the subsequent satisfaction will strengthen the bond between stimulus and fortuitous response. If a hungry rat accidentally touches a lever and receives a pellet of food, a connection between lever-pressing and food reception is very soon established. This latter kind of learning has been used extensively in therapy for autism and criminal deviance. Programmed learning using linear techniques also owes a lot to Skinnerian theories of operant conditioning.

As connections between S and R can be forged, so can they be extinguished by removing the reward which accompanies the response. Introducing an unpleasant or a neutral response as an alternative to the rewarding response is the commonest way.

Of the cognition theories, the best known and most useful for the teacher belong to the Gestalt School. Insightful learning occurs with a sudden, immediate, repeatable and transposable flash of inspiration. Tolman developed this view by showing that animals quickly learn to recognize cues and the link between these cues thus giving rise to cognitive maps which assist in the solution of problems. A hungry rat running through a maze for food is thought, by Tolman, to form a pattern of clues, each one leading to the initiation of the next stage in the solution of the maze.

Summarizing some of the main conclusions arising from these theories, we find that they agree on several vital issues. Children can be encouraged to learn using intrinsic (affiliation, exploration, manipulation, achievement) and extrinsic (incentives, praise and reproof) rewards. Immediate relevance and importance has high motivational value. Habits of thinking, that is personal and unique ways of tackling problems, are laid down in early life as learning sets (Harlow). Not only do these apply to cognitive habits, but also to social behaviour (Bandura) by imitating models of behaviour. Knowledge of results too, particularly successful results, has reinforcement value.

Whether to learn in moderate chunks or by successive, small portions depends upon the kind of material being learned. But there is support for both whole and part methods of learning. Starting from familiar, basic schemata and using analogy as a means of proceeding to the unfamiliar has much to commend it. There is also something to be said for both guided discovery and verbal reception techniques of teaching depending on the subject matter, the previous experience of the pupils, their intelligence, and the cognitive stage they have reached.

A final section on programmed learning includes a detailed discussion of programmed instruction using teaching machines. Consideration is given to the design of linear and branching programmes and their place in the growing technology of education.

ENQUIRY AND DISCUSSION

1. On teaching practice or observation, draw up a list of the factors which you consider would influence the learning habits and skills of pupils. These observations should be pooled and discussed in tutorials. To what extent have learning theories contributed to evaluating these factors?

2. Look round for examples of operant conditioning in the classroom. Is language acquisition partly dependent on operant conditioning? Examine the steps and methods which lead to teaching a child its first word.

3. Read up and write about the schedules of reinforcement used by Skinner in his work with autistic children, delinquents and criminals.

4. Take a very small topic in your main subject of study suitable for a given age and ability group. Try and draw up a short linear programme covering the topic. You will soon discover what a difficult task this can be and how much it calls on a detailed and well-informed knowledge of the subject.

5. Look for examples of 'modelling' amongst children, i.e. the imitation of novel chunks of behaviour *in toto*. Compare and contrast the techniques needed for teaching behaviours using modelling or operant conditioning.

6. Read chapter 16, 'Learning by discovery', in *School Learning*, by D. P. Ausubel and F. G. Robinson (Holt, Rinehart and Winston, New York, 1969). There are several questions for discussion and observation at the end of the chapter.

NOTES AND REFERENCES

1. W. F. Hill, *Learning: A Survey of Psychological Interpretation*, Methuen, London, 1964, 2nd ed. 1972.

2. Some of the problems raised are discussed in some detail by E. R. Hilgard and G. H. Bower, in *Theories of Learning*, 3rd ed., Appleton-Century-Crofts, New York, 1966.

3. E. A. Lunzer (also with chapters by N. Moray and J. F. Morris), *The Regulation of Behaviour*, vol. I, Staples, London, 1968.

4. For a simplified version of classical and operant conditioning see K. O'Connor, *Learning: An Introduction*, Macmillan, London, 1968.

5. The story of 'little Albert' and other children who were 'con'd' in the interests of science can be found in J. B. Watson, *Behaviourism*, Routledge and Kegan Paul, London, 1931.

6. The details of Hull's intervening variables are not too important because there is no way, at present, of verifying the details of their existence. In general, however, he postulates physiological internal needs which create *drives* (hunger, thirst), and provide activation for the satisfaction of these body needs. Another intervening variable is *incentive*, that is the strength of the reward on previous, recent occasions is likely to intensify goal-seeking activity. *Habit strength* is also said to be involved which is the strength of the bond created between S and R.

7. E. C. Tolman, *Purposive Behaviour in Animals and Men*, Appleton-Century-Crofts, New York, 1949 (recent edition).

8. E. A. Lunzer, *The Regulation of Behaviour*, vol. I, Staples, London, 1968, chapters 3 and 4 particularly.

9. A. Bandura and R. H. Walters, *Social Learning and Personality Development*, Holt, Rinehart and Winston, New York, 1963; A. Bandura, *Principles of Behavior Modification*, Holt, Rinehart and Winston, London, 1970; A. Bandura, D. Ross and S. A. Ross, 'A comparative test of the status envy, social power and the secondary-reinforcement theories of identificatory learning', *J. abnorm. soc. Psychol.*, **67**, 527–534 (1963).

10. J. M. Thyne, *The Psychology of Learning and Techniques of Teaching*, University of London Press, London, 1963. Thyne defines a habit as 'an instance of learning in which a relatively simple response is made, automatically and fairly frequently, to a relatively simple kind of situation'; H. F. Harlow, 'The formation of learning sets', *Psychol. Rev.*, **56**, 51–65 (1949).

11. R. R. Skemp, 'The need for a schematic theory of learning', *Br. J. educ. Psychol.*, **32**, 133–142 (1962).

12. J. A. Rowell, L. Simon and R. Wiseman, 'Verbal reception, guided discovery and the learning of schemata', *Br. J. educ. Psychol.*, **39**, 235–244 (1969). This paper contains a useful collection of recent researches in this field. L. S. Shulman and E. R. Keislar (Eds), *Learning by Discovery: A Critical Appraisal*, Rand McNally, Chicago, 1965; J. S. Bruner, 'The act of discovery', *Harvard educ. Rev.*, **31**, 21–32 (1961).

13. M. Wertheimer, *Productive Thinking*, Harper, New York, 1945.

14. B. F. Skinner, *Science and Human Behaviour*, Macmillan, New York, 1953.

15. See Further Reading references to programmed learning.

16. International Tutor Machines, Ltd, in their company profile of teaching machines make this claim.

FURTHER READING

W. F. Hill, *Learning: A Survey of Psychological Interpretations*, Methuen, London, 1964, 2nd ed. 1972. A sound basic text.

J. Leedham and D. Unwin, *Programmed Learning in the Schools*, Longman, London, 1965. Readable and relevant.

K. O'Connor, *Learning: An Introduction*, Macmillan, London, 1968. Tends to dwell on the conditioning aspects of learning, but contains some useful classroom points.

W. K. Richmond, *Teachers and Machines: An Introduction to the Theory and Practice of Programmed Instruction*, Collins, London, 1965.

Three recent books containing independent views about the nature and role of instruction at school which should be of interest are:

D. P. Ausubel and F. G. Robinson, *School Learning: An Introduction to Educational Psychology*, Holt, Rinehart and Winston, New York, 1969.

J. S. Bruner, *Toward a Theory of Instruction*, Norton, New York, 1966.

R. M. Gagné, *The Conditions of Learning*, Holt, Rinehart and Winston, New York, 1965.

7   Learning, retention and recall

In this chapter (1) we shall deal with some of the down-to-earth problems of acquiring, retaining and remembering which are pertinent to the activities of learners and teachers alike. The blanket term 'memory' has often been used to describe these activities and at one time it was thought to be a faculty capable of being exercised, like a muscle, in order to improve the quality and quantity of what we learn. The use of mechanical memorization in Latin, mathematics and history for instance was, and probably still is, held by some teachers to be a good means whereby pupils can flex their memories by sheer, dogged effort. The present view is that we are endowed with a capacity for memorization which is a manifestation of general intelligence, and whilst we can improve on our methods of assimilating information it can only be done within the limits of our intellectual capacities. Since we probably never reach the full extent of our capacities it should certainly be possible to improve the amount we memorize by correspondingly improving the acquisition techniques. Furthermore, there may be a case for believing that several kinds of memory exist. Some people have better rote memories than others; visual, auditory and kinaesthetic memory (that is movement memory which is helpful in touch typing or sport—any activity requiring muscle coordination) vary from one person to another.

The physiological mechanisms which accompany memorization are not really understood. We have seen in chapters 2 and 4 some postulates about the biological, chemical and perceptual nature of memory and whilst we can be fairly certain of a chemical explanation of memory storage, there is still a long way to go in our understanding of the exact processes involved.

It is convenient to divide the overall process of remembering into three phases (2). These are *acquisition* (or *reception*, i.e. learning), *retention* and *retrieval* (or *recall*). We shall deal with each in turn.

ACQUISITION (LEARNING OR MEMORIZING)

Our main concern here will be to discuss the factors which are thought to affect the efficiency of learning for retention and recall. It is taken as self-evident that the study habits, as well as the abilities of individuals, are important in determining performance in all forms of recall including conventional examinations. Yet research into the effect of different study habits has not given us any clear indications of the precise patterns best suited to individuals. This is not surprising when one considers the complexity of the studying task itself, quite apart from the cognitive and personality factors contributing to performance (3). In addition to the factors mentioned in the previous chapter (motivation, intelligence, personality, knowledge of results, and so forth), the following have been shown to affect the way we learn and how much knowledge we acquire (4). Some of the issues apply to students in higher education as well as those in primary and secondary schooling.

Organization   There is nothing more soul-destroying than to be groping from one topic to another without any clear plan of action. It is uneconomic in terms of both time and effort. Gestalt psychologists have pointed out the need for an understanding of the context within which to work and for this we need to organize and order our subject matter and methods both as students and teachers. Children quickly become confused and intolerant of situations which are unstructured and undisciplined. As students it is worthwhile forming some simple study routines which become habits, otherwise the many attractions of the non-academic life of a student can take over completely.

Place to Study   For concentration and learning it is necessary to have peace and quiet (remember the sound-proof conditions in animal experiments alluded to in the previous chapter). A noisy classroom, TV or radio in the background at home, roadworks or building noises or even the voices of others constitute a distraction for most people. Some claim that a background of music is not a hindrance, but it does constitute a source of competition for one's attention. Technically speaking, the level of extraneous sound should not reach a level which is likely to break through the threshold of one's attention. In private study, body comfort is essential, although one must avoid sleep-inducing conditions such as easy chairs or beds to work on or smoky atmospheres in students' rooms.

Time of day and length of study   No hard and fast rule applies as to the best time of day or how long one should study at a given session. Variations between individuals make it necessary for each person to discover his own optimum conditions. Some individuals like to rise early in the morning and work 'whilst the mind is fresh', but few students find themselves able to take advantage of this suggestion (Child, 4)! But there is reason to believe that personality is a significant variable contributing towards differential performance according to the time of day, and whether people work individually or in a group. Using a task in which subjects were required to cancel the letter e on a sheet of print, Colquhoun and Corcoran (4) showed that in the morning or working by themselves, introverts perform better than extraverts. However, in the afternoon, or when working in a group, the performance of introverts is the same as (or even worse than) extraverts.

   The span of attention (the length of time one can concentrate without interruption) is clearly relevant here and probably related to personality differences. This point will be elaborated in chapter 11 where there is some discussion of Eysenck's theory that extraverts normally require more involuntary rest pauses than introverts in tasks requiring concentration. Some people might be unshaken by a two-hour stint of work, whilst others need more frequent rests. The build up of inhibition to studying can be dissipated by distributing the rest and work periods. But we are not yet in a position to say with conviction how long the work or rest period should be for a given person or, for that matter, how best to use the work time. A few short breaks of about five minutes during a long study session (say of two or so hours) are essential and a longer break should be taken between tasks (see pro- and retro-active inhibition later in the chapter). One thing is certain, very few children are taught how to study or how to make a self-evaluation of their study strategies to obtain maximum efficiency. In a recent study by the author (4), 72 per cent of a sample of university, college of education and sixth form students claimed to have taught themselves how to study by the process of trial and error whilst at secondary school. Even obvious points about organization and work conditions, timetabling or avoiding fatigue are rarely mentioned by teachers.

Personal problems   Many students are adversely affected in their work by the existence of personal problems arising from emotional, social, academic and, for older students on grants, financial difficulties (see chapter 12). Learning becomes more tedious as these influences intrude on the concentration of the learner. In both young and old pupils alike, the emotional and social 'cut and thrust' of home life and friendships probably play a significant part in learning inefficiency, although the strongest evidence on this point so far comes from American research (5). Feelings of inadequacy are another source of trouble (see the sections on need achievement, level of aspiration and self-fulfilling prophecy in chapter 3). The relationship between teacher and taught is frequently held to influence the latter's attitude to learning. Where there is some good-natured friendliness with authority, derived not so much from his position as a teacher as from his knowledge of the subject, then an atmosphere more conducive to learning seems to prevail.

One aspect of pupil–teacher relationships which has not yet been researched is the influence of characteristic teaching styles on the study habits and learning skills of children, in other words the problem of compatibility of teaching and learning styles (6).

The peer group   Teachers probably underrate the extent to which study strategies are influenced by one's friends. The Americans (5) have gone some way in exploring the nature of agreements and understandings amongst secondary and higher education students about their roles as students. The topic is partly concerned with competition and cooperation between pupils in comparing work by discussing standards, require-ments and lesson content. However, it is also concerned with the motivation generated by rivalry between peers to obtain a teacher's attention, or understandings between children as to what is a 'group norm' of work (and play).

Meaningfulness of task   Grasping the meaning of a task is essential for efficient learning. Most of what we learn requires an understanding of the gist of an argument and not a follow-my-leader repetition of the argument. To see the logic of what is being learnt greatly assists in its memorization.

It is nevertheless true that some things have to be learnt by heart. There is no inherent logic in the letters of the alphabet or the actual symbols for the numbers 0 to 9. Formulae, scientific principles and laws, passages of prose or dates, zoological systems such as the cranial nerves have often to be learnt by heart, even when one understands the meaning of the facts. Some use props such as rhymes and mnemonics, that is taking the initial letters of a sequence of facts and using these initial letters to make up an amusing or memorably pornographic sentence. Most students have come across these, especially in science. For example, the colours of the rainbow can be memorized using: <u>R</u>ichard <u>O</u>f <u>Y</u>ork <u>G</u>ave <u>B</u>attle <u>I</u>n <u>V</u>ain the initial letters of which make Red Orange Yellow Green Blue Indigo Violet. The rules for finding Sines,

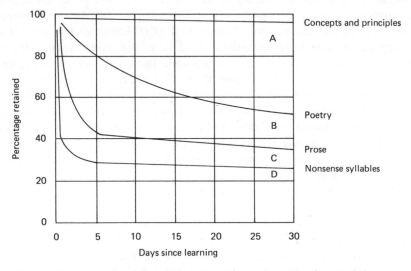

Figure 7.1   Curves of forgetting for different types of material
From H. Maddox, *How to Study*, Pan, London, 1963

Cosines and Tangents of angles are sometimes remembered using SOH CAH TOA (S = sine, C = cosine, T = tangent, O = opposite side, A = adjacent side, H = hypotenuse) from which we get <u>S</u>ine equals <u>O</u>pposite over <u>H</u>ypotenuse, and so on. Remembering the jingles is only half the battle because we have then to recall the facts they represent. However their main function is to produce a link between unrelated things. Rhymes such as 'Thirty days hath September . . .' or 'Willie, Willie, Harry, Ste . . .' for the kings of England from William the Conqueror onwards and 'i before e except after c' are also commonplace aids.

The rapidity with which we forget different kinds of material is illustrated in the accompanying figure 7.1. Note that the more meaningful topics such as laws and concepts are by far the best retained, whilst nonsense syllables are quickly forgotten.

Revision is important. Memories begin to fade with the passage of time unless we actively recall them periodically. Whilst learning a subject it is a useful idea to set some time aside both during and after the learning session for sitting back and actively recalling or committing to paper the work covered. It is believed by some psychologists (1) that we should spend at least half the study time trying to recall work we are learning. Often the time is totally taken up in reading without necessarily absorbing the work. Apart from anything else, it helps to vary the learning task and reduce the influence of reactive inhibition (the tendency not to repeat a response which has just been made). Active reconstruction and organization of learnt material helps to fix it in one's mind.

'Whole and part' learning and reading   Given a learning task requiring the assimilation of large slices of information, we may read through the information several times to get an overall picture of the content and try to memorize it. On the other hand, we may break the information down into parts and learn each part first before drawing it together again. This crudely distinguishes 'whole' and 'part' learning. The pros and cons of the two approaches have been researched and debated for several years without any resulting clear-cut advice as to the superior method. The compromise conclusion is that the nature of the material and the condition of the learner dictate the most suitable method. The holistic approach is useful where the amount of information is sufficiently small to be absorbed at one time. Also it is said to provide a better grasp of meaning and continuity between the elements of the material once the overall pattern of knowledge is understood. It is not always possible to treat large chunks of information in this way, particularly if the material is difficult and unfamiliar; consequently we must resort to breaking it down into manageable portions. The central issue is understanding; provided the total context is understood, 'part' learning can be an effective way.

One application of the 'whole' or 'part' approach to learning is found in the teaching of reading. No attempt will be made here to advise students on the teaching of reading, partly because it is not possible to do justice to the findings and arguments surrounding the subject in a few paragraphs of a basic general textbook, but mainly because no one is able, as yet, to give unequivocal directions to teachers of reading. Reading, quite rightly, takes pride of place in our junior schools and the subject deserves detailed and careful scrutiny (7) for which specific references are more appropriate.

Loosely speaking, the *decoding* methods of teaching reading, as they are called, are based on the 'part' approach and have the support of many behaviourists. The *reading for meaning* (see Goodacre, note 7) methods are holistic approaches typified by gestalt psychology.

Decoding methods include the *alphabet* and *phonic* approaches. Alphabetic teaching is carried out by first naming the letters of the alphabet and using these names to build up words. Thus the word 'pod' would first be introduced as 'pee-oh-dee gives pod'. Phonic systems use the sounds of letters in the words: so that 'pod' would be 'puh-o-duh', 'puh-od' or 'po-duh' (o is the phonetic symbol as in rock). The words are gradually pieced together from the basic names or sounds of letters. Letter recognition and the relationship between letters and their sounds in particular word contexts lie at the root of the phonic method. Its special advantage is that it can be taught systematically, starting with synthetic word building. Transferring the pronunciation of combinations of letters to similar groupings of letters (cow, now, sow) is sometimes possible, but we have so many exceptions in our language (tow, row, low) that the task is made tedious.

In 'reading for meaning' methods we find *look-and-say, whole word* and *whole sentence*. The principle is that children will remember the configuration of the whole word and associate it with a meaning—where possible a pictorial representation. The whole-word method is frequently accompanied by pictorial aids in the first stages, whilst look-and-say can be applied to non-pictorial words as well. So the word 'log', probably already in the oral vocabulary of the child, would be presented along with a picture of the object. This is good psychological thinking because we are moving from the familiar (sight of, and sound of, a familiar object) to the unfamiliar (sight of the whole word). Decoding methods, on the other hand, are said to be boring and sometimes meaningless because the phonic-taught child can piece together long words without any idea of what the words mean. However, the 'look-and-say' child does have to wait before his knowledge of words is sufficient to enable him to decipher unfamiliar looking words. Again, the teacher's help is more frequently sought (with the consequent disadvantage of long queues waiting for the meanings of words). The starting vocabulary also tends to be limited because of the amount of learning required of the child. Each word is learnt as an entity, although some transfer might be possible as with phonic methods. The whole-sentence method is an extension of the look-and-say method using sentences as the unit to be learnt. Small groups of short words giving a meaningful sentence are taught along with visual props.

It is probably the case that look-and-say methods predominate in our schools, moderated in some cases by phonic teaching. At the earliest stage of reading, children need to appreciate the shapes of letters and what they represent. Therefore to assist in establishing recognition of these shapes for their ultimate usage in meaningful words, some combination of the two approaches would seem to be a sensible way of tackling the early stages.

The Initial Teaching Alphabet (i.t.a.) was recently launched by Sir James Pitman as an alternative and more logical aid to reading. The idiosyncrasies of our language are well known to readers. Just think of the different ways in which 'ough' can be pronounced to realize how much of a barrier our *traditional orthography* (conventional spelling) is to the development of reading skills. Pitman suggested replacing traditional orthography with a consistent system of spelling derived from forty-four basic characters covering the whole of our language pronunciation. For a thorough introduction to i.t.a. see John Downing's *The Initial Teaching Alphabet*, 1965 (5th ed. Revised). There are at least six ways of representing the simple word 'and' in traditional print:

And ɑnd AND ɑND and ɑnd

because the letter 'a' can occur in lower-case as 'a' or 'ɑ' and in capitals as 'A' or 'ɑ', 'n' appears as 'n' or 'N' and 'd' as 'd' or 'D'. Try the word 'nag' to see how many combinations are possible, remembering that we can have 'g', 'ɡ', 'G' or '𝒢'. With the i.t.a. system, capitals are enlarged lower-case letters, thus 'and' appears as and (capitals), and (capital a) or and (lower-case).

By reducing the appearance of letters to one system and making each sound appear as the same combination of symbols, there are 44 characters to cover the English language. Similar sounding words with different spellings in traditional orthography such as 'eat', 'feet', 'key' and 'pier' become 'eet', 'feet', 'kee' and 'peer' in i.t.a. Similar combinations of letters such as 'ough' in 'rough', 'ought', 'bough' and 'trough' which give different sounds become 'ruf', 'aut', 'bou' and 'trof'.

The advantages and limitations of i.t.a. as a reading aid are still the subject of an active research programme. Protagonists amongst teachers are convinced that it does help children towards efficient reading more so than traditional methods. Warburton and Southgate (note 7), in an extensive comparison of i.t.a. and traditional orthography, concluded that i.t.a. was superior for teaching young children to read. Infants, apparently, learn to read earlier, more easily and at a faster rate with i.t.a. However, the advantages gained by using i.t.a. were frequently lost after transition to traditional orthography. Those not so keen on the method have reservations about the need for such an elaborate detour when ultimately the children are going to have to learn the vagaries of our language in any case. Still to be established is the value of i.t.a. in remedial cases, its long-term influence upon mature reading skills, and especially the extent to which conversion to traditional orthography, particularly in writing down words from memory as in essay writing, will cause problems.

Transfer of training   At one time, the Royal Air Force had a battery of aptitude tests for those hoping to enter as aircrew. One test presented the candidate with a board full of pegs placed in square holes. On the top of each peg, one half was painted white, the other black. The candidate was told to reverse as many pegs as he could with his non-preferred hand in a given time. Some had what seemed to be a natural skill at the game. But there were also those who had had previous experience as packers in industry (such as chocolate, biscuit or component packing) whose skill enabled them to perform this task with outstanding dexterity. Some of the skills they had learnt in one situation were now being applied in a second similar situation. This we call *transfer of training*. It is particularly apparent in physical skills and to some extent it is applicable in mental activity. Around the turn of the century there was a belief amongst psychologists and teachers that some school subjects acted as a training ground for exercising mental skills. This became known as 'the doctrine of formal training'. Mathematics was thought to develop children's powers of logic, science was seen as training children to be observant, learning Latin and historical or geographical facts was thought to exercise the memory.

These views are no longer held by the majority of psychologists and teachers. However, there is a case for believing that some skills can be transferred and that the curriculum can play a part in this. We have seen from the researches of behaviourists that stimulus generalization occurs where animals and humans are disposed to recognize a stimulus within fairly wide limits. The dogs in Pavlov's work, whilst presumably realizing that there was a difference, were prepared to respond to a range of tuning forks or bells of slightly differing frequencies as if they were all from an identical stimulus. We also saw in concept formation that we formulate our concepts flexibly within wide limits—cats come in all shapes and sizes yet we generalize our perceptions to constitute the single concept 'cat'.

A lot of research has been directed towards finding the factors most necessary for transfer (8). The most significant finding is that where there are common factors in the content or in the procedures adopted in carrying out two tasks, transfer is possible.

The content of mathematics is useful in the solution of problems in physics and chemistry. Some of the procedures of mathematics are helpful in statistics. Physical skills involving similar procedures, as in the illustration at the beginning of this section, encourage transfer. Length of training also has a long-term effect, as when a person who has concentrated his efforts on science subjects at 'A' level and at university may find that objectivity and conciseness begin to permeate into other aspects of his life requiring the assembly and dissemination of knowledge.

Three other factors which affect transfer should be mentioned. There is a better chance of transfer, assuming similarity of content and procedure, where the learner is made aware of the possibility of transfer. The author pointed out earlier in this section that transfer of training had much in common with the behaviourists' concept of stimulus generalization. Having made the point, it was hoped that what the reader had gleaned about stimulus generalization would be transferred to the subject of 'transfer of training' because of content similarity. This brings us to the second influence. The more thoroughly the first task is learnt, the more likely it is that transfer will occur, given the conditions in the previous paragraph. This is tantamount to saying that if one task is not learnt properly it is hardly likely to have a positive influence on the performance of a second similar task. Intelligence also affects transfer because more intelligent children and adults are more likely to spot the relationship between tasks.

The instances cited above have been examples of positive transfer, but it is quite possible to have negative transfer. Where the second task possesses content or requires procedures in conflict with the first task then negative transfer is likely. A commonplace example from sport is the hindrance experienced in trying to learn a second style of swimming after mastering one style. Negative transfer is also apparent in learning foreign languages where the rules of grammar (adjective position, masculine–feminine rules, etc.) differ to the point which impedes transfer (see also pro- and retro-active inhibition).

RETENTION

Because we can reproduce information once learnt, it is not unreasonable to conclude that our bodies possess retention mechanisms which we suppose to be located in the brain (though we know little of the physical changes involved, see chapter 2). How efficient are these mechanisms and how can we influence their efficiency? The study of remembering and forgetting has endeavoured to find answers to these questions. Some ideas about aids to remembering have already been discussed, so we shall now deal with the topic of forgetting.

A curve of forgetting

Ebbinghaus (9) and his associates were amongst the first to study remembering and forgetting. His famous experiments related chiefly to the rate of forgetting with the passage of time. We are well aware that most learnt material gradually fades away, and Ebbinghaus devised experiments to see if there was any pattern to the nature of forgetting. His subjects were required to learn a list of *nonsense syllables* until they could repeat the list perfectly. A nonsense syllable consists of a three-letter arrangement of two consonants with a vowel as the centre letter. The resulting combination must not be a word in the language. Such syllables as BOL, QIS, WEJ are examples. Nonsense syllables are chosen to make sure that the learners have no prior knowledge of the task— everyone starts from scratch. The criterion of learning is the ability of the subject to repeat the list of, say, ten syllables once through completely, whilst the task is being timed. At intervals of time after learning, the subject endeavours to repeat the list, and if (as is the usual case) he is unable to repeat it he is timed in the relearning of the list. The usual formula for deriving the time needed for recall is:

$$\frac{\text{original learning time} - \text{relearning time}}{\text{original learning time}} \times 100$$

This gives the ratio of time saved in relearning expressed as a percentage. A typical curve of retention (or conversely forgetting) using several time intervals is shown in

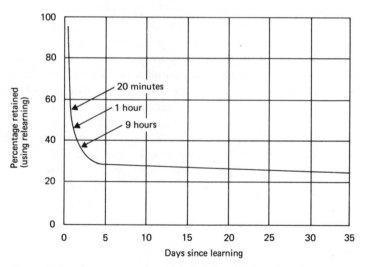

Figure 7.2   A curve of forgetting (after Ebbinghaus)

figure 7.2. The higher the percentage, the more efficient has been recall. Note the rapid fall in the amount remembered and the levelling out of the curve after about 24 hours to something like 30 per cent of the original amount retained. Earlier, in figure 7.1, we saw some marked differences in this quantity which varied according to the kind of material being learnt.

Serial learning

In a particular learning programme, the position of the material as it is presented can have a marked influence on the prospects of retention. Again, using a list of nonsense syllables which it is assumed can be generalized to meaningful material, it has been shown that the first and last few syllables are usually learnt and remembered first and the central syllables last. If we plot the number of trials required to learn a syllable against its position in the list we generate a *serial position curve*. This is most useful information for the class teacher. In devising lessons some thought should be given to the order of presentation in terms of difficulty and length, and in re-ordering for revision purposes.

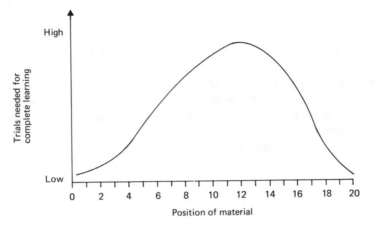

Figure 7.3   A representative serial position curve

Pro- and retro-active inhibition (or interference)

The question 'why do we forget' has generated two broad theories. One, the *atrophy theory*, is based on the belief that some chemical causing metabolic change in the 'storage' system brings decay and finally disappearance of memory traces in the nervous system. The second, and more widely supported view, *interference theory*, holds that the interplay and possible confusion in the build up of memories interferes with retention. By this means, some memories may not actually disappear altogether, but become obscured and overlaid with more recent memories. The fact of a sudden reappearance of long-lost memories either normally or under hypnosis is offered as evidence of interference theory.

In the short term, the recall of information can be inhibited in two ways. If we learn two lots of work X and Y in that order, the nature of X might influence the recall of Y and this we call *pro-active inhibition*. Underwood (10) cites an example, well known amongst teachers, in which several lists of similar material are given to a group of subjects who are required to memorize them on successive days. Performance in terms of amount recalled deteriorates progressively from the first to the last list. The correct responses remembered from the preceding lists interfere with the recall of the one being learnt.

When Y, the second task, inhibits the recall of X we call it *retro-active inhibition*. If the second learning task Y is repeated several times, each occasion makes the recall of X that much more difficult. The pro-active effect of task X on Y is gradually eliminated by repeated trials of task Y, but in so doing the extinction of task X is taking place (11).

Experiment reveals that interference is a function of the similarity of tasks X and Y and their closeness in time. In both pro- and retro-active inhibition the subject matter is similar. Even when a task of a different nature is interposed between X and Y, recall is worse than when a complete rest is taken. Sleep between learning and recall helps retention for this very reason. In view of these findings, lessons should be interspersed with a short interval of relaxation and the subject matter of adjoining lessons should not be similar. Learning just prior to bedtime (if one is not too tired), followed by a revision period first thing in the morning, is effective for some.

Reminiscence   Ballard (12) found a curious phenomenon in 1913. Some children who had partially learnt a poem were able to recall better after a period of time than immediately after the learning session. This is known as *reminiscence*. One explanation is that inhibition builds up during the task, but once the task is abandoned, dissipation of inhibition sets in and enables a better recall performance. Thus, for a short time after the learning the dissipation might proceed at such a rate as to enable the individual to improve his performance. In a research with schoolchildren the author (13) was able to show that neurotic extraverts display significantly higher reminiscence effects than stable introverts using the inverted alphabet test. The direction of this finding is in keeping with the postulates of Eysenck regarding the levels and dissipation of inhibition in different personality types (see chapter 11). As extraverts develop higher levels of inhibition than introverts, their performance will be poorer, relatively speaking, as the task proceeds. Consequently, after a break in which inhibition has dissipated, the performance of extraverts will appear as temporarily superior to introverts. Once again we see a possible connection between personality characteristics and performance which one would hope might become a valid source of information in class teaching.

Massed and distributed practice   *Massed* practice occurs when little or no rest is permitted during a task or between tasks. When intervals during the task are allowed, we have *distributed* practice. In general, massed conditions of learning are less productive than distributed conditions. A possible reason has already been broached in the discussion of interference and reminiscence where we proposed that retention is inhibited as a task proceeds and until there is some rest the inhibition continues to affect performance. A rest pause enables the inhibition to dissipate. If you have ever tried 'press-ups', you will recall that a point is reached when it seems absolutely impossible to raise the body one more time. In a way, this illustrates the effects of mental inhibition when the mind is pushed to a point where it cannot function adequately, although we rarely reach the kind of dramatic standstill as experienced in physical exercise.

No satisfactory solution has been found to the questions of how long the rests should be, or how long is a reasonable stint of work in particular school subjects. The periods normally used in school are based on a rule-of-thumb and not on scientific analysis. Choosing periods of 35 minutes in primary schools, for example, is entirely intuitive. The idea that young children can only take about twenty minutes of narration from a teacher has very little experimental support. Nevertheless, teachers have doubtless arrived at a knowledge of timing lessons from observation and experience of handling children. The signs of fatigue or work decrement are plain to see and inexperienced teachers would be wise to keep a wary eye open for such signs of inhibition.

RETRIEVAL (RECALL)

There are several recognizable ways by which we can recover information. In the first place we can dig into our memories for the answer to a problem and rely entirely on our ability to *recall* the relevant information. Examples of simple recall are given in chapter 13. This is the most difficult method of retrieving information. *Recognition* is a second method of recovering information. In this case we are given a clue or shown

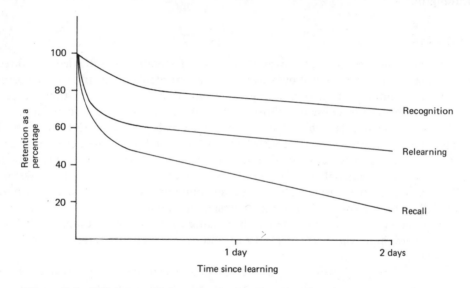

Figure 7.4   Efficiency of three methods of retrieval
After C. W. Luh, 'The conditions of retention', *Psychol. Monogr.*, **31** (1922)

the information from which we can remember something learnt on a previous occasion. To some extent multiple choice questions rely on recognition where alternative answers are offered to a question and the individual is required to select one answer. However, in many instances the solution has first to be worked out and tallied with those provided, and this involves a high level of recall. We have all experienced the occasion when we see a face in the newspaper or on TV and cannot put a name to it. Someone suggests a few names and the moment the correct name turns up we recognize it. The method is easier than recall as can be concluded from the figure 7.4 which illustrates an experiment comparing retrieval by recognition, recall and *relearning*. In the latter case a pupil is asked to relearn something after a lapse of time and his efficiency in recall is measured by finding the time taken to relearn the task. We have all experienced the greater ease of revising something already learnt.

The marked contrast between recall and recognition is worth bearing in mind not only in the design of multiple choice examination questions (examples given later in chapter 13), but in the prevalent method of question and answer teaching. Using entirely recall methods is exacting and fatiguing for youngsters and should certainly be interspersed with recognition tasks. Translation from French to English is easier than from English to French because we can recognize the English equivalents of French words much more readily than in the reverse case. Note finally that relearning something which has been forgotten gets easier on each successive occasion and this is why regular revision is a vital aspect of studying. Retrieval is aided where the original learning has been systematic, thorough and understood by the learner. Thus trying to recall material memorized by rote methods is more painful than when the material is meaningful.

SUMMARY

For the purposes of description, the overall process of remembering is divided into three stages. These are (1) the acquisition stage in which we deliberately try to memorize material; (2) retention, which is a storage stage inferred from the fact that we can reproduce information by conscious effort; and (3) the act of recalling information.

Effective acquisition of knowledge is aided in a number of ways. Organization of the material to be learned, careful control of working conditions, the absence of distractions (be they physical, emotional, social or academic), dealing with meaningful rather than nonsense material, and frequent revision interspersed in the learning session, are all of benefit to the learner. The debate surrounding 'whole' and 'part' learning was related to the teaching of reading in which decoding methods (alphabetic and phonic) were compared and contrasted with 'reading for meaning' methods (look-and-say, whole-word and whole-sentence). I.t.a. and traditional orthography were also briefly discussed.

Transfer of training was seen to be possible when the tasks involved have similarities of content, or procedures of learning, where the elements to be transferred are pointed out, when the first task is thoroughly mastered and when the ability of the learner is sufficient to enable him to see the transferable elements.

Retention has been studied using rates of forgetting of both nonsense and meaningful material. Studies have concluded that with most topics there are marked differences in the prospects of retention which depend on the temporal position in learning of the material. Material at the start or finish of a learning session is more likely to be retained than material learned in mid-session. But this generalization applies particularly where tasks are extensive or difficult. The manner of interspersing the learning sessions and the kind of activity which precedes or follows a learning task has a significant effect on the chances of retention and retrieval. Reminiscence effects and the phenomenon of massed and distributed practice were also discussed.

Reproducing what we have retained in our memories can be achieved in at least two ways—either by recall in which we are required to drag information from our minds without being prompted, or by recognition in which we are presented with clues or information from which previously learnt material can be recognized. One difference between unseen written examination papers and multiple choice items is that recall is most often employed in the former and recognition in the latter.

ENQUIRY AND DISCUSSION

1. Appended is a list of questions which the present author used in a report on study habits [see note (4) for the reference]. They will be seen to relate to general study, study prior to examinations, the influence of the peer group and the effect of attitudes and anxiety on study. Read through this list, see how you compare with the students reported in the research and note the pattern of study habits revealed in this research. Use the most relevant questions in the list to enquire of children how they study.

General study
1. When do you usually study?
2. Do you have a favourite time of day? Yes/No. When?
3. In allocated study periods do you usually work (a) all the time;
   (b) some of the time; (c) hardly at all?
4. Do you, on average, spend at each study session outside school (or in your own time at college) a *long* (more than two hours)? a *medium* (between one and two hours)? or a *short* time (less than one hour)?
5. Do you spend the same time on each subject? Yes/No.
   If No, why not?
6. Where do you usually study (note all places)?
7. Where do you most like to study?
8. Do you read in subjects beyond what is set? Yes/No.
   If Yes, why?
9. Do you make notes from your reading? Yes/No.
10. Do you re-read notes taken in class (lecture)? Yes/No.
    Do you re-write notes taken in class (lecture)? Yes/No.
11. Where did you first learn how to study?
    Who taught you?
12. How do you think you developed your present study methods?
13. Have you ever read a book on how to study? Yes/No.
14. Do your teachers give you cues to study methods? Yes/No.
    If Yes, in what way?

Examinations
15. Do you revise for exams throughout the year? Yes/No.
    If not, how long before you begin?
16. Are some kinds of notes better than others from which to revise? Yes/No.
    What sort?
17. Do you revise with someone else? Yes/No.
18. How do you discover what is the required standard for exams?
19. Do you discuss exam tactics with your friends? Yes/No.
    If Yes, what do you discuss?
20. Do you select certain areas for detailed study rather than the whole syllabus? Yes/No.
    If Yes, how do you decide what to choose?
21. Are you nervous before exams? Yes/No.
    If Yes, how long before?
22. Are you nervous during exams? Yes/No.
    If Yes, how long for?
23. Do you have difficulty expressing yourself on paper? Yes/No.

24. Do you usually manage to finish exam papers? Yes/No.
    Do you have difficulty in timing answers? Yes/No.
25. How do you divide the time?

Personal Problems and Attitudes

26. Do you feel that personal problems interfere with study? Yes/No.
    If Yes, what kind of problems (family, girls, home study conditions, etc.).
27. Do you feel that lecturers/teachers allow personal prejudices to enter into their assessment?
    Yes/No.
    If Yes, what makes you feel this?
28. Do you have periods when concentration on study seems impossible? Yes/No.
    If Yes, give examples.
29. Are you easily upset by noise or other disturbances when you study?
    Yes/No.
30. Do you hesitate to ask questions in lectures/lessons? Yes/No.
    If Yes, why?
31. Do you think your relationship with the teacher affects your attitude to study? Yes/No.
    If Yes, why?
32. What kind of relationship appeals to you?
33. Do you think that the subject matter of lessons/lectures is, by and large, a waste of time?
    Yes/No.

Student Culture

34. Do you discuss your marks with other students? Yes/No.
35. Do you compare standards with others? Yes/No.
    Do the marks of others in your group influence you? Yes/No.
    If Yes, how?
36. Do your friends persuade you to go out? Yes/No.
37. Do you feel guilty about study when you go out? Yes/No.
    If Yes, why?
38. What helps you to decide whether to go out?
39. Do you mind appearing to be enthusiastic about academic work? Yes/No.
    Or do you sometimes disguise the fact that you are enthusiastic in front of your friends?
    Yes/No.
40. If you talk about academic matters with friends, what are the most common topics of
    conversation?
41. Have you discussed with your friends what is a reasonable stint of work? Yes/No.
    If Yes, how do you decide on a reasonable stint?
42. Do your friends' views about study or exam tactics influence you? Yes/No.
43. Do you find that you can bring pressure to bear on some lecturers/teachers to 'deliver the
    goods'? Yes/No.
    If Yes, in what ways?

2. If you were helping children of a given age and ability to develop the art and science
   of study, what would be the main points you would stress? How do these points
   differ with age and ability? You will find the basic texts on study habits suggested
   in Further Reading of help.

3. Whilst on teaching practice, discover the importance attached to, and the opportunities
   given for, the following as aids to learning:

   (a) revision; (b) 'whole' or 'part' learning; (c) 'massed' and 'distributed' practice;
   (d) different methods in the teaching of reading or number; (e) transfer of training.

4. Experiments on learning and memory are most instructive. In a book edited by G. Humphrey entitled *Psychology Through Experiment*, Methuen, London, 1963, you will find a chapter on 'Remembering' which gives details of how to set up experiments on recall, recall *vs.* recognition, interference, 'set' and speed of recognition. With the help of your tutors, try these out. Most basic textbooks in experimental psychology contain information about experiments on memory, serial learning, interference and reminiscence which you will find interesting and helpful. A number of valuable experiments also appear in F. C. Bartlett's book *Remembering*, Cambridge University Press, Cambridge, 1964.

NOTES AND REFERENCES

1. A standard work on memory is I. M. L. Hunter, *Memory: Facts and Fallacies*, Penguin, London, 1957.

2. C. A. Mace, *The Psychology of Study*, Penguin, London, newly revised, 1968.

3. The subject of study and study habits has quite a useful literature for our present purposes. Of recent vintage there is H. Maddox, *How to Study*, Pan, London, 1963; D. E. James, *A Student's Guide to Efficient Study*, Pergamon, Oxford, 1967; M. Guinery, *How to Study*, Allen and Unwin, London, 1967.

4. For some recent research into study habits in higher education, see D. Thoday, 'How undergraduates work', *Universities Q.*, **11**, 172–181 (1957); B. Cooper and J. M. Foy, 'Students' study habits, attitudes and academic attainment', *Universities Q.*, **23**, 203–212 (1969); D. Child, 'Some aspects of study habits in higher education', *Int. J. educ. Sci.*, **4**, 11–20 (1970); W. P. Colquhoun and D. W. J. Corcoran, 'The effects of time of day and social isolation on the relationship between temperament and performance', *Br. J. soc. clin. Psychol.*, **3**, 226–231 (1964).

5. J. S. Coleman, *The Adolescent Society*, The Free Press, New York, 1961; N. Sanford (Ed.), *The American College*, Wiley, New York, 1962.

6. C. R. B. Joyce and L. Hudson conducted one of the few researches into this realm of student/teacher styles in a medical school, but their findings are somewhat limited and could not possibly be applied to school-based learning. The research was 'Student style and teacher style: an experimental study', *Br. J. med. Educ.*, **2**, 28–32 (1968).

7. An exceptionally good book for those needing an introduction has been written by E. J. Goodacre, *Children and Learning to Read*, Routledge and Kegan Paul, London, 1971. She is also responsible for producing a series of teaching schemes obtainable from the centre for the Teaching of Reading, 29, Eastern Avenue, Reading. There is a short reading list and glossary of terms available with these schemes which forms a very sound starting point for a deeper study of the subject. Another point of view is to be found in G. R. Roberts' book *Reading in Primary Schools*, Routledge and Kegan Paul, London, 1969.

For a primer on i.t.a., see J. Downing, *The Initial Teaching Alphabet* and *Evaluating the Initial Teaching Alphabet*, Cassell, London, 1965 and 1967. O. M. Gayford has produced a clear beginners' text entitled *I.t.a. in Primary School*, Initial Teaching Publishing, London, 1970. Research into the effectiveness of i.t.a. is reported in F. W. Warburton and V. Southgate, *I.t.a. An Independent Evaluation*, Murray and Chambers for the Schools Council, London, 1969. A very handy non-technical version of this report has been written by V. Southgate, *I.t.a What is the evidence?* Published for the Schools Council by Murray and Chambers, London, 1970. A detailed overview of reading difficulties is given in M. D. Vernon, *Reading and its Difficulties*, Cambridge University Press, Cambridge, 1971.

8. The first nails in the coffin of 'formal learning' were hammered home by E. L. Thorndike and R. S. Woodworth, 'The influence of improvement in one mental function upon the efficiency of other functions', *Psychol. Rev.*, in 1901 and since then research has concentrated on isolating the particular factors concerned in transfer. For a summary see the chapter on transfer in K. O'Connor's book *Learning: an Introduction*, Macmillan, London, 1968.

9. H. Ebbinghaus (translated by Ruger and Bussenius), *Memory*, Dover, New York, 1966.

10. B. J. Underwood, *Forgetting*, reprint from *Scientific American*, March, 1964.

11. Meaningful as well as nonsense material has been used in researches on retention. See J. Deese and S. H. Hulse, *The Psychology of Learning*, McGraw-Hill, New York, 1967, for some examples.

12. P. B. Ballard, 'Oblivescence and reminiscence', *Br. J. Psychol. Monogr.* (1913).

13. D. Child, 'Reminiscence and personality—a note on the effect of different test instructions', *Br. J. soc. clin. Psychol.*, **5**, 92–94 (1966). The inverted alphabet test requires the subject to print the letters of the alphabet upside-down from left to right as quickly as possible in a given time.

FURTHER READING

I. M. L. Hunter, *Memory: Facts and Fallacies*, Penguin, London, 1957. A readable supplementary text.

D. E. James, *A Student's Guide to Efficient Study*, Pergamon, Oxford, 1967. Apart from being a helpful study guide it also summarizes some of the evidence relating to learning and memory.

H. Maddox, *How to Study*, Pan, London, 1963. Extremely useful introduction to learning, retention and recall.

K. O'Connor, *Learning: an Introduction*, Macmillan, London, 1968. Several relevant chapters can be found.

J. M. Thyne, *The Psychology of Learning and the Techniques of Teaching*, University of London Press, London, 1963. The relevant chapters make very good reading.

8   Language and thought

Language is man's finest asset. Many essentially human activities spring from this unique characteristic by which man becomes detached from his physical world. As far as we can tell, animals normally go into action because they are prompted by physical stimuli. A cat stalks a bird which has attracted attention; a dog begs for food when it can smell or see it or when feeding rituals are set in motion. In contrast, man can indulge in reveries which take him well beyond the present reality into the realms of abstract thought. He communicates to himself in some symbolic form. Moreover, he can communicate his ideas to others by using these symbolic forms. These two uses of language, that of personal and social communication, are very important for teachers because their work is built around the efficient communication of ideas.

How far is language solely a human activity? Animals can, of course, communicate; ants, bees and primates afford well-known examples of animal contact, but the level is primitive. It is habitual, situation specific and initiated by internal or external physical cues which are not symbolic. Primates have systems of sounds for survival and emotional needs (grunts, howls) which are *not* symbolic. Starting with similar body apparatus to the primates, we have managed to produce a vast range of meaningful vocalizations. Viki, a chimpanzee belonging to the American psychologists C. and K. Hayes, took six years of hard work to learn four rather imperfectly spoken words (1). With human beings competence to assimilate a spoken language is universal and comparatively rapid.

CHARACTERISTICS OF SPOKEN LANGUAGE

Language has been defined as the term denoting '*the psychological processes which regulate speech*' (2). And speech is language behaviour. The two basic requirements of a language are that it is symbolic and systematic. We tend to regard language in a somewhat atomistic fashion by looking upon it as a collection of words strung together in sentences, each word having a separate identity and meaning. This is a false way of looking at language. In fact, the words are brought together in special ways to give a highly systematic order from which we get a meaning. Similarly, there is no one meaning for each word in a sentence. The meaning we ascribe to a sentence can change from one context to another. Altering the position of words in a sentence alters the sense of the sentence—even though the same words are there. 'The sun is shining' is not the same as

'Is the sun shining?' Language, then, is not random behaviour, but is systematic, where certain orderings are accepted as having prescribed meanings.

The raw materials of each language are the basic sounds. These give the character of the language and form one method of distinguishing different languages. The *phoneme* (3) is the term we use for the perceived basic speech sounds of a language— 'perceived' because the latitude in pronunciation within a culture may vary (compare the Scot, the Londoner and the Lancastrian), but all have the same interpretation. Certain phonemes are specific to a language. 'Th' (as in 'the') in the English language has no equivalent phoneme in French. The French pronounce it as 'z' to begin with because, as one *au pair* girl from France put it, 'I say 'z' instead of 'th' so zat I don't bite ze tongue'.

Phonemic utterances are put together to form *morphemes* which are the smallest units of a language having a grammatical purpose. They are not necessarily words as we know them. In the word 'plans' there are two morphemes—'plan' and 's'. 'Plan' is a word, but 's', which serves the useful grammatical function of converting plan into the plural, is not a word as such. Prefixes, suffixes and word endings which change the singular to plural or alter the tense are therefore morphemes. Linguists find morphemes much more useful than words for defining language content. The sentence 'The girl liked to dress her dolls' broken into morphemes would be 'The + girl + like + ed + to + dress + her + doll + s'.

The systematics of a language involve more complex combinations of symbols. Each morpheme has a particular function and the formation of sentences by combining these morphemes so that they obey rules requires a knowledge of *grammar* (some call this *syntax*). Most, if not all, readers will recall having to discover the parts of speech represented by words in a sentence and making sure that they are presented in a certain order. But combining morphemes in a specified order does not necessarily mean that the resulting sentence makes sense. The combination of morphemes to make words and arranging them together to give meaning in a particular tongue is called *semantics*. In the sentence 'the green toes fought on the apple', the grammatical structure is correct, but the sentence is meaningless in our culture. The study of semantics involves the resolution of the meaning we ascribe to systems of morphemes.

LANGUAGE ACQUISITION

How does a verbally helpless infant develop into an articulate adult? A widely held belief is that we are born with vocal equipment and a neural system which gives us the capacity to verbalize. It does not take a child very long to discover and utilize a vast range of phonemic utterances no matter which culture he happens to be born into. Equally, the speed with which these utterances are converted into meaningful (to both child and parent) and reproducible sounds during the first few years of life are convincing testimony to an inborn capacity. Contrast this with the slavish way in which Viki, the chimpanzee, was taught to say only four utterances in six years. Even then, there is very little evidence to lead us to suppose that the words are any more than the result of conditioning. Two further capacities essential to communication are the ability to reproduce utterances *at will* when required, and the realization that one is being understood.

Vocabulary growth

The earliest clues to the child's ability to comprehend his surroundings come from the use he makes of *signs*, *signals* and *symbols* [see note (4)]. The latter, as we have seen, enable the child to communicate using words. The rate at which the child is able to use and understand words is quite slow in the early stages of language development. Note that there is a difference between the number of words we actually use (*active vocabulary*) and the larger number we are able to understand (*passive vocabulary*). Of course children vary enormously in their vocabulary size and usage depending largely on intellect and linguistic opportunities. But a general picture of the average rate of vocabulary growth

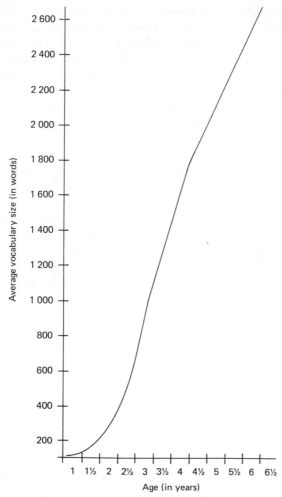

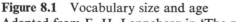

Figure 8.1 Vocabulary size and age
Adapted from E. H. Lenneberg in 'The natural history of language' (a chapter in *The Genesis of Language* edited by F. Smith and G. A. Miller)

we can expect is shown in figure 8.1. At one year of age the average word count is three or four. At one-and-a-half years the count is around twenty and at two years this figure rises sharply to about two hundred. Note how, in the Piagetian sensori-motor stage of cognitive development, progress is slow, and it is not until the transition into the stage of pre-operational thought that the child really begins to amass words. Assessing an average count is quite difficult with young children, because one is never quite sure whether all the possible utterances of which a person is capable have been made, or indeed if the utterances are understood. Morpheme counts are popularly used and an estimate of between 4 000 and 7 000 is thought to be the case for children just entering school (5), and rising to 10 000 at fourteen years of age.

Growth in the acquisition of elementary meaningful forms of our language, as in the formation of plurals and tenses (morphology), has been extensively studied. Berko (6), for example, has shown, using nonsense syllables, that at seven most children can cope with a plural formed by adding 's', but experience greater difficulty when 'es' is required. Likewise, in the formation of the past tense, 'ed' is not found to be too difficult to apply, but where a change such as 'ring–rung' is required, only a third of the seven year olds could manage. Grammatical skill, which is said to occur when a child can put two words together to form a meaningful expression, generally appears around two years of age.

The important, detailed work of Templin (7) set out to investigate four aspects of language amongst children of three to eight years of age. These were (i) articulation of speech sounds; (ii) speech sound discrimination; (iii) sentence structure; and (iv) vocabulary size. Of the many conclusions reached in this valuable work, perhaps the following are of particular note. In articulation skills, the three year old is still making, on average, 50 per cent errors, whilst at eight years he is accurate 90 per cent of the time. In five years the child reaches close to articulatory maturity. Boys usually take about a year longer than girls, and children from working-class homes about a year longer than those from middle-class homes. In speech sound discrimination, that is the ability to recognize auditory differences among speech sounds, there is a consistent increase in the ability with a gradual deceleration beyond five years of age. At the lower ages, there does not appear to be any significant difference in the ability between boys and girls, but at eight years of age, girls are better than boys. Sentence length and structure now appear to be longer and more complex than in previous studies (25 years earlier). No differences were detected for the boys and girls, but children from middle-class homes used longer and more complex remarks than working-class children. About half the remarks made by three year olds are grammatically accurate and this improves to about three-quarters at age eight. The vocabulary count presented a lot of problems and there seems to be little agreement between researchers as to methods of finding the recognition or recall vocabulary of young children. The estimates of basic vocabulary for the six to eight year olds ranged from 13 000 to 23 000 in Templin's work, although these figures seem on the high side when compared with the work of Lenneberg (see figure 8.1). The *total* vocabulary, Templin suggests, is even higher at eight and could be as high as 28 000.

A developmental view

The first stage in language acquisition, then, seems to be the building up of sounds and their consequent combination into accepted morphemes. The baby's noises which accompany discomfort (hunger, pain) or pleasure (chuckles, cooing) are no doubt the starting point. At the *babbling stage* (thought to be inherent in humans because deaf children also babble) sometimes around six to twelve months, a baby rehearses sounds such as 'dadadada' which encourage basic sound-forming skills. Perhaps more important, the baby also discovers that people, dad in the above instance, pay particular attention to him when he makes certain sounds.

Presently, the child begins to take sounds made by adults into his own system—he assimilates utterances which are both phonemes and morphemes. It is at this stage when the foundations of pseudo-concepts (see Vygotsky's work in the last chapter) are being laid down.

Later the youngster begins to discover the rules by which the system works. He learns plural endings or other morpheme combinations. Grammatical skill appears when he can put two words together (two–two-and-a-half years of age). The rules of language are acquired by hearing word positions and adult intonation and variation in word emphasis. Herriot (8) summarizes one point of view so:

> Children notice certain features of language behaviour, and use these features to form their own individual system of combination. However, the needs of communication, the requirement for more words and more complex ways of combining them, force them to approximate more and more to adult systems. So, of course, does the need to be understood by a variety of other people. When his only communicant is his mother or his twin, the child may be held back by baby language. But as soon as he needs to speak to other members of the community, the rules of the conventional code of language become more necessary.

It is not assumed that children are born with linguistic potential already laid down in the brain, but rather that as the brain develops, more elaborate regulation of language behaviour becomes possible.

Language learning and operant conditioning

An elaborate view of language acquisition is suggested by B. F. Skinner (9), an American psychologist whose work on conditioning appears in chapter 7. For him, language is a skill fabricated by trial and error and reinforced by reward (or extinguished by non-reward). The reappearance of a verbal response is conditional on the receipt of a reward. Bluntly, if there is no reward when you do something, you are less likely to repeat the activity on a future occasion. In the case of language usage, the reward could be one of many possibilities. Social approval from parents or others when a child makes an utterance is probably the most potent in the early stage of development.

Skinner distinguishes three ways in which the repetition of speech responses may be encouraged. First, the child may use *echoic* responses. In this case, he imitates a sound made by others who immediately display approval. These sounds need to be made in the presence of an object to which they may be linked. Secondly, we have the *mand*; this is a response which begins as a random sound but ends up by having meaning attached to it by others. Echoic response frequently follows a mand expression where a parent on hearing 'mama' or 'baba' uses it to form a word and encourages the child to repeat the utterance. Once the sound is firmly implanted, it gradually becomes associated with an object. Finally, there is the *tact* response (a contraction of the word contact). Where an acceptable verbal response is made, by imitation usually, in the presence of the object and the child is rewarded by approval, there is every likelihood that the response will appear again [remember Helen Keller (4)]. Clearly, these types of responses are closely related in the early stages of children's language formation. Note how imperative is the presence of other people. With no one around to show approval or test the accuracy of verbal utterances, they would soon be discarded.

Not all psychologists are satisfied with this paradigm of Skinner's. To begin with, verbal responses quickly take on much wider meaning, as indicated by the range of usage, than can be explained by operant conditioning. Again, there are many words which do not 'name' objects (they have no *referents*). Learning such articles as 'the' or 'a' is difficult to explain in Skinnerian terms. Add to this the phenomenal vocabulary count (see later) of young children accumulated in a comparatively short spell, and Skinner's theory does not appear to provide the whole explanation. Noam Chomsky (10) takes up a completely different position in asserting that there are common structural factors in all languages from the simplest native tongues to the most complex in the world. Although his interests lie in theories of grammar and linguistics, he has something to say about language acquisition.

The inheritance of linguistic competence

Chomsky could not hold with the mechanistic view of man as a computer—being fed with words (input) and reproducing them in the required order from suitable programmes laid down in childhood. Apart from anything else, the actual process is far too elaborate; not even a computer could cope with a fraction of the language capacity of man. But his theory is a difficult one and only the bare essentials are given here.

By mastering the rules governing the structure of his language (syntax), a child is able to generate for himself and understand the utterances of others even when they are completely original to the child. Language is 'open-ended' and those who can use it fluently can produce and understand sentences which they have never used or heard before. According to Chomsky, stimulus–response theories are not sufficient to account for this creative capacity in language usage. Further, it is assumed that children have a potential for linguistic skill which is inborn. The rules of language seem to come to children quite naturally even when they are of widely differing intelligence and cultural background. The rules are obeyed (within limits) without apparent understanding. Chomsky also supports the theory that man is unique in possessing linguistic aptitudes and can in no way be studied, by implication, using animal comparisons. He is qualitatively different from other animals. This view is a far cry from the developmental view of Skinner's behaviouristic outlook described at the beginning.

The evidence for the child making up his own rules is not hard to find. Listen to any child as he makes what Herriot (8) calls 'virtuous errors' by applying standard rules to irregular cases. 'Mouses' instead of 'mice', 'sheeps' instead of 'sheep' are common errors. Tense errors are also frequent—'catched' rather than 'caught' and 'teached' instead of 'taught'. These errors still arise after many learning occasions in which the correct usage has been instilled. The reason is probably that the child is still trying to apply the 'correct' rule (hence 'virtuous' error) and has not had sufficient experience to remember the irregular morphemes.

Teachers must handle these errors with care. Herriot, like many others, puts in a plea for tactful handling of mistakes in language usage arising from innocent breaking of the rules through inadequate knowledge of the exceptions. This can generally be done by repeating a *correct* version in a reply to the child without making it too obvious that you are correcting a mistake, i.e. no punishments or ridicule in front of others. Some mistakes are quite hilarious, but it is often insensitive and unproductive with young children to poke fun at their language errors. Note that structure is the all-important thing in language usage (using the system meaningfully) and not individual words or phrases. New concepts represented by single words or phrases must ultimately be set in a language context for an improvement in language skills.

Language acquisition and the environment

Children can only learn the language in the early stages of their development if, and when, they hear the language spoken. Different linguistic environments have a startlingly variable effect on language usage, not just as a regional accent or dialect, but in the systematics of the language. Mother is a particularly important figure in the early language development of her children. The frequency and content of her conversation with her babies and toddlers significantly affect their progress. Mothers who provide simple explanations in answer to the many questions which children pose, lead a dialogue or describe the host of objects surrounding the child, play games involving language usage, read stories, and buy toys which develop language skills are more likely to raise the linguistic standards of their children.

The question of language competence being inborn is still a source of controversy, but there is no doubt about the effects of social background on the development of language skills (11). Where conditions are such as to impair the progress of language growth we call the outcome *language deficit*.

Of recent theories in the study of language and social class, that of Bernstein deserves to be studied. His interests are essentially sociological, but his findings point to several possible implications for students of language and cognition. He believes that language is 'one of the most important means of initiating, synthesizing and *reinforcing* ways of thinking, feeling and behaviour which are functionally related to the social group'. Children from more articulate backgrounds, generally found in middle-class homes, not only display marked differences in the vocabulary they use as contrasted with children from working-class homes, but also organize and respond to experience in more sensitive ways (12).

Different use of language forms does seem to relate to social class. These forms have been described by Bernstein as the *restricted code* (at one time he used the term public language) and the *elaborated code* (formal language). The restricted code is used by both working- and middle-class people. The elaborated code is mostly limited to middle-class usage.

A tentative catalogue of ten basic differences between the language codes appears in a research paper by Bernstein (13). To illustrate some of these, the restricted code user has short grammatically simple, unfinished sentences with poor syntactical structure. Simple conjunctions are used repeatedly (so, then, and). Short commands and questions are frequently used. Impersonal pronouns are rarely in evidence (one, it). Terms of *sympathetic circularity* such as 'like', 'you know', 'isn't it' are often used. On the other hand, the elaborated code user has accurate grammatical and syntactical structure, uses complex sentences containing conjunctions and relative clauses and makes discriminative use of adjectives and adverbs.

The role of the family, particularly mother, in exposing youngsters to restricted and elaborated language usage is clear. The language skills of parents and the purposes for which such language is used, are dominant influences. Elaboration of the language is more likely to evolve where two-way conversation takes place as in question and answer exploration rather than one-way communication consisting essentially of instructions. Equally, opportunities and encouragement for language usage in the home in the form of books, newspapers, games involving words ('I spy') and bedtime stories are all important language contacts.

The restricted code also possesses implicit understanding through grammatically incomplete expressions (or even non-verbal communication) as well as the sympathetic circular terms and widely understood clichés. Whenever people know each other well (husband and wife, brothers and sisters), contracted verbal and non-verbal codes exist. An eye movement might be sufficient to replace a sentence! Note, however, the ability of those from middle-class backgrounds to use either code. Most mothers (and teachers for that matter), whether of working- or middle-class standing, have been heard to say 'sit down and wrap up' (restricted) as an alternative to 'do sit down and make a little less noise please darling' (elaborate).

There is much the teacher can do in extending the language range of children. Devising classroom arrangements which encourage children to use language and pave the way to more elaborate language codes should come as a necessary element in classroom activity. An elaborate code is believed by Bernstein to lead to greater potentialities in complex conceptual structures than a restricted code. By exercising language skills in class and in real life experiences (visits, rambles), the child learns to apply the language *in contexts*. Drills have a place, but they are often ready-made abstractions. Alternatively, children need to experiment with applicable concepts using, where possible, extended verbal experience in context.

Not all language deficits originate from environmental disadvantages. Several physiological conditions exist. Stammering is a case in point. It often arises from poor coordination of breathing and articulation of words. The precise cause has not been substantiated, but it may start as a mild physical deformity which when aggravated by careless handling produces emotional tension. Adult intervention (constant prompting) or ridicule with child stammerers do seem to make the complaint worse. It could, therefore, be a case of a mild defect being caught up in a cycle of tension and self-consciousness which becomes magnified beyond proportion. Other physical defects of voice and articulation organs (voice box, tongue, palate) are possible. They originate from damage to the organ, the brain or the sense of hearing. Injuries to the speech regions of the brain producing aphasia have already been mentioned in chapter 2. Be on the lookout for the 'late developer' in speech. The reasons are obscure, but we do know that some children, without any apparent evidence of physical or mental defect, are very slow off the mark only to improve quite rapidly later in their school lives. However, when the teacher spots a linguistic defect, it is wise to seek professional advice in the first place so as to eliminate the possibilities of physical or mental abnormality.

PIAGET AND VYGOTSKY ON THE FUNCTION OF SPEECH

At the beginning of the chapter we regarded speech as serving two purposes, that is personal and social communication. These two functions are technically referred to as *egocentric* and *socialized* speech. Egocentric speech is characterized by the child who behaves and talks as if all points of view were his own. He seems unable to appreciate another's point of view, to conceive things from another position. The egocentric monologue is a running commentary on the child's present situation and frequently acts as a means of self-regulation and direction. At three years of age about half a child's utterances are egocentric (the rest are socialized) and this rapidly reduces to a quarter at age seven.

Jane is two-and-a-half and lives next door to the author. An extract from a tape-recording of her chatter whilst she was alone in a bedroom illustrates some features of a little one's language. She is looking out of a window and has seen a neighbour's dog, Rajah. After a lot of chatter about visiting Rajah's house, she continues the conversation, we think, with a teddy bear or on some occasions hoping that her mother can hear. 'Look what's that man doing? You can see. Look, he's digging the soil up. Can you see him? We have to ask mummy if we can go to Rajah's mummy's house [Rajah's mummy is the owner of the dog]. We can if mummy says "yes". Can't undo this lock. Better ask mummy if we can have the paddling pool out at Rajah's mummy [thought to be the bath in which Rajah is rubbed down]. Have to try and open it. Can we go to Rajah's mummy's house?'.

'No. Get into bed', says Jane's mother.

'Jane get into bed. No. I'm bright and chirpy now. Mummy, I'm bright and chirpy now. That sock doesn't fit me. Better see if it fits Teddy'.

The first snatch of conversation seems to be socialized speech where Jane is trying to encourage someone else (probably mother, who although not there may be thought to be within earshot) to repeat what she is doing. But then she appears to direct her conversation to something else (most likely Teddy) because she talks about her mummy as a third person. There is also evidence of monologue intended largely for self-direction. On several occasions she rehearses what she is going to say or do. 'We have to ask mummy if we can go to Rajah's mummy's house', 'I'm bright and chirpy now', 'Better see if it fits Teddy' are three examples. Egocentric speech is not necessarily indicated by the recurrence of 'I' or 'me'. The question is, for whom is the speech intended? Is it intended for self-direction or is it an attempt to communicate with others?

The relative development of egocentric and socialized speech and the functions they serve was a bone of contention between Piaget and Vygotsky. The latter's position has now been accepted by most (including Piaget). Vygotsky supposed that all speech is social by implication (14) although it may not always be used as a means of communicating with others. Egocentric speech was crucial as a directive for the child's actions. It was not, as Piaget once held, a simple accompaniment to the actions with no other purpose, rather it was used by the child for laying down plans of action. Further, for Vygotsky egocentric speech was a transitional step from outward vocal socialized speech to inner speech. Interiorization of speech means that thought processes are facilitated and self-direction follows without the attendant overt speech. (It is, nonetheless, difficult to determine which comes first, a thought or the speech. When Jane talks about an action she might be reminding herself of a thought.) In short, we see a change in the regulating function of speech from external sources (like mother), through egocentric speech for everyone (including self) to hear, and ultimately to speech for communication and 'internalized speech' for the regulation of behaviour and logical thinking.

LANGUAGE AND THOUGHT

It would be impossible to speak of language development in isolation from a considera-tion of thinking skills. Important questions such as, do we need to have language in order to think or vice versa, and do language and thinking skills grow as separate entities or are they interconnected from the outset, have taxed the minds of psycho-linguists for many years. There is still no comprehensive account of the relationship between language and thought. What we have is a spectrum of views and speculations based on research evidence which is very difficult to amass. Though the relationship of language and cognition has been a contentious one, it is now generally agreed that a correlation does exist.

For some of the earliest investigators there appeared to be no problem. Watson, an American psychologist in the behaviourist tradition, concluded that thought *was* language. Accordingly, thinking is manipulating words in the mind. These word-thoughts were regarded as internal speech which showed up in sub-vocal movements of the speech organs. Elaborate experiments aimed at detecting these movements whilst subjects were thinking out the solution to a problem were not entirely convincing. The present moderate view emphasizes the role of the CNS rather than the peripheral motor system of which the speech organs form a part. The child quickly learns to suppress the peripheral nervous system, therefore motor action accompanying reading or thinking gradually (but not entirely) declines. The more difficult the verbal task, the more likely is sub-vocal movement. Again, the example of deaf people who can think without vocalizing at all is evidence that thought can occur without the agency of a language system as we know it.

Origins of language and thought

One popular point of view (Vygotsky, 15) considers language and thought as originating from different roots. At first, there is what might be described as pre-linguistic thought and pre-intellectual speech which gradually merge together as the child approaches the pre-operational stage. The 'fusion' of thought and speech, however, is not total and the crude diagram (figure 8.2) shows a continuing independence of some aspects of language and thought. Pre-linguistic thought is very much in evidence, as we have seen, in the sensori-motor activity of infants. Beyond this stage, we still employ imagery and motor skills in practical pursuits. Learning by heart without any grasp of meaning may lead to pre-intellectual speech. Jane's phrase 'bright and chirpy' is probably used with little idea of what it means (see previous section). Verbal strings implanted in the memory without any logical reasoning behind the content can produce non-intellectual speech.

A very important question to which we have no satisfactory answer is the extent to which language structure affects the way we define our world. Differences between language in terms of special idioms for which no translation is available in other languages will be familiar to anyone who has taken a foreign language. The term 'gestalten' in chapter 4 has really no precise translation into English. Many of Piaget's terms in French have no equivalent translation and authors have had to resort to literal translation. But do these language idiosyncrasies affect the way we operate in our environment?

Whorf (16) strongly upholds the belief that 'thought is relative to the language in which it is conducted'. This viewpoint is known as the *linguistic-relativity hypothesis*.

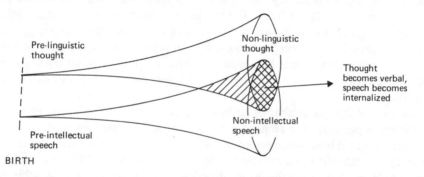

Figure 8.2 Representative model of theory relating thought and language (after Vygotsky)

'Language' he says, 'is the mould into which the infant mind is poured'. Also, 'we cut nature up, organize it into concepts' and agree 'through our speech community' to a code dependent upon the structure of the language. Whilst language differences are self-evident, there nevertheless appear to be substantial similarities amongst languages and these tend to overshadow the differences. In a review of the research on linguistic-relativity using comparisons in concept formation between native tribes, eastern, and western cultures, Carroll (3) concludes that the hypothesis 'has thus far received very little convincing support. Our best guess at present is that the effects of language structure will be found to be *limited* and *localized*' [author's italics].

Cognitive growth and representation

Another approach to the study of language in the development of thinking comes from Bruner (17). His concern is for discovering the functions of language in concept formation—the how and why of language and concepts. Piaget, as we have observed, concentrates on the description and structure of cognitive growth—the 'what happens in concept formation' approach.

How do we fix in our minds the repeated regularities of our observations? How, in other words, do we represent our experiences to ourselves? Man, in the course of his evolution, has developed systems by which he can implement his actions with increasing efficiency. First, he develops the use of tools as an extension of his *motor capacities*. A spade becomes the extension of a man's hand. He makes instruments to replace his less efficient body structures. Next, he extends his *sensory capacities* by, for instance, the use of signal systems. In order to enlarge on his sensory experience he builds telescopes and microscopes or uses radio to transmit sound over great distances. At the pinnacle of representational skills we find man's *symbol systems* for conveying experience of real (or imaginary) things in their absence. These three evolutionary changes coincide with the course of language development through *enactive, iconic* and *symbolic* representation as postulated by Bruner and they compare closely with Piaget's theorizing.

Enactive representation, the earliest stage of development, enables us to internalize repeated motor responses so that in time they become habitual. Numerous physical activities carried out in life are habitual. Opening a familiar door, driving a cricket ball, writing, walking, and so forth, do not always require conscious effort in terms of directing one's muscles to do certain things. The muscles, so to speak, seem to behave as if the memory of familiar events had been imprinted on them without the aid of mental images. The circular reactions suggested by Piaget are the beginnings of enactive representation.

When mental images enable us to build up a picture of the environment, iconic representation is possible. We amplify sensory experiences and combine these percepts to construct images. These 'internalized imitations', as Piaget calls them, are thought by Bruner to be a composite representation of several similar events. (Calling up the sound of a bell would produce a combination of bell sounds heard in the past—this point is discussed later in the chapter when we consider Osgood's work.) An exception occurs in eidetic imagery where a vivid image of a single event is recalled in great detail.

The transition from iconic to symbolic representation occurs around the age of four years, although the child begins to symbolize at about the age of two. Symbolic representation sees the use of language systems which bear no resemblance to actual objects. Symbols do more than represent reality, they enable us to transform it. This transition from iconic to symbolic representation and the central position of language is well demonstrated by an experiment of Bruner's. Children between five and seven were shown nine glasses of different sizes arranged in a pattern as shown in figure 8.3.

The children were asked to describe the arrangement, pointing out how the glasses were similar or different. The glasses were then dispersed and the children asked to rearrange them as nearly as possible to the original. Most children succeeded in this task. The glasses were dispersed again except that the glass marked A was placed in another position at X and the children asked to reconstruct the pattern with A at X. The younger children did not succeed whilst the seven years olds accomplished the task.

This and other research points to valuable conclusions for the teacher. Children who still depend on iconic representation are dominated by the images they perceive. This is in agreement with Piaget's notions of 'centering' and 'decentering' alluded to earlier. We ought, according to Bruner, to give children every opportunity to describe events in order to encourage symbolic rather than iconic representation. This is just a high-powered way of saying that we should get our children to talk or write about experiences, to express themselves in language as well as to do things. Frank's work [reported by Bruner, see chapter 5, note (8)], in which the well-known Piagetian experiment with glass vessels containing water were hidden from view apart from the tops of the vessels and children asked the typical conservation questions, demonstrates the importance of diverting the child from visual to symbolic modes of representation and testifies convincingly to the improvement in the performance of young children when we deliberately activate symbolic reasoning. Language, then, is to be encouraged as an essential accompaniment to perceptual experience.

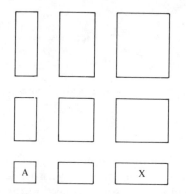

Figure 8.3   Matrix of glasses in Bruner's transposition task
Modified from Bruner by D. G. Boyle, *A Student's Guide to Piaget*, Pergamon, London, 1969

Language and meaning

We are all familiar with the feelings and characteristic reactions which can be evoked when particular signs are used. Some women recoil in horror at the word 'snake' or 'spider'. Some visibly change at the sight of a baby's photograph or even the word 'baby'. Children and adults often display inappropriate or prejudiced behaviour at the sound or sight of particular words. Occasionally one meets a reception class youngster or first-form Secondary School pupil who has developed a distorted reaction to school (especially if the parents have said 'you wait until you get to school. They'll sort you out'). But how does meaning become attached to signs?

Of the many theories extant, Osgood's (18) has received the widest currency. In a nutshell he supposes that in addition to receiving the direct stimulation from an adult, we regularly experience other kinds of stimulus which, by conditioning, become associated with the stimulus-object and become part of our response to the stimulus. Osgood gives an example of the spider. The hairy, long-legged body and quick movements representing the visual pattern received by our eyes may be encountered at the same time as a frightening description of its habits or when mother is leaping about in dread of the creature. With sufficient repetition of these extraneous reactions alongside the stimulus-object a complex behaviour response is established. As there are many and varied encounters with the stimulus-object, the total response pattern becomes very complicated. When the spoken word 'spider' occurs on some of these occasions, part of the total response pattern becomes linked with the word so that the sight or sound of the word 'spider' will provoke that part (or 'fraction' as it is sometimes known) of the total response. This system whereby a previously neutral stimulus (a sign) involves a response (or mediates between stimulus and response) is known as a *representational mediation process*. The term representational is used because the mediating response produced by the sign is only a representative portion of the whole response which would usually appear in the presence of the stimulus-object. A diagram should help to summarize the process.

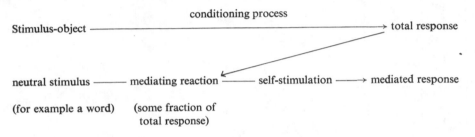

Stimulus-object ——————— conditioning process ——————→ total response

neutral stimulus ——— mediating reaction ——— self-stimulation ——→ mediated response

(for example a word)   (some fraction of
                          total response)

To quote from Osgood, 'Stimulus-objects elicit a complex pattern of reactions from the organism' and 'when stimuli other than the stimulus-object, but previously associated with it, are later presented without its support, they tend to elicit some reduced portion of the total behaviour elicited by the stimulus-object'.

It does not follow that direct association with the stimulus-object is necessary for mediating processes to arise. In fact we may never see an actual snake or giraffe and yet we develop characteristic responses to signs of these animals. Photographs or verbal descriptions of the animals are sufficient to enable a response to be formulated. Where mediation responses arise from other signs rather than from the actual object we call them *assigns*—meaning is assigned by association with other signs rather than the real thing.

NON-VERBAL COMMUNICATION

It is surprising how much information is conveyed by non-verbal means. Mime is a very common example. Friends can often carry on a wordless dialogue of meaningful nods and facial expressions. Stress, unhappiness or joy are frequently seen in certain faces without a word being spoken. Whilst speaking, people use facial and body movements which become clues to the meaning of the spoken words.

Gesture is the commonest form of non-verbal contact. It is not just hand movements, but involves facial and body movement. A clenched fist, bared teeth, frown, tongue out, stamping feet in a tantrum, voice intonation all assist in revealing the mood of a person. Sometimes gestures accompany and interplay with verbal communication adding emphasis or purpose to what is being said. Hand movements are said to portray something of the speaker (19). It has been argued that gestures are much more revealing in their psychological meaning than the speech which goes with them. Conversation is too obvious in laying bare our thoughts and feelings and we therefore tend to be guarded in what we say by the social conventions of our culture. At the same time the significance of gestures is less well understood and therefore we do not disguise them with the same subtlety as in vocalizing. You may have noticed on occasions that implicit meanings of gestures is in conflict with the explicit message of a verbal communication, as when a person is telling a lie and you can read it in their face and voice.

The skilful use and observation of gesture and expressive movement is an asset in teaching. Well-coordinated intonation and facial expressions should add to what is being said. Rather obvious movements such as prowling back and forth in front of a class can be off-putting and reminiscent of a tennis match. Also watch children's facial and body movements. These often reflect the mood and understanding of a class. In a recent research by the author (20), it seems that students at college and university were convinced of their ability to influence teachers by using facial gestures and grimaces in class where the atmosphere would allow it. On teaching practice students will very quickly notice the reaction of a class to a lesson by watching the children's faces and interpreting the silences either as a sign that they are spellbound or, conceivably, that they have not a clue as to what the student is talking about.

TEACHING ORAL LANGUAGE SKILLS

There is far more to language usage than an ability to read well. Naturally, a good reader is more likely to develop the broader language skills of communication and comprehension, but many teachers have become aware of the need for a systematic attack on basic language usage amongst children which has more to it than just reading. Most programme designers are generally agreed that at least three overlapping stages are required in order to assist language development. These are *reception* (listening with understanding), *internal symbolization* (interpreting, reasoning and concept-building) and *expression* (communicating by speaking or by writing). As we have suggested elsewhere, between reception and internal symbolization we require a process of *decoding* the incoming signals into a form which is readily interpreted in terms of previous traces in the brain. Similarly, the outcome of reasoning is thought to be converted or *encoded* into a form which enables an individual to communicate to his fellows.

The programmes (21) set out to encourage these three skills of reception, symbolization and expression. In *Concept 7–9* (for seven to nine year olds), for example, there are three units called 'Listening with understanding', 'Concept-building' and 'Communication'. Unit 'one' endeavours to help children in oral comprehension by encouraging them to attend to information which requires them to determine the position of named objects, making comparisons (which is the larger or smaller of animals for instance), 'what happens if?' or 'the reason why' questions, and items about the time. Unit 'two' employs matrices intended to help the children in the language of classification. As we have seen in chapter 5, classifying attributes is central to concept formation and the children are shown pictures which have to be rearranged according to similar attributes. The third unit on communication aims to 'increase children's oral skills of description and enquiry' by working with each other. For example, one child will describe a picture and a second child (or group) will try to draw the picture from the description. The accuracy of the drawing is taken as a measure of the effectiveness of description. This programme also contains a 'dialect kit' for West Indian Creole dialects.

The ultimate aim of *Concept 7–9*, as with all these oracy programmes, is to 'direct attention on critical aspects of oral language proficiency, and reflect the linguistic process which starts with the reception and decoding of sounds, involves the analysis of information and the development of concepts, and culminates in the production of efficient and explicit communication'. There is no doubt that teaching and research in oracy and psycholinguistic skills is going to be a major growing point in primary education.

SUMMARY

Readers do not have to be convinced that language is a most important skill for human learning and communication. There are two basic requirements of a language, namely, that it should be symbolic and systematic. The symbolic aspects were discussed in the form of phonemes and morphemes and the systematics in relation to grammar and semantics.

Templin's work on establishing norms of articulation, speech sound discrimination, sentence structure and vocabulary size amongst children from three to eight years of age was followed by a brief introduction to some contemporary views of language acquisition. At one extreme, we find the behaviourist position, illustrated from the theories of Skinner, in which language is said to be acquired largely by the processes of imitation and reinforcement of acceptable sounds. On the other hand, Chomsky, whilst not rejecting the possibility of stimulus–response learning of phonemes and morphemes, nevertheless cannot accept that the highly creative nature of language is largely derived from the Skinnerian type of language conditioning. Those with some degree of fluency are well able to create and understand entirely original sentences. Human language is far more open-ended than in other species. Whilst bees can communicate and even vary the intensity of their messages to give shades of meaning (variable activity amongst bees is commensurate with the distance of a supply of pollen), they cannot recombine their code to give original messages. With man, the potency of his communication lies in the infinite combinations possible. New rules of language can develop, or recognized rules broken, especially with young children who are still in the process of learning the rules.

Efficient language acquisition is very much dependent on the linguistic environment in which children are exposed. Bernstein has shown some marked differences in the language patterns and skills deriving from different home backgrounds and he named these patterns restricted and elaborated codes.

The function of speech was the centre of controversy a few years ago when Piaget and Vygotsky disagreed on the purposes served by the early speech of children. Now it is widely accepted that egocentric speech, that is speech intended essentially for one's own benefit, and socialized speech for the benefit of others, are the two major functions. Egocentric speech is most often used as a self-directive—giving instructions to oneself. Once this speech becomes internalized, it can regulate behaviour both for personal and social motives.

The connection between language and thought is yet another source of disagreement. However, most psycholinguists now believe that they start from different origins at birth and gradually, but only partially, merge in the early years of life (Vygotsky). Figure 8.3 summarizes the possibilities of pre-linguistic thought and pre-intellectual speech either fusing to become interdependent or remaining throughout life as non-linguistic thought and non-intellectual speech. An extreme view of Whorf, the linguistic-relativity hypothesis, which proposes that our thinking is actually determined by the language we use, would seem to be discredited by the knowledge that brain damage to the language centres does not necessarily affect reasoning and that rational thought is possible in infants who have not yet developed language skills.

We then dealt with Bruner's work on the place of language in concept formation and the theory of Osgood which proposes that 'meaning' is ascribed to stimuli in accordance with the actual sensations experienced at the time when the stimulus is presented. The representational mediation processes suggested by Osgood are responsible for the patterns of reaction (either physical or verbal) which occur on the next presentation of a stimulus.

Non-verbal communication was also held to be important to the teacher. We communicate with our fellow men not only in words, but in all our actions. Recent developments in the use of oracy programmes where children are taught skills of listening to, interpreting and communicating in the language concluded the chapter.

ENQUIRY AND DISCUSSION

1. Take tape-recordings of both monologue and dialogue of children at several ages (including pre-school children). Note:

   (i) egocentric and socialized speech;
   (ii) virtuous errors;
   (iii) restricted and elaborate code users—are they related to social class?

2. Examine the methods of language teaching in schools which you visit. Try to familiarize yourself with some of the modern programmes (SMA, ITPA, *Concept 7–9*), in action, if possible.

3. Discover what you can about non-verbal communication. Observe the non-verbal behaviour of children in the classroom and their reaction to different kinds of non-verbal activities of the teacher.

4. Read Lawton's book *Social Class, Language and Education* [note (11)] with an eye towards the problems facing teachers who are in schools where the catchment area is largely lower working class. What problems face the teacher of immigrant children? (Note the special programme for West Indian children in *Concept 7–9*.)

NOTES AND REFERENCES

1. The Gardners have had a little more success in teaching chimpanzees a hand sign language, whilst D. Premack, University of California, has managed to teach a

chimp a simple communication device using shapes which act as symbolic characters. These results can be found in N. Calder, *The Mind of Man*, BBC Publications, London, 1970. Note in both cases that the chimp must operate the system manually and not vocally.

2. P. Herriot, *An Introduction to the Psychology of Language*, Methuen, London, 1970.

3. A clear analysis of language structure can be found in J. B. Carroll, *Language and Thought*, Prentice-Hall, New Jersey, 1964.

4. The newborn relies on reflex action and soon comes to depend on direct evidence which he can assimilate from his senses. Oral contact with objects such as a milk bottle or mother's nipple will soon initiate sucking. Quickly the child begins to associate one aspect of the feeding ritual with the whole process. The sight of milk in the bottle or the sound of the bottle being prepared are often sufficient to set in motion anticipatory behaviour in advance of the actual feeding process.

   Perception, then, of some piece of the action gives the cue for the whole action. The cue which represents part of the real thing (sight of nipple or milk, smell of milk, clank of bottle) is called a *sign*. Babies become quiet when their nappies are being removed, a lead to a dog can be a sign of the prospect of a walk. Tears are a sign of joy or sorrow.

   In the discussion of intuitive thinking in children, we showed how children are often deceived by signs. By over-generalizing they take the same sign to mean that the same event is going to take place. When mother puts her coat on it may be taken erroneously to represent a sign that she is going shopping. The important thing about a sign is that it produces behaviour characteristic of the whole response to a situation.

   Certain signs become significant in the absence of the real thing. When a sign is given this special meaning in the absence of the object and it gives rise to behaviour *as if* the object were there, we call it a *signal*. Signals are often the outcome of conditioning. The hand movements, whistles, and calls which send a sheep dog cavorting round a flock of sheep are signals. Likewise, words take on the function of signals. The word 'sit' to a dog is a signal which has become part of the act of sitting down. Experiments with chimpanzees have shown that words are little more than signals. As with animals, the first childlike utterances such as 'dada' are signals acquired through repeated association and conditioning which connects word sounds with physical objects.

   When signals become endowed with meaning which bears no resemblance to the original object we call them *symbols*. Words in our language are obvious examples. The symbols actually represent things without looking or sounding at all like them. A symbol is sometimes referred to as a secondary signal because it is once removed from the real thing. Unlike commands to a dog or the first words of a child, the symbol becomes detached from physical events. Mead in *Mind, Self and Society*, Chicago Press, 1934, says that 'The vocal gesture becomes a significant symbol. . . . When it has the same effect on the individual making it that it has on the individual to whom it is addressed'. 'The same effect' is used with the reservation that no two people respond in precisely the same way.

Many stimuli not normally brought together can be represented by symbols and juxtaposed within a short space of time. Language results when these verbal symbols are brought together and organized into systems of meaningful patterns.

An unusual example of a transition from sign and signal to symbol systems is brilliantly illustrated by Helen Keller in *The Story of My Life*, Doubleday, New York, 1917. Deaf and blind from infancy, she had made little progress until at the age of seven years she was given a tutor, Miss Annie Sullivan. The tutor in their first days together got Helen to feel objects whilst they were being spelt out into the palm of her hand. But there was little realization that the shapes drawn out on her palm were labels for the objects she was touching. Helen, in fact, was not even detached from the signs around her. The moment of truth came when:

> We walked down the path to the well-house, attracted by the fragrance of the honey-suckle with which it was covered. Someone was drawing water and my teacher placed my hand under the spout. As the cool stream gushed over one hand she spelled into the other the word *water*, first slowly, then rapidly. I stood still, my whole attention fixed upon the motions of her fingers. Suddenly I felt a misty consciousness as of something forgotten—a thrill of returning thought; and somehow the mystery of language was revealed to me. I knew then that 'w–a–t–e–r' meant the wonderful cool something that was flowing over my hand. . . .
>
> I left the well-house eager to learn. Everything had a name, and each name gave birth to a new thought.

5. A. F. Watts, *Language and Mental Development of Children*, Harrap, London, 1950; E. H. Lenneberg also gives an account of word counts in a chapter in F. Smith and G. A. Miller (Eds), *The Genesis of Language*, M.I.T. Press, Cambridge, Mass., 1966.

6. J. Berko, 'The child's learning of English morphology', *Word*, **14**, 150–177 (1958).

7. M. C. Templin, *Certain Language Skills in Children*, Minnesota University Press, Minneapolis, 1957.

8. P. Herriot, *Language and Teaching: A Psychological View*, Methuen, London, 1971.

9. B. F. Skinner, *Verbal Behavior*, Appleton-Century-Crofts, New York, 1957.

10. J. Lyons, *Chomsky*, Fontana Modern Masters, London, 1970.

11. The clearest exposé of B. Bernstein's work can be found in D. Lawton, *Social Class, Language and Education*, Routledge and Kegan Paul, London, 1968. This book also gives an up to date account of findings in the field of language and social background connections.

12. At an anecdotal level, the author, in conversation with a doctor, was interested to discover that the latter preferred the more direct language approach of patients from working-class homes. Where a patient elaborates in the description of symp-toms, it is sometimes difficult to track down a diagnosis, whereas a working-class 'belly-ache' gives a crystal-clear indication of the patient's problem!

13. B. Bernstein, 'A public language: some sociological determinants of linguistic form',

Br. J. Sociol., **10**, 311–326 (1959). See as well, 'A socio-linguistic approach to social learning', in J. Gould (Ed.), *Social Science Survey*, London, 1965.

14. One source of evidence for Vygotsky's belief in speech as being social in origin is that if one puts normal children with deaf or foreign children, egocentric speech disappears. When the potential listener cannot understand, speech is no longer overt.

15. L. S. Vygotsky, *Thought and Language*, translated by E. Haufmann and C. Vakar, M.I.T. Press, Cambridge, Mass., 1962.

16. B. L. Whorf, in J. B. Carroll (Ed.), *Language, Thought and Reality*, M.I.T. Press, Cambridge, Mass., 1956.

17. J. S. Bruner, 'The course of cognitive growth', *Am. Psychol.*, **19**, 1–19 (1964).

18. C. E. Osgood, G. J. Suci and P. Tannenbaum, *The Measurement of Meaning*, University of Illinois Press, Urbana, Illinois, 1957.

19. P. E. Vernon, 'Expressive movements', in *Personality Tests and Assessments*, Methuen, London, 1953, chapter 4.

20. D. Child, 'Some aspects of study habits in higher education', *Int. J. educ. Sci.*, **4**, 11–20 (1970).

21. Several language and reasoning programmes now exist. A British example, produced for the Schools Council by the University of Birmingham, is *Concept 7–9*, Arnold, Leeds, 1972. An American programme widely used now is the *Illinois Test of Psycholinguistic Aptitude*.

FURTHER READING

J. B. Carroll, *Language and Thought*, Prentice-Hall, New Jersey, 1964. A detailed introductory text.

J. P. De Cecco, *The Psychology of Language, Thought and Instruction*, Holt, Rinehart and Winston, New York, 1967. A collection of readings from leading psycholinguists.

P. Herriot, *An Introduction to the Psychology of Language*, Methuen, London, 1970. Written for the specialist.

P. Herriot, *Language and Teaching: A Psychological View*, Methuen, London, 1971. This is a basic text intended for students and teachers.

D. Lawton, *Social Class, Language and Education*, Routledge and Kegan Paul, London, 1968.

A. Wilkinson, *The Foundations of Language*, Oxford University Press, Oxford, 1971.

9   Human intelligence

Few topics in psychology can have attracted more widespread attention than intelligence. The reasons are not hard to find. Up to quite recently, everyone's educational and career prospects hung almost entirely on standardized tests of number, verbal and general ability; the confirmation of educationally subnormal children (ESN) for purposes of providing special educational facilities has been based on IQ tests; the civil service, armed forces and even some universities of late include an IQ test in their selection procedures. The subject is also a tender spot for many social scientists who see it as having a divisive effect in social and ethnic matters, and it must be admitted that intelligence measurement has had a decisive influence on the educational and occupational life styles of many people. However, the exploration of human ability is inevitable. It is almost a platitude to say that an intelligent creature will question the nature of its intelligence.

The existence of differences in the distribution of human abilities is self-evident. Heim (1) defines intelligent activity as consisting of 'grasping the essentials in a given situation and responding appropriately to them' and we are all well aware that some can cope with certain situations better than others. Thus, the detection and measurement of differences is an important one for the teacher. It would be disastrous for children if we did not quickly recognize their cognitive strengths and weaknesses, because the intellectually dull cannot, in general, cope with the same cognitive tasks as the intellectually bright of the same age, although they may possess special skills in particular abilities. In some cases it is difficult to discover the scholastic potential of a child by observing his school work and we need to resort to standardized tests of intelligence. This chapter, therefore, will be concerned with a discussion of how far we have got in defining the nature of intelligence, in assessing intelligent behaviour and in elaborating models of the intellect.

THE NATURE OF INTELLIGENT BEHAVIOUR

The word 'intelligence' has developed some unfortunate implicit meanings over the years. In common parlance it has erroneously come to mean a possession, something one has in a fixed quantity and probably located in one's head! The concept of the intelligence quotient (IQ) is probably responsible for conveying the impression of intelligence as a quantity—'She's a bright young thing—her intelligence is 140!'.

The habit of looking on intelligence as a possession of precise dimensions (known as *reification*) has been discussed by Miles (2). He recommends that we abandon the term intelligence and replace it with the less ambiguous term 'intelligent behaviour'. In so doing we lay stress on the activity of a person exposed to certain kinds of experience and how he would respond. We can then define his behaviour as more or less intelligent. Of course, this still leaves undefined the vital question of *what* is intelligent behaviour. Nevertheless, having noted Miles' cautionary comments and the dangers of misusing the term intelligence, we shall continue to apply it in the text synonymously with intelligent behaviour.

Vernon (6), in an address to the British Psychological Society, perceived three broad categories for defining intelligence. These were (a) biological; (b) psychological; and (c) operational. Biological definitions emphasize the individual's capacity to adjust or adapt to environmental stimuli. Adaptation here refers to modifying behaviour either overtly or covertly as a result of experience. There is something of this definition in the work of Piaget. Hebb has also maintained that adaptation depends on the quality of neurological connections in the brain and CNS—high intelligence for him is founded on having a 'good' brain and CNS. Man has certainly outstripped the animals in his gift as an adaptor of, and to, environments essentially by virtue of his more advanced neural endowment in the form of a large neocortex (see chapter 2). But it still remains patently clear that many people are irreconcilably ill-adapted in particular situations. A popular, but overrated, example is that of some famous scholars, politicians and creative artists who have the utmost difficulty in catering for themselves in the mundane things of life. Another problem in studying biological adaptation as a definition of intelligence is the masking effect of man's self-made systems which have overgrown and obscured his adaptive qualities from the hard biological facts of life.

Psychological definitions stress *mental efficiency* and the capacity for abstract reasoning which requires the use of symbolic language. Spearman's famous formulation of intelligent behaviour as 'the eduction of relations and correlates' is an example of a psychological definition. This approach accounts much more for the higher abstract conceptualization prevalent in man. There is more recognition of man's verbal, numerical and spatial skills. Taking a common example from an intelligence test to illustrate Spearman's definition, find the missing word:

Hand is to arm as foot is to .   .   .   .

There are two statements here

hand is to arm .   .   .   .   (A)

foot is to .   .   .   .   .   .   (B)

The relationship we *educe* (infer) from statement (A) is based on our knowledge of limb attachments. Using this fact, we attempt to *correlate* the first part of statement (B) with the second part, in this case 'leg'.

Operational definitions involve making detailed specifications of intelligent behaviour and then finding measures of these specifications. Intelligent behaviour thus becomes expressed in terms of these measures. As Miles (2) so aptly puts it

> psychologists have devised standardized tests—it is the items in these tests which are regarded as exemplars of the word intelligent (exemplars = actual or possible manifestations of behaviour which are claimed to be intelligent). Correct responses to these items shall be deemed to constitute acts of intelligent behaviour.

The expression 'intelligence is what intelligence tests measure' is often used to describe the operational definition, although, as we shall see, it is not really as superficial as this statement would suggest.

Deciding on the specifications of intelligent behaviour has been quite a problem. Many are still not convinced that we have succeeded in tapping all man's abilities. Presently we shall look at some typical intelligence test items which exemplify the kinds of specifications already widely accepted as demonstrating intelligent behaviour. Reasoning tests containing analogies, synonyms, memory items and word or number series are very common. But there may be talents which are not yet entirely susceptible to testing in the conventional ways dictated by intelligence test design. Creative thinking (chapter 10), music or art, business acumen and cognitive development in the Piagetian tradition have still not been convincingly measured and incorporated into intelligence tests. Yet these activities would seem, at a common-sense level, to require man's higher mental processes. Also at present we know more about *what* a child can do in specified circumstances than *how* he does it. This intractable problem of defining our terms of reference arises because effects are more readily observed than causes; hence we have deliberately concentrated on measuring the outward manifestations of intelligent behaviour using test materials.

As the definition offered by Heim—intelligent activity consists of grasping the essentials in a given situation and responding appropriately to them—goes a long way towards embracing the biological and psychological views of intelligence in the design of intelligence tests whilst at the same time satisfying the common-sense view of intelligence, we shall adopt it.

The genotype and phenotype

The popular press and other mass media have become stiff with references to the 'nature/nurture' controversy surrounding the subject of intelligence (see later). The dispute centres on the dilemma of how our inherited qualities and developmental prospects affect intelligent activity. The disputants seek an answer to such questions as 'what is the relative influence and importance of inherited and constitutional characteristics in the growth of human ability?' 'Is intelligence really "innate general cognitive ability"?' (3). 'To what extent can social or ethnic disadvantages (whether inherited or developed) be influenced by educational programmes?' 'Are human beings born equally endowed and therefore entirely at the mercy of the environment in creating variations in measured intelligence (UNESCO, 1951), or in any case is the interaction of endowment and environment such that we cannot readily extricate their relative influence?'

To help define the problem, two commonly used biological terms will be introduced. These are *genotype* and *phenotype*. The genotype refers to the genetic characteristics of individuals transferred in the genes of the parents at fertilization. We have already seen in chapter 2 that many human characteristics are transferred from generation to generation by the genes which are the biological blueprints of physical and mental features found in the germ cells of the parents. Hair and eye colour, potential for height and body dimensions are examples of features carried through from previous generations into the embryo. But inherited characteristics, especially mental skills, cannot be observed and measured directly because external influences are at work from the moment of conception. The intellectual similarities of identical twins, or the variations in development which frequently occur in environments which are similar and fairly constant are just two indirect sources of evidence for believing in the inheritance of intellectual characteristics. We shall return to this point later in the chapter.

The phenotype results from the interaction of genetic potential and environmental effects from the moment of conception onwards. Thus, by the time the child is born he has already begun phenotypic development. The concept of the phenotype is frequently misused and confused with *acquired* characteristics. It is important to remember we are talking about the extent to which environmental circumstances will *allow* inborn potential to materialize and not about acquired characteristics. A young plant which is undernourished or short of light and water does not grow into a healthy plant, so the genotypic potential has been distorted to give a phenotype. The essential features of the genotype are still there, however, and an undernourished cabbage can still be distinguished from an undernourished oak. In the same way, undernourished children, in both physically and mentally impoverished circumstances, do not realize their full potential. On the other hand, we can acquire certain habits or physical injuries during life which are unique to us and die with us. If we cut off the tails of successive generations of mice we would *not* in time produce a tailless generation. This can only happen by mutation (that is distortion of the genetic material). Similarly, families with a boxing tradition do not ultimately give birth to youngsters with a boxer's nose. In short, we do not inherit acquired characteristics.

Intelligence A, B and C

Our present view of intelligent behaviour brings out this dynamic interplay between inborn potential and circumstances. One particularly instructive approach was elaborated by Hebb (4). He distinguishes between *Intelligence A* and *Intelligence B* which we can identify with the genotype and phenotype, respectively, of intelligence. For Hebb, Intelligence A represents an innate potential which depends entirely on neurological facilities and signifies the capacity of an individual to develop intelligent responses. Whether the individual realizes this capacity or not depends on his life-chances. Thus, Intelligence B represents a hypothetical level of development which has resulted from the interaction of Intelligence A and environmental influences.

Neither Intelligence A nor B can be measured directly. As we have suggested above, Intelligence A is masked by the immediate impact of experience. In the case of Intelligence B, we would have to devise a vast array of measures in order to sample the numerous aspects of man's ability. Note we would be *sampling* intelligence not measuring it directly. Intelligence B is not fixed because changes of environment produce variations during its emergence particularly in childhood and adolescence. We must consequently expect to find anomalies in the sampling of Intelligence B between cultures or sub-cultures partly arising from major differences in child-rearing habits which encourage or inhibit mental development, partly because there will be a natural variation in the genotypic distribution of intelligence between cultures (as one finds giants and pigmies), and partly because the sampling measures may favour some cultures more than others (verbal skills are often at a premium in some cultures).

Vernon (5) introduced the term *Intelligence C* to describe the sampling of Intelligence B using standardized tests. This is a very useful concept because IQ scores are often misguidedly taken as direct measures of Intelligence A or B, whereas they only result from a sampling of the latter. Much of the subsequent discussion will rest on evidence gathered using Intelligence C. It is essential, therefore, to be aware of the special relationship between it and the other hypothesized origins of intelligence. The connection between Intelligence A and C is, by definition, only fragmentary. As C samples B, and B is derived from A, we can assume a link between C and A. But it is virtually impossible to be certain of the precise relationship. Therefore, we cannot regard an IQ score as a measure of innate capacity any more than we could regard it as an accurate measure of Intelligence B.

INTELLIGENCE TESTING

The work of Binet

At the turn of the century, Alfred Binet suggested that the French Ministry of Public Instruction support him in devising a series of tests designed to pick out the mentally defective and retarded children in state schools who were unlikely to benefit from the normal system. The idea was to segregate these children and provide them with special education more in keeping with their inabilities. This principle is still in operation today. Binet's aim was to derive a scale of items answerable by about 75 per cent of children at given age intervals. The figure of 75 per cent was chosen because it was thought that the 'middle' 50 per cent (in ability) of an age group should be capable of solving the problems. Naturally the top 25 per cent should also have the ability, thus making 75 per cent in all. The performance of individual children was then compared with that of the expected performance of other age groups. If a child could answer questions for all age groups up to, say, nine years, his *mental age* was said to be nine years irrespective of his actual (*chronological*) age. Sub-tests enabled the mental age to be assessed in two-monthly intervals from three years to about thirteen years of age.

How did Binet decide on the sort of questions to ask the children? In the first place he used hunches from his observations of children in a variety of practical and theoretical tasks which appeared, at a common-sense level, to discriminate between their abilities. Items included naming or pointing to parts of the body, repeating digits or sentences, counting, producing rhymes for given words and defining familiar objects. For the most part the items were verbally biased. On referring back to his sample of scholastically bright, moderate and inadequate children he was able to chose items possessing the highest level of discrimination. The test has since undergone several revisions and translations from the French as the Binet–Simon Test, the Stanford–Binet and latterly the Terman–Merrill version (1960), all used as individual tests. To avoid publishing examples of actual test items, which would give them a wide currency and therefore make them unreliable, it is better for the college or department to show sample materials from these tests.

The concept of mental age is most useful when we express it in terms of the chronological age of the child. Stern introduced the idea of *mental ratio* which he derived by dividing the child's mental age by his actual age. The resulting ratio was thought by Stern to be a constant for a given child. We now know that mental age, and in consequence the mental ratio, may have an erratic history.

The small number obtained for the mental ratio is awkward. Terman therefore proposed that if we multiplied the ratio by 100 it would give a more convenient range of numbers to deal with. The final figure obtained is known as an *intelligence quotient*, or *IQ* for short. If a child of 5 years 0 months has a mental age of 6 years 0 months (i.e. he can answer items normally answered by six year olds), the mental ratio would be

$$\text{mental ratio} = \frac{\text{mental age}}{\text{chronological age}} = \frac{6}{5} = 1 \cdot 20$$

The intelligence quotient or IQ $= 1 \cdot 20 \times 100 = 120$. A child of six with a mental age of five would have a IQ of $83 \cdot 33$ recurring. Actually, we express IQs to the nearest whole number, that is 83 in this case.

Binet's method is only satisfactory as long as we can produce cumulative norms for each age group. But as mental development beyond fifteen or sixteen years is irregular and sometimes non-existent, it is not possible to establish a continuous yardstick for comparison in the manner of Binet. Sooner or later mental development as measured by conventional tests tails off. Around 1939, David Wechsler created the Wechsler–Bellevue tests of adult intelligence which went some way towards a scale suitable for testing beyond fifteen years of age. He included 'performance' as well as verbal tests.

Modern test design

IQs are no longer derived using Binet's method. Nowadays, the distribution of scores for each age group is found using representative samples, and they are then rescaled using a convenient mean and standard deviation (see chapter 14). Usually the mean, no matter what value it may have in the first place, is made equal to 100. The distribution of the scores on each side of the mean is then manipulated so that about 70 per cent of the scores fall within the range from 85 to 115 (i.e. 15 points on either side of the newly created mean). For this method to work properly, the distribution has to be 'normal' or very near to normal (see figure 9.1). That means the distribution of scores on either side of the mean will tail off in a regular and symmetrical fashion. If this distribution does not appear, the test is modified until it does. In other words, the normal distribution of IQ scores is not necessarily a fact of life, but a feature of IQ test design. What is more, there is no direct evidence to suppose that 'intelligence' is normally distributed in society. So many factors of upbringing, inadequate sampling of intellectual skills, etc., already mentioned above conspire against an accurate knowledge of IQ distributions. But their design is such as to impose the spread shown in the accompanying figure.

The figure 9.1 is based on a distribution with a mean of 100 and a standard deviation of 15 IQ points. There are, of course, an infinite number of means and standard deviations which are possible, but we generally adopt a mean of 100 and a standard deviation of 10, 15 or 20 points. This variation in the possible values provides the reason why we have to state the name of a test when quoting an IQ because unless the norms are the same, the scores from one test to the next will not correspond. If we were comparing IQs from tests both with a mean of 100, but having, say, standard deviations of 10 and 20, an IQ of 120 on the first would be equivalent to an IQ of 140 on the second.

At one time it was common to find verbal descriptions associated with IQ ranges. For instance those obtaining IQs greater than 140 were referred to as 'very superior' and those below an IQ of 70 (both on a scale having a mean of 100 an SD 15) as mentally deficient. In this country these unfortunate labels tend to have fallen out of use. We still employ the term ESN to refer to pupils who because of mental inadequacy are not able

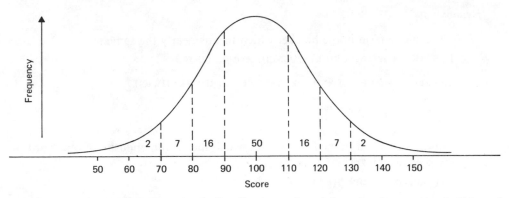

Figure 9.1 Approximate normal distribution of people using a mean of 100 and standard deviation of 15. The figures under the curve represent the percentage of people falling within the limits indicated by the dotted lines. Thus, 50 per cent fall between the scores of 90 and 110, 16 per cent between 80 and 90, or between 110 and 120, etc.

to benefit from conventional forms of education. The IQ of these children is used as one criterion, amongst other things, and a value of around 70 is regarded as critical. In the 11+ examination, a figure of 115 was often quoted as the cut-off point above which pupils were deemed suitable for a grammar school education. This amounted to roughly 16 per cent of an age group (see figure 9.1).

Intelligence test items

Over the years from Binet's earliest work, we have amassed many test items thought to reflect reasoning ability. Let us look at some of the commonest kinds of item. They have been specially compiled for the text and not taken from existing IQ tests. It will be clear to students that we cannot use standardized items from tests because they are 'closed', that is their content is subject to restrictions of both publication and circulation [see reference in note (6) for more examples]. Answers appear at the end of the chapter.

Analogies

An example has already been provided to demonstrate Spearman's 'eduction of relations and correlates'. Here are a few more.

Choose the correct alternative:
1. Rein is to rain as stem is to
   (a) item (b) twig (c) seem (d) reign

2. Male is to female as dog is to
   (a) cat (b) vixen (c) canine (d) bitch

3. Author is to words as (CONDUCTOR, COMPOSER, PLAYER) is to (MUSIC, NOTES, ORCHESTRA)

Synonyms

Choose one term in the bracket which means nearly the same as:
1. SLAKE, (GROW, DRINK, QUENCH, POUR, LOOSE)

2. PREEN (TEACH, GLAND, BE ANNOYED, TRIM FEATHERS)

Antonyms

Choose one word in the first bracket which means the opposite of one word in the second bracket:
1. (TAP, TUP, TOP)   (EWE, EYE, EVE)

Which one of the four words on the right bears a similar relationship to each of the words on the left:

2. EASY SOFT (PUTTY, HARD, SIMPLE, BRITTLE)

Memory

The subject is given digits orally and asked to repeat them. Most adults can manage to repeat around seven (telephone numbers and car registrations are about the limit). In young children, short sentences are sometimes given (Binet tests for example).

Number and letter series (Induction tests)

Fill in the missing number or letter:
   1. 60, 12, 3, 1, —, —.

   2. JFMAM ——, ——.

   3. 2, 6, 12, 20, —, —.

Ordering and classification

Arrange the following in descending order of complexity:
1. carnivore, vertebrate, animal, domestic cats, feline animals.

Which word does not belong in the list:

2. riot, subversion, turmoil, meeting, rebellion.

3. bit, piece, fraction, portion, a half.

Examples of non-verbal items are:

1. Find the patterns for the four missing pieces:

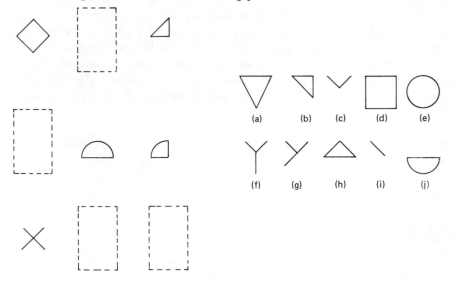

2. The two figures on the left have a feature in common. One *only* of the figures on the right has *not* the same feature. Which is it?

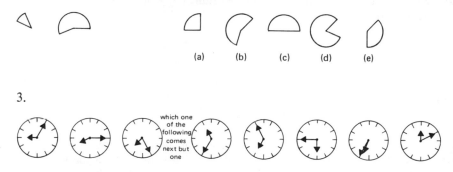

3.

     The most recent attempt to construct an ambitious scale based on contemporary ideas is at present taking place at the University of Manchester as the new British Intelligence Test (7). This individual test for the age range two to sixteen years, in addition to containing the usual verbal, numerical, spatial, memory and reasoning factors, also includes items for creative thinking (see next chapter). Another interesting inclusion under the headings of reasoning and number is a series of Piagetian sub-tests of operational thinking including measures of conservation.

SOME USES OF INTELLIGENCE TESTS

There are several ways of classifying intelligence tests. We can think of them in terms of (a) the group for whom they are intended (children or adults, low-grade or high-grade intellect, culture fair—that is 'free' from cultural biases which might depress or elevate scores unfairly); (b) whether for individual or group administration; (c) in terms of the general or special skills of those tested (verbal, spatial, performance, memory, numerical, and so forth). When we talk of intelligence tests it is most important to know and to specify which combination of these special features apply. It is also essential to note that intelligence test administration and interpretation is a skilled affair. Most tests require tuition and training before they can be used to the best advantage for reliable and valid results.

Verbal group tests (8), that is tests specifically designed for use with large numbers of children or adults, have been widely used since their introduction as a grammar school selection device. Their advantages are that large samples can be reliably tested in a relatively short time in the same conditions. They are particularly reliable for groups of older children and adults only where it is clear that written instructions are understood and motivation is likely to be maintained throughout the testing period. Where they do not prove reliable is in testing those at the extremes of the distribution. Also, with dull children the opportunity for personal contact and for elaborating on the test instructions is vital. It is also helpful to construct separate tests of high-grade intelligence (8) so as to obtain a greater degree of refinement and discrimination in the score range. This follows because where a test is intended to cover the whole range, the scores at the tail ends of the distribution cannot be sufficiently widespread to give a distinctive spectrum of scores.

Non-verbal group tests such as Raven's Progressive Matrices have been used as a supplementary and alternative measure in secondary schools. They are *not* culture fair, but they do provide additional evidence of mental competence where for some reason verbal opportunities in our culture have not been satisfactory. Specific group tests of number, mechanical and spatial skills are also available.

Individual tests are most helpful with pre-school, infant school and backward children where written communication, reading skills, motivation and concentration are amongst the particular problems which preclude group testing. The preamble to many group tests attempts to encourage continued participation during the testing session. Often the tests begin with a warming-up period to ensure that test instructions are fully understood. But even this care would not be adequate for young children. The administration of individual tests is a highly skilled and time-consuming job needing patience and knowledge of how to extract the best from young people. They form a crucial part of the diagnostic service provided by the Local Education Authority's (LEA) psychological service and student teachers should familiarize themselves with the functions of this service in relation to schoolchildren.

Tests for babies from the pre-natal stage onwards have been the focus of several researches. The best known test battery in this country was compiled by Griffiths (9) who derives an intelligence score from five major indices of infant behaviour skills. They are (1) locomotor (body movement, sitting, walking); (2) personal–social (reaction to other humans); (3) hearing and speech (response to aural stimuli, vocalization skills); (4) eye and hand (response to visual stimuli, hand–eye coordination, use of hands); and (5) performance (broadly reaction and manipulative skills in situations conjured up by the experimenter, for example if a baby is holding wooden blocks in both hands, what will it do if a third block is presented?). The norms were obtained by observing many babies and noting the average achievement for each age in the five ways mentioned above. The reliability (how close the performance is between several testings of the same child or group of children) of the scores, particularly below two years of age, is not very high. Progress in these first years is so rapid and erratic that precise measurements are not really feasible. However, as descriptive norms for use in diagnostic cases these measurements have proved to be of immense value.

In summary then, intelligence tests are used largely as diagnostic tools and as predictors of future performance. We have seen above their use with mentally defective children and their one-time place in secondary selection and streaming in both primary and secondary schools. Many schools still do use them as an aid to streaming or remediation. Vocational selection and guidance sometimes involves an IQ measure particularly for entry into the forces, civil service and occasionally into industry. Also some universities are beginning to add an IQ test to the existing selection procedures as a prognosticator of degree success.

FACTORS INFLUENCING MEASURED INTELLIGENCE

Age

We have already remarked on the complications of measuring adult intelligence. This is partly caused by the irregular development of mental ability and partly by the decline in mental ability beyond adolescence. In general, mental ability increases with chronological age up to fourteen or fifteen years of age in those of average ability. Naturally there are exceptions and irregularities in the development of individuals, but in the main the ratio of mental to chronological age is steady to mid-adolescence when a slow decline sets in until old age (10). If mental age is decreasing as chronological age increases, the mental ratio will gradually decline; hence we cannot use the method adopted by Binet and his associates for ascertaining the intelligence of adults.

There are, however, several limitations to be borne in mind when we are considering the results of research in this field. The particular methods and test materials we use to measure the ability of five year olds are conspicuously different from those for fifteen year olds or adults. Moreover, the longitudinal studies, in which the progress of an individual's mental development is plotted over a number of years, do not entirely support the evidence for this early decline in measured intelligence as do the cross-sectional studies carried out by testing different age groups at one time. Some longitudinal studies show continued development up to fifty years of age particularly in verbal skills. However, the present consensus of evidence (figure 9.2) points to a slow decline which varies with the mental stimulation experienced by the individual. Those who continue to be mentally active after mid-adolescent schooling are more likely to have continued growth in verbal ability than others (11). This fact has a special significance at a time when the school-leaving age is being raised, one consequence of which will be prolonged contact with verbal learning.

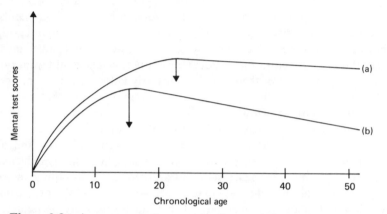

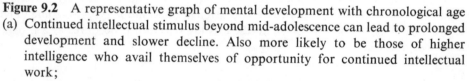

Figure 9.2   A representative graph of mental development with chronological age
(a) Continued intellectual stimulus beyond mid-adolescence can lead to prolonged development and slower decline. Also more likely to be those of higher intelligence who avail themselves of opportunity for continued intellectual work;
(b) Those who do not continue with intellectual pursuits beyond mid-adolescence experience an earlier and more rapid decline than in (a) above

Coaching (6)

Apart from the natural development alluded to above, it is possible to induce increased scores by coaching people in the ways of answering intelligence test items. Coaching for the 11+ became big business at one stage. It was possible to find primary schools with 'Intelligence' as a set period on the timetable. The abolition of the 11+ has largely dispensed with this kind of class activity. Even without coaching, one can obtain average variations on retesting children in the order of ± 7 IQ points. But coaching can create exceptional increases of a temporary nature. In some instances this has amounted to 30 or 40 IQ points, though on average the increase is in the region of 15 IQ points at the maximum. Any increase also tends to level out after several coaching sessions and to fade with time.

Effects of home and school

There are striking differences in the way people from different cultures resolve their

problems. Many may rarely, if ever, have used a symbolic code to solve abstract problems as in verbal reasoning. The perceptual emphases of a culture must also have an
influence on the solution of spatial tasks. For example, there is less preoccupation with
linearity in some African tribes than in some western cultures, consequently the latter
are more susceptible to vertical and horizontal line arrangements [and to illusions (12)].
It is hardly surprising then to find gross anomalies in the IQ measures of western and
non-western cultures. The measurement of immigrant IQs is an obvious illustration.
The art of devising intelligence tests which are reliable and valid for all cultures has
therefore never been satisfactorily accomplished. Some psychologists (Cattell, see later)
claim to have found *culture-fair* or *culture-free* items, but the overwhelming opinion
from the evidence is that there is no such thing as a culture-fair test. Whichever medium
we try to communicate in—verbally, spatially, and so forth—it is evident that cultural
differences produce variations in test results. Vernon (13) concludes that:

> while western tests often worked well in other cultural groups especially when slightly
> adapted to increase their intelligibility and acceptability, it is generally preferable to devise
> new ones locally to suit the modes of perception, the language background and concepts
> of the particular culture.

Nearer home we find similar inadequacies of conventional tests when comparing
people from different sub-cultures. Wiseman (14) in a large-scale research of fourteen
year olds in the Manchester area found, amongst other things, that an adverse environment is relatively more devastating for the intellectual development of the above-average
child. His second important conclusion, which is a strong source of controversy, is that
intelligence is more closely related to environmental factors (home area circumstances
such as birth and death rate, infantile mortality, percentage subnormal children, population density in the school catchment area) than to attainment at school. Douglas (15), in
a longitudinal study of socio-economic, physical and intellectual variables from the
prenatal stage onwards confirms the mass of evidence showing differences between the
IQs of children from different social backgrounds. Moreover, the difference widens as
the children grow older. The importance of parental encouragement and enthusiasm in
the academic progress of the children as a factor in improved performance at school is
again substantiated by his study. Other questions relating to the inequality of opportunities for children from disadvantaged homes to develop their full intellectual potential, and the effect this has on their chances of succeeding in the 11+ régime or any
selection system, are well documented elsewhere (16).

Family size has been found to correlate negatively with measured intelligence, which
suggests that children who belong to large families tend to have lower IQs than those in
smaller families (17). The reasons are still obscure. It could be that children with several
brothers or sisters have less opportunity for adult contact and are therefore restricted
in their linguistic exchanges. Again, large families may be the product of less intelligent
parents, thus giving less intelligent children. Also the smaller family might enjoy greater
economic and educational advantages than larger families.

Attempting to assess the influence of school on achievement whilst controlling for
general ability and background factors is difficult. However, Jensen (18), in a thorough,
carefully designed project, compared the influence of the school system in California

during the first eight years of schooling amongst negro, Mexican-American and white-American children. His major conclusion was that children from different ethnic groups, by and large, made similar progress. Put another way, the schools did not depress or elevate the scholastic achievements of minority groups in comparison with majority groups. Furthermore, whatever differences existed at the beginning of school life, there was no increase as time went by. Technically, a progressive increase in achievement differentials is known as a *cumulative deficit*, but Jensen found no evidence for such a deficit. He consequently concluded that as far as the Californian State system of education was concerned, children from minority groups were not cheated of achievement opportunities in conventional educational settings. Implictly, Jensen's work also points to the conclusion that children's intellectual potential has already been largely decided before formal schooling [note (19) Eysenck, 1972]. But the subject is still a source of heated dispute (19) especially where the discussion involves the differences between ethnic or social groups.

Jensen (20) also makes the interesting proposal that environmental influences obey a 'threshold' effect. That is, below a certain range of intelligence (not specified precisely) the influence of the environment is of paramount importance, whilst above the range it becomes progressively less influential. The principle is said to work in the same way as the vitamin supply to the body. The latter can only assimilate so much (up to a certain threshold) beyond which further quantities are eliminated and serve no useful nutritional purposes. Also, the very bright are proportionately more able to cope with environmental disadvantages. In the next chapter we shall see that amongst the highly intelligent it becomes difficult to distinguish the more creative minds. Further, personality may play a vital role in the expression of intelligent behaviour.

Heredity and environment

The problem of the relative contributions of inherited intellectual qualities and environmental conditions in the determination of a person's measured intelligence, the well-known 'nature/nurture' argument, has been obstinate and unresolved. In fact, the refined mathematical and methodological 'nit-picking' which the problem has generated would probably leave most students cold, and would be of little benefit in its detail. We shall, therefore, tread a middle way in looking briefly at the broad issues. There are very few who would ascribe all the variation in IQ to either environmental or genetic differences.

'Proof' that a particular proportion of measured intelligence is due to heredity or environment is not possible, and can only be estimated indirectly since the two influences are interactive from the moment of conception (see earlier in the chapter). Teasing out the threads which are 'purely' innate or 'purely' environmental is not, as yet, within the capabilities of behavioural scientists. The main indirect lines of evidence have come from the study of intellectual genealogies, twin studies, and relatives reared together and apart.

Galton's study (21) of eminent people showed that eminence seemed to be prevalent in some families more than others—evidence from selective breeding in much the same way as producing fine race horses. The study, unfortunately, did overlook the possibility that the home of an eminent person might have a marked effect on the children in terms of encouragement, availability of literature, the presence of a wide and varied collection of objects—enriched 'environment', 'intelligent' games and rituals, and so forth. At the other extreme we find the Kallikak family reported by Goddard (22). A certain Martin Kallikak (false name) had children by two women; one was feeble-minded, the other was of normal intelligence. The feeble-minded mother gave rise to a high proportion of feeble-minded descendants whilst the mother with normal intelligence had no feeble-

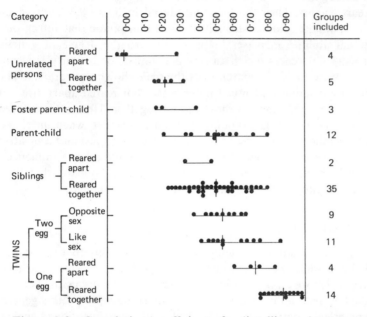

Figure 9.3 Correlation coefficients for 'intelligence' test scores from 52 studies. Some studies reported data for more than one relationship category; some included more than one sample per category, giving a total of 99 groups. Over two-thirds of the correlation coefficients were derived from IQs, the remainder from special tests (for example, Primary Mental Abilities). Midparent–child correlation was used when available, otherwise mother–child correlation. Correlation coefficients obtained in each study are indicated by dark circles; medians are shown by vertical lines intersecting the horizontal lines which represent the ranges.
Reprinted from L. Erlenmeyer-Kimling and L. F. Jarvik, 'Genetics and intelligence', *Science*, **142**, 1478, copyright 1963 with the permission of the American Association for the Advancement of Science

minded children at all. At a pinch, we could argue that the living conditions of the feeble-minded parent would be most likely to foster dull children, although the contrast in the two sets of data is rather striking.

Twin studies form the commonest line of investigation. Monozygotic twins, that is two youngsters created from one fertilized egg which has accidentally broken apart at an early stage and given two identical eggs, have precisely the same genetic endowment. Dizygotic twins occur when two separate eggs are fertilized at roughly the same time and grow in the womb side by side. They have similar genetic relationships as we might find amongst brothers and sisters (sometimes called *siblings*). A recent survey of the research literature on the correlations between the intelligence of people of varying degrees of family relationship reared together and apart has been conducted by Erlenmeyer-Kimling and Jarvik (23). It shows an impressive picture of orderly decreases in the values of correlations from high for the monozygotic twins reared together to no correlation for unrelated people reared apart. Their work is reproduced in figure 9.3 from which they conclude that the accumulated studies strongly support the opinion that 'intragroup resemblance in intellectual abilities increases in proportion to the degree of genetic relationship'. Note also the differences which can be accounted for by early environmental conditions. Take, for example, the extremes of the scale shown in figure 9.3. The monozygotic twins with, by definition, identical inheritance, but reared apart, are not so closely related in measured intelligence as those reared together. Unrelated children reared apart give, as would be expected, a random relationship whilst, when unrelated children are reared together, their similar environment is sufficient to produce a positive correlation. The intervening variable in both these examples is child-rearing influences. We are left, then, in much the same dilemma as when we started knowing that both nature and nurture are inextricably related during intellectual development.

THE STRUCTURE OF ABILITIES

A common theme throughout the study of intelligence is the possibility that we possess a fundamental general ability which we bring to bear on all problems—a kind of general level of mental efficiency which we all possess in some degree. In the discussions above, we met with several kinds of items all purporting to measure some aspect of this general intelligence. Verbal, numerical, spatial and mechanical skills were mentioned which, whilst displaying individual variations, may nevertheless be subsumed to give a level of ability we call '*g*'—general ability.

The question was first effectively examined around the turn of the century when Spearman introduced a mathematical technique called *factor analysis*. He endeavoured to determine the extent to which all the various kinds of problems thought to reflect intelligence really did possess something in common. It is not an easy subject and the reader would be advised to look at a basic text (24) if he wishes to understand the principles on which the method is based. For our present purpose, only sufficient will be mentioned to give the reader an idea of how the important models of the structure of human ability have appeared.

When two variables, let us say size of house and the income of the occupant, alter together, we say they are correlated [see note (8) at the end of chapter 14]. With the variables we have chosen, it would be safe to conclude that the larger a man's income, the more likely it is that he will own a larger house. This relationship would give a positive, but not perfect, correlation. Where an increase in one variable is accompanied by a decrease in a second (intelligence and family size), we have a negative correlation. Two unrelated variables (intelligence and eye colour) show no correlation. If we obtain a systematic change in several variables, it could well be that there is some common causal factor. For example, in the illustration using a man's income, we would probably find many other related variables especially in material possessions (car, TV, furniture, etc.), the common denominator being his salary. Applying this to human ability, suppose the scores on several tests purporting to identify intelligent behaviour were all positively intercorrelated, it could be concluded that there is a basic factor underpinning this common relationship. The mathematical procedure of factor analysis seeks to identify and isolate these common factors by using the correlations between the variables.

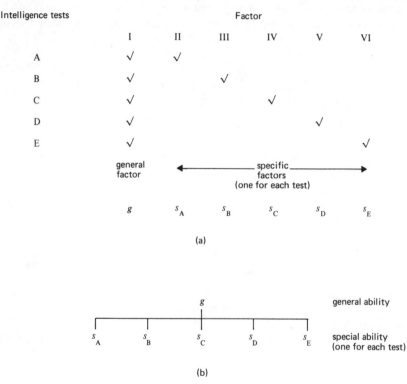

Figure 9.4 Diagrammatic representation of Spearman's Two-Factor Theory

Spearman, using a prototype factor analysis, formulated his *Two-Factor Theory* (25). His view was rooted in the assumption that general ability—referred to as '*g*' for convenience—accounted in substantial measure for differences in human performance. You will remember his belief that intelligence consisted of 'the eduction of relations and correlates'. Further, each test was thought to require a specific ability, '*s*', unique to each test. Specific ability accounted for the unevenness in an individual's score from one kind of test to another over and above his minimum competence in all the tests (*g*). A boy with high general ability would therefore be expected to perform well in most aspects of an intelligence test, whilst at the same time displaying variations in test scores arising from his special talents. Spearman's 'two factors', then, consisted of *g*- and *s*-type factors.

Figure 9.4(a) shows that all the tests deemed to measure intelligence are sufficiently intercorrelated for them to appear together as factor I. Then follows a separate column for each test to indicate that certain variations in the test scores are due to the specific and unique demands made by each. A simpler diagrammatic view is given in figure 9.4(b).

This over-simplified theory was soon superseded by the work of the late Sir Cyril Burt who proposed the *hierarchical group-factor theory* widely supported in Great Britain. Spearman's choice of test material was restricted and insufficient to allow for the existence of groups of tests which reflected common skills. Many tests, for instance, require verbal ability, in addition to a specific ability. Therefore Burt suggested 'group' factors as well as *g* and *s*. Group factors are illustrated in figure 9.5 which also attempts

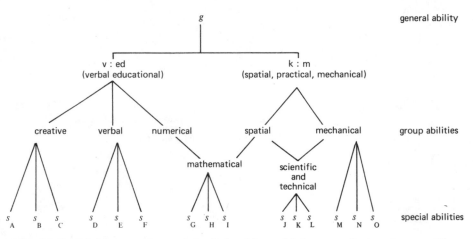

Figure 9.5 Diagrammatic model of the hierarchial group-factor theory. These include some of the main group factors underlying tests relevant to educational and vocational achievements
Adapted from P. E. Vernon, *Intelligence and Cultural Environment*, Methuen, London, 1969, p. 22

to show the tree-like connections postulated in the hierarchical theory of Burt and developed by Vernon (13).

Thurstone, an American psychologist, was not satisfied with the all-inclusive measure *g* because it revealed so little of the special talents of each person. In the 1930s he employed another factor analytical procedure which compounded *g* and *s* to give several factors referred to as *primary mental abilities*. Examples of these are verbal comprehension (V), number ability (N), word fluency (W), perceptual flexibility and speed, inductive reasoning, rote memory (M) and deductive reasoning. They are sometimes denoted by initial letters as shown in some cases above. Thurstone, it should be noted, did not deny the possibility of a general factor, but his factor approach enabled him to isolate independent mental abilities which he regarded as more productive when applied to educational or vocational guidance. For him, it was more revealing to have a broad profile of an individual's mental abilities than an overall measure.

Finally, we turn briefly to two contemporary, sophisticated models of human ability expounded by Cattell and Guilford. To understand the implications of these theories the reader would need to refer to more advanced texts, but the following very simple outline should serve as an introduction. Cattell (26) has advanced a theory in which two general factors are postulated, namely, fluid (g_f) and crystallized (g_c) general ability. g_f is regarded as a measure of the influence of biological factors on intellectual development and thought to be comparable to inherited ability. g_c represents the outcome of cultural experiences such as parental and educational contacts. Clearly g_f and g_c are not directly related to Hebb's Intelligence A and B respectively because, as we have already noted, the latter cannot be directly assessed, whereas Cattell has claimed to have measured both g_f and g_c.

Guilford's model of the intellect was first proposed in the early 1950s (27). This ambitious model postulates no less than 120 mental factors, of which he claims to have exposed about 80. He derives the mental factors from three independent dimensions which he calls *operations, contents* and *products;* that is, each intelligent act requires the individual to carry out various thinking 'operations' (such as memory, convergent thinking, divergent thinking) using 'content' media (such as symbols, figures or semantics) in order to 'produce' such things as classes, relations or implications. With this three-dimensional arrangement, 5 operations × 4 contents × 6 products, we get 120 possibilities for intellectual factors.

Both theories are speculative and the subject of criticism and controversy. Their value lies in the options which they offer in a field where there is still plenty of scope for hypothesis and experimentation. Two operations mentioned by Guilford will be central to our discussion of creative thinking in the next chapter. They are convergent and divergent thinking.

SUMMARY

The concept of intelligence and intelligence testing has been with us for some time and is probably going to stay for a good while longer. Whilst intelligence tests are by no means perfect, they are certainly amongst the most reliable of tests so far constructed. Educators and psychologists have used them extensively and with sufficient success for us to feel justified in noting their application with children.

We started the chapter on a cautious note by defining intelligent behaviour instead of intelligence. This was done to set the record straight about intelligence not being a fixed quantity, and to show that our concern should be for the quality rather than the quantity of human behaviour. Heim's definition, that intelligence involves grasping the essentials in a situation and responding appropriately to them, was used as the basis for a discussion of the subject because it incorporated the biological and psychological views of behaviour as well as serving as an operational definition.

Inborn intellectual potential cannot be assessed directly. Similarly, the influence of the environment cannot be readily estimated. Indirect sampling of some aspects of intelligent behaviour by the use of standardized tests is the nearest we have come to judging the intellectual ability and potential of individuals. The mathematical technique of factor analysis has been used to show a differentiation between the verbal, numerical, mechanical and spatial abilities of humans. These abilities have, in turn, formed the nucleus of numerous standardized tests used with both primary and secondary school children as prognostic and diagnostic tools.

But intelligence tests scores are not fixed for each person. There are many reasons for fluctuations in an individual's IQ score. The age of a person, whether he or she is coached, the ethnic and cultural experiences of social background, all contribute in differing degrees to the variability of test scores. Early childhood experiences also seem to have a marked effect on the extent to which intellectual potential finally emerges. The abandonment of 11 + selection was partly the result of anomalous IQ measures as, for example, occurred when retesting of the same children occasionally produced conflicting scores or when a child's mental age developed more rapidly than his chronological age, especially in early adolescence (sometimes known as *late development*).

The unresolved nature/nurture controversy is likewise a dispute about what a child brings with him into the world and the effect which particular home, community and school provisions can have upon his intellectual development. At present, most psychologists have tentatively settled for a middle-of-the-road policy in recognizing that interactive effects between inborn potential and environmental pressures culminate in an insoluble complex of behaviour characteristics. Twin studies and research using family trees have only partly answered the problem becuase they show equally well the effects of both inheritance and environment. In the meantime, and in the face of mounting evidence [Jensen, note (18)], teachers must continue to be optimistic about the role of the school in developing intellectual skills.

Most educators are dedicated to the task of accommodating to the individual differences displayed by children. The teacher, in the face of large classes, is set an almost impossible task of not only distinguishing the individual characteristics of his children but also of providing appropriate individual tuition to suit these characteristics. At the very least, the study and judicious application of intelligence and intelligence tests has something of value in it for teachers who wish to discover some background information about their children. IQs are not sufficient of themselves to direct the educational patterns adopted by teachers. They must be used alongside other measures of scholastic variability such as the attitudes of children to work, school and teachers, motives, interests, achievement in specific subject areas and personality.

In these days of a growing conscience about the provision for the educationally underprivileged, the gifted, the backward, and the increased use of unstreamed classes, the teacher needs every available test he can depend on. Intelligence tests, if administered satisfactorily, should provide him with a valuable piece of supplementary evidence in deciding a child's educational programme.

ENQUIRY AND DISCUSSION

1. Using whichever sources and resources are available (college or department libraries, school, tutors, etc.) discover as much as you can about the range and use of intelligence tests. It might prove helpful to invite guest speakers from the Local Educational Authority Child Guidance Service to talk about psychological testing, especially about the use made of intelligence tests. Also explore the use of IQ tests in vocational

guidance, diagnosis of educationally or severely subnormal children and selection procedures for the services, schools, and universities.

2. Discuss with the group tutor how you would set about testing a group of children (or an individual) with an intelligence test. Inspect a range of test materials for this purpose and note carefully the manual of instructions and the kind of items used. Include a consideration of:

(a) the age of the children;
(b) the tests most appropriate for your purposes;
(c) where one can obtain the tests and their price;
(d) administration and scoring procedures;
(e) how to interpret the scores and relate them to school work;
(f) other possible achievement tests.

3. What are the advantages and disadvantages of having and using a concept of intelligence in educational matters?

4. Examine the possible reasons for:

(a) the problem of defining the nature of intelligence;
(b) the negative correlation between family size and IQ;
(c) the decline of mental age with age (are there compensatory gains?);
(d) the effects of coaching;
(e) the difficulty of producing a culture-free test of intelligence;
(f) ethnic differences in measured IQ;
(g) the difficulty of measuring the ability of babies.

5. What is meant by the expression 'a child has an IQ of 105'? What other information would you require when making a statement about the child's IQ in relation to other children? Explain why you need this additional information. Is intelligence normally distributed in the population?

6. Discuss the evidence for and against the importance of heredity and environment in defining the intellectual competence of an individual.

7. What are the strengths and weaknesses of streaming according to ability? Consider the position of the mentally gifted and mentally dull in your consideration of streaming.

8. Examine the research literature with respect to the relationship between intelligence and academic achievement in one of the following sectors of education:

(a) primary schools;
(b) secondary schools;
(c) some field of higher education.

9. British psychologists, in the main, tend to favour the concept of general intelligence or '*g*', whilst American psychologists prefer to regard intelligence in terms of several distinct mental abilities. Consider the pros and cons of these two points of view (you will find the books by Butcher and Vernon in Further Reading a good starting point).

NOTES AND REFERENCES

1. A. W. Heim, *The Appraisal of Intelligence*, NFER, Slough, 1970.

2. T. R. Miles, 'Symposium: Contributions to intelligence testing and the theory of intelligence', *Br. J. educ. Psychol.*, **27**, 153–210 (1957).

3. C. Burt, 'The evidence for the concept of intelligence', *Br. J. educ. Psychol.*, **25**, 158–177 (1955).

4. D. O. Hebb, *The Organization of Behavior*, Wiley, New York, 1949 and *A Textbook of Psychology*, 2nd ed., Saunders, Philadelphia, 1966.

5. P. E. Vernon, 'The assessment of children', in *Studies in Education*, University of London Institute of Education, 1955, pp. 189–215.

6. P. E. Vernon, *Intelligence and Attainment Tests*, University of London Press, London, 1960.

7. F. W. Warburton, 'Construction of the new British Intelligence Scale', *Bull. Br. psychol. Soc.*, **19**, 68–70 (1966).

8. There are many group tests on the market. Most can be obtained from the National Foundation for Educational Research. But there are restrictions imposed on test users to safeguard the reliability of the tests and their correct usage. The NFER supply a catalogue of the tests in their stock. Several have been produced by the Foundation and Moray House. Two high-grade tests have been published for A. W. Heim under the titles of AH5 and AH6. Non-verbal tests such as Raven's Progressive Matrices and Koh's Blocks are also obtainable from this source.

9. R. Griffiths, *The Abilities of Babies*, University of London Press, London, 1954.

10. For a recent summary of the work on age and growth of intelligence see D. B. Bromley, *The Psychology of Human Ageing*, Penguin, London, 1966.

11. R. B. Burns, 'Age and mental ability: re-testing with thirty-three years' interval', *Br. J. educ. Psychol.*, **36**, 116 (1966).

12. S. Biesheuvel, 'Psychological tests and their application to non-European peoples', *Yearbook of Education*, Evans, London, 1949. Also see R. L. Gregory, *Eye and Brain*, Weidenfeld and Nicolson, London, 1967, for a discussion of illusions and their effect on Zulus.

13. P. E. Vernon, *Intelligence and Cultural Environment*, Methuen, London, 1969.

14. S. Wiseman. *Education and Environment*, Manchester University Press, Manchester, 1964.

15. J. W. B. Douglas, *The Home and the School*, MacGibbon and Kee, London, 1964; J. W. B. Douglas, J. M. Ross and H. R. Simpson, *All Our Future: a Longitudinal Study of Secondary Education*, Davies, London, 1968.

16. A summary of the writing and research into social class and educational opportunity

can be found in D. F. Swift, 'Social class and educational adaptation', in H. J. Butcher and H. B. Pont (Eds), *Educational Research in Britain*, vol. 1, University of London Press, London, 1968.

17. A review of research into family size and intelligence can be found in J. D. Nisbet, *Family Environment*, Cassell, London, 1953.

18. A. R. Jensen, 'Do schools cheat minority children?', *Educ. Res.*, **14**, 3–28 (1971).

19. Comments on Jensen's paper (note 18) made by Sir Cyril Burt, H. J. Butcher, H. J. Eysenck, J. Nisbet and P. E. Vernon can be found in *Educ. Res.*, **14**, 87–100 (1972).

20. A. R. Jensen, 'The culturally disadvantaged: Psychological and educational aspects', *Educ. Res.*, **10**, 4–20 (1967).

21. F. Galton, *Hereditary Genius: An Enquiry into its Laws and Consequences*, 2nd ed., Horizon, New York, 1892.

22. H. H. Goddard, *The Kallikak Family*, Macmillan, New York, 1921.

23. L. Erlenmeyer-Kimling and L. F. Jarvik, 'Genetics and intelligence', *Science*, **142**, 1477–1479 (1963).

24. D. Child, *The Essentials of Factor Analysis*, Holt, Rinehart and Winston, London, 1970.

25. C. Spearman, 'General intelligence objectively determined and measured', *Am. J. Psychol.*, **15**, 202–293 (1904).

26. R. B. Cattell, 'Theory of fluid and crystallized intelligence: a critical experiment', *J. educ. Psychol.*, **54**, 1–22 (1963) and 'The theory of fluid and crystallized intelligence checked at the 5–6 year-old level', *Br. J. educ. Psychol.*, **37**, 209–224 (1967).

27. For Guilford's most recent elaboration see J. P. Guilford, 'The structure of intelligence', in D. K. Whitla (Ed.), *Handbook of Measurement and Assessment in the Behavioural Sciences*, Addison-Wesley, Reading, Mass., 1968.

FURTHER READING

H. J. Butcher, *Human Intelligence: Its Nature and Assessment*, Methuen, London, 1968. A clear, detailed and well-written account.

D. Child, *The Essentials of Factor Analysis*, Holt, Rinehart and Winston, London, 1970. An introductory text for those with a little knowledge of statistics.

A. W. Heim, *The Appraisal of Intelligence*, NFER, Slough, 1970. An interesting alternative view of intelligence.

P. E. Vernon, *Intelligence and Attainment Tests*, University of London Press, London, 1960. Intended for students in psychology and teacher-training.

P. E. Vernon, *Intelligence and Cultural Environment*, Methuen, London, 1969.

ANSWERS TO INTELLIGENCE TEST ITEMS

Analogies: 1. (c) seem (first one and last two letters common to both).
   2. (d) bitch.
   3. *composer* is to *notes*.

Synonyms: 1. Slake—quench.
   2. Preen—trim feathers.

Antonyms: 1. Tup—ewe.
   2. easy, soft—hard.

Number and letter series:
   1. 1/2, 1/2. Starting with 1/2 at the left hand side, multiply it by 1, then multiply this answer by 2, and the next answer by 3, and so on.
   2. JJ (months of the year].
   3. 30, 42 (1 × 2, 2 × 3, 3 × 4, etc.).

Ordering and classification:
   1. Animal, vertebrate, carnivore, feline animals, domestic cats.
   2. meeting.
   3. a half (a word signifying a precise quantity).

Find the patterns:
   1.

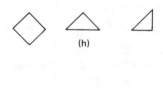

(h)

(e)

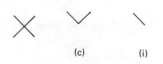

(c)   (i)

   2. (c)—the others are three-sided figures.
   3. a quarter to six (next but one!).

10   Creative thinking

There can be few students who have not encountered the concept of creative thinking in one form or another, or failed to detect the upsurge of interest in recent years. At a national level, we are told that advanced industrial societies cannot survive, develop or compete without the continued emergence of creative people in ever-increasing numbers in political, social and scientific pursuits. This has prompted many governments to sponsor research dedicated to the task of identifying, measuring, cultivating and exploiting creative talent. At a more homely level for student teachers, we find classroom practices increasingly involving such highly technical and unvalidated methods as 'creative writing', 'imaginative' work in art and drama or 'discovery methods'.

For psychologists, there are at least three factors which have contributed to the increase in enthusiasm for research in creative thinking. One is that conventional tests of intelligence have not convincingly demonstrated that they can distinguish the potentially creative from the not so creative. Teachers, incidentally, have suspected this for a long time, and the point was made in chapter 9 that Intelligence C is but a sampling of human ability. It is just possible that the kind of items we find on an IQ test demand a particular kind of thinking strategy which may not entirely tap the creative capacities of those tested. We shall return to this point later. As Liam Hudson observes in his book *Contrary Imaginations*, when you look at a class of bright boys and girls with high measures of intelligence it is virtually impossible to pick out those who will go on to be creative people from those who will not. Thus, whilst it remains true that creative individuals are amongst those with high intelligence, the relationship between creative capacity and IQ is not straightforward.

The second reason for the upsurge in enthusiasm for creative thinking is the knowledge explosion which has tended to render conventional modes of learning and teaching of limited efficiency. The teaching of science, especially in preparation for examinable subjects, has frequently taken the form of 'here are the facts, now use them'. This is not to deny the central importance of fact assimilation and recall, but where the psychologist's interests lie is in the strategies of learning and reasoning which the situation imposes on the child, and the lasting influence these might have on the way he tackles problems. Heim's definition of intelligence in the previous chapter—the grasping of essentials in a situation and responding appropriately—goes only part of the way to an understanding of creative human behaviour because there is also the important preliminary step of exploring the situation and deciding on those essentials. Learning tactical skills of approaching a task in an open-minded fashion and selecting the important aspects in arriving at solutions may well be enhanced or inhibited by the learning methods we encourage in the classroom.

Thirdly, we have long been interested in the interaction between cognitive and non-cognitive variables. Doubtless there are aspects of personality, motivation, will (that is qualities other than purely cognitive ones) which are involved in creativeness. The adoption of particular thinking strategies, in addition to being acquired as part of learning at home or in school, may also be a function of personality. Creative ability has long been associated with personality and we shall return to this point later.

DEFINING CREATIVITY

You will have noticed that I have avoided using the word *creativity* up to this point. It is amongst the most confused and misused concepts in the study of human behaviour and we need to understand this before using the term. Both American and British psychologists have been known to use it synonymously with 'imagination', 'originality', 'divergent thinking', 'inventiveness', 'intuition', 'venturesomeness', 'exploration', 'giftedness', and so on. The truth is we know very little about what makes a creative person and even less about the determinants of creativity. Consequently, there is no clear, unambiguous and widely accepted definition of creativity.

The reasons for this difficulty of definition are not hard to find. Consider, for example, the question of aesthetic enterprises in art, music, sculpture or writing. What objective criterion can we use to evaluate the 'amount' of creativity which has taken place in a work of art? Many would rightly say that it is a pointless question anyway because it depends too much upon value judgements within a cultural context. There is no sense in which we can arrive at a widely accepted judgement of creativeness since in art, music or writing one man's meat is another man's poison. For this reason, attention tends to have been directed to scientific discovery rather than to artistic creations in the study of creative thinking. There may well be a common thread running through the fabric of man's artistic and scientific creativity, but at present we have no idea what it might be. Another problem is the confusion arising from our concern to describe the processes involved in creative activity from an observation of the products. We tacitly assume that particular modes of thinking have taken place when certain kinds of response appear. Later we shall discuss 'divergent' thinking—a term which implies certain kinds of mental action. But we shall also mention a theory by Wallas about the stages in a creative act which he deduced from biographies and the introspections of creative people who were deliberately analysing in detail all the conscious physical and mental states occurring simultaneously with creative activity.

There is some measure of agreement that, at its simplest, cognitive creativity (it is hard at this point in our knowledge to include aesthetic creativity as well) results in ideas which are novel, useful and relevant to the solution of problems being examined. Novelty is used here in the sense of combining or rearranging established patterns of knowledge in unique fashions; of course, this can happen at many different levels, as when children constantly create new ideas which, for them, are completely original, but which within their culture are quite familiar. Originality at the highest level would have to occur in the much wider context of the world of knowledge. Nevertheless, many studies are based on the assumption that fluency, variety and novelty of ideas contrived by young people, using familiar material, signify a potentially creative mind.

Not all novel responses reflect creative talent. False answers are novel; so are the bizarre statements and actions of the mentally ill, but we could hardly classify these as creative in the cognitive sense. Originality, then, is not enough. There must be a measure of relevance to the solution of a problem as well. Usefulness is not quite so obvious because in science we often find that an original idea has no immediate application and must wait for advances in other fields before it becomes useful.

ASSESSING CREATIVITY

Before we can focus upon the specific sense in which we shall use the term creativity, it is necessary to give an appraisal of the attempts made to assess it. A concept which is difficult to define is difficult to measure. Consequently, a number of approaches to the study of creativity have developed in this century. Perhaps the three most promising are (1) studies of the life styles of creative people; (2) assessment, using operational definitions, of the *products* of creative activity; (3) attempts to discover the *processes* of creative activity. Of these, the first and second have been employed with somewhat greater regularity than the last, because observing people's behaviour is much less suspect and demonstrably easier than trying to discover the processes of internal mental behaviour.

(1) Creative people

The search for distinguishing characteristics and capacities of creative people has a fairly long history. In the cognitive domain, it is still widely held that creative ability is largely a manifestation of the highly intelligent. Thus, in order to find creative people you would look amongst those with high intelligence. One of the earliest and certainly the most extensive studies is that of Terman (1) whose famous longitudinal study of gifted American children is an outstanding masterpiece. 'Gifted' in this case is defined as an IQ greater than 140 on the Terman–Merrill Intelligence Test. In seeking out those with the highest IQs, Terman clearly believed in a linear connection between IQ and creative talent.

However, his, and subsequent, work is especially interesting for the light it sheds on the personality characteristics of highly intelligent and creative people. This group has been revisited periodically from the early 1920s up to the present day (2) when Oden retested a portion of the group. She compared the childhood of the top and bottom 100 men selected by compounding professional productivity, the extent of responsibility, influence and authority over others, honours and income. In other words, the status afforded by society to its most highly productive members was used to distinguish two groups for the research. A detailed interview with each individual revealed that the top group had less illness and greater stability in the home during childhood. Many more of the top group came from professional homes where parents had well-defined attitudes about education and gave positive encouragement to the children to do well at school.

Learning tended to be valued for its own sake by their parents. There was also a higher need to achieve in the top group during early childhood.

Roe (3) and MacKinnon (4), again in the United States, confirmed most of the characteristics suggested by Oden using short-term, intensive interviews of eminent and widely accepted experts from certain professions. MacKinnon, in fact, invited his subjects to a weekend gathering at which personal, social and biographical information was compiled. Biographical similarities in most enquiries in this area are quite striking. For some professional groups, for instance psychologists, architects, biologists and anthropologists, it seems that a permissive, settled, middle-class home with loose if not strained emotional ties, is the prerequisite for creative thinkers. MacKinnon (6) remarks that the parents of creative architects, for example, had an 'extraordinary respect for the child and confidence in his ability to do what was appropriate'. One exception is the scientists in Roe's work, particularly physicists and mathematicians, who seem to have had a lion's share of distress in childhood. Separation of the parents, strict and conventional upbringing (5) and illness were the commonest sources of distress. Roe's explanation is that scientists might be seeking to compensate for their earlier insecurity by choosing occupations which, superficially at least, involve convergent and clear-cut procedures leading to well-defined goals. However, this provides a reason for subject choice rather than for creative talent.

Other generalizations about the qualities of creative men and women from these and other studies depict them as singleminded, stubborn, non-conformist and persistent in tasks which engage their imaginations. Tolerance to ambiguity (7) is high—they are not perturbed when a problem has a number of plausible solutions; they may even enjoy dilemmas and searching out problems which have diverse possibilities. Risk-taking and venturesomeness with ideas appeal to the creative mind. What we are not clear about is the evidence for distinctive qualities in the thinking styles adopted by creative people when they solve problems. The work of Harvey (8) and his colleagues on patterns of concept formation goes some way towards drawing attention to the relationship between the levels of abstraction attainable by individuals and their likelihood of producing original concepts. As one might have guessed, in general the higher the level of abstraction attainable by an individual, the more creative are his concepts.

What we have done in this section is to look a long way ahead to the 'finished article' and tease out some of the characteristics of creative people which may have their origins in childhood. What has not been attempted so far, is a longitudinal study with these characteristics in mind so as to trace life histories as they unfold. Notice the importance attached to personality and the possibility that creative men and women blossom from a unique blend of both personal and intellectual qualities.

(2) Divergent thinking

The criteria for judging an eminent person's talent in his special field are fairly obvious; he must create original ideas which can be clearly recognized as pushing forward the frontiers of knowledge in his specialism. But can we devise objective tests which would predict this creative talent?

New light was thrown on this problem by Guilford in the early 1950s when he introduced his 'model of the intellect' (see last chapter). He postulated several cognitive operations amongst which he included *convergent* and *divergent thinking*. The convergent thinker is distinguished by his ability in dealing with problems requiring one conventional correct solution clearly obtainable from the information available. Problems of this kind can be found in all intelligence tests and many 'objective-type' questions in which a problem is presented with several solutions, only one of which is correct. We have seen several examples in the last chapter of intelligence test items which require the testee to focus his attention and reasoning so as to provide a single correct solution. No opportunity is given for productive thinking beyond the information supplied; in fact, items with more than one solution are discarded as unsatisfactory.

The divergent thinker, on the other hand, is adept in problems requiring the generation of several equally acceptable solutions where the emphasis is on the quantity, variety and originality of responses. Guilford's two categories attempt to discriminate between the style of problem-solving behaviour adopted in closed and open-ended problems. Although these are not exclusive processes (solving convergent problems might require a great deal of 'diverging' before a solution presents itself), in general the items of convergent and divergent thinking tests do encourage different approaches and it is this aspect which has led some psychologists to correlate divergent thinking with creative thinking. As yet, the relationship has still to be convincingly verified.

Guilford (9) has defined numerous kinds of divergent test items and there is mounting evidence to support the view (10) of there being distinct *verbal* and non-verbal (or *figural*) factors in ideational fluency. Of the verbal kind, the 'Uses of Objects' test, 'Consequences' test and the 'S' test are three of many in common usage. Here are some examples [for more detail see note (11)]:

Uses of Objects

Write down as many *different uses* as you can for a *BUCKET*. Work as quickly as possible and remember that points will be given for answers which are unusual.

Consequences

Below is given a change in the way we live. It is not likely to happen but you are asked to pretend it really does happen. Write down as many *different* results of the change as you can invent. Your score will depend on the number of *different* and *unusual* ideas as well as the *number* of ideas you can write.

The change is—we all have four fingers and no thumb on each hand.

'S' test

Write as many different five-letter words as you can beginning with S.

An example of a **number test** is:

Given the numbers 2, 3, 4, 5 and 6, construct as many different equations as you can using only these numbers (e.g. $5 - 4 + 2 + 3 = 6$).

Of the many non-verbal tests, the commonest in this country have been the 'circles', the 'squares' and the 'parallel lines' tests.

Circles   A page of circles (or squares) is presented to the subject and he is told to add lines to the circles (squares) to complete a recognizable drawing. Lines can be inside the circle, outside the circle or both inside and outside. The score depends on the number of objects, their variety and their originality. The 'parallel lines' test has a similar format.

The scoring techniques tell us quite a bit about the aims of the tests. There are three basic types of score obtainable. The first is a *fluency* score obtained by counting the number of responses given (but excluding those which are nonsensical or which do not answer the question as posed). In effect it is a measure of the speed with which the individual can summon up ideas. A second score can be obtained by grouping responses into categories. This score is known as *flexibility* and in effect measures the variety of

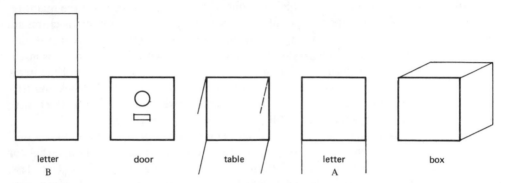

| letter | door | table | letter | box |
| B | | | A | |

Figure 10.1   Examples of answers to the 'squares' test of divergent thinking

responses given. The scorer's subjectivity enters into decisions about the groupings, but this can be partly offset by assembling the opinions of several judges and using the majority consensus [see Torrance's work (11)]. In figure 10.1 are shown five possible responses to the 'squares' test. The fluency score is five, but as the first and fourth responses fall into the same category of letters of the alphabet, the flexibility score is four. A third measure is called *originality* and is derived from the most infrequent responses. By counting the number of times a response occurs within the group under test, it is possible to arrive at a frequency distribution for each response and to allot scores for the least frequent. As these three types of score (i.e. fluency, flexibility and originality) are based on the same responses, it is not surprising to find high correlations between them.

In terms of the requirements for creativity outlined in the previous section, the divergent thinking tests leave a lot to be desired. The underlying assumption that divergent thinking scores correlate with future originality has yet to be experimentally established. Moreover, the responses are at a lower level of originality than would be required for, say, a new invention. The responses would serve no useful purpose and often display flights of fancy bordering on the grotesque, sadistic and trivial. What we have are two operational definitions of short-term thinking styles; one, the divergent kind, relying on ideational fluency in open-ended problems; the other, convergent thinking, favouring those who like homing-in on one solution. Much of the research on creativity has employed divergent thinking tests and we should bear in mind when reading the results of these researches the tenuous assumption that they give some clue to the creative ability or potential of individuals.

As we shall be referring to research in which divergent thinking scores have been used extensively it would be valuable to look at other examples of their shortcomings. Perhaps their most obvious drawback lies in the administration of the tests. They are usually timed and presented as a *test*, whereas a creative act may be time-consuming and require a relaxed atmosphere. Ideas frequently need to be chewed over before enlightenment occurs. The tension of a test situation may also militate against creative output. Wallach and Kogan (12) using untimed procedures in a playful atmosphere produced divergent thinking scores which were more clearly unrelated to IQ scores than had hitherto been obtained. Scoring the tests requires more subjective evaluation than does the scoring of standardized tests of intelligence. We saw the difficulty posed in arriving at a flexibility score, and a similar problem arises when we have to decide on the level to be chosen in awarding a score for originality using the least frequent responses. Wallach and Kogan used only unique responses (only occurring once in their sample), but others such as Torrance have accepted frequencies occurring in up to 15 per cent of their samples.

We shall return to some applications of divergent thinking tests later in the chapter.

(3) The creative process

Psychologists and teachers alike have long been intrigued by the processes of creative thought and after many years have little more than a handful of speculations. The most popular method of investigation has been the study of famous men in literature, science and mathematics using biography and interview.

Graham Wallas (13), after studying Helmholtz and Poincaré, recognized four stages in the creative cycle, namely preparation, incubation, inspiration (or illumination) and verification.

Preparation: the forerunner of the preparatory stage is the ability to spot a problem. The existence of a problem often excites and obsesses the creative mind so much that it becomes restless and disturbed. Preparation then takes place and involves a detailed investigation of all the possibilities surrounding the problem from reading, discussing and questioning to making notes and trying out solutions.

Incubation: following a period of deliberate activity in search of evidence and solutions comes a time when no conscious effort is made. This incubation period may be short or very extensive. Some authors in both arts and science have remarked on the time it sometimes takes for the germ of an idea to take shape. We have no idea what goes on during this period, but speculation has it that ideas are 'worked on' at a subconscious level to reform and evolve new combinations of ideas.

Inspiration: the sudden flash of insight; that penny-dropping sensation we all experience when a confusion of ideas suddenly takes shape. Sometimes it follows on sleep, during a walk or in the bath (Archimedes). Tchaikovsky in a letter to his patron

Frau von Merck describes his fourth symphony and makes a general comment about creative inspiration: 'As a rule the germ of a new work appears suddenly and unexpectedly. If the soul is fertile—that is to say, if the composer is suitably disposed—the seed takes root, rapidly shooting up stem, leaves and finally blossom.' We have here a classical example of the inspiration stage.

Verification: having bright ideas is one thing; they then require confirmation. Often the creator is fairly convinced of the veracity of his solution long before he puts it to the test. But there follows a stage of active revision, expansion and correction.

We see from this creative cycle that it is rarely, if ever, an event which happens over coffee. There is usually a time-consuming, tenacious and detailed period of mental activity. The inescapable conclusion from Wallas's work is that creative output needs time and effort.

DIVERGENT THINKING AND INTELLIGENCE

Following the appearance of Guilford's model of the intellect (see chapter 9) and his views on creativity (14), several researchers have attempted to confirm the independence of his convergent and divergent intellectual operations, the latter being taken as a measure of creativity. The earliest and most widely known research is that of Getzels and Jackson (15) in which twelve year olds in an American high school were given intelligence and divergent thinking tests. The scores were used to select two groups; one, the 'high creative', having high divergent and low IQ scores and the other, the 'high IQ', having the reverse of this arrangement of scores. These groups had similar achievement levels but they differed in several other important respects. 'High creatives' were less conformist, tended to overachieve and possessed a lively sense of humour when compared with the high IQ group. But the overall principal finding that IQ and divergent thinking scores were not significantly correlated, and therefore to be treated as separate entities, has been hotly contested largely on the grounds that Getzels' and Jackson's methods of analysis left much to be desired. Moreover, the sample chosen by them was restricted to the upper ranges of intelligence (average IQ score for the sample was 132), thus rendering the results somewhat untypical of the population.

Subsequent studies have tended to use more representative samples than Getzels and Jackson. The findings, in the main, have managed to show some degree of positive relationship between divergent thinking and IQ scores. Hasan and Butcher (16) carried out a close repetition of the American study using Scottish school children, but with a much wider and more characteristic range of IQ scores. The correlations between divergent thinking and IQ scores were all positive and significant, with some as high as $+0 \cdot 7$. In the few researches where no relationship has been found, the samples tend to be drawn from the upper end of the IQ range (17).

The case for or against the distinction between divergent thinking and intelligence is a difficult one to answer. Advanced mathematical procedures, such as factor analysis, and careful monitoring of test materials and their administration do tend to show a measure of separate identity, especially where the test materials involve 'ideational fluency', that is items designed and scored to show how quickly people can produce verbal or non-verbal responses. In this country, Sultan (16) was able to show a measure of independence using divergent tests which encouraged verbal ideational fluency. We have already mentioned the carefully constructed work of Wallach and Kogan (12) in which, it will be remembered, a completely tension-free and friendly atmosphere was created, no time limit was imposed, each child was questioned individually and scoring for originality responses was confined to unique answers.

In summary, the evidence at present points to a differentiation in the relationship between divergent test scores and IQ which depends on the level of IQ being considered. At low and moderate levels of IQ a linear relationship holds. Beyond a broad *threshold* of somewhere in the region of 110–120 IQ in tests with a standard deviation of 15, the relationship of intelligence and divergent scores appear to become increasingly random; in other words, the highly intelligent are less predictable in their divergent thinking ability. This tallies with Hudson's observation that in a class of bright children it is difficult, if not impossible, to pick out those who will be exceptionally creative. The basic question as to whether intelligence tests and divergent thinking tests are measuring different, partially related or the same human attributes is still a matter for psychological research.

DIVERGENT THINKING AND SUBJECT BIAS

A recurring theme in the study of convergent and divergent thinking is the possible connection between performance on the tests and arts/science bias. Hudson (18) has been most prolific in this field. He defined a *converger* as one who obtains a relatively high score on an IQ test and at the same time a relatively lower score on a divergent thinking test when compared with others in the test sample. The reverse definition was used for the *diverger*. He was able to show that science students (particularly those studying physics) tend to be convergers. Divergers, on the other hand, tend to be students of English literature, history and modern languages. The emphasis has shifted from regarding the divergent thinking tests as measures of creativity to one of looking upon them as reflecting a preferred thinking style. Hence IQ and divergent tests are more likely to distinguish science from arts specialists than to distinguish the creative from the not so creative. However, the weight of evidence from other experiments in this area (19) so far favours the convergent test as a more consistent discriminator of the science specialist with much less support for the arts–diverger connection.

The fact that science specialists do comparatively well in convergent (IQ) tests may reflect the kind of thinking strategies in which they excel. As we have indicated above, IQ items require people to take information as given and use it to arrive at a single correct answer—a procedure not unlike the traditional demands made in science lessons.

In looking for origins, Hudson (18) sees the home (cf. the findings of Roe earlier in the chapter) as the most probable source of inspiration, and in his book *Contrary Imaginations* he has this to say:

> The convergent parent . . . is probably the one who shies away from all expression of strong feeling, affectionate or otherwise. If the child demands affection, the parents do their best to provide it, but fail. In this case, either of two things may happen. The parents may guide their child into less embarrassing spheres by offering approval whenever he masters some

> safe, impersonal skill. Or, as a reaction to the embarrassment the child has caused them (out of shame or irritation or both), they become critical. Either way, the child realizes that security lies both in choosing an impersonal field within which to work, and in being right. Furthermore, the child latches on both to his parents' distaste for 'gush', and to their relief when the mood is once more safe. . . . In every sense, therefore, impersonal work and interests become a haven: from embarrassment, from criticism, and from emotions which are disruptive and inexplicable.
>
> The diverger's mother, on the other hand, is one who binds her child to her by disregarding his practical, logical accomplishments (or even ridiculing them) and by holding out a promise of love which she may or may not be able to fulfil. The child grows up addicted to people.

Notice the importance ascribed to personality development as a feature in cognitive processes. We shall refer to this point again later.

CREATIVITY AND THE CLASSROOM

This section is the least satisfactory because of the difficulty experienced in trying to define educational environments. Terms such as 'traditional' or 'progressive' give a facile black and white interpretation which rarely approximates to the truth. In fact these terms have never been satisfactorily defined. Our notions about effective and efficient 'creative' classroom conditions, for example, are largely intuitive. It is often said that a tight factual syllabus delivered by authoritarian teachers (followed in some cases by an examination requiring factual reproduction) are the ideal conditions for producing convergent thinkers (see previous section). And it seems common sense that the way in which knowledge is presented and acquired will affect the way in which it is subsequently used. Reasonable though this hypothesis might appear, there is very little hard evidence to support it.

Some American psychologists, notably Torrance and his associates in a long list of publications (20), believe that at present parents and teachers actively discourage creative behaviour in the young because it is too troublesome and time-consuming. The enquiring child needs plenty of attention; his questions are frequent, difficult to answer in simple language and sometimes embarrassing, whilst his unskilled hands lead to messiness and disorder. According to Getzels and Jackson (15), precocious children are unpopular with teachers as compared with the conformist and orderly children. A quotation from one of Torrance's many books should help to crystallize one aspect of his progressive philosophy (20):

> Many social pressures stressed at home and in the community interfere with the creative process. Consider our excessive emphasis on a success-orientation—our exaggerated fear of making mistakes. Over-emphasis or misplaced emphasis on sex roles also exacts a heavy toll on the creative thinking of both boys and girls. Consider too our tendency to overrate the finished product, the great work of art, the harmonious interpersonal relationship, the well-organized behaviour of a group. We fail to note the struggles through which these achievements come into being. We stress the importance of verbal skills, especially writing. We give credit frequently only for what an individual can write down, not recognizing that not all thinking expresses itself in verbal form. We place great emphasis upon what one knows rather than upon his attitude toward what he knows or what he can do with what he knows.

In a study of two informal, 'progressive' and two 'formal', 'traditional' primary schools in this country, Haddon and Lytton (21) demonstrated higher divergent thinking scores for the progressive schools. Lytton and Cotton (21) repeated the experiment at Secondary School level with no success. This was attributed to the inappropriateness of trying to classify secondary schools as 'formal' and 'informal' because the basic organization is much more complex than at primary level (pupils see several teachers, a wider range of subjects taught, pupils come from very different primary schools in the catchment areas, and so forth).

An interesting project on the effects of streaming in this country was carried out by Barker Lunn (22). Using a very large sample at the end of their third and again at the end of their fourth year in primary school, she was able to show that in the unstreamed schools, pupils placed with teachers who favoured 'progressive' methods showed some improvement in divergent thinking scores during the fourth year. In contrast, pupils placed with teachers who did not favour 'progressive' methods *deteriorated* in both streamed and unstreamed régimes.

Some success has been experienced where instructional methods are deliberately exploited to enhance creative abilities. Crutchfield (23), using programmed instruction in the training of creative problem-solving, was able to improve the quality and quantity of the problems solved by an experimental group of children so that they became markedly superior to the children in a control group. The effect was still apparent several months later, although its extent had decreased. This latter observation raises the question of the permanence of any training programme dealing with this subject, and Crutchfield concludes that the 'Hawthorne' effect (24) may have intruded, although it seems to the present author to be a point worth noting that change and variety in teaching techniques brings about an increase (temporary though this may be) in creative productivity.

Long-term studies of the effect of more open-ended approaches in Nuffield Science and modern mathematics are awaited. Will methods of teaching science which emphasize possibilities rather than certainties pay off in terms of understanding or in producing more creative scientific minds? Studies comparing traditional and 'new maths' using divergent thinking tests in both secondary and primary schools in Great Britain (25) reveal that children encountering modern methods do tend to produce superior divergence scores.

The interaction of intellectual styles of students and teachers is another issue relevant in the present context. Joyce and Hudson (26), in a research using medical students, felt there were some indications 'that teachers and students having similar styles (convergent and divergent that is) formed the most successful combination' in terms of examination results. This is a very important matter which, unfortunately, has not yet been indisputably supported from the large volume of American research at all levels of education. In a sense, it would be surprising if the style adopted by teachers did not have some effect on the learning of individual pupils. Both teachers and pupils seem convinced of this (27).

Clearly there are numerous unresolved issues relating to the study of creative thinking. But there remains the practical problem of how we might stimulate and encourage such thinking in school. Osborn (28), for example, makes a number of

G

suggestions cast in the form of a series of questions designed to direct the children's attention towards problem-solving: 'what would happen if "it" is made larger . . .? smaller . . .?
changes position . . .?' and so on. This skill of directing children's attention to a wide
range of possibilities is a very potent, and not a particularly commonplace, one.

There are, of course, dangers in unstructured, free-for-all episodes. Children whose
interests have not been roused can, and do, idle away their time on projects which are not
demanding. To keep things stirring in this kind of class is exhausting and requires a
vigilant, grasshopper-like creature who flits from child to child probing and directing
their energies. Learning will not take place *in vacuo* and we cannot expect children to
rediscover from scratch the wealth of knowledge already assimilated by our culture. No
matter how subtle we try to make the teaching–learning–thinking processes, well-
founded knowledge must be transmitted so that new experiences can be set against a
background of knowledge already amassed. Therefore, some structure is inevitable and
it is within this structure that we establish learning strategies. 'Free discovery' sessions
for children require careful *pre*meditation on the part of the teacher in making sure that
children's private enterprise is full, worthwhile and an important means of adding to their
existing knowledge.

To end the chapter, we shall look at some recent experimental approaches for encouraging creative thinking.

BRAINSTORMING AND LATERAL THINKING

There is a view which maintains that as our minds become cluttered with ideas so we
become inhibited in the way we re-express them. Ideas are censored and we prejudge their
value before expressing them. Osborn (28) suggests that there is a greater chance of
producing original ideas when the mind is allowed to run riot in attempting to solve a
problem. The ideas must come freely and without regard for their feasibility. In other
words—think now, evaluate later. A technique since developed by Parnes (29) uses a
group of people who concentrate on a problem, producing as many hypotheses as
possible without bothering to evaluate them. The interplay of ideas apparently sparks off
far more good ideas than conventional problem-solving techniques. The process is known
as *brainstorming*.

The idea has been tried with children of primary school age in America by assembling them around a table, presenting an open-ended problem and tape-recording the
ideas which are allowed to flow uninterrupted by the teacher. At the end of the session
the ideas are discussed for their feasibility. The point is to encourage ideational fluency
without fear of intervention or ridicule from teachers or peers. A major task in the
method with children is the preparation needed to assemble the facts as a prerequisite to
innovation (see synectics below). What is most revealing in brainstorming sessions with
youngsters is the knowledge teachers can gain about the paths a child's roving mind will
take. The central aim of the method is to produce some lasting habits of ideational
fluency in the children, though this aim has never been validated. The method certainly
improves the self-confidence of children in the presence of others, for they can express
views without fear of rebuke or derision, but a possible limitation is that it may induce
non-critical, non-factual rambling in place of reasoned judgement.

Related to brainstorming is the study of *synectics*. The word comes from the Greek and means bringing together disparate and seemingly irrelevant factors. It was first linked to creativity by the Synectics Group at Cambridge, Mass. (30). The aim of synectics is extremely optimistic, for its upholders maintain that the creative process can be described and hence a teaching methodology derived for increasing creative output. By undergoing a course of training, it is thought possible to develop more efficient and creative problem-solving. Synectics is a systematic attempt at brainstorming but differs from it in that the free thinking is always preceded by a period of concentrated searching and familiarization with all aspects of the problem.

Another approach to the problem of thinking strategies has been enunciated by Edward de Bono (31) at Cambridge. Using his collection of parlour games, he argues that logical or longitudinal reasoning is not always the most effective way of arriving at a solution. Indeed, a cold, calculating, step-wise approach to problem-solving may distract a person from experimenting and may thus obscure other more fruitful routes leading to a solution. How many times do we let our minds fixate on a certain way of solving a problem, convinced that we are on the right track, only to discover after much trial and error we could never have solved the problem in that way? This process of constantly returning to 'square one' and trying a new line of approach de Bono calls *lateral thinking*. In other words, our minds should not pursue one line of thinking (longitudinal thinking) to the exclusion of all others, but should frequently return to the information provided and try another approach. This idea of the mind flirting with ideas is also embodied in brainstorming and synectics.

SUMMARY

The last twenty or so years has seen a marked change in the philosophy of educators about the role of children in learning environments. Inflexible, formal, syllabus-bound methods are gradually being replaced by freer, child-centred methods which place more faith in exploratory and expressive activities as ploys for improving the learning skills of children than in follow-my-leader techniques. The growth of interest in creative thinking in America, and more recently in Great Britain, has played some part in focusing teachers' attention on the impact of classroom procedures on the learning styles of children.

Psychologists are not, as yet, clear about the nature of creative thinking, how to measure the quality or what can be done in the classroom to stimulate creativity in children. The efforts which have already been made are largely experimental and intuitive. Psychologists have looked at the characteristics of creative people; they have devised tests of creativity (divergent thinking tests) thought to measure ideational fluency, flexibility and originality; they have tried to analyse the creative process from a study of eminent people. But none of these methods have so far given us incontrovertible evidence or advice of value to teachers. These notes of caution are necessary in a rapidly expanding research field from which there is likely to be an avalanche of literature written with teachers in mind.

One important benefit we have reaped from the study of creative thinking is the challenge it has offered to teachers to examine the learning environments they provide in school. Do parrot-fashion methods of teaching produce different styles of problem-solving in children than do discovery methods? What is the relative efficiency of directed learning and discovery methods? Does our educational system tend to produce convergers who are looking always for one right answer, and can the system produce divergers who are just as happy with open-ended or ambiguous problems? If children are always told how to solve problems, will they be less able to meet new problem situations?

To develop an atmosphere within which children feel sufficiently free to explore and make discoveries whilst being given guidance is a difficult balance for a teacher to obtain. Too much freedom might encourage anarchy; too much guidance might produce sterile conformity. Moreover, when we encourage children to be active participants in their own learning through such media as clay, bricks, paints, musical instruments, body movement, words and number symbols in speech and writing, drama, handicraft and science, we are hopefully trying to assist them in finding their particular modes of communication which requires concentration and self-discipline. Torrance (20) believes this atmosphere can be created by the teacher who learns to recognize and value his pupils' ideas and who comes to believe in his pupils' capacity to be creative; the teacher should give his pupils every opportunity to communicate their ideas, he should encourage 'brainstorming'—a flow of ideas without evaluation—and reward unusual questions and ideas. The balance between undirected freedom and dogged rule-learning, according to recent work (32), comes when *guided discovery* prevails. Here, the major objective is to enable the child to acquire efficient ways of solving problems by free exploration whilst giving the child just sufficient framework of guidance as to help him in learning proficient methods of applying rules.

ENQUIRY AND DISCUSSION

1. In your observation of children, attempt to determine those behaviours which you consider to be 'creative'. What methods are used by the teacher to create the right atmosphere?

2. What is understood by 'discovery methods'? Are they the same for all subjects? Are there differences between primary and secondary school methods in guided discovery?

3. Organize a 'brainstorming' session with a small group of children by tape-recording their spontaneous responses to an open-ended problem.

4. Distinguish between convergent and divergent thinking. Discuss the differences in terms of curriculum content, presentation and subject bias.

5. Read up and discuss the work attempting to relate divergent thinking and school achievement.

6. Read and try out some of de Bono's suggestions in *The Five Day Course in Thinking* [note (31)].

NOTES AND REFERENCES

1. L. M. Terman *et al.*, *Genetic Studies of Genius, Volume 1: Mental and Physical Traits of a Thousand Gifted Children*. Stanford University Press, California, 1925.

2. M. H. Oden, 'The fulfilment of promise: 40–year follow-up of the Terman gifted group', *Genet. Psychol. Monogr.*, **77**, 3–93 (1968).

3. A. Roe produced a number of monographs between 1951 and 1953. The most all-inclusive was 'A psychological study of eminent psychologists and anthropologists and a comparison with biological and physical scientists', *Psychol. Monogr.*, **67**, No. 2 (1953).

4. D. W. MacKinnon, 'Personality and the realization of creative potential', *Am. Psychol.*, **20**, 273–281 (1963). See also 'Characteristics of the creative person: implications for the teaching–learning process' in *Current Issues in Higher Education*, National Educational Association, Washington, 89–92, 1961.

5. See also C. E. Schaeffer and A. Anastasi, 'A biographical inventory for identifying creativity in adolescent boys', *J. appl. Psychol.*, **52**, 42–48 (1968).

6. D. W. MacKinnon, 'The nature and nurture of creative talent', *Am. Psychol.*, **17**, 484–495 (1962).

7. B. Snyder, 'Creative students in science and engineering', *Universities Q.*, **21**, 205–218 (1967).

8. O. J. Harvey, D. E. Hunt and H. M. Schroder, *Conceptual Systems and Personality Organization*, Wiley, New York, 1961.

9. J. P. Guilford, *Personality*, McGraw-Hill, New York, 1959.

10. D. L. Nuttall, 'Convergent and divergent thinking', in H. J. Butcher and H. B. Pont (Eds), *Educational Research in Britain*, vol. 3, University of London Press, London, 1972.

11. A detailed analysis of test materials is given by E. P. Torrance in *Guiding Creative Talent*, Prentice-Hall, New Jersey, 1962. He has also produced a standardized test battery of items known as the *Torrance Tests of Creative Thinking*, Personnel Press, Princeton, New Jersey, 1966. Torrance's tests are also summarized in R. J. Goldman, 'The Minnesota Tests of Creativity', *Educ. Res.*, **7**, 3–14 (1964).

12. M. A. Wallach and N. Kogan, *Modes of Thinking in Young Children*, Holt, Rinehart and Winston, New York, 1965.

13. G. Wallas, *The Art of Thought*, Harcourt, Brace and World, New York, 1926.

14. J. P. Guilford, 'Creativity', *Am. Psychol.*, **5**, 444–454 (1950) and 'The structure of the intellect', *Psychol. Bull.*, **53**, 267–293 (1956).

15. J. W. Getzels and P. W. Jackson, *Creativity and Intelligence*, Wiley, New York, 1962.

16. P. Hasan and H. J. Butcher, 'Creativity and intelligence: a partial replication with

Scottish children of Getzels' and Jackson's study', *Brit. J. Psychol.*, **57**, 129–135 (1966). E. E. Sultan, 'A factorial study in the domain of creative thinking', *Br. J. educ. Psychol.*, **32**, 78–82 (1962). Other critical studies are well documented in the books suggested in Further Reading.

17. As well as Getzels' and Jackson's work, see L. Hudson, *Contrary Imaginations*, Methuen, London, 1966 and D. Child and A. Smithers, 'Some cognitive and affective factors in subject choice', *Res. Educ.*, **5**, 1–9 (1971). In the first case, public school boys were used; in the second, university students.

18. L. Hudson, *Contrary Imaginations* and *Frames of Mind*, Methuen, London, 1966 and 1968 respectively.

19. See for example D. Child, 'A comparative study of personality, intelligence and social class in a technological university', *Br. J. educ. Psychol.*, **39**, 40–46 (1969) and D. Child and A. Smithers *op. cit.*, note (17).

20. E. P. Torrance, *Guilding Creative Talent*, Prentice-Hall, New Jersey, 1962. Also *Education and the Creative Potential*, University of Minnesota Press, Minneapolis, © 1963. The quotation in the text is reprinted with permission from the latter book, pp. 54–55.

21. F. A. Haddon and H. Lytton, 'Teaching approach and the development of divergent thinking abilities in primary schools', *Brit. J. educ. Psychol.*, **38**, 171–180 (1968), and 'Primary education and divergent thinking abilities—four years on', *Br. J. educ. Psychol.*, **41**, 136–147 (1971). For the secondary level experiment, see H. Lytton and A. C. Cotton, 'Divergent thinking abilities in secondary schools', *Br. J. educ. Psychol.*, **39**, 188–190 (1969).

22. J. C. Barker Lunn, *Streaming in the Primary School*, NFER, Slough, 1970.

23. R. S. Crutchfield, 'Creative thinking in children: its teaching and testing', in O. G. Brun, R. S. Crutchfield and W. H. Holtzman (Eds), *Intelligence Perspectives* 1965: *The Terman–Otis Memorial Lectures*, Harcourt, Brace and World, New York.

24. The 'Hawthorne' effect occurs when as a result of introducing a novel method into a situation part of any improvement in productivity is due to the change as much as the actual method—'a change is as good as a rest'.

25. P. N. Richards and N. Bolton, 'Types of mathematics teaching, mathematical ability and divergent thinking in junior school children', *Br. J. educ. Psychol.*, **41**, 32–37 (1971), and G. S. Gopal Rao, D. M. Penfold and A. P. Penfold, 'Modern and traditional mathematics teaching', *Educ. Res.*, **13**, 61–65 (1970).

26. C. R. B. Joyce and L. Hudson, 'Student style and teacher style: an experimental study', *Brit. J. med. Educ.*, **2**, 28–32 (1968).

27. D. Child, 'Some aspects of study habits in higher education', *Int. J. educ. Sci.*, **4**, 11–20 (1970).

28. A. F. Osborn, *Applied Imagination*, 3rd rev., Schibners, New York, 1957. See also,

E. P. Torrance and R. E. Myers, *Creative Learning and Teaching*, Dodd, Mead, New York, 1970.

29. S. J. Parnes and A. Meadow, in C. W. Taylor and F. Barron (Eds), *Scientific Creativity: Its Recognition and Development*, Wiley, New York, 1963, chapter 25.

30. W. J. J. Gordon; *Synectics: The Development of Creative Capacity*, Harper and Row, New York, 1961.

31. E. de Bono, *The Use of Lateral Thinking*, Cape, London, 1967; *The Five Day Course in Thinking*, Penguin, London, 1968; *The Mechanisms of Mind*, Cape, London, 1969.

32. B. Y. Kersh and M. C. Wittrock, 'Learning by Discovery; an interpretation of recent research', *J. Teacher Educ.*, **13**, 461–468 (1962); J. A. Rowell, J. Simon and R. Wiseman, 'Verbal reception, guided discovery and the learning of schemata', *Br. J. educ. Psychol.*, **39**, 233–244 (1969).

FURTHER READING

H. J. Butcher, *Human Intelligence: Its Nature and Assessment*, Methuen, London, 1968. The book contains a well-written chapter on creativity.

A. J. Cropley, *Creativity*, Longmans, London, 1967. A concise, basic text which is easy on the eye.

J. Foster, *Creativity and the Teacher*, Macmillan, London, 1971.

J. Freeman, H. J. Butcher and T. Christie, *Creativity*, Society for Research in Higher Education, London, 1968. A technical book which summarizes the important research in the field.

L. Hudson, *Contrary Imaginations*, Methuen, London, 1966. Develops the theme of convergent/divergent–science/arts bias in an easy and amusing style.

G. F. Kneller, *The Art and Science of Creativity*, Holt, Rinehart and Winston, New York, 1965. A clearly written introduction.

E. P. Torrance and R. E. Myers, *Creative Learning and Teaching*, Dodd, Mead, New York, 1970. This is a guidebook for teachers experimenting with exploratory classroom techniques. A very readable text.

11　Personality

Why is it necessary for teachers to make a study of human personality? One reason is that we are daily making judgements about the affective qualities of ourselves, our pupils and our colleagues. We should, therefore, be fully conversant with the extent to which we can form a reliable assessment of personality using these judgements. Personality factors also affect learning and performance and although we have no precise formula, as yet, that we can apply for guiding children with diverse personal attributes, nevertheless, there is every reason why we must recognize that the differences which exist in their scholastic performance may be as much a function of their personality as of their intellect. Recognition of the mentally disturbed and immediate recourse to professional help especially in the earliest phases can prevent eleventh-hour therapy. Again, our work as teachers consists of influencing attitudes and the more we know about attitude formation and change, the better are our chances of influencing others.

Much of our time is spent in trying to weigh up the personalities of those around us and adjusting to them where possible. We observe the way people move, talk or react on different occasions; we watch their faces for clues to their attitudes and we listen to their prejudices; we find ourselves changing to suit the circumstances, so that a man amongst his friends is usually not the same as he is when being interviewed for a job or when with his fiancée or wife. But the superficial observation of how others behave in particular circumstances and its use as a means of describing personality has serious drawbacks as we shall see. This popular view of personality where we typify others in such limited terms as 'generous', 'bad-tempered', 'morbid', 'aloof', and so forth without due regard for the many other qualities which go to make up an individual's overall profile, has been unfortunate. Psychologists on the other hand have been more concerned with a description of the total organization of a person's behaviour and this chapter will be devoted to a discussion of some of these approaches.

The task of describing and defining the total organization of man is very complex. Whilst we do not find any generally agreed definition of personality amongst psychologists, one which is sufficiently comprehensive for our purposes is 'the more or less stable and enduring organization of a person's character, temperament, intellect and physique which determines his unique adjustment to the environment' (1). Note that the definition carefully distinguishes such attributes as character and temperament as well as intelligence and physique because, as we shall show next, these terms have rather special meanings in psychology.

Temperament is a quality we reserve to describe the inherent disposition underlying personality. Physiological factors, there from birth, such as variations in endocrine gland secretions in response to different environmental settings, distinguish our excitability, instability or placidity, so that temperament is closely allied to emotional dispositions which even at a common-sense level are seen to vary enormously from person to person. The evidence for inherited temperamental traits, as in our consideration of intelligence, is indirect. Like intelligence we cannot observe temperament directly because the influence of environmental factors is immediate, but the study of twins, brothers and sisters and family trees gives us a clue to hereditary influence. When we compare the response patterns exhibited by newborn babies from different families, it soon becomes obvious that even in the same situation their responses are dissimilar. In a research where babies' toes were dipped into icy water a whole range of responses ensued. Some babies took the whole sordid affair in their stride and placidly withdrew their limbs; at the other extreme, some screamed blue murder; others showed fear, horror and recoil (2).

Character, on the other hand, is an evaluative term referring to such traits as honesty, self-control, persistence and sense of justice. They relate to qualities which we can define as socially acceptable or objectionable and incorporate the development of attitudes and values. Environmental constraints accompany the expression of inherited temperamental qualities and lead to character development. The relationship between temperament and character described here is not unlike that between Intelligence A and B described in chapter 9. Having certain temperamental potentialities at birth gives a blueprint for the development of character which to some extent depends on the processes of socialization to which the child is exposed. The guidelines laid down in a permissive or an authoritarian home are thought to determine the social and moral life styles (values and attitudes to race, religion, morals, etc.) within the context of the child's temperamental possibilities.

Since our definition of personality deals with 'adjustment to the environment' it is clear that intelligence must play an important role in personality. Mention was made of this in chapters 9 and 10. Bright children do not adjust to their environment in the same way as do dull children. For one thing, the former can attain higher levels of abstraction and in consequence may face and solve life's problems in ways which contrast with the latter. *Physique* and personality will be dealt with later in the chapter.

THEORIES OF PERSONALITY

As with most unsolved problems in human experience, there are diverse theories purporting to define personality development and measurement. Not all these theories are of value to teachers, and even those which might have something to offer should be treated as possibilities and not certainties.

Interest in personality has a very long history. As long ago as the second century A.D., Galen proposed a typology of personality based on the distribution of the 'body-fluids' or 'humours' first suggested by Hippocrates (Greece, fifth century B.C.). The personality types were called the *melancholic, sanguine, phlegmatic* and *choleric*. The corresponding 'humours' and characteristics are drawn up in table 11.1. Notice that melancholics are opposite in nature to sanguines and phlegmatics opposite to cholerics. This particular fourfold scheme of personality types survives in a modified form in several contemporary theories (see, for example, Eysenck's work later in the chapter).

Table 11.1

humour	personality type	characteristic behaviour
black bile	melancholic	pessimistic, suspicious, depressed
blood	sanguine	optimistic, sociable, easy going
phlegm	phlegmatic	calm, controlled, lethargic
yellow bile	choleric	active, irritable, egocentric

Modern theories of personality structure are many and diverse. To assist in containing these we shall adopt a very useful classification compiled by Vernon (3). He sees three broad basic approaches to the interpretation of personality which he calls (a) naïve, (b) intuitive and (c) inferential. These will be dealt with in turn.

(a) Naïve approaches to personality

Naïve interpretations are based essentially on superficial, face-value observations and interpretations of overt behaviour without the use of standardized norms. What we see in other people is conditioned by our own dispositions, attitudes, motives, biases and interests and we build up a rule of thumb about human nature on the grounds of previous anecdotal experience. Some have suggested that what we perceive in another person depends entirely on the intention we ascribe to that person—in other words, we project our own interpretations of behaviour to explain the intentions of others. It is very easy, for example, to invent malicious motives for the behaviour of children when their actions are playfully and innocently disobedient. In this case, we are investing their immature actions with adult motives.

There are many behavioural cues which affect people's judgement. Two important ones are *physical characteristics* and *social response* factors. Likely physical features include facial expressions, body movements, clothes, handwriting and speech. Social response factors indicate our actual or perceived social role. We try to adopt modes of behaviour and social postures in keeping with what we think are characteristic of the circumstances. Goffman (4) thinks that, even in trivial contacts, individuals try to impersonate the image they think will fit the event and possibly satisfy the expectations of others. The implication of this kind of theorizing is that there are stereotypes which we use as models for our aspirations. The doctor or headteacher might have an image of the 'typical' doctor or headteacher which he attempts to emulate. Children may use their fathers and mothers as models of parenthood, in their approach to other people, or in solving life's problems. In short, we learn about the various roles in life by observing the important people (sometimes called 'role models') already established in these roles.

Perhaps the most extensive use made of superficial criteria for evaluating personality is in the interview. Most serious research directed towards assessing the reliability and validity of the interview as a selection procedure has been very discouraging. Vernon quotes (5) a lot of evidence against the use of interviews for selection and concludes that oral questioning and the interview are useless for assessing ability or the results of teaching. He also maintains that:

> While there is much else to be said later [in his book], particularly about clinical and counselling interviews, it may be stated here that the selection interview is at its best when it is used: (a) for expanding, checking and probing the information previously provided by paper qualifications and biographical data; (b) for assessing particular qualities, mainly physical, social and intellectual that have a good chance of expression during the interview situation. It is at its worst when it is conceived as a means for the interviewer: (a) to intuit or infer fundamental qualities of personality and character; (b) to weigh up and synthesize the evidence from diverse sources and reach a decision in the light of his 'experience' and judgement of job requirements. [note (3) pp. 70–71]

The comments were made as a result of synthesizing research findings and they raise many doubts about traditional interview methods of selection at the primary (the 'Thorn System' in the West Riding of Yorkshire), secondary (career selection) and higher (university, college and career selection) levels of education where they are sometimes used for assessing personality and ability.

Naïve interpretations of personality are doomed to failure for several reasons. These interpretations tend towards an over-simplified view of human nature, aggravated by the fact that most people create masks in order to disguise or reveal particular qualities at will and according to circumstances. They tend to employ rigid stereotypes, which are frequently based on limited and biased experience, to describe the behaviour observed. Naïve impressions of others are very much bound up with the interaction occurring between people. This interaction often rests on superficial contact in highly specific incidents. An added complication results from the *role-play* of individuals when they are trying to put over a particular image. There is also a temptation to observe the irregular because idiosyncratic behaviour is more conspicuous. Eccentricities such as voice intonation, twitches or an aggressive approach can disturb a balanced judgement. We also tend to undervalue those with a different point of view from our own. All in all, these shallow attempts at personality analysis are not likely to give us a stable, comprehensive picture of another's personality.

(b) Intuitive theories of personality

Surely the most famous psychologist of all time is Sigmund Freud (1856–1939), the father of *depth psychology* (also known as *psychodynamics* or *clinical psychology*). The theory is extensive and has had a substantial following both as an instrument of research and as the basis for therapy amongst the mentally ill. But at present much of his theorizing has limited practical value to the teacher. For those who wish to dig deeper, note (6) contains several references, but in this chapter we shall restrict ourselves to a consideration of the basic aspects of his theory which illustrate the 'intuitive' approach to personality; intuitive is here used to emphasize the subjective, and assumed unlearned, understanding of human conduct forming the basis of Freudian psychology.

Some psychologists, notably those who support the behaviourist position, have little time for the theories of Freud and his followers. They claim that his view is based largely on supposition and limited experimental evidence; an 'unsinkable theory' according to Hudson (7) which can be adjusted whenever conflicting evidence is found; his methods are said to be unscientific and employed biased samples of middle-class Viennese sex-hungry women; the proportion of 'cures' of the mentally ill brought about by psychoanalysis is little better than chance and Freud in any case exaggerated much of what he did find. These are harsh comments for a theory which has given both the layman and the psychological world a seminal framework of personality composition along with a voluminous rag-bag of terms which permeate our language (complexes, repression, ego, œdipus, etc.). More important, Freud's methods have opened up new approaches to the study of man (e.g. Piaget used techniques of a clinical kind in his earliest work) and have given a terrific stimulus to other fields of psychology such as motivation and development. Freud's gifts to psychologists and teachers were in drawing their attention to another way of looking at childhood, to the child's affiliative relationships with parents, brothers and sisters, to the existence and potency of infantile sexuality, to the possible unconscious nature of a great deal of human motivation, to the continuum between normal and neurotic behaviour, to the ambivalence of early child–parent relationships (œdipus and electra complexes) and to the enduring effects of many early childhood experiences.

Basic principles relating to Freud's work

Amongst other things, Freud's theory stresses these points:

1. The behaviour exhibited by mentally deviant people arises from the self-same motives as the mentally normal.

2. In addition to a *conscious* level of mental operations where we are fully aware of mental events, there is also the *unconscious mind* (mental traces of past experiences which were once at the conscious level). Unconscious traces can affect our behaviour without our being aware of the source. Freud considered that the unconscious was a repository consisting mainly of *repressed,* unpleasant experiences (repression means exclusion from the conscious level, see later) which could not be entertained at the conscious level. A *sub- or pre-conscious* level was also postulated consisting of traces which though not in the conscious mind can nevertheless be brought there by active recall of past experiences.

3. Unconscious motives arise from *defence mechanisms.* These we shall elaborate shortly, but they are ways of behaving which enable us to protect ourselves from conflicting and intolerable situations.

4. Early childhood experience is the key to later behaviour patterns. For Freud, the unfolding of sexual behaviour in childhood had much to do with personality formation.

We have already said something of Freud's views on the basic motivating forces of human action in chapter 3. Briefly, we noted that at the heart of man's driving force are the *libidal* (sexual) and *ego* (biological) instincts. These natural forces he referred to as the *Id*. Unleashed and uncontrolled, they would give rise to animal behaviour in violation of the cultural taboos of the child's society. Parental and societal pressures and constraints create a conscience in the developing child known as the *Super-ego* brought about by absorbing the mores of his society (*introjection*). There is also a part of his personality in contact with the Id, Super-ego and the realities of the outside world. This is the *Ego* which acts as an adjuster between the raw requirements of the Id and the censure of the Super-ego.

To bring about a resolution of the demands of the Id and the constraints of the Super-ego, the Ego resorts to *defence mechanisms*; these act as a shield against the otherwise intolerable conflicts between the naked demands of the human as an animal and the acquired conscience built up in childhood from the rules of society. The behaviour ensuing from defence mechanisms is, then, largely unconsciously motivated. Freud believed that simple slips of the tongue, pen or memory (6), serious mental disarray, dreams and fantasies in waking or sleeping are all rooted in unconscious processes. Information about these processes can be teased out by devious means such as psychoanalysis, hypnosis or the use of drugs.

Let us look at a few simple illustrations of defence mechanisms which we might find in normal life:

Compensation occurs when an individual replaces one means of expressing a motive by some other less direct means. An unattractive girl may emphasize scholarship if she has difficulty in landing a boy friend; a married couple who are childless may treat a dog as if it were a child; parents who have missed a chance in their own education may make sacrifices to ensure success for their children.

Identification results when a person is moved to regard himself as another admired person. Film or TV programmes give opportunities for some to identify themselves with the people on the screen. Sometimes children try to imitate their parents as authority figures in an effort to get their own way.

Regression is said to have occurred when an individual utilizes behaviour more characteristic of an earlier stage in life. Even amongst adults it is possible to find those who occasionally resort to stamping, weeping, overt aggression and 'going home to mother' behaviour in an effort to get their own way. The logic of this is that as children they may have sometimes been successful in getting what they wanted by stamping or weeping. As adults they regress to this earlier tactic.

Sublimation is the redirection of one's activities into similar activity when an original desire is not met. When students who may want to become doctors are unsuccessful, they often sublimate their enthusiasm in other paramedical fields (nursing, physiotherapy, pharmacy, medical social work).

Projection occurs when there is a tendency to project one's faults or wishes into others. Occasionally an adolescent girl may claim that she is being watched by boys—more as a wishful thought than a statement of fact. Countries often accuse each other of stockpiling troops and armaments on each other's borders whilst in fact doing it themselves.

We shall see in a moment that projection is one method used by psychotherapists and depth psychologists as a means of exposing hidden motives.

Rationalization, or the 'sour-grapes syndrome', is really an example of self-deception where we try to find excuses for our shortcomings—too much study ruins your eyes, if you are not fond of reading!

A final example is *repression* which is the deliberate thrusting aside, because of social inhibitions, of the libidal forces which are striving for expression. The repressed drives do not disappear; instead, they remain as traces in the unconscious and influence the actions of individuals when similar unpleasant situations arise.

All these methods of compensation occur, according to Freud, as perfectly normal reactions. Where they do get out of proportion *neuroses* develop as mental conditions such as anxiety states, phobias, obsessions or hysteria. Neuroses are the outcome of an inability to find recognized ways of adjusting to life's problems. The disorders which result affect emotional and intellectual functioning although the neurotic patient is not deprived of contact with reality. In the most serious mental illnesses known as *psychoses* (manic-depressive conditions involving delusions and hallucinations, or schizophrenia) the sufferer is completely dissociated from reality. The neurotic on the other hand has the problem of living in a real world and knowing it; the psychotic lives in quite a different mental world and his dissociation from the real world does not worry him.

Freud's theory has not stood still. His two closest disciples, Adler and Jung, stressed different sources of man's motivation such as striving for self-fulfilment and superiority (the *mastery drive* of Adler) or the desire to belong (Jung). More recently, insecurity in childhood (Horney, Fromm) and social interpersonal relations (Sullivan) have attracted the attention of the 'new' or neo-Freudians.

In addition to the criticisms raised at the start of this section, we should also note the difficulty of verifying the views of depth psychologists (8). There is also too little consideration given to man's adaptability; instead, we are led to believe that his basic personality is founded in the first few years of life and that he must live with this for the remainder of his life. The work of social anthropologists would also suggest that the aggressive drive (9) is not inevitable in man's nature. Only recently have neo-Freudians paid attention to the impact of social phenomena as a source of motivation. Later in the chapter we shall refer to some of the methods of depth psychology.

(c) Inferential theories of personality

Inferential theories depend on scientific, objective analysis and are the province of the *psychometrician.* The movement has its origins in the belief that man's behavioural tendencies can be classified as *traits* or *factors* measurable using tests and evaluated chiefly by the use of factor analysis. The idea of man possessing personality traits is not a new one. We saw Galen's typology based on the body humours; also Jung's extra-version—introversion typology arises from his conviction that there are stable patterns of personality characteristics. For the extravert the outer world is most important; he is active rather than passive; he is given more to subjective feelings than to objective thoughts. Introverts resort more to the inner, personal world and are given to introspection rather than action. This is not a complete description, but it will suffice to show how Jung first conceived the concepts of introversion and extraversion. The same terms have been adopted by later psychologists, notably Eysenck, who, as we shall see, defines the traits more extensively.

Eysenck's work

In a very long list of books (10), H. J. Eysenck has elaborated a most comprehensive objective approach to the study of personality. His theories have grown out of research with psychiatric patients at the Maudsley Hospital in London. Like the British school

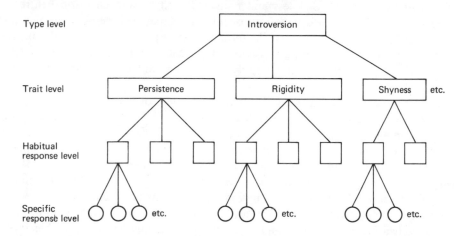

Figure 11.1   From H. J. Eysenck, *The Structure of Human Personality*, Methuen, London, 1953, p. 13

of thought regarding the structure of intelligence (see chapter 9), Eysenck holds a hierarchical view of personality. At the highest point we find personality *types* and Eysenck in fact expresses personality organization in terms of three basic types, namely, *extraversion–introversion* (sometimes contracted to extraversion for convenience), *neuroticism–stability* (neuroticism for short) and *psychoticism–normality*. He also believes that intelligence is a fourth dimension. But these dimensions are thought to be normally distributed in the population, so that the majority of people would possess an admixture of the qualities underlying the types and would therefore obtain scores around the midpoint of each dimension. In fact, Eysenck's starting point was the mentally ill, that is the extremes of the dimensions, and from these extremes he devised tests and questions which defined the dimensions. He is at great pains, nevertheless, to remind us that dimensionality implies a continuum of personality possibilities and not categorical definitions. Unfortunately, the use of such black and white terms as 'introvert' or 'neurotic' give the erroneous impression that people are either one thing or the other.

To illustrate the interdependence of personality characteristics and the way in which Eysenck envisages a connection between the levels of personality organization which underpin the fundamental type, figure 11.1 has been drawn. Qualities which characterize the introvert, such as persistence, rigidity, subjectivity, shyness and irritability, are known as *traits*. These are in turn associated with *habitual* ways of responding in similar conditions, so that in problem-solving or in mechanical tasks requiring vigilance we might expect the introvert to be, in general, persistent. In particular circumstances requiring vigilance we might find variations in the degree of vigilance displayed, but we would expect an introvert to be vigilant in most of his specific responses.

Neuroticism–Stability   The term *neurosis* was first used to describe a collection of abnormal mental conditions including anxiety, obsessions and hysteria. Thus in hysterical cases physical symptoms sometimes accompanied a mental condition (sometimes referred to as *psychosomatic* disorder). Sickness and nausea caused by apprehension before such anxiety-provoking events as examinations or interviews may well be physical manifestations of a mental condition. However, the term has developed a more particular meaning in Eysenck's model because we all possess some measure of neuroticism ranging from stability to high anxiety, worrying unduly, panicking under stress and being overemotional.

We have already seen that anxiety, a major correlate of neuroticism, has a physiological basis. The hypothalamus was noted as the centre of control for the autonomic nervous system and endocrine secretions via the pituitary gland (chapter 2). The extent of hypothalamic reaction depends on many factors not least of which are inherited autonomic functioning and the extent of the crisis which initiates anxiety. We have also mentioned how severing the frontal lobe connections of the brain has the effect of reducing the level of anxiety displayed by individuals. Arousal has also been referred to in connection with motivation. Here we saw that, in difficult tasks, high levels of anxiety could adversely affect performance and we shall say more later about a possible application of measures of neuroticism to performance in academic work.

Extraversion–Introversion   Extraverts in Eysenckian terms, are outgoing, relatively uninhibited, fond of activities which bring them into contact with other people, not attracted by solitary pursuits such as study, cravers after excitement, aggressive, unreliable, easy going and optimistic. Introverts tend to possess the opposite of these qualities. Most of us, mercifully, possess most of these qualities to some degree— ambiverts. But this has been a particularly interesting personality dimension for educational psychologists. A glance at the list of traits just mentioned will soon reveal that they bear directly on a number of qualities of advantage in traditional educational settings. However, before we deal with this matter there are one or two theoretical issues to consider.

A recent theory posited by Eysenck (11) attempts to provide causal connections between physiological brain mechanisms and the personality dimensions of extraversion and neuroticism. In chapter 2 we mentioned the ascending reticular activating system (ARAS) as the seat of arousal in response to external stimuli. Eysenck proposes that there are individual differences in the extent of arousal which can be related to extraversion–introversion. 'Arousal under identical stimulating conditions is higher in introverts than in extraverts.' The differences can, therefore, be directly related to inherited qualities in brain structure. Another part of the brain, the *visceral brain*, is thought to be responsible for individual differences in emotionality as measured using the neuroticism dimension.

The theory leads to a number of propositions which have some experimental backing. The notion that we are aroused to different levels by similar events is not new. Some people become much more 'aware' of stimulation that others. Similarly, some people take longer to 'cool off' after excitation. If Eysenck's arousal proposition is valid, introverts, by implication from our knowledge of brain functioning, are less likely to develop inhibition in a task than extraverts. Thus the former are more likely to be able to concentrate for longer periods of time in tasks requiring vigilance. We shall apply this later. Again, introverts are more susceptible to conditioning than are extraverts. This could be a decided advantage in some formal educational settings and may mean that the introvert is likely to be more readily socialized in childhood. We must not forget, however, that in using concepts such as 'introvert' and 'extravert' we are dealing with extreme cases. Most individuals are ambivert in their behaviour. For this reason, the findings we shall refer to later, in the absence of more refined measures, relate mainly to those with more extreme personality manifestations. Another complication in dealing with extraversion and neuroticism is the possibility of excessive visceral brain activity affecting the arousal mechanisms of the ARAS as well. In other words, those with high neuroticism scores are often in a state of arousal and thus we have an interaction effect between extraversion and neuroticism.

Throughout Eysenck's arguments there is unequivocal support for the inheritance of personality characteristics. The evidence and the debate surrounding this issue take on a similar form to that dealt with in chapter 9. Evidence taken from twin studies (12) shows high correlations in adulthood using the extraversion scale. Studies of the consistency in the personality profiles of babies (2) lend further support. A thorough review of the research for and against the inheritability of personality traits is given by Eysenck (13).

R. B. Cattell (14)

Another worker who has successfully applied psychometric methods, chiefly factor analysis, to explore personality organization is Raymond B. Cattell in the United States. By taking the kind of analysis used by Eysenck a stage further, he has obtained sixteen personality factors (sometimes known as the 16PF). Cattell distinguishes between what he calls *source traits* which are at the root of observed behaviour and *surface traits* which are the superficial and detectable patterns of behaviour having their origins in source traits. Neuroticism as defined by Eysenck would be a surface trait for Cattell, and the qualities which go to make up neuroticism (emotional instability, tenseness, timidity, etc.) would be source traits. Figure 11.2 demonstrates the connection between the two points of view. There are matters of detail in which the two would differ, for not all the sixteen factors of Cattell will 'compress' to give the E and N dimensions of Eysenck. Nevertheless, there is a large measure of agreement between these two.

The approach of these and other psychometricians is not without its critics. The primary source of information for the detection of the dimensions is the pencil-and-paper test (see later in the chapter) which raises several questions. Do people tend to give socially desirable responses on these tests and are there universal 'yes' or 'no' men? How total is the profile of human personality, in other words, have all the relevant questions been posed on these pencil-and-paper inventories? How stable are the factors across different groups of people or for the same person, and where variations in the scores occur are they due to unreliable test material or to genuine changes in personality from one test occasion to the next? These and many other questions are levelled at inferential personality approaches. Fortunately, the nature of the concepts and test materials makes it possible for some attempt to be made to answer the questions and they have become the subject of much contemporary research.

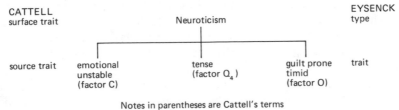

Notes in parentheses are Cattell's terms

Figure 11.2   The relationship between the terminology of Cattell and Eysenck Taken from D. Child, *The Essentials of Factor Analysis*, Holt, Rinehart and Winston, London, 1970

Kelly's personal construct theory

One attempt at a rapprochement between intuitive and inferential theories comes in the work of Kelly (15). A basic premise is that the theories man has regarding the world about him form the basis by which he perpetually seeks to 'guess' what will happen next. In this manner he construes or reconstrues his world of experience. 'A person's processes are psychologically channelized by the ways in which he anticipates events' (15). This view is in marked contrast to that of the inferential theorists because Kelly's fundamental belief is that human behaviour is anticipatory rather than reactive. Thus, we react *not* to a stimulus but to what we interpret the stimulus to be. If a man digs a piece of metal out of the ground he may construe it as a 'thing', as a lump of metal, as a coin, as a Roman coin or as a coin of particular value from the reign of Constantine the Great, depending on his personal constructs. Each man's reaction to the find is different even though the superficial sensory stimulation is the same.

By using a *triad* method of comparing our reactions to people who are significant in our lives, Kelly was able to inspect the interpersonal construct world of individuals. The triad method consists of choosing sets of three people from a larger list of significant others (mother, father, brother, sister, work friend, boss, neighbour, etc.) and requiring the respondent to select in such a way that two are alike but at the same time dissimilar to the third person in some specified way. The 'specified ways' consisted of bipolar constructs such as powerful/weak, cruel/kind, mature/immature, generous/stingy, intelligent/stupid. By a statistical procedure too complex to mention here, a construct universe can be designed for an individual which Kelly claims will define the major personality variables of that individual. Hence we see the clinical technique involving a description of *individual* personalities—sometimes called the *idiographic* approach to personality as compared with the *nomothetic* approach which endeavours to portray human behaviour in terms of 'average' tendencies or norms as in the work of Eysenck and Cattell. At present, the method has not been used with schoolchildren, but mainly in clinical psychology. However, it may well prove to attract increasing attention in the future.

NEUROTICISM, EXTRAVERSION AND ATTAINMENT

The definitions of neuroticism and extraversion given above have some clear implications for educational performance especially in a system where long periods of study and concentration both in general work or in preparation for examinations are at a premium. Personality, then, plays an important part in learning and attainment as well as the more obvious factors of intelligence, motivation and cognitive development. However, the *orectic* variables (variables other than the purely cognitive), especially personality, have, until recently, taken a subsidiary place in educational thinking. Yet it would be surprising if temperament and drive were not intimately involved in performance.

In chapter 3 we mentioned that drive and performance were connected and the Yerkes–Dodson law was one expression of this relationship. Evidence is accumulating to show that drive and anxiety are closely related. This being the case, we might expect those with high levels of neuroticism to have reserves of drive which can be harnessed for useful performance in a task, provided the task is not too problematical, in which case performance is adversely affected. In fact, the relation between neuroticism and academic attainment is not that simple. Generally speaking, in children of both primary and secondary school age the results have given negative correlations (16), whilst at university and college the connection is significantly positive (17). The explanation for this reversal is not known. It could be that older and more experienced students learn how to control and canalize their energies, or that the intellectual demands perceived by children are relatively more complex because of the children's inexperience, with the consequence that higher levels of anxiety, disadvantageous to performance, are generated. Again, perhaps the tests used for children are not measuring quite the same quality as those used with adults.

The case for a positive correlation between introversion and secondary school or college attainment is more substantial. When we look at the characteristics of the extravert in the definition, it is not difficult to imagine why he is at a disadvantage in academic pursuits. If reactive inhibition is high, then concentration in studious tasks will be marred by involuntary rest periods, and vigilance must suffer. During examination revision the extravert child will have difficulty maintaining interest in what can be a boring task. Amongst primary school children (18) introversion is not of as much advantage for girls as it appears to be for boys. But in secondary (19) and university (20) education the connection has been more frequently established. Thus we find a tendency for those in higher education to be more neurotic and introverted than the population at large. By definition, the introvert avoids personal situations and enjoys bookish and conceptual pursuits, all of which are rewarded by the present educational selection system. Given students with sufficient intelligence to cope with the demands of higher education, the examination system itself acts as a personality selection device which filters out the neurotic introverts. Moreover, amongst university students it would appear that the science specialists are even more introverted and less neurotic than the arts specialists (20 and 21).

In the present state of research in this field it would be unwise to make too much of the connections indicated above, especially at the primary level. Primarily, it is important to be aware that personality characteristics play a significant role in both the act of learning and in attitudes towards the act of learning. Variations in performance are not entirely a question of intellect, motivation or thinking skills, but may depend on the personal attributes which can enhance or inhibit the quality of that performance. This fact alone is sufficient to justify continued research in this field.

TEACHER–PUPIL INTERACTION

Our knowledge of teacher–pupil interaction and the influence of teacher personality characteristics on the learning environments created for children is alarmingly incomplete. Many attempts at categorization exist, but the results are not conclusive. One well-known classification, originally used to describe the leadership styles of youth club leaders but having obvious applicability in classrooms, was proposed by Lippitt and White (22). The *authoritarian* system is created by the teacher-centred set up in which the emphasis is on formality, teacher-directed communication and dominance, competition and punishment. In the *democratic* system, the stress is on learner participation in decision-making, on cooperation and open-ended structures in human relationships. A third system is referred to as the *laissez faire* approach in which the leader or teacher gives complete freedom for decisions and offers the minimum of guidance. Another classification already mentioned in chapter 10 is the converger–diverger style which distinguishes between the closed, single-solution problem situation and the open, multiple choice problem situation.

We noted in chapter 6 some of the effects of informal and formal classrooms on the quality and quantity of learning. In terms of discipline it is difficult to draw generalizations. Clearly, a *laissez faire* atmosphere is asking for trouble. Leaderless children find their own, usually wildly inadequate, substitute leaders (W. Golding, *Lord of the Flies*), and create their own low standards of performance. Disciplinary problems would most likely be a nightmare. Most children enjoy and prefer a democratic and divergent class atmosphere, but, as we noted in chapters 6 and 7, the propitiousness of methods depends on the purposes to be served by the content of the lesson, on the difficulty of the content, on the children's previous knowledge and on the 'styles of thinking' which one hopes to generate in the children. Given an enjoyable and meaningful classroom atmosphere, teachers may still be faced with behaviour problems. These latter have been classified into two categories of *conduct* and *personality* problems (23). In conduct problems, the pupil displays marked disobedience, restlessness and destructiveness. Personality problems are characterized by displays of self-consciousness, feelings of inferiority and emotional instability. Whilst we know these problems have to be treated in different ways, and children carefully screened to ascertain the background factors to their behaviour deviance, it remains true that psychologists are not yet able to provide us with workable solutions. Some of the research in this field is given as a point for enquiry and discussion at the end of the chapter.

THE ASSESSMENT OF PERSONALITY

The approaches to the study of personality we have been looking at have generated many methods of assessing personality and our purpose here will be to give a summary account of the better-known methods. The task facing the psychologist concerned with personality study is very complex. As we saw from the definition above, his terms of reference are broad and the intrusion of intervening variables, both personal and social, make analysis very difficult. One of the clearest expositions of the task facing the student of personality is given by Vernon in *Personality Tests and Assessment* (5, 3). In this section we shall look at physique and temperament, experimental and physical measures which relate to personality, ratings made by self or others, attitude and interest inventories and the better-known methods of depth psychology, such as projection techniques.

Sheldon's typology of physique and personality

Galen's body humours mentioned earlier constitute one of the first attempts to link physiological characteristics with personality types. More recently, Kretschmer (24) drew up a body typology which was developed and refined by Sheldon (24). The latter postulated three basic body builds having corresponding temperamental traits. The three basic body-build types are: *endomorphs* who are round, fat and soft, *mesomorphs* who have hard, muscular bodies and *ectomorphs* with a delicate, lean, linear physique. The biologists amongst our readers will recognize that Sheldon has taken the embryonic layers of endoderm (responsible for laying down the digestive system), mesoderm (lays down muscle, bone, heart and blood system) and ectoderm (lays down the surface structures such as the skin and sense organs, and the nervous system including the brain) as the predominant body systems characterizing, respectively, the body-build types of endomorph, mesomorph and ectomorph. Each body type dimension was rated by Sheldon using a seven-point scale. Therefore, a man with a normal physique would be rated 4 on each dimension, giving a profile of 4–4–4.

Sheldon claimed a close correspondence between these threefold measures of physique and the temperaments of an individual. Using nude photographs and detailed analytical interviews of individuals he concluded that it is possible to obtain a correspondence between physique and the temperaments portrayed in table 11.2.

Whilst Sheldon has obtained some convincing correlations between physique and temperament, his work has found critics who have questioned the methods and statistics he uses. Again, there does not appear to be a satisfactory explanation for the changes in physique which often occur with age and which are not accompanied by a corresponding change in temperament. Lean individuals develop middle-aged spreads without necessarily changing in temperament.

Table 11.2

Body type	temperamental traits
Endomorph (round, fat, soft)	Viscerotonia (sociable, affectionate, lover of comfort)
Mesomorph (hard, muscular)	Somatotonia (aggressive, assertive, energetic)
Ectomorph (fragile, 'linear' physique)	Cerebrotonia (withdrawn, lover of privacy and mental activity)

Physical experiments and personality

Eysenck (25) has been particularly active in finding a series of physical tests which appear to have personality correlates. The *pursuit rotor* is one such device which is said to discriminate between introverts and extraverts. A disc like a gramophone record containing a metal stud near the edge is set in motion on a turntable. The idea is to keep a metal probe, like a pencil, held on the stud for as long as possible whilst the disc is spinning. Concentration and persistence are obvious qualities for this task and those in whom reactive inhibition [see note (11)] is high will be at a distinct disadvantage. Thus the extravert is rendered less efficient at this game than the introvert, so that an electrical timing mechanism which can measure accurately the contact time over a given test period will show introverts as having longer contact time than extraverts. Many other experimental ploys have been used to assess persistence, dark-adaptation, reminiscence, conditionability, and so forth. Whilst Eysenck's hypotheses of excitation and inhibition are seminal in providing many plausible experiments to test the diversity of sensory, perceptual and learning functions of personality, there is still much to be done before we can apply the findings in educational settings.

Self-rating inventories of personality

Certainly the most popular means of measuring such dimensions as neuroticism–stability, introversion–extraversion, tender-minded–tough-minded, apprehensive–placid and the like is by the use of questionnaires. These contain items by which the individual can rate him- or herself usually by agreeing or disagreeing with the items. The following are examples typical of personality inventories:

> After each item is a space for answering 'YES' or 'NO'. Answer each item by putting a tick in the appropriate space provided at the end of each item which best expresses the way you usually act or feel.
>
> YES   NO
>
> 1. Are you a nervy person?
> 2. Do you like playing practical jokes?
> 3. Are you frequently moody?
> 4. As a child were you afraid of the dark?

5. I would rather work with things than with people.

6. I enjoy closely reasoned argument.

Using the technique of factor analysis [see chapter 9, note (24)], a pool of items is assembled which measure the same dimension. In the examples above, the items have been chosen to represent different personality dimensions, but normally one would find several items in an inventory which are typical of each dimension being measured. The commonest are extraversion, neuroticism and anxiety scales designed for eight year olds onwards to adulthood (26). Test administration and interpretation require skill and training so that it would not be possible for all and sundry to obtain copies of these tests.

Much of the research we discussed under the heading of 'neuroticism, extraversion and attainment' earlier has been carried out using personality inventories of the kind described above. Students should take the opportunity to look at test materials provided by their college and explore the kinds of questions which psychologists use for assessing personality types.

The reliability obtained from testing and retesting the same group with the same or a parallel form of inventory has been encouragingly high. The closer the testing sessions in time, the higher is the reliability. Our reservations about such inventories include the problem of knowing whether changes in the score from one occasion to the next are a measure of unreliability of the test material or an accurate measure of personality change (or both). Moreover, we cannot be certain that *all* dimensions of personality have been catered for in the selection of items on existing inventories, a problem similar to that met with in our discussion of intelligent behaviour.

Attitude and interest inventories

In a sense, a personality questionnaire of the kind described above is an attitude scale. However, the term 'attitude' is generally reserved for an opinion which represents a person's overall inclination towards an object, idea or institution. Interests differ from attitudes in at least three important ways:

 (i) interests are always positive, whereas attitudes can be positive, negative or neutral;

 (ii) interests are always active whilst attitudes can be dormant;

(iii) interests are specific and functioning here and now whilst attitudes are more generalized and may not function at all.

Attitude measurement has very wide currency. Scales have been created for attitudes to almost every aspect of our lives from soap powders to school subjects. Several techniques exist (27) of which the *Likert scale* is now the most used. It consists of an attitudinal statement followed by a scale running from one extreme of opinion to the other. Between these extremes, the respondent is given a number of points which express shades of opinion. For example, here are a few statements taken from an attitude to school questionnaire. The respondent indicates the degree of importance he ascribes to each attitude by using the following five-point scale of numbers after each statement:

1—absolutely essential
2—important but not essential
3—of only moderate importance
4—of very little importance
5—of no importance at all

For an 'ideal' school typical items might be:

1. Plenty of opportunity for sports and athletics   . . . .
2. informal relations with staff   . . . .
3. has social as well as academic activities   . . . .
4. separates the sixth-formers from the rest   . . . .
5. is concerned with preparing students for future work   . . . .

Although 5 points have been used along the scale, it is quite possible to have 7, 9 or 11; odd numbers are chosen so that it is possible to give a central neutral response.

Interest inventories have taken four basic forms (28). *Expressed interests* consist of extracting a direct statement of a person's liking or disliking for something. The answers tend to be very unstable, and subject to the transient moods of individuals. If you ask a boy 'do you like science' his answer could vary from one day to the next. *Manifest interest* is shown by an individual's participation in an activity. But this could be misleading as when one participates in an action for other motives, such as companionship. *Tested interest* is ascertained using objective measures of the information known by a person. Interest in a particular field is assumed to lead to an increase in the information known in that field. Thus some believe that a measure of acquired knowledge is a partial indicator of interest. Peel's 'general information test' or Richmond's 'culture test' are examples (29). The principle, as Peel points out, is that a youngster who is interested in an activity will not only feel pleasure when he is pursuing his interest, but will amass information while participating. Two sample questions of the kind used in general information tests are:

Here are the titles of five books. Underline the one written by Robert Louis Stephenson.

    Robinson Crusoe: Dog Crusoe: Coral Island: Treasure Island: Jungle Book.

Which of the following is true of a penguin?

    A penguin is   (a) a mammal,   (b) a bird,   (c) a fish,   (d) an insect.

Inventoried tests of interest are usually constructed for the purpose of choosing occupational preferences (see later, chapter 15). The earliest kinds required respondents to place school subjects or occupations either in rank order or as *paired comparisons* [note (29), chapter 15].

Research into the subject interests of children using the instruments mentioned has shown in general that their choices are not particularly reliable in terms of the subjects which they choose later when specialization is possible, in vocational choice or when interest is correlated with attainment. Correlations of interest with school subjects are low and add very little in the way of predicting success at school.

Projection techniques

One of the sharp dividing lines between depth psychologists and psychometricians is in the techniques the former employ in studying human personality (30). The clinical orientation of depth psychologists involves them in intuitive and subjective encounters with, in the main, mental patients. The purposes of these psychoanalytical techniques is to reach the recesses of the unconscious mind in an effort to expose inner, hidden motives which are said to be the cause of overt behaviour. Consequently, part of the secret is to disguise the purpose of these techniques from the patient by using indirect and veiled methods in the kind of questioning used. Then follows an interpretive session when the depth psychologist attempts to read into the findings the hidden causes of the patient's actions either with or without the presence of the patient. The psychoanalyst, therefore, is trying to break through the patient's defence mechanisms and discover their origins.

There are several projection techniques of which *association* has proved to be an attractive one. Free word association requires a quick pairing of words from a given one, for example, given 'knife' what would be its pair? Most people would give 'for!:' to this stimulus word, but occasionally unusual and bizarre replies such as 'cell' or 'murder' do turn up which are thought to have hidden meaning. Continuous association consists in requiring a string of words from a given stimulus word. Incomplete sentences are also used such as 'Other people . . .' or 'my father . . .' and the subject is required to finish the sentence. Whatever associations transpire are thought to arise from deep motives unrealized by the respondent.

Story telling is a second method in which a person is asked to write a pen-picture of himself. A third technique of *Thematic Apperception Tests* (or TATs) has arisen from these. TATs demonstrate a projection device in that they require an individual to make up a story from a picture he is shown and to say what might have led up to the scene in the picture, what is happening currently and what might happen in the future. By doing so he is thought to project his own problems into the characters he portrays in the story.

The *Rorschach Ink Blot Test* is very well known. Again, a set of figures, originally made from symmetrical inkblots by inking a piece of paper and folding it down the middle to give a symmetrical pattern, is presented to a subject who is asked to report on what he sees in the figures. His responses are then analysed for deeper motives which underlie his choices. Those who favour the method have devised an extensive classification of replies from large numbers of people.

The interest of these tests to the teacher is academic. Should a child ever need the help of a psychiatrist, the teacher should immediately see that this help is given. Professional psychoanalysis has its limitations, let alone amateur psychoanalysis which could well aggravate rather than alleviate a mental condition; thus teachers are wise to seek professional advice if they suspect that they have a mentally sick child on their hands.

SUMMARY

If the definition of personality involves a knowledge of the total organization of man, then most avenues of educational psychology lead ultimately towards a greater understanding of personality. A classroom is not just a cognitive habitat, but consists of intricate personal interactions which deeply affect the learning and teaching processes. The pity is that psychologists are only scratching the surface of this very complex mesh of characteristic, temperamental, intellectual and physical determinants of each person's adjustment.

In this chapter, we noted a distinction between temperament, which refers to inherent dispositions and character, which is an evaluative term associated with social behaviour (honesty, cruelty, self-control).

Three broad approaches to the study of personality were adopted from the writings of Vernon. These were the (a) naïve, (b) intuitive and (c) inferential interpretations of personality. The first kind of approach relies essentially on superficial observations of other people's behaviour. All the idiosyncratic, as well as the 'normal', experiences in our lives are compounded to give us thumb-nail sketches of how people tick, and from these we establish a theory of human personality. Intuitive theories, intuitive because they are dependent on subjective assessments of human conduct, are led by the psycho-analytical school of psychology. Freud and his followers constitute the mainstay of this movement. Whilst psychoanalytical theories were outlined, it was suggested that there were few direct applications in classroom practice. Nevertheless, the particular contribution of this line of thinking was to increase our awareness of the importance to be attached to the lasting influences of childhood experiences as a source of adult motivation.

Inferential theories were illustrated using the psychometric analyses of Eysenck and Cattell. In particular, the dimensions of extraversion–introversion and neuroticism–stability described by Eysenck were discussed in some detail and their bearing on school achievement explored. The idea was mooted of a connection between the emphases and appeal of particular educational methods and corresponding personality characteristics. Introverts, for instance, tend to prefer their own company and tend not to be as inhibited by routine tasks (study for example) as extraverts. Clearly, these are advantageous qualities for students.

Finally, the problem facing the psychologist who attempts to quantify personality characteristics was put into perspective by describing some of the assessment methods now in use. These included Sheldon's typology of physique, physical experiments, rating scales and inventories, and projection techniques.

ENQUIRY AND DISCUSSION

1. Look at school record cards and decide on the validity and reliability of the personality characteristics reported. Whilst observing children, which personality qualities would you consider to be the really important ones from the point of view of (a) learning behaviour; (b) conduct in class? What dangers exist in this kind of observation?

2. As a background to the study of conduct and personality deviance, read J. S. Konnin, W. Freisen and A. Norton, 'Managing emotionally disturbed children in regular classrooms', *J. educ. Psychol.*, **57**, 1–13 (1966), and for the role of the school in the important task of minimizing deviance see M. Power *et al.*, 'Delinquency and schools', *New Society*, **264**, 542–543 (1967) and A. B. Clegg, 'The role of the school', in

Delinquency and Discipline, Councils and Education Press, London, 1962. Also read D. H. Stott, *Studies of Troublesome Children*, Tavistock, London, 1966.

3. Get your tutor to show the group some sample personality questionnaires including projection tests. Inspect these in terms of (a) the traits they purport to measure; (b) their fallibility—are the responses superficial, can the respondent falsify his answers, how have these problems been countered by the test designer (lie detection, duplication of items, parallel forms of the tests, etc.)?; (c) their particular use (age range, intelligence, verbal skills); (d) the use to which teachers can put the results of such tests when applied to children.

4. Examine the following:
   (a) sex differences in personality which are likely to affect (i) children's learning; (ii) teaching young or older children—are women teachers more appropriate in primary schools or men more appropriate in secondary schools?
   (b) the different behaviour patterns of interest to teachers in extraverts and introverts;
   (c) aggressive behaviour in children [Bandura's work, chapter 6, note (9)];
   (d) ways of reducing and controlling anxiety and drive energy in class.

NOTES AND REFERENCES

1. The definition is taken from H. J. Eysenck, *The Structure of Human Personality*, Methuen, London, 1953.

2. A. Thomas, S. Chess, H. G. Birch, M. E. Hertzig and S. Korn, *Behaviour Individuality in Early Childhood*, University of London Press, London, 1964.

3. P. E. Vernon, *Personality Assessment: A Critical Survey*, Methuen, London, 1966.

4. E. Goffman, *The Presentation of Self in Everyday Life*, Monograph 2, Social Science Research Centre, University of Edinburgh, 1956.

5. P. E. Vernon, *Personality Tests and Assessments*, Methuen, London, 1953 and the reference in note (3) above. Also see 'The use of tests in student selection', in H. J. Eysenck, *Uses and Abuses of Psychology*, Penguin, London, 1953.

6. J. A. C. Brown, *Freud and the Post-Freudians*, Penguin, London, 1961; C. S. Hall, *A Primer of Freudian Psychology*, World Publishing, Ohio, 1954. Another interesting text written by Freud himself attempts to explain the little accidents and slips of pen and memory occurring in our daily lives in terms of his psychoanalytical theory. S. Freud, *The Psychopathology of Everyday Life*, Penguin, London, 1914.

7. L. Hudson, *Contrary Imaginations*, Methuen, London, 1966.

8. P. Kline, in a book entitled *Fact and Fantasy in Freudian Theory*, Methuen, London, 1972, attempts to survey the research in support of Freud's theory.

9. R. Benedict, *Patterns of Culture*, Routledge and Kegan Paul, London, 1935.

10. It is difficult to recommend just one text of H. J. Eysenck's which examines his point of view because they are rather technical for the beginner. The earliest fundamental texts were *The Dimensions of Personality*, Routledge and Kegan Paul, London, 1947, and *The Scientific Study of Personality*, Routledge and Kegan Paul, London, 1952. However, for a less technical book, readers might like to try R. Lynn, *An Introduction to the Study of Personality*, Macmillan, London, 1971.

11. H. J. Eysenck, *The Structure of Human Personality*, 3rd ed., Methuen, London, 1970. In this book, Eysenck outlines a new approach which overlaps and partly supersedes a previous view of his in which Hull's theory of learning played a large part. Because this latter theory still appears in the literature and still finds a place in contemporary educational journals, it is briefly mentioned here. There are two basic postulates which involve the use of the concepts of *excitatory potential*, that is the tendency to make a response to a given stimulus, and *reactive inhibition*, that is the tendency not to repeat a response which has just been made. The two postulates are:

(a) human beings differ in the speed and strength with which excitation and inhibition are produced and the speed with which inhibition is dissipated;

(b) individuals in whom excitatory potential is generated slowly and relatively weakly and in whom reactive inhibition is developed quickly and strongly, but dissipated slowly, are thereby predisposed to extravert patterns of behaviour. The reverse is true of the introvert.

The notion expressed in (a), that we are aroused to different levels by similar events, is widely accepted. Some people become much more excited by certain pleasant or unpleasant events than others. Similarly, some people take longer to 'cool off' after arousal than others. What Eysenck has done in (b) is to relate these differential levels of excitation and inhibition to the extravert and introvert personality. The extravert experiences far more involuntary rest pauses than the introvert. Because excitatory potential is generated slowly and weakly whilst inhibition is quick and strong, the actual excitation will not be high unless the driving force which is motivating the activity is very high. The important point to remember from Eysenck's work is that extraverts possess high levels of reactive inhibition and this tends to make them less able to concentrate for any length of time in tasks requiring prolonged concentration. They require more lapses or *involuntary rest pauses* in carrying out a task, although these breaks are fractions of a second. The longer the task, the greater is the inhibition which accumulates.

By a similar argument, introverts are more readily conditioned than extraverts. The reason is that the involuntary rest pauses which the latter experience more frequently than the former interfere with the concentration necessary for conditioning to occur.

12. J. Partanen, K. Brunn and T. Markkanen, 'Inheritance of drinking behaviour', *Finnish Foundation for Alcohol Study*, **14** (1966); J. Shields, *Monozygotic Twins*, Oxford University Press, Oxford, 1962.

13. H. J. Eysenck, *The Biological Basis of Personality*, Thomas, Springfield, Illinois, 1967.

14. R. B. Cattell, *The Technical Handbook to the 16 PF*, Institute for Personality and Achievement Tests, Illinois, 1970.

15. D. Bannister and J. M. M. Mair, *The Evaluation of Personal Constructs*, Academic Press, London, 1968.

16. For example, L. M. Terman *et al.*, *Genetic Studies of Genius, Volume I: Mental and Physical Traits of a Thousand Gifted Children*, Stanford University Press, Stanford, California, 1925; D. Child, 'The relationships between introversion–extraversion, neuroticism and performance in school examinations', *Br. J, educ. Psychol.*, **34**, 187–196 (1964); N. J. Entwistle and D. Cunningham, 'Neuroticism and school attainment—a linear relationship?', *Br. J. educ. Psychol.*, **38**, 123–132 (1968). For a recent summary, see N. J. Entwistle, 'Personality and academic attainment', in H. J. Butcher and H. B. Pont (Eds), *Educational Research in Britain*, vol. 3, University of London Press, London, 1972.

17. For example, R. Lynn and I. E. Gordon, 'The relation of neuroticism and extraversion to intelligence and educational attainment', *Br. J. educ. Psychol.*, **31**, 194–203 (1961); W. D. Furneaux, *Report to the Imperial College of Science and Technology*, 1957.

18. N. J. Entwistle and S. Cunningham, 'Neuroticism and school attainment—a linear relationship?', *Br. J. educ. Psychol.*, **38**, 123–132 (1968).

19. For example, M. P. Callard and C. I. Goodfellow, 'Neuroticism and extraversion in school-children as measured by the Junior Maudsley Personality Inventory', *Br. J. educ. Psychol.*, **32**, 241–250 (1962); D. Child, *op. cit.*, note (16).

20. For example, *op. cit.*, note (16) and D. Child, 'A comparative study of personality, intelligence and social class in a technological university', *Br. J. educ. Psychol.*, **39**, 40–46 (1969).

21. D. Child and A. Smithers, 'Some cognitive and affective factors in subject choice', *Res. Educ.*, **5**, 1–9 (1971).

22. R. Lippitt and R. K. White, 'The "social climate" of children's groups', in R. G. Barker, J. S. Kounin and H. F. Wright (Eds), *Child Behaviour and Development*, McGraw-Hill, New York, 1943.

23. A. Morrison and D. McIntyre, *Teachers and Teaching*, Penguin, London, 1969.

24. E. Kretschmer, *Physique and Character*, Harcourt, Brace, New York, 1925; W. H. Sheldon and S. S. Stevens, *The Varieties of Temperament: A Psychology of Constitutional Differences*, Harper, New York, 1942. An extract from this book appears in B. Semeonoff (Ed.), *Personality Assessment*, Penguin, London, 1966.

25. Most of Eysenck's books contain examples of apparatus designed to measure physical correlates of personality such as persistence, endurance and conditionability. Look at H. J. Eysenck, *The Scientific Study of Personality*, Routledge and Kegan Paul, London, 1952.

26. Amongst the commonest inventories are Eysenck's personality inventories of extraversion and neuroticism, Cattell's 16PF or 16 personality factors and his anxiety scale for adults. A children's form has been devised by W. D. Furneaux and H. B. Gibson under the title of *The New Junior Maudsley Inventory*, suitable for mental ages of 11 to 16 years. Eysenck and his wife have also prepared a junior form. Both these junior inventories measure extraversion and neuroticism.

27. Two good introductory texts are A. L. Edwards, *Techniques of Attitude Scale Construction*, Appleton-Century-Crofts, New York, 1957 and A. N. Oppenheim, *Questionnaire Design and Attitude Measurement*, Heinemann, London, 1966.

28. D. E. Super, *The Psychology of Careers*, Harper and Row, New York, 1957.

29. Several psychologists in the 1940s set out to discover predictors of success in school subjects in the form of information tests. E. A. Peel, 'Assessment of interest in practical topics', *Br. J. educ. Psychol.*, **18**, 41–48 (1948) and T. F. Fitzpatrick and S. Wiseman, 'An interest test for use in selection for technical education', *Br. J. educ. Psychol.*, **24**, 99–105 (1954) were amongst the earliest to devise 11+ examinations to assist in the selection of pupils for technical grammar schools. As it happens, these tests were never adopted throughout the country.

30. Eysenck has little time for depth psychology. He feels that psychoanalytical sessions give an opportunity for the mind of the analyst to run riot in seeking to make sense out of the mumbo-jumbo of semi-consciousness. A. R. Jensen, 'Personality', *Ann. Rev. Psychol.*, **9**, 295–322 (1958) found little by way of validation for projection techniques and Eysenck doubts whether they are any better than chance in helping to cure the mentally ill.

FURTHER READING

R. Lynn, *An Introduction to the Study of Personality*, Macmillan, London, 1971. A basically written text with the emphasis on psychometric studies of personality.

A. N. Oppenheim, *Questionnaire Design and Attitude Measurement*, Heinemann, London, 1966. Very useful for those who want to know more about the design and pitfalls of attitude scales.

C. Rycroft (Ed.), *Psychoanalysis Observed*, Constable, London, 1966.

B. Semeonoff (Ed.), *Personality Assessment*, Penguin, London, 1966. Contains many extracts from the writings of well-known researchers in the area of personality.

P. E. Vernon, *Personality Assessment: A Critical Survey*, Methuen, London, 1966 and *Personality Tests and Assessments*, Methuen, London, 1953. Both these texts provide a thorough examination of the problems of personality assessment.

12   Educational handicap

The title of this chapter needs a word of explanation. In everyday language, the term 'handicap' is often used to signify a physical defect—limb paralysis, partial or total blindness, and so forth—which renders the individual incapable of living in quite the same way as the normally endowed. We will use the term in a much wider sense to include the intellectual, emotional and social as well as physical disabilities and disadvantages which are likely to cause learning hardships especially in orthodox educational settings. We are none of us, of course, completely equipped for all eventualities in life, yet most of us manage to survive either because some of our assets can be used to compensate for our inabilities or because we are able to avoid situations where our weaknesses are exposed. There is, however, a small number of children whose handicaps are so extreme that they are unable to benefit from our regular educational facilities and therefore must receive special provision. It is to these children that the present chapter will be devoted. Whilst the education of the educationally handicapped may never fall within the responsibilities of the majority of teachers, it remains true that it is almost impossible to go through one's professional life without meeting several cases of handicap both in and out of school.

THE AIMS OF SPECIAL EDUCATIONAL PROVISION

All teachers are concerned with the mental progress of children by promoting intellectual skills in the acquisition of knowledge. Further, they attempt to encourage individual children in their efforts to adjust both personally, in preparation for adult life, and socially, as a member of a community. These same aims are true of special educational provision except that the order of priority must take into account the exceptional disadvantages of each child. The key to special educational provision is to help each handicapped child in adjusting and compensating for his disability as well as in fulfilling the broader aims suggested above. The mentally dull will grow up, find work, run a home and have many exacting responsibilities for which they must be prepared. Work which is other than skilled is becoming harder to find and the business of budgeting for a family taxes the ingenuity of most people, let alone those with mental backwardness. Sometimes the physically disabled are prone to emotional and social side-effects because they have difficulty coming to terms with the inadequacy they feel in comparison with others. Problems of this kind require different emphases and careful handling which only special, individual education can provide.

For ease of description later, we shall consider four possible categories of educational handicap, but it should be made clear from the outset that it is now unfashionable to attach too much importance to this separation; the symptoms and remedies are so often interrelated and the provision frequently geared to the particular problems of each child. Although institutions still exist where specialist attention is provided (schools for the educationally subnormal, partially sighted, etc.), they all recognize that a stereotyped pattern of educational facilities would be totally inadequate for the range of problems one can find within each kind of institution. Frequently those with one major handicap suffer in other ways. A physically disabled child may also be mentally backward, have language difficulties or suffer from emotional and social problems; the emotionally disturbed, in addition to faltering in their school work, sometimes display socially deviant behaviour.

To meet these difficulties of classification, Gulliford, in an important textbook on the subject of special educational needs (1), suggests that we might do better to consider the education of the handicapped in terms of the resources and purposes served by the special forms of education available. He lists three forms of provision, namely, *special*, *remedial* and *compensatory* education.

(a) Special education serves those who need a special environment for medical, teaching and curriculum purposes. Full- or part-time residence or day special schools are common features of this kind of educational provision. Where the home or a traditional school is inadequate to cope with the unusual demands of the child, custom-made facilities have to be provided in special centres. Catering for the education of the blind, the severely physically handicapped, the severely mentally subnormal and the maladjusted is often better done away from home, although where it is at all possible parental affection, support and encouragement add a very important dimension to the child's development. Nevertheless, where there are multiple handicaps requiring medical aids and treatment, or where the home is not able to create a helpful atmosphere, as in maladjusted cases, residential facilities are desirable.

(b) Remedial education is usually offered as a part-time and short-term provision for individual children who are experiencing particular difficulties in scholastic or mechanical skills. Remedial work in reading is quite common, but speech therapy, drawing, writing and other language skills also form an important task. Remedial lessons are usually school based for groups or individual children. Either teachers are specially appointed to a school for the task, or peripatetic teachers (travelling teachers— 'have skills, will travel') call in at the school or members of the School Psychological Service through the Child Guidance Centres visit the school or take the children at the centres. The education offered is *in addition to* the normal schooling as a sort of 'topping up' process. In fact, at one time the remedial service was intended for those who were thought to be underachieving (not reaching a standard commensurate with the child's performance on standardized tests of ability), but the service does not now limit itself to remediation in backward children.

(c) Compensatory education is provided in the belief that the home and environmental circumstances of some children are so limited that programmes concentrating particularly on language and social skills are necessary. Development is thought to be retarded by cultural deprivation. In some cases the entire school may be oriented towards remedying the disadvantages of the neighbourhood circumstances. These areas are sometimes referred to as *educational priority areas* (e.p.a.) because of a high prevalence of intellectual and social deprivation in addition to inadequate amenities (too much noise and grime and not enough green space and privacy when required). In other cases, one or two classes in a school are given over to the children from disadvantageous backgrounds. Social as well as educational services play an important and active part in the liaison between home and school. More will be said later on these matters.

At the end of the Second World War and following smartly on the heels of the Butler Education Act of 1944 came the Handicapped Pupils' and School Health Service Regulations, 1945, which formulated several categories of handicap in need of special educational treatment. Table 12.1 shows these categories along with some recent statistics taken from the Plowden Report (2) highlighting the magnitude of the problem. The table includes educationally subnormal children who are by far the largest group amounting to nearly one per cent of the seven and a half million children of school age, but it omits both the most seriously mentally deprived group now known as severely subnormal (SSN), which includes some 21 000 children, and the significant army of slow learners in normal schools totalling 10 to 15 per cent of all schoolchildren.

Table 12.1   Numbers of handicapped pupils receiving and awaiting special education (in special schools, classes, units, in hospitals and at home) and prevalence per 10 000 of the school population in England and Wales, 1966. From the Plowden Report with the permission of Her Majesty's Stationery Office.

Categories	1966	
	No. of children	Prevalence per 10 000 of school population
Blind	1 337	1·7
Partially sighted	2 326	3·0
Deaf	3 281	4·2
Partially hearing	3 296	4·2
Physically handicapped	11 616	14·8
Delicate	10 418	13·3
Maladjusted	8 548	10·9
Educationally subnormal	55 514	70·9
Epileptic	877	1·1
With speech defect	224	0·3
Total	97 437	124·4

For convenience, in the following pages we shall divide handicaps into four categories and consider each in turn. It should soon become apparent that they are not mutually exclusive. The four are: mental, emotional, social and physical handicaps.

H

MENTAL HANDICAP

Most of the cases we are likely to consider in this chapter, whether they be physically disabled, emotionally disturbed or culturally deprived, exhibit some degree of mental handicap where scholastic performance is below the average expected of a child's age group. Most teachers who deal with average and below-average pupils, especially in infant and primary schools, meet with children who do not seem to profit from the usual educational methods and content provided. Mental handicap in the present context is being reserved for those who are *backward*, or to use a more recent and acceptable term, *slow learners*. Where a child is not coping with the work normally expected of his age group, he is said to be a slow learner (3).

Whilst the sources of backwardness are many, complex and diverse, it is possible to perceive two broad distinctions made in the HMSO pamphlet No. 46 on *Slow Learners at School* (4). There are children who by nature have limited intellectual endowment and who would not be expected to become bright adults after receiving specialized education. These are referred to as *mentally dull* children. But there are children whose achievements are depressed by causes other than low mental ability and who could in fact with careful handling and remedial aid be expected to do better (quite remarkably in some cases). These are *retarded* children. With dull children, we need to give special education either within the normal school setting or in special schools. Retarded children most frequently require remedial education to discover their particular problems and provide additional educational support to normal schooling.

Detecting cases of backwardness is usually left to the teacher. Children with severe subnormality, disability, blindness or deafness are readily noted and reported by parents, but mental backwardness is not always noticed especially in mentally dull homes. The first intimations come from either medical services—doctors, clinics, social workers—or from teachers in the first few months at school. Often the parents of backward children particularly those who have not helped their children in language, number or play prior to school, are blissfully unaware of their children's standing (largely because they have little or no yardstick for judging their child's ability in relation to other children) and it is left to the reception class teacher to spot intellectual underfunctioning or dullness.

When suspicions are aroused, the head teacher is informed and the procedure then involves the parents, the Local Education Authority, the Child Guidance Clinic and whatever previous medical evidence is available (5). As well as medical evidence, intelligence tests and performance in basic school subjects, simple manipulative skills, language usage and social adjustments are other variables which are considered.

The distinction between mentally dull and retarded children is generally confirmed using intelligence tests. Also a clue to the degree of dullness can be obtained from the IQ score, although we should remember that IQ scores are not constant and retesting is an advisable part of the programme. We saw in chapter 9 that IQs are distributed 'normally' in the population. There are a few very bright and very dull individuals— some so mentally deprived that mental testing is impossible. When a mean of 100 and standard deviation of 15 have been used in test design, something approaching 70 per cent of the population would obtain an IQ between 115 and 85 IQ (standard deviation is dealt with later). Dull children are usually found to have IQs lower than 85–90. Retarded children, on the other hand, may, in fact, be quite bright and their IQ scores could be much higher than 90.

At one time it was conventional to group children according to measured intelligence before it was realized that intelligence was neither fixed nor entirely innately determined. Such unpleasant sounding labels as 'imbecile' (IQ range 25–50) and 'idiot' (less than 25) were in common usage. Though we still use IQs as a criterion for deciding on a child's level of educability, the interpretation of IQ value has wide limits. We have tried to convey this in figure 12.1 which shows the present approximate IQ ranges existing amongst those who are slow learners, educationally subnormal and severely subnormal. Note there is overlap between these to demonstrate that, for example, children with IQs of 80 might be receiving an education alongside other children as slow learners in

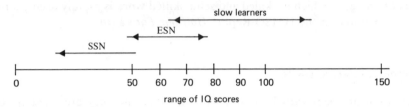

Figure 12.1   Range of IQ scores (mean = 100, SD = 15) giving a rough idea of IQ ranges within which we find slow learners, ESN and SSN children

an ordinary school, with a special class, or with ESN children in a special day or residential school. Having noted the limitations of intelligence measures, it remains true that they are an important means of assessing the severity of mental handicaps.

Slow learners: mentally dull

The majority of dull children find their way into primary and non-selective secondary schools. A few are sent to day special schools for ESN children. As stated before they form between 10 and 15 per cent of schoolchildren and consequently demand a substantial investment in teachers' time and effort. The special education offered endeavours to find and provide ways by which the mentally subnormal can fulfil whatever limited potential they possess. Sometimes they are placed in a separate group or class, but it is often possible, especially in unstreamed class groups, to find them with brighter children (2). Provided the class is small enough, which is rarely possible in present circumstances, individual help from a sympathetic and adequately trained teacher can be effective in unstreamed classes. Where circumstances permit or when class sizes are too large, remedial education using part-time or visiting teachers often becomes an additional source of educational provision. Dull children's involvement in the normal school setting, where this is at all possible, is to be encouraged. Most of them grow up to be useful members of a community consisting of people from all walks of life and of varying intellectual skills; therefore segregation early in life could militate against the slow learner taking a responsible part in the community.

Mentally dull children need tactful, resourceful and skilful teaching of basic language and number skills together with a programme of *activities* with the emphasis on children doing things in craft, art, drama, movement and communication. The curriculum is very much concerned with the concrete and practical aspects of scholastic work rather than with abstract thinking. Both from our definitions of intelligent behaviour and from Piaget's view of concept formation it follows that mentally dull children are intellectually operating at a level well below their actual age. Some dull children may rarely, if ever, operate abstractly in the sense used by Piaget in concept formation. Nevertheless, dull children still have to grow to adulthood facing similar problems of earning a living, providing for a family and taking leisure. Clearly the examination system is quite unsuited to the needs and abilities of these pupils and the raised school-leaving age must be used to provide children with competence to meet the demands of an age in which unskilled and semi-skilled work is rapidly disappearing. This problem is explored in the HMSO Report *Half our Future* (6).

Slow learners: retarded pupils

Some children are backward in school work not because they are mentally dull, but because their ability has been depressed by some environmental cause. Implicit in remedial education is the notion that there is going to be an improvement after a short- or medium-term remedial programme intended to remove or counteract the source of trouble and recover lost ground in the scholastic attainment of the child to a point more in keeping with his potential ability. It is quite possible to find children with IQs of well over 100 in need of remedial teaching.

The conditions which accompany retardation tend to resolve into physical–personal (other than mental dullness as we have noted above), environmental and emotional difficulties. Personal factors include long illness or absence from school, undetected physical defects such as partial sight and hearing, mild aphasias (see chapter 2); environmental variables range from poor home facilities for learning speech and reading skills, low quality and quantity of food, shortage of sleep and adverse parental attitudes towards education to poor or inappropriate opportunities at school such as large classes, poor teaching of basic skills (going too quickly, choosing inadequate or advanced material), incompatibility between home and school, repeated changes of school and consequent changes in teaching styles and content (changing from i.t.a. to traditional orthography or from 'new maths' to conventional number teaching). Emotional states will be dealt with later under the heading of maladjustment, but here we should mention dislike of teacher through clashes of personality, negative parental attitudes to school creating in the child similar adverse attitudes, failure in school snowballing into feelings of inadequacy and subsequently depressing the child's confidence and need to achieve, and extreme timidity and anxiety giving rise to poor levels of attainment.

Remedial education for the retarded generally takes the form of individual or small group tuition by skilled teachers or educational psychologists from the School Psychological Service. The commonest subject is reading, but speech therapy, number and writing also figure.

Educationally subnormal (ESN)

Where there is serious mental deficiency it is not always appropriate for a child to remain in a State school. When the measured intelligence is below about 70 IQ, it usually becomes necessary to refer children for special education in day special schools or residential special schools for the educationally subnormal. We do, nevertheless, find a few children of low IQ in special classes in State schools where facilities are possible (some rural comprehensive schools, for example, have day classes for ESN children). ESN children total just under one per cent of school-aged children of which about 45 000 [in 1966, Plowden Report, p. 301, reference (2)] were in special schools and 10 000 were in State schools awaiting a place in a special school.

Whilst we all agree with circular 276 of the Department of Education and Science (1954) that 'no handicapped child should be sent to a special school who can be satisfactorily educated in an ordinary school', it is often in the best interests of the ESN child to attend a special school which can cater for individual needs using skilled and specially trained staff as few State schools are able at the moment. Where possible ESN children attend the day special school, but when (i) home conditions adversely affect the child's development; (ii) special services such as medical or psychological treatment are necessary; (iii) rural children have no local day special facilities; and (iv) there are emotional complications aggravated by home circumstances, the children are sent to a residential special school.

With intelligence quotients in the range 45 to 80, children cannot profit from the same educational provision found in classes of mentally average children. Small classes (ideally no more than twelve) are in evidence and the school size is rarely more than 200. The curriculum is less verbal and more practical. The three Rs are taught with a view to helping children in the difficult task of adjusting to a normal life in society (7).

Severely subnormal (SSN)

Children whose intellectual competence is very low (often associated with an IQ of less than 50) and who are not capable of taking advantage of the type of education found in either State or ESN schools are referred to as severely subnormal children. Special schools for the SSN have replaced the junior training centres ('training' was an unfortunate term anyway for the kind of education provided) and they are now under the jurisdiction of the Department of Education and Science through the Local Education Authority. These schools, along with hospitals for the subnormal (when a child has physical complications as well and cannot care for himself), cater for children who would get no benefit from academic kinds of schooling.

Until recently these children were considered to be ineducable, but it has been shown that some of the more able can learn simple reading and writing skills. The priority is to help them in motor, perceptual and simple language skills so that they can gain some personal competence in looking after themselves (feeding, dressing, toilet, homely routines), and social competence in communicating with others and possibly engaging in some kind of simple manual work. There are some unfortunates who are hospitalized and never attain even these basic human competences and must depend on others for their daily routines.

In addition to poor genetic potential, there are organic disorders which lead to low mental competence. During pregnancy the brain may be damaged, or diseases of both mother or foetus can lead to degeneration of brain tissues. These are congenital disorders of mental functioning. Injury during birth is also a possible, but comparatively rare, cause nowadays. These give spastic and cerebral palsied conditions. Diseases in early childhood can leave a permanent mental scar if they are serious and remain untreated (measles, scarlet fever and several others). Also mongol children usually have low IQ scores, although one can find wide variations (8).

In summary then, we have:

Table 12.2   Summary of educational provision for the mentally handicapped

Mental handicap	Educational provision	Approximate IQ range
Slow learners — mentally dull	(a) ordinary primary and day schools (b) special classes attached to (a) (c) individual teaching (d) occasionally in ESN schools	90–60
Slow learners — mentally retarded	Individual or group remedial classes taken by specialist teachers or psychologists from the School Psychological Service	100 →
Educationally subnormal	(a) special classes attached to primary and secondary day schools (b) day special schools for the ESN (c) residential special schools for the ESN	80–45
Severely subnormal	(a) residential special schools for SSN (b) hospitals for the subnormal	50→

EMOTIONAL HANDICAPS

Emotional disturbance is commonplace. All of us at some time have experienced symptoms of emotional stress and disturbance without their unduly affecting our daily lives. Temporary effects such as lack of concentration, quick arousal to anger or tears, temperamental fickleness or fecklessness are soon overcome. There is a small group of children and adults who are unable to overcome their emotional problems. In a submission from the Plowden Committee (2) it would seem that upwards of 15 per cent of schoolchildren in primary schools experience strong debilitating influences from their emotional stresses.

When emotional handicaps reach the stage of being so grave as to affect social development leading on to behaviour disorders (and frequently influencing school work), we term this *maladjustment*. The definition enunciated by the Handicapped Pupils' and School Health Service regulations of 1945 suggests that maladjustment is exemplified by 'pupils who show evidence of emotional instability or psychological disturbance and require special educational treatment in order to effect their personal, social and educational readjustment'. Cases requiring special facilities, as indicated in table 12.1, amounted to 8 548 in 1966, although, as we have noted above, far more children than this do need help in this direction without it ever coming to the notice of the authorities. Definitions of maladjustment also imply that behaviour is judged in terms of a society's existing standards. Thus, what is commonly acceptable to a society at one time (take our own at present compared with the beginning of this century) might be thought of as quite unacceptable at another time. Young children talking about sex might have been regarded as promiscuous or precocious fifty years ago; in this permissive age it would be tolerated if not encouraged as being forthright, honest and frank. Again, changes in attitude as a result of the processes of maturity should not be taken as signs of maladjustment. Adolescents in search of adult standards, values and privileges may appear to some parents as suffering from behaviour disorders, whereas, in fact, the onset of these attitudes is a healthy developmental sign.

The Underwood Committee (9) looked at the whole question of maladjustment and educational provision. They set out six groups of symptoms commonly associated with maladjustment. The appearance of any one of these symptoms does not of itself signify maladjustment. Nor are these symptoms necessarily permanent. They range from mild to severe and many cases can be dealt with in the normal school setting by teachers aware of the problems and possible solutions. Examples of the six groups of disorders are:

1. *Nervous disorders:* Fears and anxiety; marked solitariness and timidity; depression and obsession; excitability–apathy; hysteria and amnesia;

2. *Habit disorders:* Speech defects and stammering (other than those caused by physical defect); excessive daydreaming, sleeplessness and nightmares; facial and body tics, nail-biting, rocking; bed-wetting and general incontinence; physical symptoms such as asthma and allergies;

3. *Behaviour disorders:* temper tantrums; destructive, defiant or cruel; stealing, lying, truancy; sex abberations;

4. *Organic disorders:* neurological dysfunctioning—head injuries; brain tumours; epilepsy;

5. *Psychotic disorders:* Hallucinations; delusions; bizarre behaviour;

6. *Educational and vocational difficulties:* lacking concentration; unable to hold down a job; irregular response to school discipline; slow learning—retarded in reading particularly.

Looking around a class of children (or just contemplating one's own earlier characteristics) will soon reveal the presence of some of these symptoms without it necessarily signifying maladjustment. Many children have an eye or facial twitch, bite their nails or have sleep problems. But when these symptoms accumulate we normally have a maladjusted case on our hands. Some symptoms such as psychotic and organic disorders are quite conclusive in their effects.

Apart from the obvious organic disorders mentioned above, the origins of maladjusted behaviour are not understood. It might be, as we noted in chapter 11, that some individuals are predisposed to maladjustment given the right conditions. Home and school could therefore present problematic situations which might provoke emotional discord. Frustration and strained relationships between parent and child, teacher and child or between the children will influence some children more than others. Withholding affection or generating feelings of insecurity are likely to precipitate maladjustment in some children. Inability to cope with school work or teachers whose approach is too demanding or intimidating are also likely causes of maladjustment.

Maladjustment is frequently dealt with whilst the child is attending a primary or secondary school. Close liaison between the school and home to discover the background to the child's problems and the involvement of social psychiatric workers, psychiatrists and psychologists from the Child Guidance Service are necessary in determining possible causes and in some cases preventing the situation from worsening. School attainment often shows a marked improvement as a consequence of detecting and tackling the cause. This is sometimes accomplished by visits to the home and school from the Child Guidance workers. At school or at the clinic the child receives lessons and treatment in keeping with the causes. Where the home is clearly not suitable in its influence on the emotional development of the child, the child is sent to a residential special school for the maladjusted designed to provide a therapeutic environment. Cases of retarded mental development are given remedial help (1).

Autistic children (10)

Autism (from the Greek *autos* which means *self*) has only recently been isolated as a specific handicap (Kanner in 1943). Many views as to its nature and causes have been suggested of which the most recent is that autism is caused by a disability in interpreting sensory experiences, particularly hearing and seeing. Symbol interpretation is especially difficult. Autistic children seem to lack the ability to symbolize and therefore have great difficulty acquiring language. Other causes which have been proposed are brain damage and inherent emotional bleakness, but the evidence is not convincing.

The most conspicuous symptom of autism to an outsider is the lack of contact, either with eyes or in speech, between the child and others (even parents). Speech, where it appears, is grossly retarded and unusual ('echolalia' where the child repeats something which has just been said). Excessive and persistent movement such as rocking in a chair and banging the head against the back of it or flapping hands with or without a piece of string are characteristic. Some perceptual experiences are ignored (sights and sounds and even heat and pain) whilst other perceptual experiences seem to become hypnotic (music and regular beats) [for other symptoms see note (11)].

The special provision for autistic children has not been clear cut. The numbers involved are about 3 000 throughout the country receiving attention in hospitals for the subnormal, special schools for ESN and SSN children and a few in normal day schools. A few special schools have been established by the National Society for Autistic Children. This haphazard organization is partly the result of uncertainty as to the assistance which can be fruitfully afforded to these children. If the supposition that autism involves impaired perceptual interpretation in mainly the visual and hearing modalities is correct, it would seem appropriate to explore the other senses—touch, movement, olfaction. A stable environment where a close watch can be kept on each child to capitalize on those sensory channels which he can appreciate is also recommended [(10) Furneaux].

SOCIAL AND CULTURAL HANDICAP

This is a vast topic which is an important province of the sociologist and social psychologist and should be fully dealt with in these areas. We shall content ourselves with a summary of the major factors in educational backwardness which have psychological significance in a social context.

The potent influence of cultural background on scholastic performance, social and emotional development, and competence in adult life is not a new discovery. A number of psychologists and teachers back in the twenties, highlighted by Burt (12), recognized the place of home circumstances as a causal factor in educational backwardness and behaviour problems which sometimes culminated in delinquency. However, it is really since the last war that a systematic assault on the origins of, and possible compensations for, cultural deprivation has been launched. Most of the major reports in education have presented evidence and suggestions relating to the life-chances of children. The Crowther and *Early Leaving Report* (13) point to several cultural differences which have led to a shortfall in the numbers of children from working-class homes going on to higher education compared with those from middle-class homes. Furthermore, the former seem to be losing ground in their school attainment as they move through the school (14). The Plowden Report on primary schools (2) devotes a whole chapter, well worth reading, to *Educational Priority Areas* (e.p.a.'s) where some children (not necessarily all children) are handicapped by home and neighbourhood conditions (both physical and mental), where schools are starved of amenities and high turnover of staff is disturbing to the stability of the children, where, in a nutshell, educational handicaps are reinforced by social handicaps.

To cope with the social and cultural casualties, a series of programmes has been devised which emphasizes strategies in the presentation of content designed within a conducive atmosphere and aimed at counteracting the disadvantages of the child's social background. These programmes are referred to as *compensatory education*, about which more will be said presently.

Some social disadvantages

From the earliest work of Burt to the present time, a lot has been written about the social factors thought to conspire against successful progress in and beyond school. Whilst there will undoubtedly be those of low intellectual ability amongst the children from deprived backgrounds, there is strong evidence for believing that many are under-functioning—as in the case of those receiving remedial education. However, remedial education is not enough to compensate for the many overlapping cultural factors at work and a total educational programme is required from the earliest possible moment in the child's life.

Several summaries of the characteristics of disadvantaged children have been compiled (15) from which the following has been freely adapted.

(a) Poverty and inadequate care often mean cramped and improverished living conditions, overcrowding, low income (and pressure on children to start earning) and feelings of insecurity;

(b) restrictions in language experience (see chapter 8) often disable the child from a working-class home when he comes to forming abstract concepts. The character of the language and its content are obvious barriers to scholastic success as we know it. There are few books around in the home and conversation is neither informative nor extensive. Immigrant children in some cases have the added problem of living with the language of their parents (sometimes called L1—pronounced 'L one') and trying to learn a second language (L2) which is the language of transmission of knowledge in the school;

(c) sensory deprivation is often the case in homes with little in the way of sensory stimulation. There is often a shortage or absence of toys or surrounding objects offering some variety of stimulation (see chapter 4);

(d) a hedonistic outlook is very common ('why put off till tomorrow what you can do today?'). There is little medium- or long-term planning and this reappears in the secondary school when decisions have to be made as to whether the pupil will stay on for several years to obtain a qualification (perhaps until 21 or 22 years of age) or whether he will leave and earn a living (13). Deprived children often succumb and leave school. The signs are also seen in a lack of perseverance in school work;

(e) parental attitude to school and a clash of values between children and their schools often gives rise to disillusionment and reduced motivation to do school work;

(f) performance at school, especially in standardized tests, tends to deteriorate as children proceed through school life (14);

(g) emotional deprivation arising from inconsistent and inconsequential parents, broken families or loss of a parent can give rise, as we have seen, to maladjustment;

(h) large families sometimes produce a greater possibility of poverty, language deprivation (parents have not the same opportunity to converse with their children and there will be more communication between less verbally mature siblings). IQ is also negatively correlated with family size (16)—as the family size increases the average intelligence decreases;

(i) children from socially deprived homes tend to develop poor self-images. The 'self-fulfilling prophecy' in chapter 3 is an example of the way in which a poor self-image can soon be nourished in children, who have little in their backgrounds to be confident about, by teachers, who are insensitive to children's potential.

Compensatory programmes (17)

Research into approaches to the teaching of disadvantaged children is a fairly recent feature, and far more has been done in America than in this country. Some programmes emphasize language habits (19) and use drill methods in order to create a firm foundation for symbolic reasoning. Another approach adopts the developmental stages postulated by Piaget with the emphasis on cognitive development to ensure that the child's progress is paced and punctuated with active participation in learning.

All the programmes seem to have certain objectives in common. Enrichment is provided in language, perceptual and social skills. Plenty of talk about stimulating objects and events, tape-recordings, films, visits to places of interest to children (zoos, parks, famous places) and abundant opportunity for reading materials are the order of the day. School must offer a stable and secure atmosphere, a place where children want to be and to work. An adequate self-image needs to be fostered through encouragement and the feel of success. Personal standards and development in terms of cleanliness and social behaviour are frequently the subject of compensatory programmes. But this sphere is still the subject of lively research effort (20).

Delinquency

> Our youth now loves luxury. It has bad manners, contempt for authority, disrespect for older people. Children nowadays are tyrants. They contradict their parents, chatter before company, gobble their food and tyrannize their teachers.

In the broadest terms, a delinquent act is any behaviour on the part of a juvenile (under eighteen years of age) to which the more senior members of a society object. Couched in these terms, we have all been delinquents at one time or another. Judging from the quotation at the beginning of this section, it would seem that things were not much different in the days of Socrates who wrote it in 329 B.C. The kinds of non-indictable offences for which young people can be brought to justice as delinquents are truancy, taking and driving a car, vandalism, stealing, trespassing, sex misdemeanours (girls– prostitution) and youths who are beyond parental control. The testimony of Burt (12) in *The Young Delinquent* and other research since (18) shows that most delinquents are not mentally unbalanced nor completely devoid of moral standards. Many do not persist in crime and a high proportion are never caught.

The causes are as yet little understood [Wilkins (18)]. One school of thought lays stress on the punitive, poverty stricken or broken home giving a bad example to children. Another school of thought feels that a permissive home with spoilt and lonely children could be a cause. Others lay the blame on personality deviance. These views have been summarized according to the emphasis on underlying psychological assumptions. The three important approaches are (i) family influences; (ii) personality delinquency; and (iii) 'sociological' or situational delinquency.

In the familial kind of delinquency, the significant determinant of anti-social behaviour is thought to be family conflict [Burt (12) Bowlby (18)]. Such factors as defective home management, immorality, drunkenness, criminality, broken homes, poverty and the child-rearing practices and experiences during the first five years of life are thought likely to precipitate delinquent behaviour. There is a small number of delinquents who have personality deviances. Psychopathic conditions and character disorders through excessive emotional stress, chiefly at home, are seen as causes [Stott (18)]. Finally, situational delinquency [Cohen (18)] lays great stress on the influence of the environment in city sub-cultures and the formation of gangs where the individual is able to create an identity which is respected and gives him status. There is also a negative correlation between delinquency and social class (although the statistics are not all that convincing because middle-class parents are usually in a better position to get their children 'off the hook'). All the culture theorists of delinquency, however, give pride of place to life styles either in the home or in the surrounding sub-culture.

EDUCATION OF THE PHYSICALLY HANDICAPPED (1)

There are many forms of physical disability which are classified as handicaps. Children with loss of limb functioning causing them to be chair- or bed-bound, profound deafness, blindness, spasticism, spina bifida, polio, cerebral palsy, delicacy and other disabling malfunctions generally need to attend special schools which can cater medically as well as provide educational services. There are cases, and we have probably all met some, of children with physical handicaps still able to attend normal day school, but these cases are rare. Special schools for the blind, deaf and physically handicapped cope with some 25 000 children between five and sixteen years of age. The ability range is wide because there are many cases of physical disability which are not accompanied by mental handicap. Team work in special schools is very necessary. The paramedical staff (nurses, physiotherapists, occupational and speech therapists) work alongside the teaching staff to give individual help to the child. Where children are able to go on to more academic work every encouragement is given. There are now several cases of blind, deaf and chair-bound adults who have found a place in higher education and in work demanding high intellectual skills.

Some have complications arising from their physical handicaps which make communication difficult—speech organ deformities or hand paralysis preventing writing for instance. Emotional and social problems can soon arise from the frustrations of immobility unless carefully handled. Where possible, family life is encouraged, for parents can do a great deal in providing a secure and stable background for their children. Central to all their efforts is an attempt to give the child as much self-assurance and independence as he is capable of and, where possible, to draw on the child's capacities to enable him to take some part in community life.

SUMMARY

There is now a substantial investment of time and effort in our educational system devoted to the task of providing for the educationally handicapped. Strictly speaking, children who, by virtue of exceptional physical, mental, emotional or social attributes, are not always able to benefit from conventional State day schools are included in the official definition of the educationally handicapped. We do, however, meet children in need of special education in our daily work, partly because some can benefit more from the companionship of normally endowed children both in work and play, and partly because special educational facilities are not always available for those who are in need of them. We will all have to deal with slow learners, the occasional partially disabled, the gifted, epileptics, delinquents and the emotionally disturbed within the traditional State school.

Children with special needs are catered for in broadly three ways, namely, by special education, remedial education and compensatory education. Special education serves those who must have a purpose-built environment because conventional facilities at home or school are inadequate. Physical disadvantages such as blindness, severe physical handicap, SSN and severe maladjustment often require the expert attention of professionals in medicine, clinical psychology and special education. Remedial education is most often a part-time, short-term affair for those with particular problems in scholastic or mechanical skills. Reading and speech difficulties are amongst the commonest subjects for remedial education. Outside help from a child guidance unit is frequently necessary. Compensatory education is most needed when the environmental circumstances have to be compensated for by the use of enrichment programmes aimed at giving disadvantaged children the right kind of conditions. The socially disadvantaged are fast becoming the subject of new programmes of compensatory education. The help available often takes place in part of a school in the form of special classes, or the whole school is involved in providing an atmosphere intended to enhance social and communication skills.

Slow learners, those children who are not coping with work normally expected of their age group, are generally either low in intellectual endowments as compared with their contemporaries (mentally dull) or through impoverished educational opportunities, emotional hazards at home or other mentally disabling circumstances have fallen behind their peers (retarded). It would be futile to take the same syllabus for a given age group and to give it to dull or retarded children at a slower pace. Adjustment in presentation methods and curriculum content are frequently necessary. The emphasis is 'local', active and practical, although the curriculum must include language and those abilities which enable an individual to cope sufficiently with the concrete problems of daily life. Children who are mentally dull need to be weaned from isolation to taking a useful place in the community. Those whose capacities have been artificially depressed by circumstances require remedial help intended to recover lost ground in the basic skills of reading and communicating.

The educationally and severely subnormal, those with low measured intelligence amongst other things, usually require special school provision, although this has not always been possible in our crowded school conditions. The gifted, those with unusually high IQs, are less frequently given special education in this country, whilst in the USA and USSR there are special centres where accelerated programmes are provided.

Children who display emotional instability or psychological disturbance sufficient to warrant professional treatment are said to be maladjusted. A teacher who suspects that he has an emotionally disturbed child on his hands must be in a position to decide on the seriousness of the problem and whether he can deal with it or will need to obtain the help of the psychological service.

Delinquency amongst children has been with us for centuries. Delinquent children are in a somewhat unfortunate position in that their 'disabilities' are also a source of anti-social behaviour. Fortunately their plight is rarely permanent and our job must be to make sure that the passage of young people through difficult times of behavioural deviance is quick and complete. Offering trusted ears and gradually re-educating delinquents in terms of moral and social values are often arduous and thankless jobs in which the community, the school and the teacher have a stake. The ultimate aim is to create conditions in which our youth find delinquency an irrelevance. In particular, the school must look at the motivational problems which currently beset us in the secondary sector, especially in these days of the raised school-leaving age.

ENQUIRY AND DISCUSSION

1. Whilst on school visits or practice try to meet and observe children in some of the following categories. Also discover if there is any special provision for the children.

    (a) Educationally subnormal;
    (b) gifted;
    (c) maladjusted;
    (d) culturally disadvantaged;
    (e) retarded;
    (f) mentally dull.

2. Try to arrange visits to the relevant institutions or invite speakers who can give specialist information about the identification and education of children provided by the following:

    (a) ESN and SSN special schools;
    (b) branches of the Child Guidance Service;
    (c) services related to delinquency;
    (d) schools and homes for the physically handicapped;
    (e) educational priority areas.

3. Consult the *Newsom* and/or *Plowden* Report(s) for their comments and suggestions relating to the educationally handicapped.

4. What are the arguments for and against the segregation of educationally handicapped children?

5. The gifted child, often defined in terms of intelligence rating, is considered as an exceptional case in the USA and USSR. Examine the literature to discover the nature of the provision made by these countries. What is the case for and against such provision?

6. Read up and discuss the psychological and sociological theories associated with delinquency.

NOTES AND REFERENCES

1. R. Gulliford in *Special Educational Needs*, Routledge and Kegan Paul, London, 1971, has written an admirable textbook which covers the problems of educational handicaps in just the right detail for those wanting a sound knowledge of the subject.

2. The Plowden Report: *Children and their Primary Schools*, vol. I, HMSO, London, 1967, p. 299.

3. C. Burt defined a backward child as one unable to cope with work normally expected of average children in the year below the child's age. But in the less formalized settings existing in our infant and primary schools, the definition is not as meaningful as it used to be. The definition appears in *The Backward Child*, University of London Press, London, 1937.

4. *Slow Learners at School*, Education pamphlet No. 46, HMSO, London, 1964, p. 10.

5. *Op. cit.*, note (4), the Appendix gives an outline of the procedures often used when a child is thought to be backward.

6. The Newsom Report: *Half Our Future*, HMSO, London, 1963.

7. *Op. cit.*, note (4). The HMSO pamphlet devotes several chapters to conditions and curriculum content in special schools.

8. Mongolism is now thought to be the result of chromosome excess. In the normal human cell we find 46 chromosomes, but when 47 chromosomes appear, mongoloid characteristics result. These characteristics include stunted size, flattened bridge on the nose, slanting eyes, dry, open lips, a squarish flat face and short neck. They occur in about one in every thousand births and are more often born to older women.

9. *Maladjusted Children*, A report by the Underwood Committee into maladjustment, HMSO, London, 1955.

10. B. Furneaux, *The Special Child*, Penguin, London, 1969, chapter 9; S. Elgar and L. Wing, *Teaching Autistic Children*, College of Special Education, 1969. See also *Aspects of Autism* by P. J. Mittler, British Psychological Society Publication, London, 1968.

11. M. Creak *et al.*, 'Schizophrenic syndrome in children', *Br. Med. J.*, **2**, 889–890 (1961).

12. C. Burt, *The Causes and Treatment of Backwardness*, 4th ed., University of London Press, London, 1957. Also see *The Young Delinquent*, University of London Press, London, 1925 as evidence of some early thinking about the effects of social deprivation on educational performance and behaviour.

13. *Early Leaving*. HMSO, London, 1954, The Crowther Report: *15 to 18*, HMSO, London, 1959.

14. J. W. B. Douglas, *The Home and the School*, MacGibbon and Kee, London, 1964.

15. A thorough elaboration of social deprivation appears in M. Chazan, *Compensatory Education: Defining the Problem*, Occasional Publication No. 1, The Schools Council London, 1968. A useful summary also appears in a chapter by G. Williams, 'Compensatory education', in H. J. Butcher and H. B. Pont (Eds), *Educational Research in Britain*, vol. 2, University of London Press, London, 1970.

16. J. D. Nisbet, 'Family environment: a direct effect of family size on intelligence', *Eugenics*, Occasional Paper No. 8, Eugenics Society, London, 1953.

17. For a summary of compensatory programmes see A. F. Laing, *Compensatory Education for Young Children*, Occasional Publication No. 1, The Schools Council, London, 1968.

18. L. T. Wilkins, 'Juvenile delinquency—a critical review of research and theory', *Educ. Res.*, **2**, 104–119. Also see M. Willmott, *Adolescent Boys of East London*, Penguin, London, 1969; J. Bowlby, *Forty-four Juvenile Thieves*, Bailliere, Tindall and Cox, London, 1946; D. H. Scott, *Studies of Troublesome Children*, Tavistock Publications, London, 1966; A. K. Cohen, *Delinquent Boys*, Routledge and Kegan Paul, London, 1956.

19. C. Bereiter and S. Englemann, *Teaching Disadvantaged Children in the Pre-School*, Prentice Hall, New Jersey, 1966.

20. Projects have been mounted by the University of Swansea (Schools Council sponsorship) and the Educational Priority Area Research Unit under the Directorship of A. H. Halsey.

FURTHER READING

Compensatory Education: An Introduction, Occasional Publication No. 1, The Schools Council, London, 1968. A sound little book for beginners and those wanting further reading references.

B. Furneaux, *The Special Child*, Penguin, London, 1969.

R. Gulliford, *Special Educational Needs*, Routledge and Kegan Paul, London, 1971. A splendid textbook containing an up to date analysis of the whole field of educational handicap.

Slow Learners at School, Educational Pamphlet No. 46, HMSO, London, 1964. A brief and readable book containing a discussion of the curriculum as well as the background to special and remedial education.

E. Midwinter, *Projections: An Educational Prority Area at Work*, Ward Lock Educational, London, 1972.

13   Educational assessment

Attempting to assess the quality and quantity of learning has been, and probably always will be, a regular feature of classroom practice. Whilst experts argue the toss about the efficiency or desirability of examinations, teachers will continue in their own way to establish whether their pupils have been learning. There are many ways in which teachers might try to assess progress, ranging from simple observation or conversation to standardized testing. It will not be possible to touch on all the multitude of methods which could be adopted. Instead, this chapter will tend to draw on the more acknowledged methods of assessment employed by examining bodies and teachers, although many of the arguments can be applied equally well to less formal classroom procedures.

The public examination system continues to grow in size and importance year by year (1). Prior to the late 1960s the vast majority of the country's eleven year olds sat the 11+ entry examination to grammar schools. Now with the evolution of the Certificate of Secondary Education (CSE) and the raising of the school-leaving age, the emphasis has shifted from 11+ to 15+ when ever-increasing numbers of young people are becoming involved in public examinations. In 1967, for instance, no fewer than half a million pupils in the age range from fifteen to seventeen years sat some form of public examination—usually GCE 'O' and 'A' levels, CSE and various technical exams. This figure is about a third of the age group. As the CSE is made available to more and more pupils, and both higher education and many industries continue to be geared to an examination system, it is inevitable that numbers will swell over the next few years. It has been suggested (2) that about 75 per cent of the fifteen to seventeen age group will be involved in some form of examination by the mid-1970s. With these and other factors in mind, we need to stress the importance of knowing the pitfalls and limitations which accompany examinations.

SOME PURPOSES OF EXAMINATIONS

A system which is used so extensively should have substantial justification. Let us therefore look at the important purposes which the protagonists of conventional examinations would claim. Later it will be necessary to re-examine some of these points to assess the extent to which these purposes are achieved.

Attainment One of the teacher's objectives, amongst others, is to stimulate the acquisition, understanding and application of knowledge. It therefore seems perfectly reasonable and desirable that the teacher should also want to explore the extent to which these objectives have been achieved. Indeed, in any walk of life, a time comes when we have to expose our knowledge and have it evaluated. This evaluation of attainment at a given time is one of the central aims of examinations.

Beyond the classroom there are employers and professions who require some assurances about the level of competence reached by prospective entrants. These assurances must be expressed in terms which are readily understood by all concerned. Examination marks are thought to provide one such criterion, although, as we shall see, marks can just as readily be misunderstood. When an organization external to the school is engaged, it adds a measure of objectivity and credibility to the marks obtained.

Diagnosis   By comparing the attainment of a group of people having taken the same examination, it is possible to draw some conclusions about the strengths and weaknesses of individuals. Of course, we have only measured the effects and not the causes of success or failure in the exam. Detecting the origins of failure is no easy task particularly if the exam is not all that it should be. Essay-type papers, for example, are less useful when we want to see how extensively a pupil has covered the syllabus. An objective-type test which endeavours to cover a good portion of the syllabus is more likely to be of value in this kind of diagnosis. Again, the failure of a large number of pupils to give an adequate answer to particular questions could arise from inadequate teaching.

The teacher's task of using examination scores as one source of pupil- and self-analysis, known as *feedback*, is very important and requires careful scrutiny of the scripts. Insufficient attention is given to the feedback made possible by this kind of analysis. In school examinations pupils should be allowed to see their scripts after being marked. The opportunity for pupils to see where they have gone wrong, to evaluate their competence and to set realistic goals is a most important function of well-designed examinations.

Prediction   Success in public examinations opens the door to a number of careers. Whether we agree or not with the validity of this process, most external exams are used to assess the potential of the examinee. If a student obtains so many 'O' levels he is deemed suitable for 'A' level studies; 'A' level successes are taken as the basis for choosing an academic or professional course; authority and professional status are placed in the hands of those who succeed in conventional examinations (3). The tacit assumption in all these cases is that examination results are valid predictors. The 11+ entrance examination was probably the most widespread prognostic device ever used in our educational history. Success in standardized tests of numerical, verbal and reasoning ability was said to indicate those children who would most benefit from an academic schooling.

Providing and maintaining standards   A carefully devised examination can be set at whatever level one chooses. It can be arranged that, say, 'O' level chemistry exams are of the same standard from one year to the next or from one examining Board to the next, although this latter claim has been hotly contested in recent research (4). Establishing standards of attainment is inevitable in a society which demands minimum levels of competence as a prerequisite for certain qualifications. How would we find our next generation of teachers if the last generation of teachers abandoned the idea of distinguishing between the qualities of their pupils? A public exam system is also an admission that we cannot trust each other. Its presence gives an air of impartiality and respectability to whatever standards are obtained.

Motivation   Learning is not easy. It requires self-discipline and hard work. Interest is obviously a good starting point, but this often comes as a product of becoming competent in a subject (5). One major source of motivation is the long-term prospect of obtaining a qualification and a good job (6). It is thought by some teachers that the CSE has injected new life and purpose into the work of moderately able secondary pupils who not long ago would have impatiently played out their last school years longing to be wage earners at the end of the fourth form. The motivational qualities of exams need hardly be mentioned to student teachers who have all experienced the annual retreat into studies and libraries (around Easter time usually) and the feverish activity which preceded the exams.

Development   Examinations have been said to bring out qualities of perseverance and industriousness. They are thought to give practice in expressing ideas lucidly, fluently and quickly. They compel students to organize their ideas and develop systems of study and concentration which may be adapted for service in later life.

Social (and administrative) engineering   By making examinations available to anyone who feels capable, it is possible for social mobility to take place. At one time, favouritism and patronage played a large part in the life-chances of young people entering schools, universities or business. Now nepotism (favouring relatives irrespective of their qualities) no longer has any significant effect. The 11+ was seen by many as promoting social justice and enabling the children from less fortunate home backgrounds to enter grammar schools. Robbins (7), in a report on higher education, foresaw the existence of 'pools of ability' largely consisting of able youngsters leaving school before attempting to get into higher education. Examinations at 'O' and 'A' level have since revealed these pools and most establishments of higher education are now busy mopping them up!

These aims should not be regarded in isolation from each other. They are complex and interrelated. The student should question these assumptions in the light of his or her experience and reading and make some decision as to whether there are more suitable alternatives. The following sections should help to pinpoint some of the limitations imposed by exams.

LIMITATIONS

There are many drawbacks to conventional examinations. Much research energy (8) (in particular the Schools Council and the National Foundation for Educational Research) has been directed to finding ways of improving the present system including the introduction of alternative forms of assessment. These other forms will be mentioned later in the chapter. For the moment we shall look at three criteria which play a particularly important part in defining the adequacy of examinations. They are *reliability, validity* and *comparability*.

Reliability   Let us first define this term as applied to examinations. A reliable exam is one which will give a consistent score from one occasion to the next for the same individual or group irrespective of the person who marks it. We are dealing here with the adequacy of the measurement and not the content. A simple example should suffice. If a teacher gave her primary school class a home-made arithmetic test on two separate occasions and the two scores for individuals were irregular, she would be justified in suspecting that the test was unreliable. If most of the scores increase on the second testing, it may mean that the children have had some practice in the meantime or they have remembered some answers and left more time for the solutions of other questions. If, on the other hand, the scores for some children are higher and for others lower, then it could mean that the questions are poor or the marking inconsistent, and these are the kinds of inconsistency which give rise to unreliability of tests.

Firstly, there are inconsistencies arising in one examiner's marks for a particular paper when he marks it on different occasions. This occurs primarily because of fatigue, mood, time of day and inadvertent changes in interpretation of an answer from one script to the next. Therefore, on marking the same batch of scripts on two occasions, two different sets of scores for each candidate or variations between candidates who have given similar answers could result.

Secondly, different examiners often have different interpretations and expectations of the candidates' answers. An essay-type answer is especially prone to varied interpretations because examiners can look for so many differing qualities. Some might be influenced by a fluent and witty style even when the content is thin; others might reward grammatical structure. An 'Impression' mark is also decidedly open to criticism for the high degree of subjective judgement involved.

As evidence of the fluctuations in essay marks which happen when a panel of markers is used, the famous research in the 1930s by Hartog and Rhodes (9) will be quoted. For subjects like French, English essays, history and mathematics at levels from junior school to university, Hartog and Rhodes invited panels of expert examiners to mark sets of papers. Table 13.1 shows the marks awarded to six candidates in the Entrance Scholarship Examination to university by five examiners. These have been chosen from a larger table given by the authors because the range of discrepancy, 25 marks, is the same for each candidate. Often one finds in a panel of examiners consistently generous or mean individuals. But notice the irregularity with which the highest (ringed) and lowest (boxed) marks have been awarded, although examiner (b) appears to be heavy-handed. The maximum discrepancy for a candidate was 36 as shown in the last line of the table. These results speak for themselves by exposing enormous differences in the marks allotted to candidates by different examiners on the same essay, particularly where there was no coordination between examiners. However, these findings from the mid-thirties have only partial relevance today. A great deal has been done by examining bodies to overcome unreliability by making improvements in marking procedures. For example, it is now common practice for examiners in a subject to meet and coordinate a marking scheme. Decisions are made about the allocation of marks and the range of answers which the panel will accept and these are adhered to by them all. Marked scripts are sampled and re-marked by a second examiner, usually the leader of the team. Borderline candidates' scripts are always re-examined. Very little is now left to chance in public examinations.

Table 13.1 Disparity in examiners' marks in an essay question

Candidate No.	Examiner					Discrepancy range
	a	b	c	d	e	
9	48	30	55	55	40	25
13	67	50	45	42	52	25
23	42	35	60	58	47	25
34	65	52	40	60	55	25
47	32	36	35	55	30	25
25	60	32	65	50	68	36
Mean score	52·3	39·2	50·0	53·3	48·7	

Extracted from Table 96, p. 143 of *The Marks of Examiners* (1936) by P. Hartog and E. C. Rhodes. Reprinted with the kind permission of the publishers, Macmillan, London and Basingstoke.

The idea of re-marking, particularly essay-type answers, has the support of research. Wiseman (10) has suggested from his work that several examiners should mark each paper, thus obscuring the idiosyncrasies of individual examiners. Recent work published by the Schools Council (11) on *multiple* marking in English composition at 'O' level using a combination of marks for impression (three independent assessors) and mechanical accuracy (one assessor) reveals an improvement in reliability over the official mark awarded by an examining Board. There was also closer agreement with a continuous assessment given by the schools of the candidates.

Mathematics can also be subject to variation from one sitting to the next. Dale (12) found several disconcerting movements in the marks obtained by candidates at 'O' level in successive June and September (resit) examinations. He gives four examples of increased marks which seem to go far beyond what one might reasonably expect as a result of concentrated effort in the time between the two exams. Table 13.2 is a reproduction of his findings.

This kind of unreliability is of particular interest for it calls into question the comparability of test papers which, superficially at least, are thought to be similar. In mathematics there is an additional problem that candidates may spend disproportionate amounts of time on a few questions without necessarily being successful in solving them.

Apart from a stricter control of marking schemes and increasing the number of examiners, it is also possible to improve the reliability by increasing the length of the examination paper. This is usually the case in multiple choice tests as we shall see.

Table 13.2   Differences in mathematics marks between June and September (resit)

Candidate	June	September	Range
	Marks as percentages		
A	27	58	31
B	25	63	38
C	32	59	27
D	36	76	40

Reproduced from *From School to University* 1954, by R. R. Dale, p. 141. With the kind permission of the publishers, Routledge and Kegan Paul, London.

Validity   If a test achieves what the originators intended it to achieve, it is a valid test. There are several kinds of validity (13), but we shall be concerned here with *content* and *predictive* validity. Before describing these, it ought to be noted that there is a connection between the validity and reliability of a test or examination paper. If a test is unreliable, then plainly it cannot be valid for any purpose. On the other hand, if it is highly reliable it need not necessarily be valid—in other words, it might be highly reliable at measuring something which the designers never intended! Briefly, tests can be reliable and invalid but they cannot be unreliable and valid.

(a) *Content validity*   For an examination to have content validity it must contain qualitative and quantitative representation in the sampling of the whole syllabus. This rests upon the judgement of the examiner in compiling questions from the syllabus. Essay-type papers often fall short of this requirement. It is very difficult to cover a significant portion of a syllabus using only ten or so questions. Multiple choice designs overcome this difficulty to some extent by setting a large number of short questions covering a major part of a syllabus. However, there is more to content validity than merely making sure the syllabus content has been adequately sampled. We also need to know whether the questions are set in such a way as to fulfil the purposes and aims of the course. The teaching has been geared to certain objectives (see chapter 16). Have these objectives been realized in the choice of questions and the answers given? Unfortunately, there are no formulae for finding content validity. The teacher must make up his mind about it from experience with the material and by using, where possible, a second opinion because this is a qualitative rather than a quantitative activity. Deciding on objectives and setting appropriate questions is a difficult business. In this respect, Bloom's *Taxonomy of Educational Objectives* (14) is quite helpful in defining the scope and extent of the purposes we ascribe to educational procedures and in providing the kinds of questions appropriate for them.

(b) *Predictive validity*   We saw earlier that one function of many public examinations is to enable us to select people for certain occupational or scholastic pursuits. The predictive validity of an examination is characterized by its ability to forecast those who might succeed in these pursuits. For example, 'A' level results are used by universities and colleges as a major source of evidence of a student's capacity for coping with the course requirements. A degree is often taken as evidence that a man has the ability to cope in industry.

The results of research into the predictive value of examinations has not been encouraging. Investigations into the prognostic use of 11+, 'O', 'A' levels, teachers' certificates and degree results (15) have all, at one time or another, provided conflicting results. The reasons for this confused picture are complex, but one fairly obvious cause of low correlations is that some occupations demand qualities which are not disclosed by traditional written examination papers.

Comparability   This is closely linked with reliability, but it is so often neglected that a separate discussion was felt to be needed. Basically, if we want to compare results of an individual on two or more tests or the results of several groups using the same test, we have to make sure that the comparisons are legitimate. For example, given two parallel forms of a French or arithmetic paper, are we justified in comparing the raw scores obtained by an individual on the two parts? This depends on a number of factors. Have the tests similar content? Do the scores for each group have similar means? Are the scores spread out in a similar fashion in both tests? Before we can draw conclusions about the relative performance on the two forms, we have to standardize the scores. This will be dealt with at greater length in the following chapter.

Up to this point the emphasis has been on the suitability of the measuring device and the problems encountered in scoring it. However, there are other criticisms which have been levelled at examinations and we shall now consider some of the important ones.

The examinee   There are many intellectual, personal and social reasons which impose limitations on the performance of students but which have little or nothing to do with the setting or marking of the papers. Whether we could in some way allow for these variables is an extremely difficult and unresolved matter. They exist, and we should at least be aware of them. There are several obvious reasons which need little comment. Some people are over-optimistic about their talents and have not really the necessary skills. Choosing the wrong subject is at the root of some students' problems. Few people are entirely consistent in their mood from one examination to another. The physical and mental condition of a candidate can affect performance, and in some cases candidates do not do themselves justice. Others are capable, but do not work, often through lack of motivation or over-confidence. Poor study strategies, lack of guidance about the requirements or faulty examination technique, all of which can be remedied, are common sources of trouble. Sometimes a teacher has a style of presentation which is incompatible with the style of learning of the pupil (cognitive style). Student teachers out on school practice will have experienced those blank looks on a child's face when something is being described, even when the student is convinced that the presentation was simple and logical. The art of simplification and discovering the modes of thinking of pupils is a skill which every teacher has to cultivate.

Some have argued that examinations engender an unnecessary spirit of competition between pupils. However, in most public examinations where an external paper and examiner are employed, the pupil and the teacher are, in some respects, in partnership. They cooperate in an attempt to meet the external demands of the examination system.

Recent research (16) suggests that those who succeed in conventional written examinations may have particular personality predispositions. It would be surprising if this were not the case. Characteristics such as persistence, a theoretical turn of mind, fondness for solitude and reflection are clearly beneficial to a student. These characteristics have been associated with the introverted personality, and research has shown that introverts abound in higher education where theoretical, solitary study is at a premium.

Another influence arises from the fact that our exam system tends to over-emphasize the written word. More recently an effort has been made to vary the means whereby students can communicate their skills and knowledge besides the two- or three-hour written paper. Practicals, vivas, project work and orals (some of which have been in use for a long time) are amongst the commonest methods.

Curriculum To what extent are syllabuses determined and restricted by the existence of an examination? How are teaching methods affected by syllabus demands? Are there important educational needs (social, moral and intellectual) which are not examinable and which have to be sacrificed in favour of examinable themes? It has been suggested by many teachers that both they and their pupils have to make many omissions in their work because they get caught up in the frenzied scramble towards 'O' and 'A' levels. For many years the teaching of mathematics and science was designed to provide routine strategies for problem-solving without arousing any exploratory interest in these subjects. The phenomenon of the examination dictating the content of the curriculum and methods of teaching is known as the 'backwash' effect. It is a subject with which every teacher should be familar.

Question 'spotting' (guessing in advance the content of the exam questions) is commonly practised by pupils and teachers. Some teachers have developed the art to a high degree by juggling the questions on back papers with great dexterity. Unfortunately it makes nonsense of a syllabus intended to give a comprehensive grounding in a subject.

KINDS OF ASSESSMENT IN USE

There has been a marked growth in the use of alternative forms of academic assessment to essay questions in recent years. The most important development has been in devising multiple choice or *objective-type tests* and standardized ability tests as distinct from conventional written examinations. But let us first take a look at some variants of the latter kind of examination.

Conventional written examinations It is hardly necessary to remind students of the design of traditional exam papers. We are all too familiar with the rubric 'Answer 3 from 7 in 3 hours: careless and untidy work will be penalized'. But a number of interesting variations have been tried. Some universities, for instance, are experimenting with 'open-book' methods where the candidate is allowed to take specified texts into the exam room (if he finds time to use them). Some candidates have been given the actual questions in advance or have been allowed to set their own papers. Naturally, the tendency is to set questions which make greater demands of the students if they are being given the advantage of a preview. The questions require answers which are less factual, more analytical and not unlike essays. Continuous (or continual, but really intermittent) assessment involving mainly essays and projects is now in widespread use from CSE to university level. With the sting of the three-hour unseen exam paper drawn, it is felt by some that learning is more effective and less anxiety provoking. Essays allow us to expose our ability to produce, organize and express ideas, to integrate information from several directions, to pose and solve problems and evaluate ideas. Marking, on the other hand, is more subjective and attempts the near impossible task of measuring complex learning skills from what is usually a combined effort between the essay writer and his reference sources. Clearly, the advantages and shortcomings of continuous assessment, particularly where this requires essay-type answers, is still an important area of investigation. At the end of the day, we must continue to ask ourselves whether the pupils have been learning and understanding in the most efficient, effective and enjoyable way.

A great deal of evidence is still required before we are able to evaluate the various kinds of assessment now being adopted. Several questions still need to be answered. Are all these methods measuring more or less the same qualities—thus obviating the need for such an elaborate array of methods—or do they inspire different modes of learning and thinking? Have continuous assessment methods an inhibiting effect on students in fear of prejudicing their assessment? Nisbet (17) makes the point that

> The advantages of a prescribed examination over informal or continuous assessment are that the examination is, to some extent, a public occasion, revealing at least some of the bases of assessment; and that the examination identifies the occasions when the student is on trial and thus gives him freedom at other times. Examinations impose on students occasions of submission, but they also define areas of freedom.

Again, we might ask whether continuous methods are less reliable because they are more susceptible to manipulation than formal examinations. These and many other problems are the focus of research at present.

Objective-type examinations (18)   In essay questions the student is free to plan out his own answer using whatever knowledge he can recall usually without any clues from the question. In objective questions the information given (or 'stem' of the question) is posed in such a way that there is only one acceptable answer which can either be recalled from memory or recognized from a collection of probable answers. They are called 'objective' because the questions and answers are carefully predetermined rendering the responses free from the personal biases of the examiner. Designing items is a skilled job (19), as we shall see in the next chapter. Item analysis is required to provide a measure of the difficulty of each item for a given ability group, and to determine the discriminative qualities of the item.

In this country the use of objective tests has been gathering momentum. CSE and GCE General Studies papers now contain many items of this kind. The Schools Council has been most prolific in the researches it has sponsored, and its publications relating to many important aspects of the whole field of educational assessment make important reading for students and teachers (8).

Several examples are given below (answers at the end of the chapter) to give the student some idea of the scope of objective test items now available. They by no means cover all the variations in use, but represent the commonest. For convenience, we might make a broad distinction between items requiring straightforward *recall* and those requiring the *recognition* (or choice response) of an answer, although some designs require both these mental activities.

(I) *Recall* items, as stated above, require the candidate to remember a simple correct answer without it appearing on the answer sheet. Some factual essay questions require just this, except that the answers are buried in continuous prose. There are three basic kinds of recall item.

(i) *Simple recall:* here the candidate must recall a single fact (or series of facts) as in the following example taken from a recent CSE paper.
example:
  (a) 'Here am I; send me'
  (b) 'I do not know how to speak, for I am only a youth'
  Each of these sentences was spoken by a prophet when God called him. Name the prophets.
  (a)   (b)
(West Yorkshire and Lindsey Regional Examining Board for the Certificate of Secondary Education, Religious Knowledge, 1970)

(ii) *Open (or sentence) completion:* the candidate fills in an incomplete phrase or sentence.
example:
  Jeremiah said that the Lord 'Will give all Judah into the Hand of ....'
  Complete the sentence.
(From the same paper as the example for simple recall)

(iii) *The unlabelled diagram:* used extensively in science, particularly biology, where candidates are asked to recall parts of an organ or apparatus.
example:

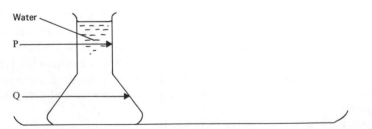

  The diagram shows a conical vessel full of water. Show, on the diagram, the jets of water which occur when small holes are made in the vessel at the points marked P and Q; assume that air resistance is negligible.
(University of Cambridge Local Examinations Syndicate, GCE 'O' level physics, 1970)

(II) *Recognition* items require the candidate to choose a correct answer from two or more possible answers which are given. There are a number of ways of presenting this kind of item and four will be illustrated below.

(i) *True/false* items give the candidate a stem and he is required to say whether it is true or false.

example:

Place a tick in either the 'True' or 'False' column after each statement depending on which you think is the appropriate answer.

	True	False
1. Intelligence may be defined as inborn all-round mental efficiency.		
2. Intelligence is largely a product of the culture in which a child is reared, and the stimulation he receives.		
3. Intelligence is entirely distinct from attainments or acquired information, and education received.		
4. The IQ (if tested by a reliable test) remains constant to within about 5 points either way throughout school life.		

(Taken from a questionnaire by Professor P. E. Vernon in *The Bearings of Recent Advances in Psychology on Educational Problems*. Evans, London, 1955)

(ii) *Multiple choice* responses are the commonest form of objective test. Usually there are five or so alternative answers provided for each item. It is possible to have more than one acceptable answer in some cases.

Examples having one correct response:

You are asked to underline the appropriate item in each case.

1. The chief danger from FALL-OUT comes from	Cosmic dust, fission fragments, fusion fragments, cosmic rays, disturbance of the atmosphere, any of these, none of these.
2. ALTAMIRA attracts visitors for the same reason as	Palmyra, Nimes, Alicante, Bonn, Lisieux, Lascaux, Arles, none of these.
3. Which of these has the most complex MOLECULAR STRUCTURE?	Salt, sugar, starch, protein, petroleum, potassium permanganate, nitrous oxide.
4. One of these Shakespearean characters is out of keeping with the others.	Iago, Macbeth, Cassius, Claudius, Feste, Richard III, Timon.

(Taken from a 'culture test' by W. K. Richmond, in *Culture and General Education*, Methuen, London, 1963)

Example having several correct responses:

Place a tick in the box opposite each correct response.

Plaster of Paris is often used to immobilize fractures because of the following advantages

(a) It is relatively cheap ☐

(b) It is unaffected by water ☐

    (c) It is relatively light   ☐
    (d) It is non-toxic and non-inflammable ☐
    (e) It is easily moulded to fit the part   ☐

(Trial multiple choice question for Physiotherapy students. With the kind permission of Mr. J. L. Low, St. Thomas' Hospital, London)

Example using the 'best reason' method:
    Answer the question implied in the following statement by selecting the answer A, B, C, D, or E which best completes the sentence.
    A metaphorical expression
    A. is allowable in poetry but not in prose
    B. is never used except for rhetorical ornament
    C. falsely likens one thing to another
    D. is always in the form 'A is B'
    E. implies a comparison

(Joint Matriculation Board, GCE 'A' level General Studies—Paper I, 1968)

(iii) *matching items and rearrangement* are self-evident from the examples below.
    Example of matching items:
    The names of some composers are given below. Which of these composed the opera named in question a to e?

A. Berg	a. La Bohème
B. Beethoven	b. La Traviata
C. Britten	c. Peter Grimes
D. Gounod	d. The Magic Flute
E. Mozart	e. The Mastersingers
F. Puccini	
G. Rossini	
H. Verdi	
I. Wagner	

(Joint Matriculation Board, GCE 'A' level General Studies—Paper I, 1968)

Example of rearrangement:
    Write in the box alongside the statement in the second column the letter which is given to the structures in the first column which is best related to that statement.
    Also write in the name of the structure that has been omitted from the first column in the question.

(a) DNA	Carries information from nucleus to cytoplasm	☐
(b) Chloroplast	Combines loosely with oxygen	☐
(c) Haemoglobin	Every plant and animal has a fixed number of these structures in the nucleus	☐
(d) RNA	Contains 'coded information' from parents	☐
(e) _____	Absorbs light energy for photosynthesis	☐

(West Yorkshire and Lindsey Regional Examining Board for the Certificate of Secondary Education, Biology, 1970)

The unlabelled diagram with labels provided for insertion is another form of this method.

Case History and interpretive questions have a particular relevance in examinations for applied fields such as medicine, teaching and management. The case history technique provides the candidate with sufficient information about a case to enable diagnosis, indicate complications and offer treatment or decisions. Hubbard and Clemans (20) in a book about multiple choice examining in medicine give a number of examples of this approach. The 'A' level General Studies papers have also adopted a similar procedure. The questions are usually long winded because a thorough exposition of all the symptoms or observations must be given in order for the student to select answers. Very complex and searching questions are possible using this design chiefly when the candidate is required to recall and evaluate rather than recognize the answer.

Standardized tests

There are now many standardized tests of ability and attainment in a wide variety of subjects designed for use with children from four to sixteen years of age. Several of these tests are compiled with teachers in mind so that the tests can be administered by the teacher in his or her own class either individually or as a group test. For obvious reasons, the tests are only available to legitimate persons who have a need for them and who are able to use them properly. Of the publishing firms and organizations in this country, the National Foundation for Educational Research has undoubtedly built up a tradition as designers and suppliers of well-standardized test material. Their publication *Educational Guidance in Schools: Standardized Tests for the Use of Teachers*, contains a very comprehensive selection of ability and attainment tests covering reading, comprehension, word recognition, number, arithmetic or mathematics, verbal and non-verbal reasoning interest and practical skill tests. A similar selection of tests is available in *A Teacher's Guide to Tests and Testing* by S. Jackson (Longman, 1968). We shall deal more extensively with the concept of standardization in the next chapter.

Ability tests have already been alluded to in chapter 9. They attempt to measure the all-round mental efficiency of a person, without necessarily indicating specific subject skills. Verbal and non-verbal reasoning tests are amongst those ability tests most used in schools. As we have seen, they have been used to define broad classifications of pupils for streaming or selection purposes in the belief that pupils so classified should, in general, be capable of coping with academic work of a given standard. But they do not tell us *in particular* if a child is better at physics than at history. They are most efficient when it comes to showing the extremes of mental functioning, that is the very dull or the gifted.

Attainment tests, whilst they correlate to some extent with ability tests, are designed principally to sample achievement in specific school subjects, having first been tested out on a large representative group of children. The sampling usually occurs over a smallish age range (three or four years at the most) to enable a fairly accurate estimate of attainment to be made. In the next chapter on standardization, we shall look more closely at the method of standardizing the age norms. These are commonly used in primary schools as a means of estimating the progress in specific basic subjects such as reading, arithmetic, and word recognition. *Aptitude tests*, are more often concerned with spatial and mechanical skills necessary for a particular task. We find aptitude tests in science and various professions requiring skills in manipulation or hand–eye coordination.

Diagnostic tests are constructed in a similar way to attainment tests, but they are intended to give a more detailed picture of the weaknesses in a school subject. They are common in basic subjects such as reading and arithmetic where they usually consist of several sub-tests constructed to show the finer details of the difficulties experienced by children. Their application is particularly helpful in cases of retarded development.

ADVANTAGES AND LIMITATIONS OF OBJECTIVE EXAMINATIONS

Advantages

Many more questions can be set in a given time than is possible in essay examinations. Some writers (21) have suggested that about 100 items per hour, without a choice, is a reasonable pace. As a consequence, more extensive sampling of syllabus content is practicable and this gives a corresponding increase in the reliability of the score. Marking is made much easier because responses are short, to the point and systematically arranged on the answer sheet. Clearly there is complete impartiality in the marking, although mistakes are still possible as happens when adding is incorrect, two pages are turned by mistake or when accidents occur in the marking. Some American test agencies (22) are now able to automate the marking and totalling.

Less time is spent by candidates in writing out their answers. This, hopefully, leaves more time for thinking! There is little opportunity for padding or writing long, elaborate answers to questions which the examiner had not set.

As we shall see in the next chapter, the construction of objective tests enables a careful control of the difficulty levels associated with each item. In this way, we can decide in advance the spread and frequency of each level of difficulty. With essay answers, the level of difficulty experienced by candidates is discovered in retrospect once the marks have been awarded. Much time and skill is required to accumulate an 'item bank' containing questions of known difficulty for a given ability range. The NFER has recently undertaken a study (19) into the feasibility of creating item banks or libraries of examination questions. They were concerned with establishing a pool of items suitable for school based mathematics exams at CSE level. Ultimately, teachers would be able to draw out of the bank a number of items covering specified fields at known levels of difficulty.

By taking a large number of items covering small sections of a syllabus it is easier to detect and counsel a pupil's (or teacher's) weaknesses. This has an added advantage in that students not only have knowledge of results, but a detailed analysis of the shortcomings. Essays are not easy to analyse in this way.

Limitations

Although scoring is made easy, setting the questions is a difficult business. Badly constructed tests can have a disastrous effect on the study and morale of students. Poor design often reflects the subjective element which enters into the choice of questions. So we see the position in 'objective' questions is the reverse of essay-type questions—the former require subjective judgement in the setting, the latter in the marking. Panels of judges for question setting will overcome this problem to some extent.

There is something deceptively comforting about a paper which provides the answers as well as the questions. It is certainly easier to recognize an answer than to recall it from memory (see chapter 7). But not all questions need be of this kind. In medical questions, for example, and presumably in any applied field, the student can be given information from which he must provide evidence not only of knowledge but reasoning and judgement. Advanced level General Studies papers contain many examples of questions requiring comprehension, interpretation and application of knowledge. Nevertheless, there is limited opportunity for disciplined expression.

The short, sharp question and answer require a particular kind of behaviour which can be developed. Sophistication in answering these questions is also a criticism levelled at the IQ test where concentrated practice can give rise to increased scores. A corollary of this is the influence that practice may have on the whole pattern of study. There could be serious distortions if only this kind of question is used.

Little opportunity is afforded for imaginative and creative work. The emphasis is on fact rather than fancy and little, if any, account is taken of the *quality* of thought which has led to the answer. Consequently only certain subjects, chiefly factual areas of mathematics, sciences, history, geography, and so forth, lend themselves to objective assessment. Skills such as organizing and presenting knowledge in a lucid, concise and fluent manner are not in evidence. In fact, the examinee spends rather more time reading than writing. The obvious way round this criticism is to make sure that essays are included somewhere in the examination.

Guessing is quite possible in multiple choice answers, but it is not the problem which some people have supposed. It must first be made quite clear to the candidates that they must not attempt a question which they cannot answer and that guessing will be penalized. A formula can then be used to counteract guesswork. It is derived in the following way. Suppose a test consists of 10 questions each having 5 alternative answers of which only one is correct. A candidate who could only answer 5 correctly would obtain only 5 marks if he followed the instructions. However, if he guesses at the remaining 5 answers he would, by chance, obtain one more mark because in a five-way choice with one correct choice there would be a one in five chance of being correct. His total would therefore be 6. The formula devised to overcome guessing should give us a total of five because this extra mark was a guess.

$$\text{Total mark} = \text{number of correct items} - \frac{\text{number of incorrect items}}{\text{number of choices in an item} - 1}$$

In our example, number correct $= 6$

number incorrect $= 4$

number of choices in each item is 5

$\therefore$ Total mark $= 6 - \dfrac{4}{5 - 1} = 6 - 1 = 5$

which is exactly the mark he deserves. A modified formula is available for two-way choice items such as the true/false kind where the total mark is given by:

number correct $-\frac{1}{2}$ number incorrect

Finally, a word about *anxiety* and *stress* aroused by the tensions which accompany an examination system. Whenever there is a fear of failure (23) and a threat to one's self-esteem, anxiety is inevitable. In turn, anxiety states will have some influence on learning and performance. Intellectual and personal factors interact in a complex fashion not yet understood by psychologists and the direction of influence is still not predictable. In some circumstances a moderate level of stress may provide drive energy which can be harnessed to good effect. In other cases, the level of stress may be so high as to be disruptive (driving tests have a bad habit of doing this!). This deleterious influence has been shown, for example, in higher education (24), where increasing numbers of referrals for temporary mental disorganization are a testimony to the growing problem. Malleson (25), at university level, has managed to reduce examination panic by carefully designed interviews in order to gain a thorough knowledge of the individuals concerned and the specific source of their disturbance.

Most teachers soon discover those pupils with a nervous disposition. It is up to teachers to put pupils at ease by showing sympathy and a willingness to talk through the problems. The anxiety generated by examinations, especially public exams on which one's future career might hinge, is a regular source of trouble. Similarly, younger children get worked up about standardized tests. Teachers should do all in their power to allay excessive tension. Where possible, the test or examination should be held in familiar surroundings in the school with familiar faces as invigilators; if the examination can be fitted into the normal school routines, all well and good. The atmosphere in an examination room should not be unduly tense and distant, but relaxed, quiet and conducive to concentration. Pupils should have a clear idea what is expected of them and this can frequently be achieved by making sure they understand the rubric of their papers without unduly prolonging the period of preparation before the exam.

ASSESSMENT AND RECORD KEEPING IN SCHOOLS

We have discussed a number of ways by which a teacher is able to estimate the learning progress of his pupils. But how, and to whom, are these estimates communicated? In both the primary and secondary schools it has been traditional to convey terminal and annual reports to the next teacher or school through the Local Education Authority and to communicate the results in a contracted form to the parents either by parent–teacher meetings or on a written report. Many Local Education Authorities require their schools to complete a cumulative record card for each child. The main object of the card is to compile a systematic record as the child passes through a school so as to establish a profile of development for the benefit of teachers and parents. The format of the record card varies between authorities, but they are usually divided up (or appear on separate cards) according to the level of school attended (Infant, Junior, Middle, Secondary).

Most records contain the following information: (a) biographical details of name, age, sex, birthdate, address and general information about schools attended; (b) health and home conditions such as illnesses or handicaps which may affect a child's progress or require regular treatment; (c) attainments in general ability, verbal reasoning, word recognition, reading, comprehension and arithmetic taken at various ages in school along with the name of the test; (d) interests such as music, drama, sport, social activities or practical skills; (e) attendance; (f) behaviour and personality including deviant behaviour (delinquency, truancy) and emotional disturbance; (g) other general comments by the teachers or headteacher.

In secondary schools, subject reports are also sent to the child's parents. These very familiar school reports, containing (frequently unstandardized) exam marks with teachers' comments, have uncertain utility. Research into the value of school reports, both from the school's and parents' points of view, has been very scant up to now. At the least, they are intended to convey to the parents a measure of their child's progress and standing in particular subjects and to indicate any strengths or weaknesses. Whether parents interpret the marks and comments in quite this way is open to question. However, reports coupled with personal contact between the teacher and the parent can often resolve some of the instrumental questions ('will he get a decent job?', 'has he a chance of passing "O" levels?') running through the minds of parents.

SUMMARY

Evaluating pupils' learning is a necessary step in any formalized educational system. We need to have some valid and reliable assessment of a child's progress, his standing relative to his peers and his potential. At the same time, the assessment should be in a form which is readily understood by pupils, teachers, parents and, where necessary, employers. Examinations provide, with varying degrees of success, an estimate of attainment and a means of diagnosing weaknesses and misdirections in the pupils' studies. They are used with the intention of predicting aptitude for further study or entry to work. Examinations provide an opportunity for upward mobility for the successful, but they can produce feelings of inadequacy in the unsuccessful as an unfortunate spin-off. They are used too as a gauge in predetermining and maintaining standards as well as measuring the efficiency of a teacher's content and methods. Revision for examinations acts as a means of reinforcing the learning of the content.

These ambitious suggestions as to the purposes of examinations must be considered along with two important criteria. Any evaluation must measure what it is supposedly designed to measure—it must be valid—and if it is valid, the evaluation must be consistent when used with the same or similar pupils—it must be reliable. But the potency of examinations also depends on conditions external to the design of the test material. Amongst these, the psychological condition of the pupil is paramount. Too little is known about the interaction of personality attributes and performance, although we are well aware that excessive anxiety can adversely affect a pupil's achievement. The presence of unfamiliar people or conditions, lack of understanding of what is required and undue pressure from parents or teachers to perform well can all take their toll. Faulty learning strategies are similarly effective in depressing performance.

The range of evaluative instruments and methods is now quite extensive. Amongst these are the essay-type tests, projects, vivas, practicals, attainment tests and objective tests, of which the last mentioned are becoming very significant alternatives to the well-established unseen essay paper. The method does compensate for several criticisms levelled against essay-type questions, but the preparation of objective-type questions is a highly technical and time-consuming job for the outcome to be of value. Assessment is largely used as a means of communication between a pupil and his teacher. Therefore, we should endeavour to give a pupil every opportunity of using as many communication media as possible. The emphasis in our system has been on the written word produced over a timed period. It would seem equally important to encourage children to communicate their knowledge in oral or practical ways where this is feasible.

Often assessments have to be formalized so that we can convey to others the level of attainment and progress made in particular school subjects. Other teachers, parents, Local Education Authorities and employers need to know this information. School reports are the commonest methods of conveying the information to parents. Many authorities also provide a cumulative school record card on which attainments, amongst other helpful details, are recorded by the child's teacher. Regular insertions on these records enable an extremely useful profile to be compiled for each child.

ENQUIRY AND DISCUSSION

1. On school practice or school visits, investigate the following:
   (a) school and Local Education Authority (LEA) record cards. What are they for? How are they compiled? What use do teachers, LEAs and employers make of them?
   (b) discuss with teachers their methods of assessing children both in term time as part of continuous assessment and in end of term tests. What difficulties do they experience? What use do they make of these assessments? Are they reliable and valid? How does assessment vary with the subject?
   (c) school reports and 'parents' day are routine features in most schools. How do teachers overcome the tricky task of telling parents about their children's shortcomings? How do parents respond? Do parents have difficulty in evaluating how their children are developing or how they are progressing in relation to others?
   (d) discover pupils' views of the public examination system and continuous assessment;
   (e) inspect and compare intelligence, attainment and diagnostic tests. Look also at some examples of objective-type tests. If at all possible, try to become involved in the administration of a test programme. Have a look at the instruction manuals of these tests.

2. Examine the place of assessment in either (a) junior or (b) secondary or (c) higher education. What forms might it take? What are the purposes served by such assessment? Are the purposes achieved?

3. Read *The Rise of the Meritocracy* by Michael Young [note (3)] or *Education or Examination* by T. Fawthrop (published by the Radical Student Alliance, 1968). Discuss these provocative glimpses into the future.

4. Read up, write about or discuss the following:
   (a) the effects of anxiety or fear of failure in examinations;
   (b) the role of ambition in examination motivation;
   (c) validity and reliability of 'home made' examinations in primary or secondary schools;
   (d) the evaluation of project work or 'creative writing';
   (e) the distinction between ability and attainment tests.

NOTES AND REFERENCES

1. For a detailed statement on the origins of our present examination system, the student is advised to read R. J. Montgomery, *Examinations: An Account of Their Evaluation as Administrative Devices in England*, Longmans, Green, London, 1965.

2. The Beloe Report, a report of a Committee appointed by the Secondary School Examinations Council in July 1958 whose brief was to look at *Secondary School Examinations other than the GCE* (HMSO, London, 1960), contains several interesting figures. Up to 20 per cent of the sixteen year old age group may be expected to attempt (though not necessarily pass) GCE 'O' level in four or more subjects, in the next most able 20 per cent of the age group we might expect pupils to attempt four or five CSE subjects and a further 20 per cent of the age group of round about average ability might attempt fewer than four subjects in the CSE. Adding to this percentage those school leavers who might be sitting RSA (Royal Society of Arts) and other technical or commercial subjects, a figure approaching 75 per cent is not inconceivable.

3. For a thought-provoking fantasy about where present trends are leading us, have a look at M. Young, *The Rise of the Meritocracy 1870–2033; an Essay on Education and Equality*, Penguin, London, 1961.

4. A. Hewitt in Occasional Publication 27 of the Joint Matriculation Board comments on differences between successive English 'O' level papers in 1965. In an article by H. B. Miles and G. E. Shipworth in the *Times Educational Supplement* (2.10.70), results from five Boards show some marked discrepancies.

5. Some researches have shown little or no correlation between interest and attainment. Interest, by its very nature, is subject to change and does not always depend on competence. The work of R. G. Rowlands, 'Some differences between prospective scientists, non-scientists and early leavers in a representative sample of English grammar school boys', *Br. J. educ. Psychol.*, **31**, 21–32 (1961), is an example. L. Cronbach in *Essentials of Psychological Testing*, Harper and Row, New York, 1964, in an extensive summary of this field of investigation concludes that:

   > Correlations of interest with grades in specific fields or courses of study are generally below $+0\cdot30$ which implies that interest tests add only a small amount to formulas predicting grades. (p. 428)

6. We are told by sociologists that this ability to postpone an immediate gratification for a long-term goal such as a qualification is more characteristic of children from

middle-class homes than from working-class homes. This is one of many social reasons why early leavers come largely from working-class backgrounds.

7. The Robbins Report: *Higher Education*, HMSO, London, 1963.

8. The Schools Council has produced a series of working papers and examinations bulletins published by HMSO. They are written by teachers with teachers in mind and are exceptionally readable. The National Foundation for Educational Research (NFER for short) has initiated many research projects which are reported from time to time. It also produces a journal, *Educational Research* and a newsheet—both intended for practising teachers. Students and teachers are well advised to keep in touch with the publications and findings of these organizations.

9. P. Hartog and E. C. Rhodes, *The Marks of Examiners*, Macmillan, London, 1936.

10. S. Wiseman, 'The marking of English compositions in grammar school selection', *Br. J. educ. Psychol.*, **19**, 200–209 (1949) and 'The use of essays in selection at 11+. Reliability and validity', *Br. J. educ. Psychol.*, **26**, 172–179 (1956).

11. Schools Council Examinations Bulletin No. 12, *Multiple Marking of English Compositions*, HMSO, London, 1966.

12. R. R. Dale, *From School to University*, Routledge and Kegan Paul, London, 1954.

13. F. N. Kerlinger, *Foundations of Behavioral Research: Educational and Psychological Inquiry*, Holt, Rinehart and Winston, London, 1969, pp. 444–454.

14. B. S. Bloom (Ed.), *Taxonomy of Educational Objectives. Handbook I: Cognitive Domain*, Longmans, London, 1956.

15. For a summary of American work, see D. E. Lavin, *The Prediction of Academic Performance*, Wiley, New York, 1967. In this country, a paper by L. Cohen and D. Child entitled 'Some sociological and psychological factors in university failure', *Durham Res. Rev.*, **22**, 365–372 (1969), points to researches in higher education. Comments about the 11+ are numerous and both the Newsom Report: *Half our Future*, HMSO, London, 1963 and the Plowden Report: *Children and their Primary Schools*, HMSO, London, 1967 have something to say on this subject. More critical views appear in J. E. Floud, A. H. Halsey and F. M. Martin, *Social Class and Educational Opportunity*, Heinemann, London, 1956, and B. Jackson, and D. Marsden, *Education and the Working Class*, Routledge and Kegan Paul, London, 1962.

16. Using personality measures such as the Eysenck dimensions discussed in chapter 11, it appears that introverts (and in some circumstances those who score high on neuroticism) tend to succeed at both school and in higher education. See for higher education R. Lynn and I. E. Gordon, 'The relation of neuroticism and extraversion to intelligence and educational attainment', *Br. J. educ. Psychol.*, **31**, 194–203 (1961) and for children D. Child, 'The relationships between introversion–extraversion, neuroticism and performance in school examinations', *Br. J. educ. Psychol.*, **34**,

187–196 (1964). Also, N. J. Entwistle and S. Cunningham, 'Neuroticism and school attainment—a linear relationship?' *Br. J. educ. Psychol.*, **38**, 123–132 (1968).

17. J. D. Nisbet, 'The need for universities to measure achievement', in *Assessment of Undergraduate Performance*, which was a report of a conference convened by the Committee of Vice-Chancellors and Principals and the Association of University Teachers, 1969, pp. 15–18.

18. For a splendid introduction to the problems of objective testing, the reader is recommended to read the Schools Council's Examinations Bulletins 3 and 4. Bulletin No. 3 is *An Introduction to Some Techniques of Examining*, HMSO, London, 1964 and Bulletin No. 4 is *An Introduction to Objective-type Examinations*, HMSO, London, 1964.

19. R. Wood and L. S. Skurnik, *Item Banking: A Method for Producing School-based Examinations and Nationally Comparable Grades*, NFER, Slough, 1969.

20. J. P. Hubbard and W. V. Clemans, *Multiple-choice Examinations in Medicine: A Guide for Examiner and Examinee*, Kimpton, London, 1961.

21. P. E. Vernon in the Schools Council Examinations Bulletin No. 4—see note (18).

22. P. D. Groves, 'Marking and evaluating class tests and exams by computer', *Computer J.*, **10**, 365–367 (1968).

23. R. C. Birney, H. Burdick and R. C. Teevan, *Fear of Failure*, Van Nostrand Reinhold, New York, 1969.

24. F. Zweig, *The Student in the Age of Anxiety*, Heinemann, London, 1963.

25. N. Malleson, 'Treatment of pre-examination strain', *Br. Med. J.*, **2**, 551 (1957) and 'Panic and phobia', *Lancet*, **1**, 225 (1959).

FURTHER READING

R. Cox, *Examinations and Higher Education: Survey of the Literature*, Society for Research into Higher Education, London, 1966.

S. Jackson, *A Teacher's Guide to Tests and Testing*, Longman, London, 1968.

R. J. Montgomery, *Examinations: An Account of their Evaluation as Administrative Devices in England*, Longmans, Green, London, 1965.

D. Pigeon and A. Yates, *An Introduction to Educational Measurement*, Routledge and Kegan Paul, London, 1968.

Schools Council's *Examinations Bulletins* and *Working Papers*, HMSO, London, from 1963 onwards.

P. E. Vernon, *The Measurement of Abilities*, University of London Press, London, 1956.

S. Wiseman, *Examinations and English Education*, Manchester University Press, Manchester, 1961.

World Year Book of Education, *Examinations*, Evans, London, 1969.

M. Young, *The Rise of the Meritocracy 1870–2033: An Essay on Education and Equality*, Penguin, London, 1961.

ANSWERS TO TEST ITEMS

Recall:

(i) Simple recall: (a) Isaiah (chapter 6), (b) Jeremiah (chapter 1).

(ii) Open completion: 'the king of Babylon' (chapter 20).

(iii)

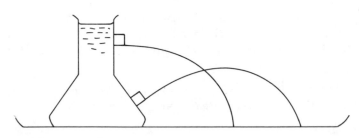

Recognition:

(i) True/false: (1) False, (2) True, (3) False, (4) False.

(ii) Multiple choice—one correct: (1) fission fragments, (2) Lascaux, (3) Protein, (4) Feste.

several correct: responses (a), (d) and (e).

best reason: response E.

(iii) Matching items: (a) La Bohème—Puccini, (b) La Traviata—Verdi, (c) Peter Grimes—Britten, (d) The Magic Flute—Mozart, (e) The Mastersingers—Wagner.

rearrangement: (a) d, (b) c, (c) no response, (d) a, (e) Chromosomes and b.

14   Standardization and item analysis

This chapter is offered as an optional extra for those who wish to know more about the statistics of standardizing test scores and the fundamentals of item analysis. It is not an attempt to introduce students to statistics. That would require a whole text book, some of which are recommended in note (1) and the Further Reading list at the end of the chapter. Even so, students without any mathematical background or with a phobia about mathematical concepts are likely to find this chapter somewhat intimidating. The author, nevertheless, believes that every student should at least attempt to fathom basic statistical concepts in order to make his reading of the research literature more meaningful as well as helping to expose for him some of the dangers inherent in the design and use of standardized tests. In this respect, colleges and departments have an important role to play in providing suitable introductory courses in statistics for students in training.

STANDARDIZATION OF EXAMINATION MARKS

Teachers are often faced with the task of pooling several sets of marks sometimes for the same school subject, sometimes between different subjects. But there are good reasons why it is not always justified simply to add all the marks together and use the total, or average, as a measure of the relative competence of pupils. The standard of marking varies for an individual from one occasion to the next. Standards also vary between teachers and between subjects. Often the marks are widely spread in subjects such as science and mathematics with well-defined expectations in the answers, whereas essay marks tend to bunch round the average mark. The average itself is also affected by the leniency or severity of the marker or the content of the examination questions. Even when the standards for each subject are the same, one may question the sense of adding the marks of such disparate subjects as French, arithmetic and needlework. What we shall do in this section is to demonstrate a method for adjusting the marks in two subjects so as to make them comparable. This process of converting the raw marks to a common scale is known as *standardization*.

Tabulation   Suppose a form teacher has received two sets of marks (variously referred to in the following text as raw marks and scores) one for arithmetic, the other for English. When the marks are assembled for each pupil, the list will have the chaotic appearance of Table 14.1. Gathering systematic information would be impossible from the confusion of figures as they appear in this table.

The first task is to rearrange the scores to provide us with a concise picture of the *distribution*, that is the frequency with which successive scores occur. The best and most easily interpreted arrangement is a *tabulation* obtained by writing down all the possible scores in ascending or descending order. By working through the list of marks we *tally* each one against the appropriate mark to build up a tabulation looking something like

Table 14.1   Marks for arithmetic and English ($N = 50$)
(Maximum score $= 10$)

Pupil	Arithmetic	English	Pupil	Arithmetic	English
1	9	3	26	4	8
2	1	9	27	4	6
3	4	8	28	3	7
4	8	4	29	7	7
5	7	5	30	2	7
6	4	7	31	5	5
7	2	2	32	3	4
8	4	8	33	5	8
9	6	6	34	4	8
10	5	7	35	6	7
11	3	5	36	0	6
12	4	6	37	1	3
13	8	7	38	5	8
14	7	6	39	6	7
15	10	3	40	5	8
16	4	7	41	2	7
17	3	8	42	5	4
18	2	7	43	4	9
19	5	9	44	5	8
20	4	6	45	6	2
21	3	6	46	1	6
22	6	7	47	3	5
23	4	4	48	2	4
24	3	5	49	7	7
25	4	5	50	6	9

table 14.2. The fifth tally mark is drawn through the first four, like a gate, and a second set started with the sixth occurrence of the mark. This has the advantage of breaking the scoring into convenient units of five, thus making for easy additions at the completion of the tally.

Where the range of marks involved is extensive, as would most likely be the case for a percentage scale, the tabulation of single numbers is not sufficiently compressed to give a clear picture of the frequency distribution nor is it convenient for the calculation of statistical quantities. In this case, we group the marks in useful *class intervals*. For a percentage scale the interval might be five consecutive marks such as 0 to 4, 5 to 9, 10 to 14 and so on. A score of 8 would be tallied in the class interval 5 to 9. In subsequent calculations the mid-point of the interval is then used to represent the interval. For example, the mid-points of 0 to 4 and 5 to 9 are 2 and 7 respectively, convenient whole numbers which result from taking class intervals containing an odd number of scale points such as five.

Table 14.2 Tabulation of arithmetic and English marks

Mark	Arithmetic Tally	Arithmetic Frequency	English Tally	English Frequency
0	│	1		0
1	│││	3		0
2	₪	5	││	2
3	₪ ││	7	│││	3
4	₪ ₪ ││	12	₪	5
5	₪ │││	8	₪ │	6
6	₪ │	6	₪ │││	8
7	││││	4	₪ ₪ │││	13
8	││	2	₪ ││││	9
9	│	1	││││	4
10	│	1		0
	total	50	total	50

Graphical representation Although we can now see some semblance of order, there is an even more graphic way of presenting the information. If the frequencies of table 14.2 are plotted against the corresponding marks in the form of bars we have a *histogram* as portrayed in figure 14.1(a). For each mark along the horizontal axis of the graph we erect a block whose height represents the frequency of the mark. Figure 14.1(a) is the histogram for the arithmetic distribution. At a glance we can see that the frequencies for arithmetic accumulate around a mark of 4; for English the most frequent mark is 7.

An alternative method of presenting the frequencies is the *frequency polygon*. If instead of bars we join up the mid-point at the top of each bar as in figure 14.1(b) a frequency polygon is generated. In the histogram the base of the bar is one mark unit wide with the actual mark value at the centre of this base whilst in the frequency polygon the points to be joined correspond to the centre of the base at the mark value. The lines joining the points are straight. However, with large numbers and a good spread of marks the lines joining the points take on the appearance of a continuous *curve*. For ease of presentation the subsequent illustrations will be smoothed; readers should appreciate that the curve will have been derived from a less regular distribution.

Distributions The shape of the curve tells us a lot about irregularities in the distributions.

Many statistical formulae rely on the fact that the distribution of data is *normal*. A normal curve has a symmetrical appearance of frequencies regularly diminishing on either side of the most frequent score. Figure 14.2(a) is a normal distribution; our distributions in arithmetic and English are close to normal. Intelligence tests are designed to give normal distributions when administered to a random sample of a population.

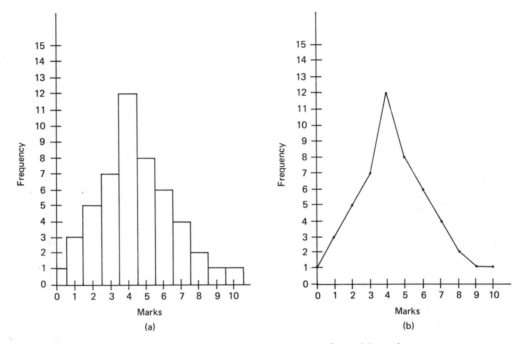

Figure 14.1   (a) Histogram and (b) frequency polygon for arithmetic

Test items are chosen so as to give this kind of distribution. Consequently, it is meaningless to suppose that intelligence tests can 'prove' intelligence to be normally distributed in a population because the tests are manipulated to make normality inevitable.

The English marks tend to fall towards the high end of the distribution and where this becomes exaggerated, as shown in figure 14.2(b), it is known as a *negative skew*. A preponderance of scores towards the low end of the scale gives a *positive skew* as in figure 14.2(c). When two obvious maxima occur in a distribution as would result if we plotted 1, 3, 7, 10, 17, 14, 14, 17, 11, 5, 1, a *bimodal* distribution is said to exist. Bimodal distributions are common where there are two clearly defined groups in the sample chosen—clearly defined because they give rise to conspicuously different maximum frequencies. The figures chosen above are in fact the totals of frequencies for the marks between 0 and 10 in arithmetic and English. As we saw in table 14.2 the maxima for these subjects are different and this is reflected in the overall distribution of the totals shown in figure 14.2(d). Heights or weights of men and women if combined would also tend to give bimodal curves, one maximum connected with the men and the other with the women.

Means The difference in the distributions and maxima for arithmetic and English makes it highly improbable that we can make direct comparisons of the raw marks for each pupil. If we wanted an overall mark we could not simply add the raw scores. We must first convert the distributions to some common standard—a technique known as standardization and used, for example, in the 11+ examination where verbal, numerical

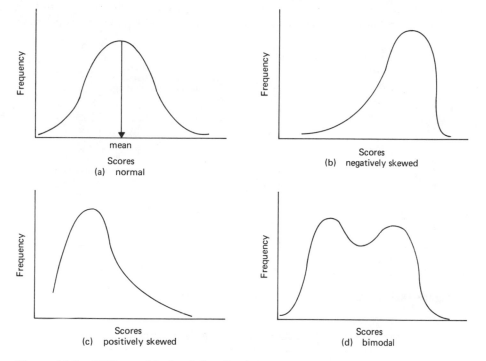

Figure 14.2   Different kinds of distribution

and general ability scores were first adjusted before being added to get a grand total. Occasionally, it is achieved by altering one distribution to comply with the second (see the discussion of cumulative frequencies later) or, as in the following case, by converting the two scales to a third common scale. To do this, we need to know two things about the marks; we need (a) the *mean* or average of each distribution—sometimes known as a measure of central tendency along with *mode* and *median* [see note (2)] and (b) the spread or *standard deviation* of the marks in a distribution—sometimes known as a measure of dispersion. These two important statistics are closely connected to the distribution and provide an accurate way of describing it. Where the scores give a small standard deviation, the curve is steep and high, whereas a large spread would give a flat curve; both are illustrated in figure 14.3.

The popular way of finding a mean is to add all the figures and divide by the total number of figures involved. Unfortunately this is a laborious job if there are numerous figures to contend with. One short cut is demonstrated in table 14.3.

The weird and wonderful symbols employed are in very common usage. X represents the raw mark, $\bar{X}$ (pronounced 'ex bar') is the mean, $\bar{X}_A$ is the particular mean for arithmetic, Σ means 'the sum of' so that Σf is 'the sum of all the frequencies' which is bound to equal the sample size, N. ΣfX means 'the sum of all the separate *frequencies times the marks*'. If one inspects the table it will become clear that each fX saves the trouble of having to add all the separate marks together, that is, instead of adding twelve lots of the mark 4, one has $12 \times 4 = 48$. With our simple example not much saving is apparent, but if the numbers were larger there would be considerable economy

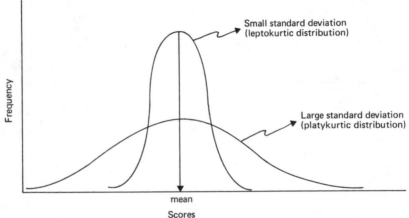

Figure 14.3   Extreme kinds of normal distribution

Table 14.3   Finding the mean for arithmetic

Mark (X)	Frequency (f)	fX
0	1	0
1	3	3
2	5	10
3	7	21
4	12	48
5	8	40
6	6	36
7	4	28
8	2	16
9	1	9
10	1	10

$$\Sigma f = N = 50 \qquad \Sigma fX = 221$$
$$\text{The mean } \bar{X}_A = \Sigma fX/N = 221/50 = 4 \cdot 42$$

of effort. The reader might like to calculate the mean for the English marks using the same technique as shown in table 14.3. The value $\bar{X}_E$ should be 6·20.

Note that if a class interval system had been used, the mid-point of the interval would be taken to represent the range of marks falling within the interval. Thus the interval 0 to 4 is represented by 2, 5 to 9 represented by 7 and so on. The term fX would then be found by multiplying the frequency of marks within a given interval by the mid-interval score. For any one interval this procedure may be slightly inaccurate as we see in table 14.4.

Table 14.4 Calculating a mean using class intervals for arithmetic marks

range	mid-point	f	fX	(actual totals of fX)
0–4	2	28	56	82
5–9	7	21	147	129
10	10	1	10	10
			$\Sigma fX = 213$	221

One would never dream of calculating a mean using the very small range in our example, but it does illustrate the effect on fX of taking the mid-interval point. For the range 0–4, mid-point 2, the product fX would be 56. In fact, it should be 82 if we consider the marks separately as in table 14.3. The inaccuracy is lessened by the second range and the total for fX comes very close to the true value. With a greater number of class intervals the minor variations in fX tend to cancel each other out.

Standard deviation   The second important statistic we need to know is the standard deviation. A knowledge of the central tendency of the marks, the mean for instance, tells us nothing about the way in which the marks are distributed on each side of the mean and the next stage will be devoted to finding the dispersion of the marks. In the following, we will concentrate on the *method* of finding a standard deviation rather than the reasons for the procedures we adopt—in a similar manner to using a cookery book! As was observed above, one would really need a course in statistics to understand the reasoning behind the mathematical manoeuvres.

The stages necessary for the calculation are (a) find the mean; (b) find the difference between the mean and each mark; (c) square the difference obtained in (b); (d) multiply the square from (c) by the frequency f if this applies; (e) find the sum of the results from (d); (f) divide the answer from (e) by the number of pupils in the sample; (g) find the square root of the answer in (f). This gives the standard deviation of the marks. Using symbols again, let the mean be $\bar{X}$, let the raw mark be X, then (a) to (g) would be represented by (a) $\bar{X}$; (b) $\bar{X} - X$; (c) $(\bar{X} - X)^2$; (d) $f(\bar{X} - X)^2$; (e) $\Sigma f(\bar{X} - X)^2$; (f) $\Sigma f(\bar{X} - X)^2/N$; (g) $\sqrt{\Sigma f(\bar{X} - X)^2/N}$. The headings and calculations in table 14.5 follow this pattern. Stage (f) is $\Sigma f(\bar{X} - X)^2/N = 222 \cdot 36/50 = 4 \cdot 447$ and the standard deviation σ (sigma) $= \sqrt{4 \cdot 447} = 2 \cdot 11$. Notice that we include the correct sign in the column $(\bar{X} - X)$ and when this is squared in the next column the sign becomes positive.

Squaring, therefore, overcomes the problems of a negative sign. Readers may like to try their hand at a similar calculation for the standard deviation of the English marks. The answer should be $\sigma = 1 \cdot 82$ using a mean, $\bar{X}_\mathrm{E}$, of $6 \cdot 20$.

Table 14.5 Finding the standard deviation for arithmetic $\bar{X} = 4 \cdot 42$

Mark (X)	Frequency (f)	$\bar{X} - X$	$(\bar{X} - X)^2$	$f(\bar{X} - X)^2$
0	1	4·42	19·54	19·54
1	3	3·42	11·70	35·10
2	5	2·42	5·86	29·30
3	7	1·42	2·02	14·14
4	12	0·42	0·18	2·16
5	8	−0·58	0·34	2·72
6	6	−1·58	2·50	15·00
7	4	−2·58	6·66	26·64
8	2	−3·58	12·82	25·64
9	1	−4·58	20·98	20·98
10	1	−5·58	31·14	31·14
$\Sigma f = N = 50$				$\Sigma f(\bar{X} - X)^2 = 222 \cdot 36$

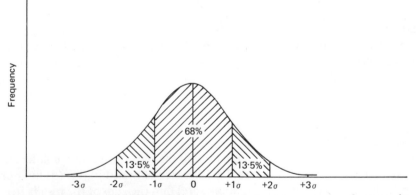

Figure 14.4 Standard deviation related to percentage of cases in a normal distribution

σ is the symbol for standard deviation

In the area between -1σ and $+1\sigma$ there will be about 68 per cent of the cases

One interesting fact about standard deviations for distributions approaching normality is that the percentage of the sample falling within one standard deviation on both sides of the mean is approximately 68 per cent of the total sample. Figure 14.4 is a diagrammatical expression of this fact. The mean for arithmetic was $4 \cdot 42$ and one standard deviation of 2·11 above and below this value gives a range from 2·31 to 6·53. We were operating with whole numbers and this range would include values between 3 and 6. Reference to table 14.2 shows that for arithmetic 33 pupils obtained scores between these limits, that is 66 per cent of the sample. Two standard deviations on both sides of the mean would enclose about 95 per cent of the sample. Three standard deviations on both sides encloses almost the whole sample as shown in figure 14.4.

Standardization Armed with the means and standard deviations of the two subjects, we are now in a position to equate the two sets of marks. But what standard are we going to choose for the third scale? To make life easy in the transformation calculations, it is usual to take whole numbers for the new mean and standard deviation. A convenient mean would be 5 with standard deviation of 2. The common quantity which links all the scales together is the *standard score* (z). This is obtained by dividing $(\bar{X} - X)$ by the standard deviation (σ). For the arithmetic marks

$$\frac{\bar{X}_A - X_A}{\sigma_A} = \frac{\bar{X}_S - X_S}{\sigma_S}$$

Where $\bar{X}_S$, X_S and σ_S are the mean, new standardized mark and standard deviation for the new scale. The only unknown quantity in this equation is X_S, the new set of standardized scores.
Rearranging the equation we get

$$X_S = \bar{X}_S - \frac{(\bar{X}_A - X_A)\sigma_S}{\sigma_A}$$

Suppose we want to standardize a score of 9/10 in arithmetic, then substituting in the formula above for $\bar{X}_S = 5$, $\sigma_S = 2$, $\bar{X}_A = 4.42$, $X_A = 9$ and $\sigma_A = 2.11$, we obtain

$$X_S = 5 - \frac{(4.42 - 9)2}{2.11} = 5 + 4.34 = 9.34$$

Referring to table 14.1 will reveal that pupil 1 obtained 9/10 for arithmetic. He also managed 3/10 in English which converts to 1·48 when standardized using $\bar{X}_E = 6.20$ and $\sigma_E = 1.82$. In fact, pupils 1, 4, 5, 9 and 10 have all obtained a raw score total of 12 when arithmetic and English are added. Yet on standardizing their marks, a rank order is created as shown in table 14.6. Wider variations in the means and particularly the standard deviations than those cited here can produce conspicuous changes when scores are adjusted.

Table 14.6 Marks before and after standardization

Pupil	Raw marks			Standardized marks		
	Arithmetic	English	Total	Arithmetic	English	Total
1	9	3	12	9·34	1·48	10·82
4	8	4	12	8·40	2·58	10·98
5	7	5	12	7·45	3·68	11·13
9	6	6	12	6·50	4·78	11·28
10	5	7	12	5·55	5·88	11·43

Cumulative frequency   Short-cut methods of finding an estimate of standardized scores are available. Students are recommended to read a pamphlet by J. C. Daniels entitled *The Standardization of School Marks* in which these are described. Where there is some doubt regarding the normality of a distribution, it is possible to employ a *cumulative frequency graph* or *ogive* (usually pronounced 'ohjive'). For this solution the frequencies are arranged as in table 14.2 but with the lowest score or mark at the bottom of the column. The frequencies are then added in succession starting at the lowest score. For arithmetic the cumulative frequency (*cf*) is given in table 14.7. The highest *cf* should equal

Table 14.7   Cumulative frequency of arithmetic marks

Mark	Frequency (*f*)	Cumulative frequency (*cf*)	Percentage (*cf*)
10	1	50	100
9	1	49	98
8	2	48	96
7	4	46	92
6	6	42	84
5	8	36	72
4	12	28	56
3	7	16	32
2	5 ⟵—gives—→ 9		18
1	3 ⟵—gives—→ 4		8
0	1	1	2

the sample size giving 50 in the present case. To construct a cumulative frequency graph, plot the marks along the horizontal axis against the *cf* along the vertical axis. For our purposes a percentage cumulative frequency graph is required. To convert *cf* into percentage *cf*, simply divide the value of *cf* by the sample size and multiply the result by 100. At a mark of 5 in arithmetic the *cf* is 36. Hence the percentage *cf* to this point in the distribution is 36/50 × 100 which gives 72. The graph of percentage *cf* against marks from table 14.7 has the appearance of figure 14.5. Note the characteristic shallow S-shaped curve of the ogive.

To produce a conversion graph, first draw percentage cumulative frequency curves for arithmetic and English on the same graph (figure 14.5). In this case we are going to convert marks in one subject to a comparable scale in the other subject. To convert 5/10 in arithmetic so that it has a comparable mark in English, first draw a vertical line from 5 on the mark scale until it reaches the curve for arithmetic—marked B on the graph. Then draw a line horizontally from B until it meets the curve for English—marked C. Drop a line from C on to the mark scale and this reading gives the corresponding mark, which in English is 7·1. Notice that both these marks occur at the 64th percentile as indicated on the percentage cumulative frequency axis.

Standard scores and percentage of a population

Whenever we have a normal distribution of test scores, it is possible to calculate the percentage of cases (number of people for instance) falling between given scores on the scale. This is a very useful piece of information, particularly when we want to discover the number of people who, for example, might have IQ scores greater or less than given values. The figures 14·4 and 9·1 were both calculated using this knowledge.

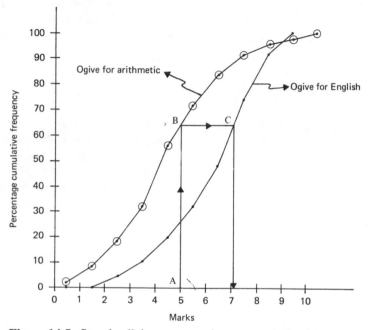

Figure 14.5 Standardizing scores using a cumulative frequency method

The first stage involves the calculation of the standard score corresponding to the range of scores required and using this standard score to determine the percentage for the range chosen. The following table gives a series of standard scores and the corresponding percentages of the population falling in the range *between the mean and a point along the scale of scores* which would give the standard score.

Table 14.8 Percentage of cases under a normal curve using standard scores from the mean

Standard score	0·5	1·0	1·5	2·0	2·5	3·0	3·5
Percentage of cases	19·15	34·13	43·32	47·72	49·38	49·87	49·98

Let us suppose we wanted to know how many in a population of children would obtain IQ scores between 100 and 115 on a test which has a mean of 100 and a standard deviation of 15. The standard score for 115 is:

$$\frac{100 - 115}{15} = -1$$

Ignoring the negative sign, which merely tells us which side of the mean we are operating on, the percentage of cases falling between the mean of 100 and one standard score higher (115) according to table 14.8 is 34.13. From the mean to the far end of the distribution on either one side or the other would incorporate half or 50 per cent of the population. Thus, if we wanted to know the percentage from a point along the scale to the end, let us say 115 and greater, we could subtract the percentage obtained in the method just described from fifty per cent. Hence we would find $50 \cdot 00 - 34 \cdot 13 = 15 \cdot 87$ per cent above 115 IQ points on a scale having a mean of 100 and a standard deviation of 15.

ITEM ANALYSIS

Several references have already been made to item design and analysis as the starting point in the production of multiple choice test papers. In the next few pages we cannot do more than suggest some important considerations which are taken into account when these tests are required. It is not anticipated that students will be able to construct their own items after reading this brief description. For details the reader is referred to the Schools Council's publications and other references made at the end of this chapter. One particularly relevant description appears in the work of a research unit at the University of London which is investigating test materials for the Nuffield Science Teaching Project. We shall draw on the team's work in 'O' level chemistry to introduce the student to item design and analysis (3).

Test blueprint (4)

Before we can design a set of items we must have a clear idea of the aims, objectives and scope of the subject matter (see chapter 16) as well as making explicit the kinds of student ability and behaviour we wish to exploit. Rather than pulling topics out of a hat or dreaming up essay titles whilst watching TV, it is essential to make a detailed map of the nature and content of the whole paper, having regard to the activities and abilities being tapped. We have to decide if our pupils are required to use comprehension or evaluative techniques in the questions posed. Are they to apply knowledge to novel problems? What proportions of these skills do we hope to represent in the questions? In a nutshell, we have created a syllabus to bring about the growth and development of behavioural skills in our pupils; the examination should aim at testing these skills.

Once these skills and the subject matter through which they are expressed have been defined, a *blueprint* is required which incorporates all the essential features of test design. The blueprint consists of a grid which must include all the attributes so defined. For the purposes of building this grid, the Nuffield Project team decided to use some of the educational objectives proposed by Bloom (5) as a workable classification of student behaviours.

The categories chosen were knowledge (recalling facts), comprehension (calculating, translating, interpreting and making deductions to solve problems with familiar solutions), application (applying knowledge to unfamiliar situations) and analysis/evaluation (analysing information for the purpose of making value judgements). These skills represent one important dimension to be accounted for in item design.

A second dimension is, obviously, the content of the syllabus, and this should be divided into conveniently discrete areas of similar material. A third possibility results when the content is classified according to the operations or 'activities' required by the wording of the problem. In Nuffield chemistry the activities postulated were (i) composition and change in materials; (ii) practical techniques; (iii) patterns in the behaviour of materials; (iv) essential measurements; (v) concepts. These can be seen as broader groupings of the syllabus content.

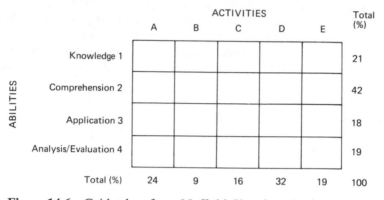

Figure 14.6   Grid taken from Nuffield Chemistry Project (page 4)

If we consider the 'activities' and 'abilities' dimensions as shown in figure 14.6 a grid is generated. The cells of the grid are used to guide us in accounting for whichever combinations of the categories we desire. Not all cells will necessarily be represented. It may transpire that some topics cannot be expressed in all forms of activity. The important point to remember is that we can scrutinize in detail the distribution of the syllabus content and the behaviour we wish to evoke from the questions. Sorting out the proportion of items to appear in each cell is rather complex and rests on value judgements made by the test designer. Weighting of specific categories along the two-way table is a starting point and these have been inserted along the sides of the grid. By judicious manipulation of these marginal proportions we obtain the individual proportions to be assigned to each cell according to the emphases we wish to observe. If nothing else, blueprint design is a most effective way of getting a teacher to examine and define his or her purposes in providing a particular course.

Test item design

Having created a ground plan of the skills, topics and activities we wish to examine in a predetermined proportion, we must devise appropriate items. There are two important indices which help in forecasting the suitability of test items. These are the *facility index* which shows whether the candidates have found an item easy or difficult and the *discrimination index* which shows how far an item distinguishes the high from the low scoring candidates. In all that follows, we are assuming that large samples are involved, certainly more than 30 individuals.

Facility (or difficulty) index It is plainly important to know the level of difficulty experienced by a group of candidates in answering each item. In setting traditional examination questions chance plays a major part in the choice of easy or difficult questions. What appears easy to a teacher in the setting may be very difficult for the pupil in the execution. The teacher's comprehension of a subject often makes it difficult for him to assess, before the fact, the quality of the answers he will receive. To overcome this problem, the questions are initially tried out with a similar group of pupils—referred to as a *pilot sample*. Usually a teacher has neither the time nor the resources to embark on this kind of venture. Consequently, research is under way to test the feasibility of creating 'libraries' or 'banks' of items covering specified ability levels and school subjects (4).

For an examination of the facility and discrimination indices, the following example has been taken from the Nuffield Project (3).

Directions: The group of questions below consists of five lettered headings followed by a list of numbered phrases. For each numbered phrase select the one heading which is most closely related to it. Each heading may be used once, more than once, or not at all.

Classify the following changes into one of the categories, A–E
A Radioactive decay
B Catalysis
C Hydrolysis
D Cracking
E Oxidation
1. The conversion by heat alone of an organic liquid consisting of one compound only, into a mixture of compounds which are gaseous at room temperature.
2. The production of thermal energy from the fossil fuels.
3. Changes in the nuclei of atoms.

The originators of this item are testing comprehension, their argument being that the questions require not just simple recall but an understanding of the chemistry in the example and the terms used for sorting out the type of change involved. Note also that the activity involved in questions 1 and 2 is 'composition and changes in materials'; for question 3 it is 'concepts'.

Dealing only with question 1, three hundred and forty-eight candidates took the paper and eight did not respond to this question. The remaining candidates gave one of the alternatives A to E as set out in table 14.9.

The step before this table was built required the pupils to be arranged in rank order according to the total mark obtained on the whole paper. The order was then divided into five equal, or almost equal, groups shown as fifths in the table.

Table 14.9 Distribution of responses to question 1 ($N = 348$)

Students classified by total test score	Alternative						
	A	B	C	D*	E	Omits†	Total
Lowest fifth	5	17	11	13	21	3	70
Next lowest fifth	4	7	7	33	16	3	70
Middle fifth		8	8	37	15	2	70
Next highest fifth	2	3	7	47	11		70
Highest fifth	1	2	4	56	5		68
Total	12	37	37	186	68	8	348

* Correct answer.

† Number of students who reached question but did not answer it (i.e. omitted the question).

Look first of all at the column totals. Not surprisingly, alternative D attracted the highest proportion of respondents because it was the correct answer. Expressed as a percentage, 53 per cent of the total sample ($186 \times 100/348$) got the question right. The proportion (0·53) of respondents giving the correct solution is known as the *facility index* (F or p). If only 20 per cent had managed to get the right answer, the question would clearly be a difficult one. Higher percentages or F values would signify easy questions. The inverse of the facility index is known as the *difficulty index*. Whether items are included which give a wide distribution of facility levels depends on the purposes of the test. Nevertheless, indices which are lower than 0·10 or higher than 0·90 are often caused by badly worded questions or, as we shall see, by alternative answers distracting the respondent. The inclusion of a few easy items may help the less confident to settle down or the less able to gain some benefit from the test; difficult items, which are frequently analytical or evaluative, may reveal the 'high-fliers' in a group. But most papers possess a substantial proportion of items with near to average facility levels (ranging from roughly 0·30 to 0·70).

The totals for the alternative answers are also very important. An incorrect answer which attracts a large proportion of respondents is known as a *distracter* and should be treated with caution. In multiple choice items, it is common practice to select alternatives which give the appearance of being plausible. If the alternatives were superficial and ridiculous, the candidate could arrive at the correct solution by a process of elimination. On the other hand, the inaccurate answers should not readily draw the candidate off the scent. There is a very real danger that distracters arise through poor and inaccurate teaching or ambiguity in the wording of the question. In our example, alternative E has the largest response rate, apart from the correct answer, and claims some 20 per cent of answers. There are no hard and fast rules governing the limits set for distracters and test designers create their own standards from experience. If distracters are appealing to better candidates they should certainly be replaced. Ideally in the multiple choice item we are looking for alternatives which would be equally attractive to someone with little knowledge of the subject being tested. Thus if the brighter candidates are being fooled by distracters it is wiser to discard and replace them.

Discrimination index (D) It seems obvious that an item should be answered correctly most often by those with the highest overall mark. It would be a curious question indeed if it was answered correctly by poorer candidates and incorrectly by the better ones. The *discrimination index* gives us a measure of how far an item distinguishes between high and low scoring candidates. A formidable collection of methods now exists for estimating discrimination. Of these, it will suffice to mention two and to direct the student to Anstey's book, *Psychological Tests*, for a thorough exposition of the subject.

The simplest measure, and one adopted in researches sponsored by the Schools Council, can be used when the numbers involved are high (certainly not less than 30 and preferably over 100) and when the high and low scoring groups contain the same number of individuals. The formula is simply $p_1 - p_2$; where p_1 is the proportion of high scorers getting the question correct and p_2 the proportion of low scorers getting the question right. The number of high and low scorers must be the same. So we could find p_1 from the highest 2/5ths and p_2 from the lowest 2/5ths. Extracting the values from table 14.9:

$$p_1 = \frac{\text{number getting questions right in highest 2/5ths}}{\text{total in the highest 2/5ths}}$$

thus $p_1 = 103/138 = 0 \cdot 747$
and $p_2 = 46/140 = 0 \cdot 328$
then $p_1 - p_2 = 0 \cdot 747 - 0 \cdot 328 = 0 \cdot 419$

The closer this D value is to $0 \cdot 5$, the better is the discriminative power of the item. Again no rule about limits exists, but many test constructors avoid D values outside $0 \cdot 3$ to $0 \cdot 7$ (6).

A second and more sophisticated measure of discrimination can be obtained by correlating an individual's correct or incorrect response to an item with his total score. When this is performed for the whole sample, a high correlation means that generally speaking those who obtained the correct answer to the item also obtained a high overall score (and vice versa for the low scorers). For a discussion of correlation see note (7). The value obtained from table 14.9 is $+0 \cdot 54$. Interpreting the significance of the correlation coefficient depends on the size of the sample. For $N = 100$ or more a value of at least $0 \cdot 20$ is needed, although most item users would look for somewhat higher values than this if at all possible. With a D value of $0 \cdot 419$ by the first method and $0 \cdot 54$ by the second, question 1 appears to discriminate satisfactorily whichever method is applied.

The final decisions in fabricating a test paper depend largely on the pool of items available. It pays to start with a large number of well-formulated questions so as to create a store of items with adequate facility and discrimination levels. The final test can then be assembled with an eye to satisfying the blueprint and at the same time introducing questions with know standards of difficulty. But there are many pitfalls which confront the would be test designer. These are discussed in the books recommended for further reading at the end of the chapter.

SUMMARY

In order to make school marks meaningful and to justify the comparison of marks from different subjects it is necessary to standardize them. The technique of standardization is also used in the design of objective and intelligence tests (see chapter 9). In this chapter we have lightly touched on some of the basic statistics involved in standardization processes to help students in their interpretation of marks and scores obtained from examination and test material. Such fundamental concepts as tabulation, distribution, mean and standard deviation are mentioned. Item analysis is also mentioned in the hope that it will serve as an aid in the understanding of objective test construction and as a preliminary to our further discussions of curriculum design in chapter 16.

ENQUIRY AND DISCUSSION

1. On school practice or school visits, investigate the following:
   (a) does the school use a system of mark standardization? Explore the reasons for its presence or absence. How do the teachers view the prospect of standardizing the marks for the terminal or annual reports?
   (b) how do teachers *actually* devise examination questions? What attempts are made to sample the syllabus and the skills required in answering questions?

2. Investigate:
   (a) the work of the Schools Council on examinations;
   (b) other current research into question design and item analysis;
   (c) a blueprint analysis of a recent college examination paper. What, roughly, is the percentage of the syllabus covered by the paper? What student skills are being tapped by the questions?
   (d) the contrast between the histogram and frequency polygon for the arithmetic and English marks given in this chapter. Also check on the mean and standard deviation of the English marks. You should get $\bar{X}_E = 6\cdot20$ and $\sigma_E = 1\cdot82$.

3. In chapter 12 it was suggested that children with IQs less than 70 on a scale having a mean of 100 and SD of 15 would usually require some special form of education. What percentage of the population of children would this involve? Using the same scale, and taking 145 IQ and above as the criterion of giftedness, what percentage of children would you expect to be gifted, assuming always that intelligence is normally distributed? Again with the same scale, what percentage of the population would you find between IQ 85 and 115? Compare your answer with the value quoted in figure 14.4. You should now be in a position to check the other values in this figure.
   [*Answers:* number of cases less than 70 IQ = $2\cdot28$ per cent;
   number of cases greater than 145 IQ = $0\cdot13$ per cent;
   number of cases between 85 and 115 IQ = $68\cdot26$ per cent.]

NOTES AND REFERENCES

1. It is not an easy matter to advise students on the best books to read in statistics without knowing their previous experience in mathematics and the availability and quality of the guidance they might receive at college. D. M. McIntosh, *Statistics for the Teacher*, 2nd ed., Pergamon, London, 1967, and D. G. Lewis, *Statistical Methods in Education*, University of London Press, London, 1967, are probably the best for the student still 'cutting teeth' in statistics. See also H. T. Hayslett, *Statistics Made Simple*, Allen, London, 1970. More adventurous students might like to look at the advanced texts suggested in Further Reading.

2. Mode and median are alternative ways of describing central tendency. The mode is the value along a scale or set of marks which has the maximum frequency. The mode for marks in arithmetic (table 14.2) occurs at mark 4 where the frequency of 12 is higher than at any other point. Likewise, the mode for English is at mark 7 it having a maximum frequency of 13. Hence we can trace the origin of the term bimodal in this chapter which refers to a distribution with 'two maxima'. The median is the point along a scale with exactly half the number of cases above it and half the cases below it. In arithmetic the median can be found directly from the cumulative frequency curve in figure 14.5 by reading off the value of the mark corresponding to the 50th percentile. The value is 4·25 in arithmetic and 6·60 in English. Where the distributions are normal the mean, mode and median occur at the same point along the scale. In the present case, the mean for arithmetic is 4·42 and English is 6·20. These values are at odds with those obtained for the modes and medians, thus showing some variation from normal distribution.

3. Pamphlets have been prepared for teachers and candidates by the Research Unit of the School Examinations Department, University of London as a result of their research into the Nuffield Science Teaching Project in Chemistry at ordinary level, 1967.

4. See, for example, the use of test blueprint techniques adopted by R. Wood and L. S. Skurnik in *Item Banking*, NFER, Slough, 1969.

5. B. S. Bloom (Ed.), *Taxonomy of Educational Objectives. Handbook I: Cognitive Domain*, Longmans, London, 1956.

6. Examinations Bulletin No. 7 concerned with *The Certificate of Secondary Education: Experimental Examinations—Mathematics* 2, HMSO, London, 1965, employs these criteria.

7. Correlation is undoubtedly the most widely used statistical concept. It has even crept into common usage in a great variety of forms. Fundamentally, it tells us in a numerical form known as the correlation coefficient the extent to which two sets of measures for the same group of people are related. If we take as an illustration the length of people's legs compared with the length of their arms, we would expect tall people to have long limbs and short people to have small limbs. In other words, there is a direct connection between the two measures. If this relationship was perfect, that is for each

slight variation in arm length there is an exact corresponding variation in leg length as we pass from one person to another, the numerical value obtained would be a 'positive correlation' of +1. With two measures in which one increases whilst the other decreases in exact steps we obtain a 'negative correlation' of −1. But things are never that perfect. We will always find the 'sports' with long arms and short legs (or vice versa) tending to give a correlation somewhat less than +1. In fact the numerical value can be anything between +1 through 0 to −1. A value of 0 or thereabouts represents 'zero correlation', the sort of value we might obtain if we compared the size of shoe which a person takes with his hair colour.

To give some idea of typical values, if we gave a group intelligence test to a class of 100 pupils and retested them a week later, the correlation for a good test between the scores obtained on the first and second occasions by each person would be about +0·90 to +0·98—a very good value. If now we compared the marks obtained in a school physics examination with intelligence test scores we might get a value in the region of +0·50. In a research by the author the correlation between IQ and biology came to +0·14 which as we shall see below is not much different from zero. Negative correlations are less common in behavioural studies than in natural sciences, but one often quoted example is the relationship between intelligence test scores and the number of children in a family. The value is around −0·25 and is taken to mean that the larger the family the lower the measured intelligence. Another topical negative correlation occurs between the cost of living (rising) and a person's spending power (falling) given a constant wage.

We were careful in the last paragraph to mention the number of pupils involved. It is most important when interpreting a correlation coefficient to take the sample size into account. This is obvious because if we obtained a correlation of +0·20 for a sample of five people we would not treat it with the same assurance as for a sample of 500. In fact +0·20 for five sets of data is *not significant*, that means the correlation is no better than zero. For a sample of five we would have to obtain a correlation coefficient of + or −0·88 for us to place any reliance on it being a significant positive or negative correlation. For 500 the value need only reach plus or minus 0·12 for it to be significantly better than zero. The value of +0·14 between IQ and biology quoted above proved to be insignificant once the sample size was taken into account.

Another important point to watch is the interpretation we place on the underlying causes of the correlation. All the correlation tells us is the extent and direction of a relationship and not the reason for it. As an example, just think of the many reasons for the negative correlation of minus 0·25 between family size and measured intelligence—it would be impossible to arrive at a single causal relationship from this information alone.

FURTHER READING

E. Anstey, *Psychological Tests*, Nelson, London, 1966.

J. C. Daniels, *Statistical Methods in Educational Research* and *The Standardisation of School Marks*, University of Nottingham, Institute of Education, 1953.

J. P. Guilford, *Fundamental Statistics in Psychology and Education*, McGraw-Hill, New York, 1965.

H. T. Hayslett, *Statistics Made Simple*, Allen, London, 1970.

J. P. Hubbard and W. Y. Clemans, *Multiple-choice Examinations in Medicine: A Guide for Examiner and Examinee*, Kimpton, London, 1961.

D. G. Lewis, *Statistical Methods in Education*, University of London Press, London, 1967.

D. M. McIntosh, *Statistics for the Teacher*, 2nd ed., Pergamon, London, 1967.

D. A. Wood, *Test Construction*, Merrill Books, Columbus, Ohio, 1960.

R. Wood and L. S. Skurnik, *Item Banking*, NFER, Slough, 1969.

15   Vocational development and guidance

Almost everyone has to find employment at some time. With few exceptions this happens immediately after secondary or higher education. But the important role of our educational system in forming and directing occupational preferences has not, until recently, been fully appreciated in this country. The many psychological and sociological influences brought to bear on young people by the family, the school and society helping to shape their career life-chances tend to have been ignored in our educational arrangements. In America (1), career and personal counselling has become well established as a necessary element in the educational system and there is no doubt that its value has at last been recognized in this country. The coming years (2) will see a growth in vocational guidance in our schools with teachers playing a conscious part. In this respect, there will be a growing dependence on psychological material and its evaluation.

Perhaps the most striking feature of occupational choice in the past, if 'choice' is really the appropriate term in this context, was the apparent haphazard or coincidental way in which young people ended up in jobs. Talent matching, either cognitive or affective, between individuals and the work they undertook was more a matter of chance than choice. Work choice was, and still is to some extent, governed far more by availability in such circumstances as geographical distribution of industries, regional manpower needs or the financial position of the family and its willingness to be mobile in pursuit of work than in medium- or long-term analysis of talent (3). The emergence of guidance and counselling in our schools is of course in response to a great many related factors. Craft (4), for example, believes that changes in political ideology towards an egalitarian system which attempts to provide for the underprivileged and adds a measure of security in employment is one set of reasons. Again, the growth of our economy requires employees who are more adaptable to work situations and more highly skilled than previous generations. With fewer unskilled and semi-skilled jobs available, it becomes important to seek out the talents of people to avoid wastage. But the really crucial point is for individuals to find work which is personally satisfying whilst being useful to the community.

This chapter can do no more than introduce students to some elementary theories of occupational development and their bearing on vocational guidance in schools. In addition, we shall look at the systematic attempts to discover useful psychological factors in vocational choice.

THEORIES OF VOCATIONAL DEVELOPMENT

Prior to the 1950s, no thoroughgoing theory describing occupational development had been formulated. No one had drawn together the rapidly accumulating results of research, chiefly in the States, to provide a working model. To this time, three broad approaches had been suggested based more on speculation than on empirical research. These are known as 'accident', 'impulse' and 'talent-matching' methods of occupational choice. Some people are convinced that their entry into a career results from some unexpected incident thought to be beyond their control. 'I was watching my teacher one day and suddenly thought that I wanted to do a similar job.' This accident hypothesis takes no account of personal and social factors which in unperceived ways might have rendered one range of jobs more appealing than others. Impulse theories stress the unconscious drives laid down in childhood and their pervading influence on the pattern of occupational choice. In later life, particular occupations will gratify particular personality needs. Galinski (5) was able to show that discipline in the early lives of physicists was rigid, stressed obedience and was consistent and predictable whilst, for clinical psychologists, childhood discipline had been flexible, unpredictable and appealed more to 'feelings'. Impulse theory shifts the emphasis to internal factors and early influences. Both this and the accident viewpoint place the individual in a somewhat passive role—helplessly drifting in the currents of chance or the irrevocable influence of infantile experience. The third approach of talent-matching attempted to fit a person's expressed occupational interests with previously determined interest profiles of people already established in occupations. Strong (6), who produced a vocational interest questionnaire, was a pioneer in this field and we mention the application of these questionnaires later in the chapter. Their weakness is the limited information they afford. It is not possible to evaluate from the responses why or how a person arrives at a choice of job, so vital when we want to know the effect of educational or home circumstances. The information they provide is very much 'after the fact'. Again, interests tend to be unstable in early life, hence one cannot be certain about the lasting appeal of a choice. However, interest inventories have certainly a place as part of the picture we build up about an individual's occupational possibilities.

Ginzberg's theory (1951)

It is to Ginzberg and his associates (7) that we owe the earliest detailed formulations. Their main interest was to elucidate a sequence of developmental stages leading to entry into an occupation. The model was based on three postulates which they regarded as basic conditions in the process of vocational choice. These were (i) occupational choice is a developmental process consisting of three periods covering fifteen or so years from early childhood; (ii) the process is largely irreversible; (iii) compromise is an essential aspect of every choice.

(i) *Occupational choice as a developmental process* is seen to last from four or five years of age to early adulthood. This time span embodies three periods of *fantasy choices* (thought to coincide with the Freudian latency period from six to eleven years of age), *tentative choices* (between eleven and seventeen years of age) and *realistic choices* (between seventeen and the early twenties). The timing of these periods depends to some extent upon other aspects of development (intellectual for instance), cultural variations such as school-leaving age and the availability and complexity of work, to mention a few.

During the period of *fantasy choices* the child believes that he can become anything he desires. If you ask a young child what he wants to be when he grows up, his answer will probably be based on recent experience watching someone at work or hearing a description of work, and his preference will have no regard for the skill or qualification necessary. The child can think himself into any role without having to bother about such grown-up complications as training or physical strength. His dream world of play does much to obscure the realities of working life. Frank and Hetzer (8) discerned two stages in this period. Younger children were more concerned with satisfying some specific pleasure they might experience in a job. Bricklaying might appeal because of the enjoyment the child can have in mixing up and splashing around in the cement and water and sticking the bricks together; shopkeeping might appeal because the child could rifle sweets or cakes at will. Frank and Hetzer referred to this earliest kind of motivation as 'function pleasure' and noted that pleasure was based on superficial observation of the enjoyable aspects of work. The later stage was thought to be motivated by more socially oriented notions of doing work which gave self-satisfaction derived from helping or pleasing others. Nursing would enable the child to help other people (notably parents) back to health; bus drivers could carry people where they wanted to go.

The essential features of this period are the lack of regard for medium- or long-term outcomes of the choices made and an almost complete disregard for the skills or qualifications required. There is no connection in the child's mind between means and ends. Often children centre on pleasant or simple beneficial aspects of a job whilst being able to ignore the less pleasant, complicated or routine nature of the work. The child fantasizes about work in the same way he would any other activity he sees around him.

The period of *tentative choices* coincides roughly with the period of adolescence from eleven to seventeen years of age. The onset of a transition from the fantasy period varies according to the experiences and personal maturity of the individual. It is characterized, like many other features of adolescent life, by uncertainty, exploration and self-conscious analysis. Wisely, the young adolescent makes few firm commitments about occupational choices, although exceptionally one meets a very determined youngster who has an occupation in mind, often conditioned by parents, and sticks to it. The period sees the gradual awareness of the need for criteria by which the adolescent can make reasoned choices. It is, nevertheless, a most difficult time because often many decisions have to be made from the flimsiest evidence; our educational provisions demand it. Secondary school pupils often have to choose between several subjects at thirteen or fourteen; they may have to decide whether to stay on at school and take certificate examinations or whether to make an early start in an apprenticeship. Directions chosen at this time are often irrevocable in a system which values the specialist.

Ginzberg divides the period into four stages of (a) interest; (b) capacity; (c) values; and (d) transition. Taking them in order, at the *interest stage* around eleven and twelve years of age, children begin to realize that they will be required to make a decision about their future jobs. Their outlook is not too serious and their choices are primarily based on interests and hobbies. New subjects at school often act as a temporary spur to choosing a job; starting technical drawing or science usually produces a short-term rash of potential draughtsmen and scientists. Father's occupation also intrudes at this age and the influence of parents making suggestions about future employment is beginning to take effect.

Soon the adolescent realizes that interest is not enough. Enthusiasm for an interest or hobby does not guarantee success. Consequently what he sees of the skills required in occupations directs his attention to his own *capacities* and his career pattern becomes oriented towards those things he is good at. Teachers, as well as parents, now become influential because they are the means whereby he can discover his capabilities, chiefly from feedback in school subjects. He also begins to recognize more clearly that education has a role to play in helping future career decisions.

At the *values* stage around fifteen or sixteen years, the adolescent begins to relate his capacities and skills to the satisfaction he might realize from the range of occupations suited to his abilities. Value complexes, which have built up in childhood and adolescence from personal and social influences, make their appearance and help to guide the adolescent in choosing which of his capacities and skills he might want to apply. Such questions as the personal satisfaction offered, prospects (in very sketchy terms), income, scientific orientation become important. However, questions of status or leadership opportunities do not appear voluntarily at this stage. The need for indirect satisfaction is also in evidence. The desire to be a doctor for the sake of doing something for others is an instance. Also the value of work for its own sake becomes an intrinsic desire, thought by Ginzberg to satisfy an emotional need and a desire to do something constructive. This is in contrast with earlier stages of development where a boy or girl might say, 'I want to do so-and-so because I am interested in (or good at) it'. Now he or she would say, 'I want to do so-and-so because I think I might like to do it—it has value for me and others'.

The final stage in the tentative period of occupational choices is known as the *transition* stage because it is at this time when the realities of impending work prospects, opportunities and demands begin to assert themselves. A consideration of values, interests and capabilities alongside the hard facts of work conditions tends to complicate rather than simplify the decision-making process; a period of consolidation and adjustment is therefore needed. The age at which transition occurs is largely determined by the school-leaving age. Ginzberg's analysis was carried out using evidence from the American scene where large numbers of seventeen year olds are still at school, many of whom will move on to some form of higher education. The transition stage, whenever it might appear, is clearly a time in which realistic goal-setting in relation to achievement becomes increasingly important. At the same time, these older and more stable adolescents have begun to realize that they will have to wait until they have sampled work before an intelligent decision can be made. For those leaving for work, there is a preoccupation with what is in store. Likewise those going into higher education are waiting in anticipation, having made a tentative choice to enter on a degree or profession. Ginzberg calls this a time of 'restrained suspense about the future'. Concern about work conditions, length and nature of preparation and the financial returns are uppermost in their minds. In a word, youth becomes more 'instrumental' in outlook.

The stages very briefly outlined above are cumulative and not mutually exclusive. The point has been made of a gradual build up in the realization of personal strengths and limitations and a growth of self-knowledge, all of which help the youngster in occupational decision-making. A burning interest in an occupational task at twelve soon begins to die when the child realizes that certain abilities are required to carry out the task adequately. Again, the ability to perform a task is no guarantee that the child would want to do it for the rest of his life. Routine work probably would not appeal to most bright adolescents. They are likely to aspire to more mentally exacting work for personal satisfaction and reward. Here we see values operating. We can readily discern how home and school play a critical part in the development of values. Contrast the short-term hedonistic philosophy in some working-class homes with the long-term, cold, calculating, almost ruthless view of occupational preparation prevalent in middle-class homes (3). This has often in the past been demonstrated by the early school-leavers who are disproportionately represented from working-class backgrounds, whilst many who stay on from middle-class homes, a number with modest intellectual means, succeed and go to college or university. The way in which a boy or girl handles occupational choice is a measure of his or her level of maturity—Super called it *vocational maturity* (9).

The period of *realistic choices* during early adulthood marks the final stage in Ginzberg's developmental hypotheses. It is important to note that he derived these later stages using students in higher education and this accounts, in part, for the examples he chooses. The period is divided into three stages of (a) exploration; (b) crystallization; and (c) specification.

The individual passes from the uncertainty inherent in the transition stage, when he is changing from school to work or another educational institution, through an experimental stage in which he explores in some detail the occupational horizons open to him. During the *exploration* stage, the individual gains experience by looking closely at the intellectual or physical requirements within the band of jobs available to him. The focus has narrowed because he has chosen a job or subject area with specific demands. But he will still search within the narrow band of possibilities for those aspects which are likely to give greatest satisfaction and prospects.

When the individual becomes increasingly conscious of the attractions of particular aspects in his work or studies he has reached the stage of *crystallization*. For students in higher education, Ginzberg found this stage at around twenty to twenty-two years of age. It may happen at a different, and probably earlier, time for young working men. It is a time when, rightly or wrongly, an individual feels himself to be in possession of sufficient information about himself and his potentialities to make a firm decision about entering a career. The distinguishing feature from earlier stages is the firm commitment, a series of compromises having culminated in an unswerving choice.

Having crystallized their views in broad terms, the individuals in Ginzberg's sample now select a *specific* occupation which calls for particular requirements. Having settled for history, they might choose to teach the subject or enter politics or become an archaeologist. The characteristics of this last stage are a willingness to state a speciality and to possess a determined dedication to the idea of a specific occupation. Obviously, many students are still in need of guidance, which in this country is conducted by Appointment Services within the universities. Appointments officers are kept busy with clients who need help finding work in keeping with their specific aspirations. Some clients may not have reached the stage of crystallization, whilst others may even want to change direction.

Moreover, Ginzberg observed a greater degree of variation in the *pattern* of development during the period of realistic choices than in other periods.

It appears (7, pp. 133–159) that a similar pattern existed in the tentative period for young people who were not going into higher education. However, there were fundamental differences in the expectations and values held by school-leavers. They tended to be looking for work which offered more money than their fathers were earning, steady employment, skilled work so that in time they could become their own bosses and a job free from serious accident risk. Ginzberg says little of the realistic period for normal school-leavers. He does, however, show that this final period is somewhat different for women. To quote:

> the general theory of occupational choice developed on the basis of our study of the men seems to require no major change for interpreting the behavior of the girls throughout the tentative period. . . . From that point on, the strategic influences on the girls are decidedly different from those on the men by reason of one major consideration: the girls are thinking of and planning for their future primarily in terms of marriage: everything else falls into a subsidiary position. Because of this they are not deeply concerned about an occupation.

As with most developmental theories, it is not claimed that these periods and stages are rigid in their emergence. We only need recall our own experience in occupational terms to be aware that variations and omissions in the pattern outlined above are quite feasible. Ginzberg showed a number of variations in his own researches. Some youngsters had a clear idea of the work they wanted to do from an early age and not only stuck to it, but reached a high level of accomplishment. Others with special aptitudes such as musical, mathematical or mechanical skills also displayed singlemindedness in their desire to achieve an occupational aim once they had recognized their talents. For teachers, a major concern must be vocational *immaturity*, that is where young people have arrested or omitted essential stages in occupational development giving rise to inappropriate choices later on. A person who 'gels' in his development at an early stage or who is inadequately informed about aptitudes or work availability is at a serious disadvantage. As Super suggests, work is a way of life and if one has to live with it for so many years it is imperative to have made a decision which is likely to give some lasting satisfaction.

(ii) The *irreversibility of occupational choice* is a second postulate of Ginzberg. The longer one is engaged in the preparation or execution of a career the harder it is to see one's way to changing it. The dilemma of a second-year college of education student affords a good illustration of this statement. Having entered college by the conventional academic route of 'O' and 'A' level successes of a moderate standard, and having discovered that teaching is not what had been anticipated, what can a student do? Does he or she leave college with a possible feeling of failure at having got two-thirds of the way towards a professional qualification and with the prospect of starting afresh in some other area, or should the student stay on in the knowledge that the next forty years or so may have to be played out in an occupation which does not appeal? It becomes increasingly more difficult to reverse the investment in time and effort as one continues along a given occupational route. Psychologically, feelings of failure can have a devastating effect on self-esteem and security.

The prospect of irreversibility is notably acute in a system where specialization is at a premium. Industry and higher education entry requirements are often translated in very narrow terms, leaving the less successful in very insecure positions. The more we can do to help schoolchildren in becoming informed about their potentials, intellectual, practical, and occupational, the better. As we shall see later in the chapter, the work of vocational counsellors involves this kind of service.

(iii) *Occupational choice is the outcome of compromise.* The main point here is that the vast majority of young people are engaged in decision-making and risk-taking as a product of assembling what information they can muster. Each step usually requires a compromise between two or more possibilities, as when a youngster has to balance his interests against his talents, or later when he needs to contemplate the subjects he will need in order to enter a profession—even though it may involve him in the study of subjects not necessarily to his liking. Medical students need to have sciences other than the biological sciences. The greater an individual's vocational maturity in terms of the information available to him, the more enlightened is likely to be his compromise decision.

Super's view of occupational development

One of the best known names in the field of occupational choice is that of Super (10). His researches have partly been incorporated in the theory proposed by Ginzberg, although he has several points of criticism. He felt that the Ginzberg theory did not take account of all the relevant research which had preceded it, particularly in the use and value of occupational interest inventories. The use and interpretation of the word 'choice' left much to be desired. In some cases it was used to signify *preference* for an occupation in the absence of any urgency to enter that occupation—as when a twelve year old says he would like to be a plumber without having the obligation to stand by his decision. This hypothetical kind of choice has a different implication and meaning from that made by someone seeking a job who having made a choice must act on it and *enter* on a career. Another drawback of Ginzberg's formulation was the absence of a detailed analysis of the compromise process. For the purposes of guidance and counselling, Super rightly claims that we need an elaboration of the variables and the routes by which people arrive at, and enter, an occupation.

Super was also responsible for a life-stages model of occupational development, details of which can be found in the references (11). The time spans are compared with Ginzberg's in figure 15.1. Super regards the whole of life in five major stages of growth, exploration, establishment, maintenance and decline of occupational choice. Further, he makes ten propositions which he feels are central to any enlightened theory of vocational development. They are considered here very briefly. Students will notice that they are incorporated in one form or another into later models (12).

(a) Individual differences should be considered such as abilities (both general and specific), interests and personality.
(b) 'Multipotentiality' exists in all of us whereby the attributes mentioned in (a) above qualify us for a number of occupations by which we can succeed and gain satisfaction. These can be discerned using occupational interest inventories.

K

(c) Occupational ability patterns are present in us all. A characteristic pattern of abilities, interests and personality is more appropriate for some occupations than for others.

(d) Vocational preferences and competencies change with time and experience thus making choice and adjustment a *continuous* process.

(e) This process can be expressed as a series of life stages outlined in figure 15.1 [see note (11)].

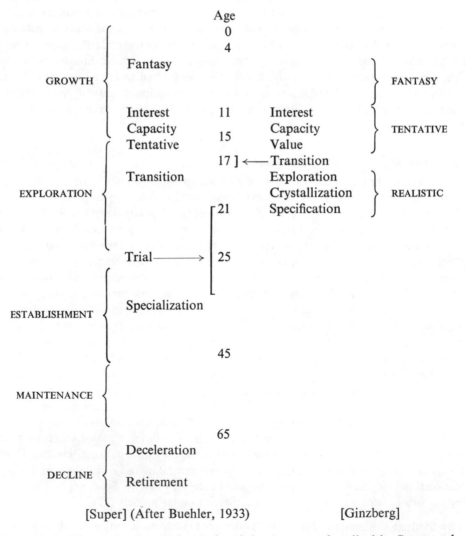

Figure 15.1   The main stages of vocational development described by Super and Ginzberg
Reprinted with permission from B. Hopson and J. Hayes, *The Theory and Practice of Vocational Guidance*, Pergamon, 1968

(f) A career pattern, that is the level, sequence, frequency and duration of trial and stable jobs, is determined by external factors such as socio-economic background, work opportunities, and internal factors such as mental abilities, achievements and personality.

(g) Progress through life stages can be guided by counselling in which self-knowledge of abilities and interests, aptitudes and career prospects are encouraged.

(h) The process of vocational development is essentially that of developing and implementing a self-concept; it is a compromise process in which the self-concept is a product of interaction of inherited aptitudes, neural and endocrine make-up, opportunity to play various roles, and evaluations of the extent to which the results of role playing meet with the approval of superiors and fellows.

(i) The role playing suggested in (h) above is a process of compromise between one's self-concept and the realities of external social factors.

(j) Work is a way of life. Adequate vocational and personal adjustment are most likely when both the nature of work and the way of life that goes with it are congenial to the aptitudes, interests and values of an individual.

Super stresses the interaction effects of personal and social factors and the part they play in forming a self-concept. The latter has a crucial influence on the choice, entry, maintenance and satisfaction gained from work. Another point is his emphasis on development as a continuous process following a sequence of characteristic stages only loosely connected with chronological age. For the counsellor, awareness of the level of developmental maturity attained by a client is important, for it is only when the client's vocational maturity is known that steps can be taken to decide on a course of guidance.

Holland's Theory

A number of developmental theories have appeared since these earlier ideas of Ginzberg and Super (see Zytowski reference in Further Reading). But there are other approaches worth noting for their attempt to go beyond a developmental paradigm to a detailed consideration of causal influences in vocational decision-making. The work of Holland (13) and Blau *et al.* (14) are of particular interest.

Holland gives a very useful model because it demonstrates a convenient link between the theoretical formulations already described and the practical issues of defining occupational interest profiles for the benefit of counsellors. His theory

> assumes that at the time of vocational choice the person is the product of the interaction of his particular heredity with a variety of cultural and personal forces including peers, parents and significant adults, his social class, American culture, and the physical environment.

Holland postulates six *occupational environments* (Table 15.1) or major kinds of work situations typical of Western cultures. Others have attempted to define occupational categories and some will be discussed later in the chapter under vocational interest inventories.

Each person has a life style compounded from values, interests, aptitudes, personality factors, intelligence and self-concept which helps to orientate him or her in differing degrees towards the six occupational environments. In fact, for everyone, we can arrive at a rank order of these orientations by using measures of occupational interests, personality, values, needs, and so forth. The orientations are given the same names as the occupational environments and the rank order of these orientations is referred to as the *developmental hierarchy*. Figure 15.2 should help to clarify the description. The occupational environments are illustrated at the top of the diagram and the developmental hierarchy shows the person's particular rank order of occupational preferences. Of the six possible orientations, the person exemplified has chosen a motoric field as his first priority. According to Holland he would enjoy work involving the use of physical strength, motor coordination and skill; those with a motoric orientation 'prefer dealing with concrete, well-defined problems as opposed to abstract, intangible ones'.

Table 15.1 Holland's occupational environments

Environment	Illustrative occupation
1. Motoric	labourer, machine operator, truck driver
2. Intellectual	physicist, anthropologist, biologist
3. Supportive	social worker, teacher, vocational counsellor
4. Conforming	secretary, book keeper, clerk
5. Persuasive	salesman, politician, publicity officer
6. Aesthetic	musician, poet, writer, photographer

Within each vocational field, there are several possible levels of entry partly determined by the ability and self-evaluation of the individual. In the motoric orientation we find jobs ranging from civil engineer to motor mechanic or welder. Both ability and self-evaluation can be found using tests of intelligence and status scales. These latter measure a person's perception of competence and the worth he attributes to himself with respect to others. The two internal factors of ability and self-evaluation are supposed by Holland to interact in a manner which has not yet been worked out, but he derives a crude formula to represent the interaction: occupational level = (intelligence + self-evaluation) where self-evaluation includes socio-economic origins, need for status, education and self-concept. Four levels are postulated—arbitrarily chosen—and these he calls the *level hierarchy* as shown in figure 15.2.

The picture as it stands is grossly over-simplified. The reader should not be put off by the appearance of precise numbers of levels. They are not intended to impose limitations on the general structure of Holland's model, but simply to bring home the fact that there are different occupational expectations, some of which are beyond the capacities of some people.

There are many other mediating factors which affect the ultimate direction and level of entry. One important internal process is *self-knowledge* or the amount of information a person possesses about himself. The diagram shows how ability and self-evaluation are seen as the contributory elements of self-knowledge. From without, environmental influences like the social pressures from family, friends and school, the economic position and work availability also intrude on the final choice. Holland shows in his diagram the social pressures of peers, siblings and parents directed towards the person. The picture might have been more accurate if another intermediate process had appeared between the person and the occupational areas, thus representing the fact that self-knowledge is not enough when external manpower demands and work opportunities have to be considered. This has been shown in figure 15.2 in the dotted line block marked 'external selection agencies'.

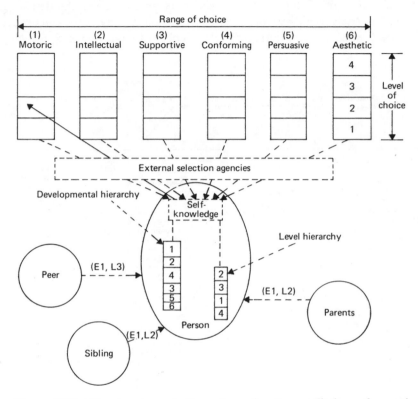

Figure 15.2 Constructs and dimensions for the prediction of vocational choice Reprinted from J. C. Holland, 'A theory of vocational choice', *J. counsel Psychol.*, **6**, 35–43 (1959), with the permission of the American Psychological Association

Blau's conceptual model

Throughout the previous discussion the emphasis of the theorists has been on the development and *processes of choice and entry* to an occupation. Blau and his colleagues (14) rightly point to a second major determinant in the *processes of selection* by external agents (employers, university and college authorities) in response to the demands of the economy or the availability of places in higher education. These decisions are somewhat out of the hands of those seeking entry. Blau in his model is concerned to show the equally dominant role of social agencies in shaping a person's hierarchy of preferences. He notes that

the social structure—the more or less institutionalized patterns of activities, interactions, and ideas among various groups—has a dual significance for occupational choice. On the one hand, it influences the personality development of the choosers; on the other, it defines the socio-economic conditions in which selection takes place.

The overall effect of this dual interaction is demonstrated in figure 15.3.

The most useful feature of this conceptualization is its regard for the details of factors which effect the 'how' and 'why' of career choice. It adds body to the framework proposed by Holland, particularly with regard to the effect of environmental agencies.

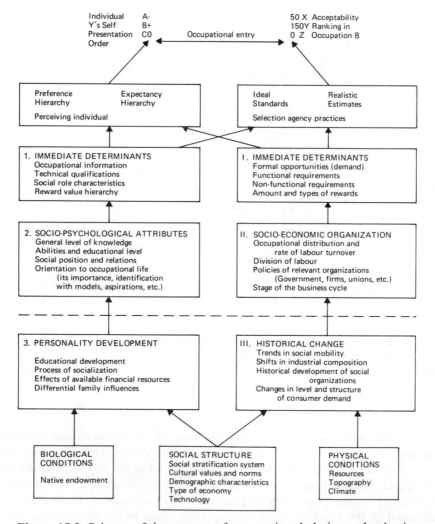

Figure 15.3 Schema of the process of occupational choice and selection Reprinted from D. M. Blau, J. W. Gustad, R. Jessor, H. S. Parnes and R. C. Wilcock, 'Occupational choice: a conceptive framework', *Industrial and Labor Relations Review*, **9**, No. 4 (1956), copyright © by Cornell University. All rights reserved

It also raises the important issue of socio-economic and labour requirements which mediate in the selection process.

The theories outlined above are presented as a pattern of increasing complexity starting with a developmental description and ending with a scheme which attempts to pinpoint causal influences in job choice. There are several other approaches; some emphasize self-expression and self-concepts (15); some lay great stress on childhood experiences of a direct (16) or psychoanalytic nature (17); others have approached the problem using decision-making theory (18). But sufficient has already been said to indicate the primary considerations facing those who are responsible for guiding and counselling young people in their career decisions.

VOCATIONAL AND EDUCATIONAL GUIDANCE

In this country, there has been a long tradition of amateur counselling in our schools alongside the Youth Employment Service provided by the Government and the National Institute of Industrial Psychology (19). Well-meaning teachers have in the past offered advice or been approached by pupils and parents bewildered about prospects. Naturally, the one thing which teachers know most about is higher education where they have been most able to help pupils. Even in this respect, the problem is becoming complicated; youngsters have to push their way through an ever-increasing jungle of subjects offered at school and match their achievements in some of these subjects to an ever-increasing number of career possibilities. Most teachers, however, have only a limited knowledge of employment outside that offered after higher education, and it is here where we find the majority of our pupils.

In America (20) the picture is quite different. Personal counselling is a serious business, undertaken, as far as possible, by trained professionals. Their widest aims are to promote personal, social and educational development to a point where the young people they help, *clients*, can make adequate decisions about careers for themselves and *not* just to place them in employment. The American ideals of counselling are admirably summarized by Daws (21), and discussed in relation to the setting in Great Britain by the Schools Council's working paper No. 15 (2). These ideals, six at least, insist that good counselling practice should include: (a) *continuity of concern*—involving long-term contact between the client and counsellor; (b) *globality of concern*—implying that a counsellor should busy himself with the whole social context as well as the personal, educational and vocational qualities of clients; (c) *active client participation*—by which is meant encouraging independence and decision-making capabilities within the client; (d) *unity of role*—suggesting that the job of counsellor and teacher should not be undertaken by one person. There may be incompatible roles for the teacher as an authoritative figure in one breath and a friendly guide, comforter and confidant in the next; (e) *preventive orientation*—occurring when choice emerges as the end-product of thoughtful, long-term counselling in preference to 'crisis counselling' at the eleventh hour; (f) *coordination of school activities*—the counsellor should be in a position to call on the resources of the school to help a particular child or to call on outside agencies where necessary, e.g. School Psychological Service.

These suggested functions of the personal counsellor go well beyond anything attempted in Great Britain. In addition, Daws (21) recommends that we recognize two broad concerns. These are *educational and vocational counselling* on the one hand and *therapeutic counselling* on the other.

Educational and vocational counsellors

Those specializing in 'matters of scholastic development and vocational thinking' would have two clear goals. 'Firstly, to ensure the fullest development of the child's capacities in school by guiding him on curriculum choice, and secondly, to help the school child to choose a career.' This kind of service is attempted by the few careers guidance personnel in our schools and will no doubt be the important growing point in the future in order to avoid the haphazard and inexpert part played by schools in the past. This is not to deny the effective and professional aid given by the Youth Employment Service, but as we saw in the developmental findings of Ginzberg and Super, there is ample justification for believing that vocational choice is a cumulative process which requires regular guidance in the formative years. Only a full-time member of the school would have the time, close contact and knowledge of the pupils to do this. We noted above the American policy to avoid last-minute guidance not only to prevent chancy vocational choices but to give time for evaluation on the part of the counsellor and self-knowledge on the part of the client.

In summary, Daws (21) suggests that the counsellor needs to discover and transmit information 'about jobs, about entry qualifications, about skills required and satisfactions offered, and about the various forms of higher and further education and their occupational relevance'. He also needs to provide the client with knowledge about his abilities, aptitudes and limitations

> and make sure he understands it. He would rely upon his own cumulative record cards which would record scholastic progress, the comments of class teachers, and psychological test results. He would need to be familiar with at least a few of the environments in which working life is lived and able to command either in memory or at his finger tips a large store of occupational information. He would have some skill in the use and interpretation of psychological tests to enable him when necessary to probe his clients more fully in occupationally relevant aspects. He would also understand our educational system thoroughly and the relevance of particular courses to particular vocational ends.

This gives in a nutshell the major functions of a vocational counsellor.

Therapeutic (personal) counsellors

No mention has been made so far of how we might deal with pupils showing signs of stress and mental disturbance. A whole range of problems come under this heading such as truancy, withdrawn behaviour, underachievement, exam nerves, delinquency. Whoever takes on this work must have acquired psychological training and skill in distinguishing the symptoms of different disturbed conditions both in nature and intensity. Mild cases, where a usually normal child experiences mental distress, would be dealt with by the therapeutic counsellor. Severe morbidity would have to be referred to the School

Psychological Service for psychiatric treatment. Clearly this work requires a highly competent and well-qualified person.

There are very few of this kind of counsellor in Great Britain basically because the School Psychological Service, with its attendant Child Guidance and Psychiatric Units, has dealt with the situation. It is in the milder forms of mental deviance where a school-based counsellor would have an important function. A major task is to prevent the development of serious cases from mild beginnings rather than to provide cures. The small-scale pressures which beset young people and occasionally assume undue proportions can often be contained by well-timed treatment and understanding. In this respect, the parents are frequently an important element in the treatment, and sometimes in the cause of disturbances. This requires skills on the part of the therapeutic counsellor in handling other significant people as well as the client. It is vital to repeat that this role, apart from demanding particular personal qualities, requires people qualified in psychiatry.

Some determinants used in vocational counselling

Returning to the work of the educational and vocational counsellor, there now exists a growing number of devices whereby a client's capabilities, values and aspirations can be assessed and his knowledge of work opportunities and demands widened. A formal or informal discussion with a client is rarely, if ever, the only means used and would not be sufficient for a scientific appraisal of his career profile and possibilities. Many schools, in addition to providing literature and talks about regional employment or higher education, have schemes for industrial visits together with the services of the Youth Employment Office.

But a systematic exploration of a client's occupational potentialities is also a necessary prerequisite. One fruitful format has been devised by Rodger (23) for assembling and classifying information about the career patterns of clients under the title of *The Seven Point Plan*. The resulting profile can be matched against the profiles of people already in work and against the special intellectual, physical or social challenges of the work itself. This is not the only format (24), but it is sufficiently comprehensive to overlap with all the others. Its particular merit is in directing our attention to some really essential factors which affect occupational choice. Rodger's seven points, although examined separately, should ultimately be considered together. Also, the results represent a poorly focused snapshot in the life of the client at a time when, as Ginzberg observed, his choices are still only tentative and partially informed. Let us look at Rodger's seven points of physical make-up, attainments, general intelligence, special aptitudes, interests, disposition and circumstances in some detail.

(i) *Physical Make-up* It is self-evident that certain physical attributes are essential for some jobs. Small stature bars a man or woman from entering the police force, although a small man may be at a premium for work as a jockey! Physical handicaps place limitations on the kind of work people can attempt. The loss of limbs or senses imposes some restrictions. Physical stamina obviously plays a part in fitting a boy or girl for jobs requiring tough constitutions. A knowledge of physical prowess is more likely to operate in a negative sense in excluding people with deficiences or disabilities from certain jobs rather than in deeming them suitable. Physical or personal attractiveness, along with an ability to handle people, are useful qualities for work involving contact with others as in the case of shop assistants and social work.

(ii) *Attainments*   Bearing in mind the limitations referred to in the chapter on examinations, scholastic achievement is one source of information. To begin with, the level of education and success at school are widely used by employers as a measure of potential competence. Certification, amount and quality of schooling and progress through the school are most commonly used as evidence for suitability and entry level to industry or higher education. The counsellor needs a well-documented record card of his clients' achievements together with background information from teachers and parents. Knowledge of weaknesses is just as valuable as knowledge of strengths—clients having difficulty with, say, number skills might be discouraged from entering certain occupations requiring these.

(iii) *General intelligence*   Our educational system has for many years used general ability as one of several criteria for choosing or excluding children from certain kinds of educational opportunity—at least in the early stages of secondary education. An up to date assessment of a client's *general* level of ability can give a clue to broad occupational horizons which may satisfy his intellectual powers. Obviously a pupil with low general ability would not even obtain the level of attainment needed for a career in medicine. A bright boy or girl *might* be dissatisfied with a job requiring little use of the intellect particularly if it involves routine concrete operations. Research has shown (25) broad ranges of general ability within occupational areas and minor differences in the averages between these occupational areas. But this could *not* be used as a precise indication of a client's suitability, only as a guide to his potential. Taking a measure of intelligence is also a recognition of the fact that some people underachieve at school; we need, therefore, a more objective estimate than is provided by school marks or teachers' assessments.

A number of intelligence tests, provided they are individual ones which take account of numerical, spatial and mechanical skills as well as verbal fluency, are satisfactory and many have already been mentioned in the chapter on human ability. A popular test in recent years in this country has been the Morrisby Differential Test Battery (1955) both for general intelligence and, more particularly, special aptitudes. It takes a long time to administer because it includes a wide-ranging collection of intellectual and motor tests admirably suited to discovering aptitudes.

(iv) *Special aptitudes*   As we saw in the chapter on human ability, there are a number of specific capacities such as memory, spatial perception, number manipulation, manual dexterity, artistic ability and verbal fluency which may be present to a greater or lesser extent in individuals in spite of a modest overall general intelligence. Combinations of these aptitudes can give composites such as clerical and musical talent. Possession of a special aptitude can compensate to some extent for a deficiency in general intelligence, provided, of course, that the deficiency is not marked. The aptitude may be pressed into service in certain kinds of work (26). For example, even moderate intellectual power together with numerical aptitude can be an advantage in work requiring manipulation of numbers as in accountancy, but not necessarily in higher mathematics which requires a high general intelligence. The Morrisby Battery mentioned above is suitable for assessing special aptitudes.

(v) *Interests* Vocational interests questionnaires have become the stock in trade of vocational counsellors. Their design has been the focal point of a rapidly expanding research field (27), whilst their administration and interpretation is the subject of several courses. Super (28) has given a handy classification of interests in terms of the methods applied to their assessment. He suggests four categories of expressed, inventoried, tested and manifest interests [see note (28) for definitions]. Of these, we are concerned with inventoried interest tests.

Commonly, the client is required to make a choice between two occupations, or two activities involved in an occupation, over a wide range of vocations [sometimes known as the method of *paired comparisons* (29)]. The same occupation turns up in combination with all the others so that an order of preference can be obtained. We saw an example of occupational categories in Holland's model. The most comprehensive to date is given by Miller (30), consisting of twelve 'stereotype categories and representative occupations'. Examples are given in note (30). In this inventory a ranking method is used between the twelve categories.

The evidence for a marked positive connection between success in an occupational pursuit and a stated interest using an inventory is by no means conclusive. In general, it seems (Strong, 31) that interest patterns of young people of fourteen years are beginning to look like those of adults (compare Ginzberg). Thus the inventories can be used to identify the general direction of vocational aspiration (and assumed concomitant success). In addition, the inventory profile points to wider occupational horizons than would be the case if the client simply stated his job preference.

(vi) *Disposition* Here we should consider the personality of the client. This includes temperament, character, attitudes, values, prejudices, and so on. Personality tests (see chapter 11) such as those devised by Cattell and Eysenck are only just beginning to be used to any extent because we are not certain about the relationship between personality factors and occupational preferences. There are some indications from research (32) that those who are actually engaged in scientific work in laboratories or in higher education tend to be oriented towards things rather than people, do significantly better on intelligence tests when compared with 'arts' specialists (especially in spatial tests) and tend toward 'convergent' rather than 'divergent' thinking strategies. Hudson (33) notes that science specialists in sixth forms as contrasted with arts specialists tend to be conformist, less emotional, interested in practical hobbies and outdoor pursuits, somewhat humourless, pacifist and careful. But these studies relate specifically to the extensive categories of arts or science orientation. We know little about dispositions in particular occupational categories.

Tests of general and occupational values have been devised. Rosenberg (34), using a large sample of American college students, found three major value orientations. First, he found a 'people-oriented' value complex preferred by those who view work in terms of pleasure derived from personal contacts. Ideally, they like a job which offers an opportunity to work with, and be helpful to, other people. The second is an 'extrinsic reward-oriented' value complex appealing to those who emphasize rewards obtained for work done. They prefer a job to offer a chance to earn a lot of money and give prestige and status. The third value complex Rosenberg called 'intrinsic-reward oriented'. Those responding to this value viewed work as an opportunity to be creative and self-expressive. They looked upon work as a chance to permit them to use special abilities and be original.

Clearly, the direction of a client's values and beliefs in terms of social and personal relationships, his need for status, leadership, scholarship, aesthetic experience or autonomy are central to an understanding of the kind of work which might appeal to him.

(vii) *Circumstances*   The home background of a client is a most important determinant in his career choices. The ambitions, values and actual employment of parents will have had some effect on the client. The economic position of the family, whether they are willing to forgo another wage packet and encourage their children are important considerations. As Rodger (23) declares, it is only by looking at the social and economic conditions in which a client has been raised that we can evaluate his past performance and forecast his future prospects.

An elaborate speculation about childhood experiences as occupational determinants has been suggested by Roe (35). Broadly, she relates the child-centred and over-protective or over-demanding upbringing to ultimate choice of person-oriented work such as social service, persuasive, cultural and aesthetic occupations. Those from rejecting, neglecting and casual backgrounds tend not to be oriented towards people and choose scientific, outdoor or technological fields. The evidence in support of this claim is not altogether convincing (35).

SUMMARY

If we took work and leisure away from adult life, there would not be much left. Our life-chances are so closely tied to the nature and demands of our work that we cannot escape from the need to consider, as scientifically as we can, the adequacy and influence of our educational provisions on career choice. Whilst many teachers may feel that their influence in, and opportunity to assist children in, selecting a career is marginal, an awareness of the effects of school life and school work on career choice is most important. This is not to suppose that each teacher should feel himself obliged to act in the capacity of a 'citizens' advice bureau', but he must at least be alive to the relevance of his contribution in the career structure of his children. There is no doubt about the increasing importance which will become attached to those aspects of the curriculum dealing with career prospects in these days of prolonged schooling at adolescence.

We have seen in this chapter some of the important psychological and social factors which profoundly influence, or which are profoundly influenced by, the work we choose. Ginzberg and his colleagues pointed to some valuable conditions present in the process of vocational development and choice which have since been elaborated by Super. Basically, occupational choice is preceded by a gradual developmental process from childhood through adolescence. The process is largely irreversible and the final choice is essentially a compromise between several possibilities available at the moment of choice. For an understanding of the part played by home and school, we need to know something about individual abilities, interests, personality, occupational interests, self-concepts and self-knowledge in order to ascertain whether a choice is realistic and appropriate for a particular person. The question of irreversibility is a constant source of concern to most people. Because work possesses our lives so substantially, it might make better sense if we reorganized the time devoted to educational and career matters so that we dispersed them during a lifetime, rather than having a 'grand slam' of education in childhood and thus having to commit ourselves so early in life. With the system as it exists at present, Ginzberg and Super have provided a theoretical framework which must be set against a background of such practical problems as manpower demands, geographical distribution of work, guidance facilities available and other external agencies.

Counselling in schools can take many forms. We pass from the informal, 'over coffee', chat to a full-blooded analysis of educational and occupational potential. Where counselling is taken seriously, it appears to have at least six objectives. Counselling is a long-term and continuous process from primary school onwards; counselling is wide in its concern about social as well as personal characteristics; it is the pupil who must ultimately make the decision and he must, therefore, be led to a position of independence in order to make such a decision adequately; counsellors should be specialists and not necessarily teachers; there should be no room for last-minute decisions; counsellors should be able to call on all the resources of the school and community in helping each child. It must be remembered that counselling to school-leavers is a very small part of the task. The work extends well beyond the boundaries of finding jobs for the boys and girls. Advice on curriculum choice, achievement and motivation, are but a few additional concerns of the educational and vocational counsellor. There are also behaviour problems and anxieties for which specialist therapeutic counsellors are required who have undergone training in psychology. Behaviour deviance in the delinquent, minor neurotic or anxiety states prior to examinations or as a result of social relationships in class, truancy and underachievement are the kinds of difficulties with which a therapeutic counsellor might be faced.

There is still much to be done in this relatively new and complex area of vocational guidance and counselling before we can place it on a firm scientific footing. We have at our disposal a number of psychological tools which can give us information about physical make-up, attainment, intelligence, special aptitudes, interests, temperamental and cognitive dispositions. The coming years should see an increase in the refinement and use of these instruments.

ENQUIRY AND DISCUSSION

1. By using visits and/or inviting speakers, become familiar with the structure and functions of:
   (a) the Youth Employment Service;
   (b) the School Psychological Service to include the Child Guidance and Psychiatric Unit;

(c) the Child Care and Probationary Service.

What links are usually forged between these services and the schools? See as much of the test materials in (b) as you can.

2. Ask children from a range of ages what they would like to be when they grow up and why they chose it. Do the answers fit into Ginzberg's sequence of developmental stages?

3. Discuss the possible terms of reference of a career counselling service within the school framework. Is there a need to devise pre-work experience in the later years at school, such as industrial visits, social studies about the Trade Union Movement, work communities, and so on? If so, what other experiences, beside those mentioned, do you consider important?

4. Investigate:
   (a) occupational interest inventories and their uses;
   (b) personality and various occupational groups—are there generalizations about certain jobs suiting certain kinds of personality profile [see notes (32) to (35)]?
   (c) the reaction of teachers to career counselling.

5. As a group, discuss how each of you came to decide on your present career choice. You will probably have some difficulty recalling the precise details or the precise moment of decision, but try to discover *who* or *what* influenced you the most in arriving at the decision. Now that you are 'on course', what information would you have liked prior to coming on a course of teacher-training? How might this information have been conveyed to you whilst in the sixth form (or whenever you had to make the decision)?

6. Discuss with your tutor the methods which might be used to investigate 'job satisfaction' amongst non-professional workers.

NOTES AND REFERENCES

1. There is a growing technical and research literature produced largely in America. See summaries in D. G. Zytowski, *Vocational Behavior: Readings in Theory and Research*, Holt, Rinehart and Winston, New York, 1968; B. Hopson and J. Hayes, *The Theory and Practice of Vocational Guidance*, Pergamon, Oxford, 1968. H. J. Peters and J. C. Hansen, *Vocational Guidance and Career Development*, Macmillan, New York, 1966.

2. Several counselling courses have been established in British Universities. Keele, Exeter and Reading Universities are amongst the first. See H. Lytton and M. Craft, *Guidance and Counselling in British Schools*, Arnold, Leeds, 1969. B. M. Moore, *Guidance in Comprehensive Schools*, NFER, Slough, 1971; Schools Council Working Paper No. 15, *Counselling in Schools*, HMSO, London, 1967.

3. For example *Early Leaving*, HMSO, London, 1954; The Crowther Report: *15 to 18*, HMSO, London, 1959.

4. H. Lytton and M. Craft, *Guidance and Counselling in British Schools*, Arnold, Leeds, 1969.

5. M. D. Galinski, 'Personality development and vocational choice of clinical psychologists and physicists', *J. counsel. Psychol.*, 299–305 (1962). See also B. Vachmann, 'Childhood experiences in vocational choice in law, dentistry and social work', *J. counsel. Psychol.*, 243–250 (1960).

6. E. K. Strong, *Vocational Interests in Men and Women*, Stanford University Press, California, 1943.

7. E. Ginzberg, S. W. Ginsburg, S. Axelrad and J. L. Herma, *Occupational Choice: An Approach to a General Theory*. Columbia University Press, New York, 1951.

8. M. Frank and H. Hetzer—a reference given by E. Ginzberg *et al.* in their book mentioned in note (7), p. 61.

9. D. E. Super, 'Dimensions and measurement of vocational maturity', *Teachers College Record*, **57,** 151–163 (1955).

10. Over the years, D. E. Super has written extensively on the subject of occupational psychology. See, for instance, (a) *Vocational Development: A Framework for Research*, Teachers College Press, Columbia University, New York, 1957; (b) *The Psychology of Careers*, Harper, New York, 1957; (c) 'A theory of vocational development', *Am. Psychol.*, **8,** 185–190 (1953).

11. The model is elaborated in reference 10 (a). Apparently, the five stages are taken from a pattern described by Buehler as the five possible socio-economic expectations of an individual, in C. Buehler, *Der menschliche Lebenslauf als Psychologisches Problem*, Hirzel, Leipzig, 1933.

12. See reference 10(c).

13. J. L. Holland, 'A theory of vocational choice', *J. counsel. Psychol.*, **6,** 35–43 (1959); *The Psychology of Vocational Choice: A Theory of Personality Types and Environmental Models*, Ginn, New York, 1966.

14. P. M. Blau, J. W. Gustad, R. Jessor, H. S. Parnes and R. C. Wilcock, 'Occupational choice: a conceptual framework', *Industrial and Labor Relations Rev.*, **9,** 531–543 (1956).

15. D. E. Super, R. Starishevsky, N. Matlin and J. P. Jordaan, *Career Development: Self-Concept Theory*, College Entrance Examination Board, New York, 1963.

16. A. Roe, *The Psychology of Occupations*, Wiley, New York, 1956.

17. S. J. Segal, 'A psychoanalytic analysis of personality factors in vocational choice', *J. counsel. Psychol.*, **8,** 202–210 (1961).

18. T. L. Hilton, 'Career decision making', *J. counsel. Psychol.*, **9,** 291–298 (1962); D. B. Hershenson and R. M. Roth, 'A decisional process model of vocational development', *J. counsel. Psychol.*, **13,** 368–370 (1966).

19. *The Work of the Youth Employment Service* is the title of a pamphlet prepared by the Department of Employment and Productivity (HMSO). In it we are told the declared aims of the service are to provide information of educational and employment opportunities to pupils and parents in collaboration with careers teachers, to give direct guidance to pupils and employers to find the most suitable employer and employee and to follow up the occupational progress of young people giving help where needed. See also C. Avent, 'The School Counsellor and the Youth Employment Service', in H. Lytton and M. Craft (Eds), *Guidance and Counselling in British Schools*, Arnold, Leeds, 1969.

   The following extract from a pamphlet distributed by the National Institute of Industrial Psychology entitled *Choosing a Career* should give students a background to the Institute's functions. The NIIP 'is a non-profit making organization concerned with the scientific study of people at work. Its aim is to improve working methods and conditions, selection and training, supervision and management, indeed everything that affects people's adjustment to their work and to their fellow workers.' This service has been running now for over fifty years.

20. H. Lytton, *School Counselling and Counsellor Education in the United States*, NFER, Slough, 1968.

21. P. P. Daws, 'What will the School Counsellor do', *Educ. Res.*, **9**, No. 2, 83–92 (1967). Two other papers appear in this issue under the title of 'The counselling function: a symposium'. They are J. M. Raynor and R. A. Atcherley, 'Counselling in schools—some considerations', 93–102 and J. A. Fuller and D. F. Juniper, 'Guidance, counselling and school vocational work', 103–104.

22. The Schools Council Working Paper No. 15, *Counselling in Schools: A Study of the Present Situation in Great Britain*, HMSO, London, 1967.

23. A. Rodger, *The Seven Point Plan*, Paper No. 1, National Institute of Industrial Psychology, London, 1952. See also a paper by R. M. McKenzie, 'An occupational classification for use in vocational guidance', *Occup. Psychol.*, **28**, 108–117 (1954).

24. See, for instance, W. V. Bingham's nine point plan in *Aptitudes and Aptitude Testing*, Harper, London, 1942; R. M. McKenzie mentioned in note (23); D. E. Super's psychological and social factors in *Appraising Vocational Fitness*, Harper, New York, 1949.

25. P. E. Vernon, 'Occupational norms for the 20-minute Progressive Matrices Test', *Occup. Psychol.*, **23**, 58–59 (1949). Also P. E. Vernon and J. B. Parry, *Personnel Selection in the British Forces*, University of London Press, London, 1949.

26. P. E. Vernon offers some evidence from his researches relating to aptitudes and the differentiation of jobs in *The Structure of Human Abilities*, Methuen, London, 1950.

27. Research continues and the number of questionnaires increases. Amongst the best known American examples are the Strong Vocational Interest Blank, Kuder Preference Record, Thurstone Interest Schedule. In this country we have the Rothwell–Miller Interest Blank, The Connolly Occupational Interests Questionnaire,

The Factual Interest Blank and more recently the APU Occupational Interests Guide developed by the Applied Psychology Unit, University of Edinburgh. The Careers Research and Advisory Council (CRAC) is very active in providing courses and encouraging research including the production of the Connolly and Crowley Occupational Interest Blanks.

28. D. E. Super, *The Psychology of Careers: An Introduction to Vocational Development* Harper, New York, 1957. 'Expressed' interests are disclosed by asking a person to name directly his choice. In younger children, these choices are subject to change and therefore not reliable, although exceptions exist where, for example, family pressure leaves little to chance in career expectations for the children. Ranking and rating methods fall into this category where pupils are presented with a list of school subjects or occupations and are asked to re-assemble them in order of preference. 'Inventoried' interests are examined using questionnaires endeavouring to discover preferences by objective methods. The vocational interest inventories of Strong, Kuder and Thurstone are based on this principle and make the assumption that a person with interest patterns similar to those already committed to, and successful in, an occupation is most likely to follow that occupation. 'Tested' interest relies on the assumption that an interested person will learn more about a topic than one who is not motivated. By sampling a person's knowledge it may be possible to assess his ultimate preference. 'Information' and 'Culture' tests are examples which seek to discover the level of accumulated knowledge as a measure of interest. Finally 'Manifest' interest is revealed by a person's strength of participation in activities, such as an interest in sport which leads a child to playing that sport. But this method of assessment can be highly unreliable in that the centres of this kind of interest often show marked changes. See also pp. 215–216.

29. As a sample example of how *paired comparisons* works, let us imagine that we give a client three occupations in every possible combination of pairs presented in the following way:

Place a tick against the one of each pair of occupations you would probably prefer:

| doctor | ☐ | bricklayer | ☐ | commercial traveller | ☑ |
| commercial traveller | ☑ | doctor | ☑ | bricklayer | ☐ |

Preferences clearly fall into an order with commercial traveller = 2, doctor = 1, bricklayer = 0. Straightforward counts of the number of times each activity is given preference is used for a profile. Note that calculating such quantities as a mean is pointless where the scores obtained are interrelated. Apart from anything else, the scores are *relative* to each other—as 'commercial traveller' has 2 endorsements, it would be impossible for either 'doctor' or 'bricklayer' to have the maximum of 2. Therefore the profile must be viewed as a whole and not in isolated parts.

30. K. M. Miller, *Manual for the Rothwell–Miller Interest Blank*, NFER, Slough, 1968. Illustrations from this inventory are here given to demonstrate the categories in use. The twelve categories are: 'Outdoor' (e.g. farmer, surveyor, physical education teacher); Mechanical (civil engineer, motor mechanic, petrol pump attendant, weaver); Computational (auditor, cashier, income tax clerk); Scientific (industrial

chemist, laboratory assistant, geologist); Persuasive (sales manager, insurance salesman, radio announcer); Aesthetic (artist, photographer, window dresser); Literary (journalist, librarian, book reviewer); Musical (music teacher, pianist, music shop assistant); Social Service [teacher (primary), social worker, missionary]; Clerical (bank manager, office worker, town clerk); Practical (carpenter, house decorator, cook); Medical (doctor, physiotherapist, pharmacist).

31. E. K. Strong, *Vocational Interests in Men and Women*, Stanford University Press, California, 1952, and 'Nineteen-year follow-up of engineer interests', *J. appl. Psychol.*, **36**, 64–74 (1952).

32. Some confirmation can be found in A. Roe, 'A psychological study of eminent psychologists and anthropologists and a comparison with biological and physical scientists', *Psychol. Monogr.*, **67**, No. 352 (1953); D. W. MacKinnon, 'The personality correlates of creativity: a study of American architects', *Proc. XIVth Int. Congress Appl. Psychol.*, Munksgaard, Copenhagen; D. C. McLelland, 'On the psycho-dynamics of creative physical scientists', in H. E. Gruber *et al.* (Eds), *Contemporary Approaches to Creative Thinking*, Atherton, New York, 1962; C. Bereiter and M. B. Freedman, 'Fields of study and the people in them', in N. Sanford (Ed.), *The American College*, Wiley, New York, 1967; L. Hudson, *Contrary Imaginations*, Methuen, London, 1966, and *Frames of Mind*, Methuen, London, 1968.

33. L. Hudson, 'Personality and scientific aptitude', *Nature*, **198**, 913–914 (1963). See also D. Child and A. G. Smithers, 'Some cognitive and affective factors in subject choice', *Res. Educ.*, **5**, 1–9 (1971).

34. M. Rosenberg, *Occupations and Values*, The Free Press, Glencoe, Illinois, 1957.

35. A. Roe, 'Early determinants of vocational choice', *J. counsel. Psychol.*, **4**, 212–217 (1957); *The Psychology of Occupations*, Wiley, New York, 1956. Research using the theory does not strongly support it. See D. G. Zytowski, *Vocational Behavior*, Holt, Rinehart and Winston, New York, 1968, pp. 240–255 for papers relating to Roe's theory.

FURTHER READING

B. Hopson and J. Hayes, *The Theory and Practice of Vocational Guidance*, Pergamon, Oxford, 1968. A thorough textbook which is up to date. Intended for all those who want to study the subject in depth.

R. Jackson and D. F. Juniper, *A Manual of Educational Guidance*, Holt, Rinehart and Winston, London, 1971. Another full text which also deals with some of the bread and butter problems facing the teacher–counsellor in school.

H. Lytton and M. Craft, *Guidance and Counselling in British Schools*, Arnold, Leeds, 1969. Discusses many of the current problems and worries of teacher–counsellors.

Ministry of Labour, *The Future Development of the Youth Employment Service* (The Albemarle Report), HMSO, London, 1965.

B. M. Moore, *Guidance in Comprehensive Schools*, NFER, Slough, 1971.

Schools Council Working Paper No. 15, *Counselling in Schools*, HMSO, London, 1967.

'The Counselling Function: A Symposium' in *Educ. Res.* (NFER), **9**, 83–104 (1967).

16   The curriculum

We have evolved a tradition in our primary schools and non-examination classes in secondary schools of being the masters of our own curricula chiefly in having considerable freedom to choose what we do and how we do it. This freedom to sell wares in whichever way takes our fancy places a great responsibility on the shoulders of teachers. But as public interest in education increases, as qualifications become ever more important as a passport to work, as our mode of living increases in complexity and the knowledge explosion imposes increases both in the quantity and levels of abstraction, we must recognize the need for a systematic appraisal of school curricula. Assumptions about what is worth teaching, priorities in subject matter, order of presentation, how a subject might be presented, what forms the evaluation of learning experiences for the children or teaching methods of the teachers might take are but a few major considerations. It should come as no surprise to student teachers that this book includes a chapter on some factors bearing on curriculum development. One of the first and inescapable jobs of a teacher is to design a curriculum. Students on teaching practice also have to devote many hours to the preparation of their lessons.

For most teachers the main concern has almost inevitably been what to teach and how to teach it (1), with some, though diminished, regard for evaluating the effectiveness of content and method. In effect, teachers have broken into their curriculum planning at the 'contents' stage, taking for granted that the material chosen is justified and relevant. In secondary education, this state of affairs is largely a legacy of an exam-oriented system. In a régime where external, public examinations are compiled and tested by long-established agencies external to the teacher and his school, there is little wonder that teachers have taken most syllabuses as read. Mode III of the Certificate of Secondary Education attempts to overcome this tendency by placing the responsibility of syllabus design and evaluation in the hands of teachers. Apart from this novel idea, which has not caught on at the rate originally envisaged (presumably because it is very much harder than allowing someone else to do it), the secondary schools are tied to a system of external curriculum design and assessment.

Even at the primary level, the long-standing traditions of what and how to teach, the folk-lore of primary education, are sometimes devoid of a rationale defining the reasons for choosing a particular content area or method. Yet clarity in the aims and objectives of an educational programme would seem to be an obvious starting point if we are to justify a public educational system

THE MEANING OF CURRICULUM

But what do we mean by curriculum? Is it that timetable pinned to the staffroom notice board or in the back of a diary looking for all the world like a bookie's price list of runners with the times of each race? Is it the syllabus or the lesson notes? In fact, the curriculum is more than these. Neagley and Evans (2) propose that the curriculum is *all of the planned experiences provided by the school to assist pupils in attaining the designated learning outcomes to the best of their abilities.* Hirst (3) puts it another way: programmes of activities designed so that pupils will attain, so far as possible, educational ends or objectives.

Implicit in most definitions of the curriculum are at least four important elements. The order is not fortuitous, although, as we shall see, there is a very necessary interplay between the elements in the construction of a curriculum. Tyler (4) expresses these elements in the form of questions:

1. what educational purposes should the school seek to attain?
2. what educational experiences can be provided that are likely to attain these purposes?
3. how can these educational experiences be effectively organized?
4. how can we determine whether these purposes are being attained?

These four questions often appear in contracted form as:

$$\text{Objectives} \rightarrow \text{course content} \rightarrow \text{methods} \rightarrow \text{evaluation.}$$

Note that Tyler prefers to talk about 'educational experiences' in preference to course content because experience involves not only the substance of what is taught,

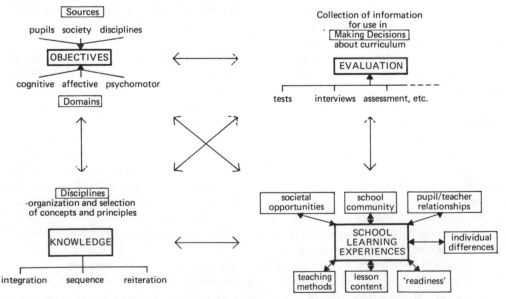

Figure 16.1   A model for curriculum theory
Reprinted from Professor Kerr's inaugural lecture, 'The problem of curriculum reform', University of Leicester, 1967, with kind permission of the author

but the processes by which the pupil learns. In other words educational experience involves content *and* what the pupil does.

As was hinted above, before deciding what to teach, we have to settle the matter of the reasons for it being taught in the first place and the outcomes we anticipate. Why teach reading to youngsters? What purposes are served by studying art in the secondary school? It is also necessary to make a regular appraisal of whether the purposes of a curriculum are being fulfilled.

The simple linear representation of Tyler's questions gives an over-simplified view of the interaction of these components of curriculum design. It gives the impression that evaluation is the end of the line, but as Richmond remarks (5) 'Death is the only terminal behaviour'! A more comprehensive and dynamic demonstration of curriculum theory can be gained from Kerr's model (6) containing similar components to Tyler but presented in a cyclical pattern. This is shown in figure 16.1. Note the interrelationships between the components demonstrated by the arrows. There are, of course, dangers in selecting just one model *if* we forget that it is only representative of complex processes. Also, we get no idea from the model of the relative importance attached to each component.

OBJECTIVES

When we specify the behavioural changes we anticipate as a result of learning experiences, the specifications are said to be *objectives*. They usually begin with a verb, thus emphasizing that certain behaviours are hoped for; 'to recognize . . .', 'to acquire . . .', 'to apply . . .', 'to understand . . .' are examples. Returning to a question posed in the previous section, what are the objectives of teaching children to read? There are several possible objectives; for example, children learn to read (a) to gain knowledge and understanding; (b) to reap satisfaction from being able to read; (c) to assist their work and leisure, and so forth. Some activities are more specific, as when we teach Newton's laws of motion to help in an understanding of the generalizations applying to bodies which move on earth with low or moderate velocities. There could be other objectives subsumed under the ones suggested above and applying to each of Newton's three laws of motion. But, clearly, defining objectives is a skilled occupation requiring a careful consideration of the knowledge we wish to transmit to our children and the impact this knowledge will have on them.

The term 'aim' is sometimes used as an alternative to objective. However, it is more accurate to distinguish between the two. Aims are much more general and frequently refer to philosophical issues in the wider context of education. They also tend to refer to the end product of the system. We might find expressions of the aims of a course couched in more general terms such as 'to produce technologists' or 'to educate for leisure'. Objectives relate to the route as well as the goal, whereas aims usually relate to the goal.

How do we decide on the skills, attitudes and activities we wish to promote in our pupils when we are trying to specify objectives? Some curriculum planners start with a consideration of human needs (see chapter 3) which encompass both personal and social needs (7). Moreover, these decisions, especially where aims are involved, are made within a very wide context of opinion. Goodlad (8) sees three levels of decision-making in curriculum design. These are (a) Societal—largely through central government and local education authority decisions sometimes based on Government reports (Robbins, Newsom, Plowden); (b) Institutional—representing school, college, or university; and (c) Instructional—at 'shop floor' level in the classroom culminating in the teacher's decisions. The reorganization of secondary education, for instance, leaves local education authorities with the freedom to decide on the system to adopt whether it be comprehensive, three tier or whatever. In the short term, these decisions have an effect on curriculum design. For example, middle schools inherited from a primary school tradition may give rise to a different scheme of objectives than a middle school inherited from a secondary school tradition. In the latter, one might see a specialist programme including science, mathematics, handicraft, domestic science for the nine year olds not at present typical of primary schools. In the former one might find greater use made of the integrated day or non-streaming. Our existing curricula also bear the marks of our history and we shall return briefly to this point later in the chapter.

Bloom's taxonomy (9)

Nowadays, it would not be possible to write about objectives without making some reference to the work of Bloom and his associates on a taxonomy of education objectives. Broadly, he classified objectives into three major domains: (1) *cognitive objectives* placing the greatest emphasis on remembering, reasoning, concept formation and creative thinking; (2) *affective objectives* emphasizing emotive qualities expressed in attitudes, interests, values and emotional biases; (3) the *psychomotor objectives* emphasizing muscle and motor skills, and manipulation in all kinds of activities such as handwriting, speech, physical education, and the like. This latter domain has not yet been fully developed by Bloom. A brief gallop through the full list of objectives in the cognitive or affective domain would do very little to assist the student in understanding Bloom's intentions. The only way of really getting to grips with his views would be to refer to his books. However, one illustration will be given to show how the taxonomy operates.

Bloom and his associates organized their taxonomy (or classification) of cognitive factors under six major headings. The six are arranged hierarchically to demonstrate that the objectives are cumulative, so that higher classes are built on the skills involved in lower classes. Briefly, the six classes involve *knowledge* which emphasizes those processes which require recall of such things as specific facts, terminology, conventions and generalizations. Clearly, if one has no fund of knowledge, one cannot operate cognitively. *Comprehension* represents a low level of understanding sufficient to grasp the translation and meaning of mathematical or verbal material for the purposes of interpretation or extrapolation. *Application* employs remembering and combining material to give generalizations for use in concrete situations. *Analysis* means the breakdown of material into its constituents in order to find the relationships between them. Note this requires all the previous classes before analysis is possible. *Synthesis* necessitates the putting together of the constituents by rearranging and combining them so as to give an arrangement not apparent before. Lastly, *evaluation* requires value judgements about materials, ideas, methods, and so forth. To perform this operation satisfactorily would need all the skills of knowledge, comprehension, application, analysis and synthesis for a valid judgement to be made possible.

Devising curriculum objectives

Designing a curriculum has a salutary effect on teaching provided the job is done properly. It is all too easy to end up with a somewhat vague and amorphous list of statements having little operational value. It should be possible in most cases for the objectives to be stated in such a way as to lend themselves to systematic evaluation. One cannot measure what one cannot define. Plainly there are occasions when we wish to 'pilot' or try out a new method in a spirit of 'let's see what happens' (scientists employ this method in addition to conventional scientific enquiry). But apart from occasional pilot runs, we ought to know precisely where we are going and what we hope to achieve on the way.

As an illustration of curriculum design in action, a recent study of curriculum objectives in teacher-training by a team in the Leeds area, will be used (7). A panel of representatives from schools, colleges of education and universities was assembled as experienced informants from the teaching profession. Their first task was to compile a provisional working definition of the teacher's role and to work back from this definition to the learning experiences provided in colleges of education. It was decided that to be effective, teachers must command:

(a) a range of *professional skills and techniques* which are directly related to the day-to-day work of a teacher;
(b) *knowledge and understanding* of subject matter and the appropriate methods of teaching it to children;
(c) *personal qualities*.

A closer examination of these professional qualities should prove to be beneficial in providing a rationale for college work as well as showing how these objectives are related to classroom practices.

(a) *Professional skills and techniques*   Taking their cue from research in the area of the probationary year in teaching and teacher-opinion of college courses, the team drew up a list of skills and techniques along with corresponding reasons for choosing the list. As suggested earlier, one way of breaking into this ground is by looking at children's needs particularly those they must acquire (to be found in chapter 3) in order to cope with their environment. Four particular kinds of experience were defined in terms of curriculum subject areas and these were *language skills*, *human studies*, *science studies* and *expressive arts*. For example, language skills would include subject studies in English, foreign languages and mathematics (regarding this subject as a form of symbolic language). Children were also considered in three groups following roughly the pattern of the three-tier system with children in early years (3 to 9), middle years (9 to 12) and later years (12 onwards). Each group had representative members of the panel. The total picture would look like table 16.1.

Within each curriculum element for each age range would be an elaboration of children's needs and some corresponding professional skills required by the teacher.

Table 16.1

		Language skills	Human studies	Science studies	Expressive arts
			Curriculum elements		
Age range	Early (3–9) Middle (9–12) Late (12–)				

Table 16.2 is a selection from the entries for the early age range in human studies set out with children's needs opposite the teacher's professional skills.

These are just a few of the recommended needs to give readers a clue to the findings. Students and teachers might have something to gain from looking at the full lists (7) and analysing them in terms of their own work.

(b) *Teacher's knowledge*   What areas of knowledge should a teacher possess in addition to his personal subject knowledge required as part of his own education? For those teaching children in the early years at school, the panel postulated six areas of knowledge. These were knowledge of (i) philosophical considerations; (ii) the four curriculum areas in sufficient depth for teaching purposes; (iii) human development and other psychological issues relevant to teaching; (iv) the formation of human relationships; (v) the country's system of education past and present; and (vi) the various welfare services. The middle and later school years are similar except that later school years should include a knowledge of the work conditions which prevail for children leaving school.

(c) *Teacher's personal qualities*   For many years research into those qualities which distinguish 'good' teachers from others has attracted great interest. The findings are frequently disappointing and unhelpful because the characteristics which appear to be popular might equally well describe a secretary or a bank manager. Taylor (10) found with primary and secondary school children that cheerfulness, good temper and a sense of humour were especially important qualities for teachers to possess. In America, Ryans (11) carried out a massive study of teacher characteristics in junior and high schools and their relationship to teacher effectiveness. Three patterns of teacher-behaviour stood out from all others and they were (i) friendly (warm, understanding, friendly vs. aloof, egocentric, restricted), (ii) organized (responsible, businesslike, systematic vs. evading, unplanned, slipshod) and (iii) stimulating (imaginative, surgent, vs. dull, routine). According to Start (12) high general intelligence, dominance, relaxed security, introversion and conservatism are the hallmarks of a superior teacher. From this rag-bag of qualities, the Leeds team chose the following:

(i) *professional attitudes* including a sense of responsibility, strong moral sense, punctuality, and appropriate standards of dress;

Table 16.2 Human studies

The needs of children	The professional needs of the teachers
Opportunity for play, which helps to fulfil the needs for: adventure cooperation knowledge of one's own and other people's reactions experience in accepting responsibility for one's own actions learning to accept others and be accepted by them an awareness of one's own ability in relation to the ability of others the control of one's own feelings, etc.	Knowledge of the use of play in this context and skill in exploring its possibilities Knowledge of the social development of children and skill in applying this knowledge in the classroom Knowledge of the customs, etc., of people from cultures different to our own Knowledge of different cultures within our own community: their clothes, food, religions, etc.
Opportunity to learn about people and to satisfy curiosity about them. within one's own family within one's own class at school within one's own neighbourhood and about: people and where they live people in other lands people in the past by means of: stories, films, television, books, pictures, etc.	Skill in the use of materials and resources in the classroom Skills in writing, printing and drawing on the blackboard, etc. Skills in assessing children's work and progress in Human Studies Knowledge of children's work (particularly in Human Studies) in the next stage of their education at school

(ii) *flexibility and adaptability* involving appropriate attitudes to learning, enthusiasm, motivation, imagination, resilience, vitality, courage, a sense of humour, curiosity;

(iii) *confidence*.

Unfortunately, lists of qualities of the kind described here are not all that useful unless we know more about the particular combinations which prove to be effective. It would not be feasible for a teacher to possess all these qualities. They tend to read like a reference for the post of Archangel!

We have spent some time looking at an analysis of objectives partly to see the way in which this analysis was approached and also because the findings are of value to intending and serving teachers. Note that implicit in some of the objectives of teacher education is a view of what is important in the education of children.

Defining objectives

Several authors have laid down guidelines which will assist the curriculum planner during his attempts to establish curriculum objectives (13, 14). When we are planning a course, the objectives must be:

(i) realistic, appropriate and capable of being translated into learning experiences in the classroom. Plans are laid after we have borne in mind the limitations imposed by, for example, the intellectual development of children, their home circumstances and school background. There is no point in specifying objectives which cannot be operationally defined. For instance, the term 'creativity' is sometimes used in primary and secondary curricula without any clear indication of its meaning in this context, or of the processes by which it can be achieved, or for that matter precisely how or when it *has* been achieved.

(ii) specified in terms of behaviour which is recognizable. Aims as we have defined them above are often not capable of being recognized in the short term. 'To educate a child so as to enable him to play a useful part in a community' would require some very careful defining of terms such as 'useful' and 'community' so that we could pin down the learning experiences necessary in the curriculum. Bloom's taxonomy of educational objectives is useful in providing recognizable behaviours.

(iii) capable of being evaluated. Needless to say, if it is intended to bring about behavioural change in learners, we ought to be able to assess the quality and quantity of this change.

EVALUATION

Curriculum evaluation is the servant by which we clarify and substantiate the effectiveness of our objectives, learning experiences and content. The idea that evaluation is an on-going process is conveyed in Kerr's model (figure 16.1) by the dotted arrows leading from the evaluation component to all the other components. Evaluation should be seen as a tool to assist in refining learning processes as well as in measuring the acquisition of knowledge.

Thus, evaluative techniques should do more than examine a pupil's knowledge. They should also help in locating the factors which influence performance such as the conditions and procedures in the classroom. Two kinds of evaluation have been defined which draw attention to this dual function (14). *Formative evaluation* takes place during the developmental stages of a curriculum and is seen as a continuous process, whilst *summative evaluation* occurs when the curriculum is established and we are measuring the achievement of those on the course as well as the effectiveness of the course. Even with established courses, formative evaluation would still be an essential aspect for reappraising the curriculum.

Mention has already been made of evaluation techniques in chapter 13. In most instances the teacher has to devise his own instruments. There are a few standardized tests in mathematics, English, reading and spelling for a wide age range (NFER, 15), but these have a special function and require, like all standardized material, very careful handling.

A necessary first step in evaluation is to prepare a blueprint (see chapter 14). This is a carefully designed breakdown plan of the content areas and objectives showing their relative importance in terms of hours (or units of time) allotted to each section. A blueprint should be assembled *before* the course commences. As we saw in chapter 13, multiple choice items are particularly favoured for evaluation although oral, written essays and practical work may be used provided they can be validated and made reliable. Other forms of evaluation have been tried with limited success; custom-made attitude and interest scales and interviews are amongst those currently being tried.

It is important to remember that our primary aim in using evaluative methods is concerned with the value of the course using group performance of the pupils in knowing, understanding and applying the skills specified. We would not necessarily be concerned with diagnosing pupils for selection or with finding their rank order of achievement.

KNOWLEDGE OR SUBJECT CONTENT

Deciding what to select from the whole spectrum of content in a discipline in order to achieve our stated objectives is the central concern in this stage of curriculum planning. But what do we hope will be the essential influence of the content? Taba (13) supposes there are two schools of thought which we might term *structure-oriented* and *task-oriented*. There are those who see each subject as having its own brand of mental discipline quite apart from the teaching methods employed. Physics, for example, demands a different mental attitude and cognitive style from literary criticism. Expectations in art are not the same as those in history. With this in mind, the proponents of structure orientation tend to concentrate on the theoretical aspects of the subject to illustrate the characteristic way of thinking afforded by the nature of the subject itself.

Task-oriented teachers view the subject matter as a means of acquiring learning skills such as memorizing (historical dates, chemical formulae, poems) or developing manual skills (play with material which is manipulated, physical education, handicraft). There is a good deal of faith placed in the concept of transfer of training.

However most curriculum planners steer a course between these extremes in allowing that some subjects demand specialized cognitive strategies whilst recognizing certain similar cognitive demands which cut across subject disciplines. In fact there is a decided move towards more integrated syllabuses, although there is little research of any kind to show the advantages or disadvantages of combined courses. Teaching number skills to a junior class, quite apart from the basic numeracy of the children or their developmental level, presents special problems which contrast sharply with, say, the teaching of reading. Yet both these subjects involve memorization or relational thinking.

LEARNING EXPERIENCES

Few would now deny the importance of purposeful activity by the learner as an aid to learning. We pay a good deal of attention to methods of presenting material, so much so that we often forego the content. Vast methodological researches and school programmes have been mounted—Nuffield Science, integrated day methods, 'free activity' methods—all testifying to the enthusiasm generated. Less emphasis is now placed on transmission of knowledge and more on the processes of assimilation by developing skills in understanding.

Psychology has much to offer in this respect. Considerations of learning, individual capacities, motivation, personality, the growth of thinking skills, 'readiness' are all major issues in devising learning experiences for pupils. In one sense this aspect of curriculum planning draws together many threads in the syllabus of educational psychology.

Our view of childhood has altered and has in turn affected the teacher's approach to structuring learning situations in the classroom. A greater recognition of individual worth and differences has brought a corresponding recognition that individual help is a vital alternative to class teaching. Our knowledge of child development and our changed attitudes towards the young have revitalized learning procedures. They have converted us from regarding the child as a passive receptacle to seeing him as an active participant in learning.

Theories of instruction, already mentioned in chapter 7, have grown in response to the need for 'prescriptions' of learning and teaching instead of 'descriptions' so prevalent in learning theories. The work of Bruner (16) is well known, although Skinner (17) and Gagné (17) have also made considerable contributions. As we saw, Bruner pays attention to the most effective 'sequence' in which materials should be presented and goes on to argue that optimal sequences need to be judged in terms of an individual's speed and power to learn, transfer possibilities, economy of learning in keeping with the 'cognitive strain' imposed and the ability of the material thus learnt to help in generating new ideas.

The impact of social psychology has rapidly made us aware that children's learning processes are markedly influenced by social factors and group dynamics. Studies of home background, the school community and teacher–pupil interaction are leaving their mark on the methods we are adopting. Experimentation with open-plan schools in streamed classes, sixth form colleges and schools where the local community is being drawn into the life of the school are but a few recent examples.

CURRICULUM PLANNING AND THE TEACHER

Establishing a new curriculum is really a combined effort requiring expert advice in the aspects we have discussed above. However, there is also the task of keeping a close watch on our existing programmes and modifying or changing parts of them as the need arises. In the light of what has been said above, we might apply one method suggested by Taylor (1) who recommends that the teacher should keep a double-paged 'ledger' account of his syllabus topics with a column for answers to each of the following questions:

    (i) what am I expected to teach, and in what order? (CONTENT)
    (ii) what educational purposes is my teaching to serve? (AIMS)
    (iii) what teaching methods are known to achieve these purposes? (METHODS)
    (iv) what standard of achievement am I expected to aim at? (OBJECTIVES)
    (v) how will I discover whether the course I've been teaching has been successful or not?
       (EVALUATION)
    (vi) what can I usefully be told about the abilities, interest and attitudes of the pupils I am
       to teach? (PUPILS)
    (vii) COMMENTS about alternative possibilities.

As Taylor comments, the purpose of the ledger is 'to help the teacher understand the nature and purpose of the course, not to determine the form and style of his teaching'.

CURRICULUM TRENDS

The present state of affairs in curriculum design is part of a chain of events in the development of educational practices in this country. Looking back over the history of our present curriculum, there seem to be at least two major strands in the development of educational practices in this country. One strand arises from the public school system of the past which permeated the grammar school system. The other strand arises from legislation relating to the elementary school system of education for all.

The classical tradition of Latin and Greek with a little geography, history and mathematics prevailed through many centuries. Latin, in the first instance, was very important because most of the literature was written in that tongue, including law, medicine and theology. However, in time it became symbolic of a particular way of life serving to distinguish the gentry, leaders with 'cultivated' minds, from the serving classes. Where the latter were able to receive an education it consisted of an iron ration of the three Rs—just sufficient to enable youngsters to serve God and the factory owners. Later, the 1902 Act also insisted that children should be fitted to meet the practical as well as the basic intellectual demands of a working life. However, this century has seen rapid and extensive changes in elementary education emerging as the present day primary and secondary systems.

As the student's work in the History of Education will show, a long train of education acts and Government reports (Plowden and Newsom for example) has had a marked effect on the direction of curriculum designs. Consider the effect of the Spens and Norwood Reports on the 1944 Act. The Reports saw children as falling into three categories of academic, technical and practical for which the Secondary Grammar, Secondary Technical and Secondary Modern Schools were created. Curriculum designers attempted to build into their schemes a style of teaching and special emphasis in content designed to satisfy the supposed characteristics of 'academic', 'technical' and 'practical' children.

Since the 1944 Act, we have seen the gradual evolution of a system dedicated to giving pupils an equal chance to benefit from whatever education would be satisfying and serviceable. Theoretically, there also seems to be a strong desire to extend the syllabus to give more attention to moral and social education: the behavioural sciences at secondary level (psychology, sociology and anthropology) and what might be termed the 'survival sciences' such as demography, pollution and conservation, race relations, peace studies, contraception, V.D., and health studies. In practice, the emphasis, as seen by teachers, has been largely on intellectual and moral development. Musgrove and Taylor (18) asked primary, secondary modern and grammar school teachers to rate the relative educational relevance of moral training, social training, intellectual training (instruction in subjects), education for family life, social advancement and education for citizenship. Grammar school teachers had a more confined outlook than secondary modern teachers and viewed their role as limited to intellectual and moral education ('character training'), with indifferent regard for social training. Surprisingly, primary school teachers likewise seemed to place less emphasis on social than on intellectual and moral training.

Parents of university students also have some clear ideas about the roles which universities should serve through their curricula. Child (19) showed three aspects of university life which were uppermost in the minds of parents: (a) students should be worked hard in a few specialized subjects with a supporting cast of academic counsellors; (b) the University should be primarily concerned with preparing and guiding students for a career; (c) the University should help in developing students' skills in dealing with other people. The study of knowledge 'for its own sake' and without regard for its practical application was placed right at the bottom of the list of priorities. Here we see an important dilemma between the teachers' cognitive outlook and the parents' highly businesslike vocational and instrumental order of priorities.

SUMMARY

One of the most important jobs for any teacher is to plan what to teach, how to teach it and how to evaluate the outcome of teaching. But it is no accident that a chapter on the curriculum appears at the end rather than at the beginning of the book. Curriculum design is a difficult task requiring a profound knowledge of psychological principles apart from content knowledge. So that whilst it is one of the first things to confront a student on school practice or fresh out of training, curriculum planning is most effectively done as a consequence of accumulated information and skills in handling children and the subject area.

The curriculum is erroneously thought of by many as the subject matter of a course. This is a very limited view. In fact, the curriculum represents the interaction of all the activities aimed at assisting pupils in reaching specified educational objectives. In short, curriculum planning involves specifying objectives, devising appropriate content, arranging educational experiences for presenting the content, and evaluating the processes of learning which have taken place along with testing the suitability of the content in relation to the stated objectives.

This is a tall order. To begin with, we have to know a lot about children in terms of their interests, motives, intellectual competence or what they have done already in school in addition to making judgements as to what is most suited to their skills and needs at a particular stage in their development. Hence, it is clear that objectives can only be specified against this background of information in order to make them realistic, appropriate and capable of being expressed in terms which can be transposed into learning behaviour. Vague, all-inclusive statements are not appropriate when they cannot be converted into activities. Again, objectives must ultimately be put to the test—they must be capable of evaluation because all educational objectives lead to learning and we must be in a position to assess whether learning has taken place.

Evaluation is an on-going process. It enables us to review and modify, if necessary, the objectives should they prove to be inappropriate. Mention is made in chapter 13 of methods of evaluation. Selecting content demands both a knowledge of particular cognitive structures inherent in a subject area and a knowledge of general learning tactics common to all disciplines.

Needless to say, much of the earlier part of the book has concentrated on the individual qualities and learning habitats of children most likely to influence learning. Such factors as motivation, attention, retention, recall, language skills, cognitive developmental stage, intellectual abilities and personality are frequently the source of variability and interaction in the learning experiences of the individual child.

The next few years will see greater demands being made of teachers to examine their curricula. Innovation is now almost a routine in education and the teacher should be in a strong position to examine the worth of the many new ideas which will flood into his working life.

ENQUIRY AND DISCUSSION

1. Take a close look at the topics you have been asked to teach on school practice in terms of objectives, content, methods of teaching and learning and evaluation. Enquire of teachers their reasons for giving particular topics.

2. What do you consider to be the important criteria when deciding on the methods or 'educational experiences' you would offer a specified group of children in a given topic. (You may have to think out a solution to this problem for a mixed ability group or in an integrated subject area.)

3. The *Plowden* and *Newsom* Reports contain a section entitled 'recommendations' giving many suggestions for curriculum reform. Examine the psychological assumptions implicitly or explicitly connected with the recommendations in one or both of these reports.

4. Try to read *Report No. I: The Objectives of Teacher-Training* [see note (7)]. Note the implications in terms of classroom practices.

5. Engage your tutor in a group discussion on the objectives of various aspects of the

education course, e.g. Philosophy, 'Methods' of Education (if such a course exists), Sociology, Psychology, History, Comparative Education.

NOTES AND REFERENCES

1. The conclusion that teachers tend to lay greatest stress on content and method is demonstrated in a research report by P. H. Taylor, *How Teachers Plan Their Courses*, NFER, Slough, 1970.

2. R. L. Neagley and N. D. Evans, *Handbook for Effective Curriculum Development*, Prentice-Hall, New Jersey, 1967.

3. P. H. Hirst, 'The contribution of philosophy to the study of the curriculum', in J. F. Kerr (Ed.), *Changing the Curriculum*, University of London Press, London, 1968. This is a very useful and readable book of individual papers.

4. R. W. Tyler, *Basic Principles of Curriculum and Instruction*, University of Chicago Press, Chicago, 1949.

5. W. K. Richmond, *The School Curriculum*, Methuen, London, 1971. A thought-provoking book, in part light hearted, in part serious.

6. J. F. Kerr, in *Changing the Curriculum* gives a model which has much to commend it. The diagram appears in his chapter 'The problem of curriculum reform' [*op. cit.* note (3)].

7. The University of Leeds Institute of Education has recently embarked on a curriculum project relating to colleges of education. Stage I, which considers the objectives of teacher-training, uses as its starting point a model of individual needs (material and experiential) by which to isolate the professional skills needed by teachers and thus to indicate the appropriate curriculum in colleges. *Report Number I: The Objectives of Teacher-Training*, The Institute of Education, University of Leeds, May 1971.

8. J. I. Goodlad, in *Curriculum Innovation in Practice*, The Schools Council, HMSO, London, 1968. See also S. Wiseman and D. Pigeon, *Curriculum Evaluation*, NFER, Slough, 1970.

9. B. S. Bloom *et al.*, *Taxonomy of Educational Objectives. Handbook I: Cognitive Domain*, Longmans, London, 1956 and *Handbook II: Affective Domain*, 1964.

10. P. H. Taylor, 'Children's evaluations of the characteristics of the good teacher', *Brit. J. educ. Psychol.*, **32**, 258–266 (1962).

11. D. G. Ryans, *Characteristics of Teachers: Their Descriptions, Comparison and Appraisal*, American Council of Education, Washington, D.C., 1960.

12. K. B. Start, 'The relation of teaching ability to measures of personality', *Brit. J. educ. Psychol.*, **36**, 158–165 (1966).

13. H. Taba, *Curriculum Development: Theory and Practice*, Harcourt, Brace and World, New York, 1962.

14. S. Wiseman and D. Pigeon, *Curriculum Evaluation*, NFER, Slough, 1970.

15. The National Foundation for Educational Research has designed several standardized tests suitable for use in primary and secondary schools. A Test Catalogue published by the NFER gives details of their function and availability to teachers.

16. J. S. Bruner, *Toward a Theory of Instruction*, Norton, New York, 1966. See also *The Process of Education*, Harvard University Press, New York, 1962.

17. B. F. Skinner 'The science of learning and the art of teaching', in A. A. Lumsdaine and R. Glaser (Eds), *Teaching Machines and Programmed Learning*, National Educational Association (USA), Washington D.C., 1960; R. M. Gagné *et al.*, 'Factors in acquiring knowledge of a mathematical task', *Psychol. Monogr.*, No. 76 (1962). For a research on discovery methods see J. A. Rowell, J. Simon and R. Wiseman, 'Verbal reception, guided discovery and the learning of schemata', *Brit. J. educ. Psychol.*, **39**, 233–244 (1969).

18. F. Musgrove and P. H. Taylor, 'Teachers' and parents' conception of the teacher's role', *Brit. J. educ. Psychol.*, **35**, 171–179 (1965).

19. D. Child *et al.*, 'Parents' expectations of a university', *Universities Q.*, **25**, 484–490 (1971).

FURTHER READING

M. R. Bar (Ed.), *Curriculum Innovation in Practice*, Edge Hill College of Education, 1969.

A. G. Howson, *Developing a New Curriculum*, Heinemann, London, 1970. A readable introduction to new developments in schools.

J. F. Kerr (Ed.), *Changing the Curriculum*, University of London Press, London, 1968. A useful collection of papers.

W. K. Richmond, *The School Curriculum*, Methuen, London, 1971.

H. Taba, *Curriculum Development: Theory and Practice*, Harcourt, Brace and World, New York, 1962.

P. H. Taylor, *How Teachers Plan Their Courses*, NFER, Slough, 1970.

R. W. Tyler, *Basic Principles of Curriculum and Instruction*, University of Chicago Press, Chicago, 1949.

S. Wiseman and D. Pigeon, *Curriculum Evaluation*, NFER, Slough, 1970. A profitable introduction for teachers.

Working papers and curriculum bulletins of the Schools Council provide a very good source of contemporary thinking in curriculum research and development. For instance Working Paper No. 10—*Curriculum Development: Teachers' Groups and Centres*, HMSO, London, 1967; Working Paper No. 33—*Choosing a Curriculum for the Young School Leaver*, Evans/Methuen Educational, London, 1971. Another valuable publication is *Curriculum Innovation in Practice*, a report by J. Stuart Maclure for the Schools Council, HMSO, London, 1968.

L

17   Psychological research and education

The strongest tradition adopted by the majority of workers in the psychology of education is that which employs the methods and assumptions of the sciences. The bulk of the experimental evidence offered in this textbook has its origins in scientific method. As we have seen in previous chapters, there are limitations imposed such that answers to the kinds of questions of significance to practising teachers are not clear cut. In fact, a few psychologists in education have questioned the suitability of scientific method in its purest form as the appropriate technique at this stage in our hazy knowledge of human behaviour. They ask, 'are the highly sophisticated methods of science too refined for the unchartered realms of complex human conduct?' However, the alternatives of inspired (and uninspired) guesswork, speculation or teaching folk-lore are hardly likely to provide us with the foundations from which decisions in the classroom are made possible.

Of course there are differences of approach even within the bounds of scientific method. Some psychologists are concerned with the study of the mind, whilst others concentrate on the observable products of man–environment interaction. Some restrict their observations to description, classification and generalization, whilst others venture to suggest causal relations from which prediction and control are envisaged. Some make a point of individual 'eyeball to eyeball' analysis (idiographic studies), whilst others prefer elaborate statistical designs for group analysis from which to derive norms of behaviour (nomothetic studies). In all these cases, we meet up with the problem of research design and the applicability of the results to classroom procedures. The increasing criticism of traditional research methods in educational psychology stems from this difficulty of bridging the gap between the theoretical findings and the practical 'nitty-gritty'. We shall return to this dilemma later in the chapter. At this point, we shall look briefly at the methods and intentions of scientific method as applied in the behavioural sciences (psychology, sociology, political science, anthropology, economics) and at some of the cautions necessary when interpreting and appraising the findings. For a sound introduction to this topic, students should see one of the books recommended in note (1).

Generally speaking, researchers in the behavioural sciences have adopted the methods of the natural sciences. Dewey (2) has outlined the main stages of this 'scientific method' as follows:

(i) the recognition of a problem which has not been solved before;

(ii) an experiment is designed in such a way as to define the problems clearly, then information is accumulated through careful observations;

(iii) the information is organized to see if regularities exist;

(iv) explanations for such regularities are suggested—this is known as setting up hypotheses (that is tentative theories);

(v) experiments are designed to test the hypotheses;

(vi) the hypotheses are used to predict new effects which are in turn put to the test.

Probably very few experiments take this precise form. Nevertheless, broadly speaking the method has been used as the basis for many research findings which are quoted in this textbook. Where the psychologist has a special difficulty is in setting up hypotheses and experiments in which he is in control of all the variables operating. It will repay us, therefore, to look at some of the important methods used for gathering information. One useful way of classifying the assembly of information [suggested by Kerlinger (3)] is (a) *experimental*; (b) *ex post facto* and (c) *survey*. In all three we are dealing with *variables*. These are qualities or attributes which can have differing values. In psychology and education we meet with variables such as type of school, motivation, sex of pupil, aptitude, extraversion, achievement and a host of others dealt with in this textbook. Some are referred to as *independent variables*, that is systems or methods used in education such as the comprehensive system or initial teaching alphabet (i.t.a.), which are presumed to be causal variables. *Dependent variables* consist of measures which fluctuate and 'depend' for their value on the independent variables; in other words, dependent variables are the supposed effects of variations in the independent variables. These latter are of special interest to the teacher for they include the methods he would employ in the classroom. The most common dependent variable in education is achievement or the amount of learning which has taken place as a consequence of given methods.

In the experimental set up we deliberately hold constant, or *control*, most of the independent variables and just vary one or two (Burroughs, 1). For example, if we wanted to test the efficiency of the i.t.a. as a means of teaching youngsters how to read as compared with a more traditional method, the independent variables would be the i.t.a. and the traditional orthographical method of teaching reading. The relevant dependent variable, that is the children's reading ability, would have to be tested for both groups either after or before and after a trial experiment, whilst all other independent variables on which the children's reading performance might also depend, such as intelligence, home background and school experience, would have to be the same for both groups. However, strict experimental control does not, unfortunately, appear all that often in educational research. The difficulty of controlling and experimenting when we are dealing with people and situations of great complexity is not easily surmounted.

Animals are frequently the subjects for this kind of strict laboratory approach. But there are obvious dangers in transferring the results of animal experiments to human situations. The presence of different levels of physiological organization, intellect and motivation amongst other things are certain to give rise to difficulties when interpreting human in terms of animal behaviour.

Ex post facto research, which translated literally means 'from what is done afterwards', involves an examination of events which have already occurred in the hope that such examination will reveal significant generalities. We cannot manipulate the independent variables because they have already happened. Take as an illustration a field study of juvenile delinquency (dependent variable). The starting point has been to take a group of attested delinquents and look at their life histories (presumed independent variables) in terms of family background, friendship networks, relationship with parents, personal and intellectual characteristics and compare these with a group of non-delinquents. The independent variables of delinquency have already occurred and we must inspect these to see which might have a bearing on the problem (4). Clearly, in some cases it is no easy task determining which of the possible independent variables are relevant. Research in education relies extensively on this method of analysis because of its convenience in cases where we cannot carry out controlled experiments with people as subjects.

There are two main forms of field studies relying on *ex post facto* techniques which along with survey methods, to be described next, are sometimes referred to as *descriptive research*. These two are *case* and *developmental* studies. In case studies, 'clients', either as individuals or in small, well-defined groups such as the family, are examined in great detail. Background information about home, school and community is gathered, together with interviews and in some cases standardized test scores. The method is popular in clinical settings and social work. Developmental studies involve a detailed description of selected variables at different stages in the lives of children and adults. We may look at the same group of people at intervals in their lives; this is a *longitudinal study*. Or we may take samples at different ages covering the range we are concerned with and test each sample on one occasion; this is a *cross-sectional* study. Developmental studies have been of great service in theories of the growth of thinking skills and vocational choice, both of which have been discussed.

In the survey technique, the results of which are now used extensively in educational policy-making at Government level, the object is to collect information about readily obtainable facts from a total population or a representative sample of the population. A national census affords a well-known example of a fact-finding survey of existing conditions. Most of the data consist of 'head counting' or frequency determination. A statement of the number of boys and girls in primary education between the ages of five and eleven years on the last day of July 1970 would be a fact obtainable by survey techniques. Successive Governments have increasingly employed survey reports such as those of the Crowther, Robbins and Plowden Committees (5).

LIMITATIONS OF RESEARCH IN PSYCHOLOGY OF EDUCATION

Behavioural research is still a long way from reaching the level of experimental sophistication of the natural sciences. Medawar (6) in summarizing some of the problems facing scientists put his finger on many shortcomings in 'scientific method' which apply equally well to behavioural sciences. According to him, the formulation of theories purporting to be scientific start with, one assumes, the 'unvarnished and unembroidered' evidence of the senses. Initial observations should be simple, unbiased, unprejudiced, naïve and innocent. From evidence through the senses we should end up with simple declarations which express, in an orderly fashion, the laws of nature. The ornithologist unobtrusively watches nature in the raw without disturbing the facts as they exist. In the same dispassionate way, the behavioural scientist would like to be regarded as a 'man watcher'.

These high aims are bedevilled by many set-backs which the cautious teacher should bear in mind when he is studying research and its implications for his work. Some of the questions posed in education are as large as life itself. Sociological themes sometimes have this awkward habit of depending on so many independent variables as to render controlled research impossible. The terms of reference are never as clear cut as might be found in physics or chemistry. Our subject matter is cumbersome with variables; our methods are messy rather than elegant and clean; our results are tentative and rarely capable of direct application to classroom practice. Nevertheless, such small steps forward are essential if we are to put the psychology of education on a firm scientific footing.

How unbiased can research be? The act of choosing a subject for research nearly always reflects a bias. Fashions come and go in educational research as the climate of opinion about values in education changes. With limited resources, this means that some topics have to be ignored. Selecting methods of measurement, analysis and interpretation requires decisions which often call for biased judgement. The experimenter brings to his research a lifetime of prejudices and predispositions about man's nature thus making it difficult to be objective about research design and interpretation.

In educational research there is a marked dependence upon introspection. When questions of attitude or opinion are asked, the responses depend entirely on the selective memory of the person being asked. Some of our behaviour is moderated by attitudes of which we may not even be aware. The way in which the questions are posed may influence the answers given. The answers also depend on the communication skills of individuals and this is particularly difficult with children.

Ex post facto methods necessarily lead to an emphasis on the products of our behaviour. We look at the outcome of a perceptual task or examination results and make assumptions in retrospect about what might have been taking place in the process of perceiving or studying for the examination. On the other hand, many of the teacher's problems focus on processes, assumptions about which can be used to modify and make efficient the learning behaviour of children.

THE NATURE OF EDUCATIONAL RESEARCH

Education is an applied science and as such it must draw inspiration and knowledge from theories which are serviceable. Ausubel (7) draws attention to three ways in which we have attempted to use knowledge from research in educational decision-making. In the first, *basic science research*, the experimenter is concerned with discovering general principles as ends in themselves. In the case of education, the fundamental principles derived in psychology, sociology or philosophy would be the source of information. One problem here is that the principles are commonly discovered using controlled experimental designs which bear only a marginal, if any, similarity to the situation which exists in a classroom. The level of complexity in a classroom frequently militates against the direct application of fundamental findings using animal or controlled human experiments. Again, the researcher is often not particularly concerned to find laws or generalities which have predetermined applications. In fact, where attempts are made to take the findings and apply them directly to classroom settings they sometimes fail because the level of generality is at a much higher point than is required in a classroom where knowledge of individual differences is crucial. The real contribution made by basic research findings is in directing our attention to what is possible in the way of generalizations about behaviour, and in generating possible hypotheses for the direction of behaviour. For example, the Yerkes–Dodson law mentioned in chapter 11 is an example of a basic science research finding. It shows that there is a predictable relationship between performance and drive provided we can specify the conditions under which a task is being conducted. All manner of conclusions are possible from a knowledge of the law which are particularly relevant to classroom practices. But, we still have some way to go in determining the details of the conditions which influence the relationship.

A second approach defined by Ausubel is the *extrapolated basic science research* in which the experimenter sets out with a specific practical problem in mind and designs an analogous basic science research from which he can extract general principles. The original research is rarely carried out in the applied setting for which it is being used and suffers from much the same shortcomings as in applying basic research. We draw on studies from the psychology of language acquisition and apply these to the classroom. Operant conditioning, for example, can be used in language learning in the junior school. The fault is in the tendency to extrapolate from basic research and apply the results to pedagogical problems without first of all finding out the extent to which this link is valid.

The third suggestion Ausubel calls *research at an applied level* by which he means performing research *in situ* and in the conditions which normally pertain in schools. Action research in the classroom involves the identification and exploration of learning environments *as they exist* in terms of such variables as motivation, facilities, personal relationships, and so forth. Naturally, this approach presents far more difficulties because of the complex nature of the task than would be the case in classical controlled researches. However, Ausubel believes that the pay off for teachers would be much greater than exists at present.

There are the beginnings of a shift in emphasis from the study of individual differences to the study of learning environments in education (8). We need to know far more about the characteristics by which we can describe educational environments and the significance of these to the processes of behaviour change and the job of teaching. To some extent, the social psychologist in education has been concerned to detect the influence of these environmental variables on individuals, but rarely has this occurred with the classroom as the environment. It is not just the content of lessons which the teacher manipulates, but the whole background of the classroom. We need to discover how these manipulations influence performance in different environmental structures. The detailed scientific study of life in classrooms (9) is a growth point about which we are going to hear more. But before we get carried away with enthusiasm for the future of educational research, let us reflect on the fact that we are already standing on the ground laid down by the psychologists alluded to in this book.

SUMMARY

In this final chapter we have looked at some of the basic attitudes and problems which beset the researcher in education. Psychology is still in its infancy as a scientific enterprise and its contribution to our understanding of children as cognitive and social creatures must be viewed with cautious optimism. The teacher's role remains one of diagnostician both in the sense in which he treats the findings of others and in the way he assimilates and interprets the evidence before him in the classroom. Psychological research has gone only so far, within the limitations discussed in the chapter, in providing generalizations about human nature. It still remains for the teacher to keep abreast with new knowledge and to devise courses of action from all the sources of evidence available to him.

ENQUIRY AND DISCUSSION

1. Read the paper by L. S. Shulman, 'Reconstruction and educational research', *Rev. educ. Res.*, **40,** 371–396 (1970) and note in particular his suggestions for alternative methods of researching into classroom behaviour. What are the snags in these approaches? Why have they not been adopted before now?

2. Observe the psychological assumptions of teachers on school practice. Are they based on psychological theory or teaching folk-lore?

3. Initiate a group discussion with a tutor on the applicability of educational psychology emanating from (i) basic science research; (ii) extrapolated basic science research; and (iii) research at an applied level. In what ways will the 'learning environments' approach take us nearer to an understanding of the teacher's role?

NOTES AND REFERENCES

1. G. E. R. Burroughs, *Design and Analysis in Educational Research*, University of Birmingham, 1971; J. D. Nisbet and N. J. Entwistle, *Educational Research Methods*, University of London Press, London, 1970; K. Lovell and K. S. Lawson, *Understanding Research in Education*, University of London Press, London, 1970.

2. J. Dewey, *How We Think*, Heath, Boston, 1933.

3. For those who want detail, F. N. Kerlinger, *Foundations of Behavioral Research: Educational and Psychological Inquiry*, Holt, Rinehart and Winston, London, 1969, is an excellent text.

4. Another topical example of independent and dependent variables is provided by the increase in lung cancer (dependent variable) and the possibility that smoking (independent variable) is the cause. This is a very good case of *ex post facto* analysis. We cannot manipulate the independent variable once cancer has appeared; we can only look in retrospect at the possibilities which might distinguish cancer from non-cancer sufferers. Kerlinger, mentioned in note (6), devotes a whole chapter to *ex post facto* research.

5. The Plowden Report: *Children and their Primary Schools*, HMSO, London, 1967; The Crowther Report: *15 to 18*, HMSO, London, 1959; The Robbins Report: *Committee on Higher Education*, HMSO, London, 1963.

6. P. B. Medawar, 'Is the scientific paper a fraud?', *The Listener*, 1962 and *Induction and Intuition in Scientific Thought*, Methuen, London, 1969.

7. D. P. Ausubel, 'The nature of educational research', in W. J. Gephart and R. B. Ingle (Eds), *Educational Research*, Merrill, Columbus, Ohio, 1969.

8. L. S. Shulman, 'Reconstruction of educational research', *Rev. educ. Res.*, **40,** 371–396 (1970).

9. P. W. Jackson, *Life in Classrooms*, Holt, Rinehart and Winston, New York, 1968.

FURTHER READING

G. E. R. Burroughs, *Design and Analysis in Educational Research*, University of Birmingham, 1971. This book is a detailed introduction primarily intended for serving teachers. But there are several sections of value to student teachers.

W. J. Gephart and R. B. Ingle (Eds), *Educational Research*, Merrill, Columbus, Ohio, 1969.

F. N. Kerlinger, *Foundations of Behavioral Research: Educational and Psychological Inquiry*, Holt, Rinehart and Winston, London, 1969. An advanced text for the strong in heart!

K. Lovell and K. S. Lawson, *Understanding Research in Education*, University of London Press, London, 1970. Both this and the next text are written with students in mind.

J. D. Nisbet and N. Entwistle, *Educational Research Methods*, University of London Press, London, 1970.

Author index

Subject index